Law and the Built Environment

Law and the Built Environment

Douglas Wood
BA, LLB, LLM, Solicitor
Senior Lecturer, Staffordshire Law School, Staffordshire University

Paul Chynoweth
BSc, LLB, Solicitor
Senior Lecturer, School of the Built Environment, University of Salford

Julie Adshead
LLB, LLM
Senior Lecturer, Salford Law School, University of Salford

Jim Mason
LLB, Solicitor
Senior Lecturer, School of the Built and Natural Environment,
University of the West of England

WILEY-BLACKWELL
A John Wiley & Sons, Ltd., Publication

This edition first published 2011
© 2011 Douglas Wood, Paul Chynoweth, Julie Adshead and James Mason

Blackwell Publishing was acquired by John Wiley & Sons in February 2007. Blackwell's publishing programme has been merged with Wiley's global Scientific, Technical, and Medical business to form Wiley-Blackwell.

First edition published 1999 by Macmillan Press Ltd
Second edition published 2011

Registered office
John Wiley & Sons Ltd, The Atrium, Southern Gate, Chichester, West Sussex, PO19 8SQ, United Kingdom

Editorial office
9600 Garsington Road, Oxford, OX4 2DQ, United Kingdom
The Atrium, Southern Gate, Chichester, West Sussex, PO19 8SQ, UK
2121 State Avenue, Ames, Iowa 50014-8300, USA

For details of our global editorial offices, for customer services and for information about how to apply for permission to reuse the copyright material in this book please see our website at www.wiley.com/wiley-blackwell.

Library of Congress Cataloging-in-Publication Data

Law and the built environment / Douglas Wood ... [et al.]. – 2nd ed.
      p. cm.
   Includes bibliographical references and index.
   ISBN 978-1-4051-9760-1 (alk. paper)
  1. Construction industry–Law and legislation–England.   2. Construction contracts–England.   3. Real property–England.   4. Landlord and tenant–England. 5. Building laws–England. I. Wood, Douglas, 1948–
   KD2435.L39 2011
   346.4204'3–dc22

                                                                    2010029197

A catalogue record for this book is available from the British Library.

Set in 10/12pt Minion by Thomson Digital, Noida, India
Printed in Singapore by Ho Printing Singapore Pte Ltd

1   2011

Contents

Preface

This is a law book with a difference. It has been written, not for law students, but for those on vocational university programmes studying for careers in the property and construction professions. Specifically, it aims to provide a single source of reference for students studying the core law modules on these programmes.

Built environment students have particular needs when it comes to a law textbook. Competence in the law is an essential ingredient for success in their chosen careers. But it is not the only one. They must also develop competencies in a diverse range of other subject areas, as well as the ability to draw effectively upon each of them in confronting real-life challenges in their professional environments.

We hope that this textbook responds to these needs. It seeks to provide a depth of coverage of the core legal topics which is appropriate to those embarking on careers in the built environment. It recognises that they must fully understand the legal environment in which they operate, and be able to discuss legal issues with their counterparts in the legal profession, whilst rarely being called upon to provide specialist legal advice themselves.

The book provides an introduction to the key legal principles that underpin the professional and commercial lives of those who provide advice to clients in the property and construction sectors. Although many of these are equally applicable to professionals in other areas we have sought to illustrate these principles throughout by reference to examples, statutes and case law which are of most relevance to the built environment. In the specialist areas of built environment professional practice – for example construction contracts and rent review – we have also gone into greater detail than would normally be encountered in a more conventional legal textbook.

Each of us has been teaching built environment students for many years and we know how difficult it can be to find a single, succinct and easily understandable textbook covering the law modules in sufficient depth, and with appropriate emphasis on property and construction. With this in mind we have attempted to produce a book that satisfies the demand for a specialist law textbook catering exclusively for built environment students.

We are grateful to colleagues Brodie McAdam and Paul Tracey for reviewing preliminary draft chapters for us. We have endeavoured to state the law as at 1 February 2010 and any errors or omissions are, of course, entirely our own.

Douglas Wood
Paul Chynoweth
Julie Adshead
Jim Mason

Table of Cases

Table of Statutes

Table of Statutory Instruments

1 The Administration of Law

1.1 The nature of law

Any system of law is basically a method of trying to enforce order and a reasonable standard of fair play. In any community, rules will develop to control the relationships between individual members. The law acts as a set of rules that protects the rights of individuals and organisations while at the same time imposing obligations on the community at large. There must be some method of enforcing these rules and ensuring that the system is flexible enough to respond to the need for change where and when it is necessary. This book is concerned primarily with rights and duties that affect those in the landed and building professions. These are areas of life that have long had to comply with legal formalities and requirements. As society has evolved and become more complex, the laws governing such activities have increased in number and become more sophisticated. The aspects of law to be considered in this book have application in England and Wales. Some of the principles apply in Scotland and Northern Ireland as well, but in areas such as the organisation of the court system and the methods of transferring land, there are significant differences. This first chapter looks at the English legal system and outlines just how the law is made and applied. This provides an essential foundation for the areas of law that are considered in later chapters.

1.2 Divisions of law

1.2.1 Civil and criminal law

A fundamental distinction is made in the English legal system between the criminal law and the civil law. *Criminal Law* is the body of law made by the state to preserve society and uphold law and order. Its object is to punish conduct of which the state disapproves and to act as a deterrent. The punishment may take the form of a fine, imprisonment or some other form of penalty. A person or organisation who infringes these laws commits a criminal offence for which the consequence can be prosecution by the state. Criminal cases are initiated by the state, normally via the police and the Crown Prosecution Service, although occasionally private citizens

Law and the Built Environment   by Douglas Wood, Paul Chynoweth, Julie Adshead and Jim Mason
© 2011 Douglas Wood, Paul Chynoweth, Julie Adshead and Jim Mason

bring such cases. The state (the *prosecution*) is responsible for bringing a case against the person alleged to be responsible for committing the criminal act (the *defendant* or *accused*). As the United Kingdom is a monarchy, proceedings are brought in the name of the Crown. Consequently, in England and Wales a criminal case is described in the following manner:

> *Regina* (latin for Queen) versus the person or organisation alleged to have carried out the criminal offence (for example, *Regina v David Cameron*). If the monarch is a king, the case will be described as *Rex* (latin for King) versus the person alleged to have committed the criminal offence (for example, *Rex v Wayne Rooney*). In order to shorten the description of the case it may appear as *R v David Cameron* or *R v Wayne Rooney*, as appropriate, when a record of the case is made.

Where the state is a major participant in the legal process, as in criminal cases, or the government is at the centre of such matters, the appropriate law is known as *Public Law*. Those who work in the professions relating to construction and the management of land and buildings may well encounter the operation of the criminal law in the course of their work. For example, a property developer who disobeys the rules relating to obtaining planning permission for a new building, or who contravenes regulations relating to building activities or environmental protection, can commit a criminal offence. Similarly, a builder who allows an unsafe system of work to continue or disregards the law relating to health and safety may be the subject of a criminal prosecution. Other aspects of public law are frequently encountered by those involved in matters relating to land and buildings and these are dealt with in Chapter 6.

The *Civil Law* governs rights and obligations between individuals. Individuals may include a business, trade union, company or other form of organisation. Private individuals and organisations initiate such cases because they have a dispute with another person or organisation. The civil law attempts to resolve disputes and to give a remedy to the person or organisation that has been wronged (the *injured party*). Money is the essence of civil cases. Such cases are initiated with the intention of compensating the injured party who has suffered some form of financial or physical loss because of the actions of the other person. The civil law does not insist that the case be brought and the person bringing it may discontinue the process at any time. In a civil action the *claimant* brings the action against the *defendant*. For example: *Cameron v Rooney* would describe a civil case brought by Mr Cameron against Mr Rooney while if British Steel Corporation brought a case against Cleveland Bridge & Engineering Co Ltd, it would be described as *British Steel Corporation v Cleveland Bridge & Engineering Co Ltd*[1]. Because this area of law is concerned with relationships between citizens and organisations and disputes personal to them it is known as *Private Law*. This is because, in the main, such disputes only affect the individuals involved in the proceedings. As a general rule, any area of law that does not come within the scope of the criminal law is categorised as being part of the civil law. Most civil law relates to the law of contract and the law of tort. Many different subject areas fall within the civil law. Property

---

[1] [1984] 1 All ER 504

law, company law, commercial law and employment law provide some examples of areas of civil law.

Sometimes the same events give rise to both criminal and civil proceedings. A prosecution in a criminal court may well be brought against the driver of a vehicle under the Road Traffic Acts while the compensation aspects will be determined in a separate action brought by the claimant in a civil court. A similar situation could arise where an employer has been negligent in looking after the safety of an employee and as a result there has been injury. The employee may wish to bring a claim for compensation (*damages*) against the employer, while out of the same set of facts the employer may be prosecuted for breaches of or non-compliance with the Health and Safety at Work etc. Act 1974 (see Chapter 6, paragraph 6.10). Where this situation arises, the two sets of proceedings are kept separate and the matters are dealt with in different courts. There are numerous other situations where this dual liability arises. Whether a case is a criminal or civil matter, an appeal may be made to a higher court against the decision of the original court. In such circumstances the person bringing the appeal is known as the *appellant* and the person against whom the appeal is brought is known as the *respondent*. It is common for legal systems to govern particular procedures which have to be carried out within a legal framework even though there is no dispute or any matter which is *contentious*. The transfer of a house, making of a will or drafting of a contract are all good examples. These *non-contentious* matters are governed by rules developed by the civil law, although there is no conflict between the parties.

1.3 Evidence in civil and criminal cases

Whether a dispute is a civil or a criminal matter, the action will not succeed unless there is sufficient evidence to support the case. Generally it is for the prosecution or the claimant, as appropriate, to substantiate the case and not for the defendant to disprove it. This obligation is known as the burden of proof. When a case is heard in a court of law, the judge must determine the correct facts of the case and then, if necessary, apply the law to those facts. The legal principles can be straightforward or complex. Often, it can be more difficult to ascertain what the correct facts are than to apply the relevant law. In a criminal case the standard of proof which is required is that the prosecution must put foward sufficient evidence to show that the accused committed the crime beyond all reasonable doubt. In a civil action the claimant must prove the facts relied upon and is required to prove the issues on the balance of probabilities. This means that it is likely, after reviewing the evidence, that the defendant did commit the act complained of. The outcome tends to reflect which party's evidence the judge believes to be true. The vast majority of civil actions are settled between the parties at some time before the judge's final decision. In a civil case there are a number of methods by which the facts may be proved. The claimant has to put forward sufficient evidence for all the relevant facts necessary for the case unless the other party has accepted the appropriate evidence. An established method of pursuing or defending a case is through the use of witnesses giving oral evidence at first hand on oath. This is in addition to any documentary evidence which may be available, or real evidence such as a mechanical device or a photograph of a building site where an accident has taken place. In civil cases, evidence is given by a sworn statement, made on oath, known as an *affidavit*. A witness must not give an opinion on the facts at issue unless he is an expert witness (see paragraph 1.18.6). Hearsay evidence is evidence which is not perceived by the witness but stated by some other person. Following the Civil Evidence Act 1995 hearsay evidence is generally admissible in civil proceedings. However, there are restrictions upon allowing hearsay evidence in criminal cases.

1.4   The common law

Most legal systems in Europe are based upon Roman law but England and Wales are subject to the so-called *Common Law*. This expression is used to describe English law and the other legal systems, such as those of Australia or the United States of America, which adopted the type of law to be found in England. The expression *Common Law* can also be used to describe the law made by judges in courts of law as opposed to that made by Act of Parliament. A third interpretation is that it means the body of law which became common or uniform to the whole of England and Wales after 1066. Up to that date, the laws of England and Wales varied from area to area as there was no unified legal system. Each court operated in isolation. There were no centralised institutions exercising either administrative or judicial control over the legal system. This changed with the Norman Conquest in 1066 when William the Conqueror (William I) proclaimed himself King of England, replacing the Saxon kings. The object of the Normans was to establish a national system of law, which would apply to all persons alike, wherever they were situated geographically and whatever their status in society. This law became based on the law which they brought with them from France and on those English customs which were found to be widespread after the conquest.

One consequence of the Norman Conquest was the introduction of the King's Council or *Curia Regis*. This was the central government of the Kingdom which exercised administrative (*executive*), law-making (*legislative*) and judge-like (*judicial*) functions without distinction. In the period immediately after the conquest, the common law developed on an *ad hoc* basis with each problem being settled as it arose. The Normans developed a strong central government and gradually the old local customs began to disappear, with their place being taken by the King's Council. From this court, special courts were instituted to deal with particular types of cases in which the King's justice was sought. As new courts developed, the *Curia Regis* diminished in importance. Three major common law courts administered the new common law:

1.   The Court of King's Bench.
2.   The Court of Exchequer.
3.   The Court of Common Pleas.

These courts were able to compel the attendance of parties involved in the disputes, and also of witnesses. The process began whereby judges, appointed by the King, acted as Royal Commissioners throughout the country. These judges dealt with civil and criminal matters wherever they arose. This process continued during the reign of Henry II (1154–89) and eventually it led to the development of the assize system, whereby judges toured the country on regular circuits in an attempt to deal with civil and criminal disputes in the regions. This process existed until 1971 and in a modified form still exists today. From the reign of Henry II, civil actions in the common law courts had to be started by writ. This royal command had to be obtained from the King's Chancellor. For every civil case there had to be a separate writ, and the claimant had to select the particular writ which fitted the facts of the case. These original writs were simply documents containing an order from the King addressed to the defendant, the County Sheriff or the Lord of the Manor, requiring the defendant's attendance at court to answer allegations against him. The different types of writ were said to give rise to different forms of action. This meant that the method of trial and the procedural rules which were applicable depended upon the nature of the writ used to start the case. Much of the civil law was built up through defining the circumstances in which the various writs could be brought.

1.5 Equity

By the end of the reign of Edward I (1272–1307) the shortcomings of the common law were becoming apparent. The writ system had become very formalised. Writs were not available to cover every set of circumstances and the rule was that, unless there was an appropriate writ, there was no remedy. No action could succeed unless the correct court was chosen. Technicalities dominated common law procedures. These had become very complex and an action might fail because of a slight error in the preparation of the documents required to start off a case. Another problem was the lack of appropriate remedies to fit every set of circumstances. A successful claimant in the common law courts had only the remedy of damages. Claimants who were dissatisfied with the common law, if they needed to go to law, began to petition the King in an attempt to redress their grievances. By the end of the fourteenth century there were so many petitions that the King referred them to the Lord Chancellor. From this process, the courts of equity emerged, presided over by the Lord Chancellor. The Chancellor granted remedies which he thought were just and equitable depending on the circumstances of the case. This process became so popular that eventually other judges needed to be appointed. These Chancellor's Courts, or Courts of Chancery as they became known, provided an alternative set of courts to those of the common law.

Equity offered new remedies as alternatives to a claim for damages. Initially, the Chancellor was able to grant any remedy which was thought appropriate to fit the circumstances of the case. Eventually, the Courts of Equity became as formalised as the common law, with the availability only of certain specific remedies with guidance from previous cases. Equity offered new remedies such as *specific performance* (a court order to compel the performance of the contract), *injunction* (an order requiring a person to stop doing something they should not be doing in the first place or requiring a particular action) and *rescission* (the right to withdraw from a contract) (see Chapter 2, paragraph 2.12). The basis upon which equitable remedies operate has always been different from the availability of damages as a remedy in the common law courts. Equity has never been a complete system of law. Instead, it has acted as a gloss on the common law by filling in gaps. Equitable remedies are discretionary and are not automatically granted even if the claimant has proved the case in issue. At common law, once the case is proved the claimant is automatically entitled to damages irrespective of any other aspects of the case. If an equitable remedy is sought, the so-called *Maxims of Equity* are applicable. These are a set of rules which regulate the basis upon which remedies are granted. The conduct of the plaintiff, in particular, is very important where an equitable remedy is claimed.

In the nineteenth century a number of reforms were made to the legal system, resulting in the Judicature Acts 1873–75. These Acts set up, to a large extent, the system of courts as it is today. Existing court structures were reorganised and at the same time it was established that matters governed by the common law and equity could be dealt with in the same court. In most modern day cases, a court will have to consider the common law position initially and then see if equity affects the position in any way. The Acts ordained that where the rules of common law and equity conflict, the rules of equity will prevail (Supreme Court Act 1981 s49). Although the common law and equity were fused for administrative purposes, they still retained their own individual characteristics and both aspects are present today in the same system.

1.6   The sources of law

Before the common law system can be properly understood it is necessary to consider the ways in which English law developed and to find out where the law actually comes from. Most continental European countries have a legal system whereby much of their law is contained in written codes which are amended as the need arises. The *Code Napoléon* in France is a good example. English law has been developed from a number of sources, each arising as the situation required. Although most new law is produced by Act of Parliament to meet the complex requirements of contemporary society, a large part of English law has developed from the rules and principles pronounced in the decisions of courts throughout the centuries. The other major domestic source of law which is referred to is *custom*. This was originally a source of law of great importance and is where the common law originated. Its practical importance nowadays is slight, but on those occasions when a case does come to court questioning the legal validity of a custom, it tends to concern rights over land or buildings, so it is appropriate to consider it here.

1.6.1   Custom

A custom is a right or duty that has come to exist through the consent of the population. Traditionally, a custom could either be general (applicable to the whole country) or local (applicable to a particular area). Nowadays, only local customs are of any importance, as general customs have either fallen into disuse or have become incorporated into the law. Such rights are exercisable by members of a particular community such as a parish[2] or a town[3]. A person who wishes to prove the existence of a custom, never previously recognised by the courts, must satisfy a number of tests relating to the alleged right.

(A) Time immemorial

The custom must have existed since *time immemorial*. This is historically fixed as 1189. In most cases it is impossible for those claiming the custom to show conclusively that it existed in 1189, so this requirement is satisfied by evidence that the custom has existed within living memory or at least without interruption for twenty years. This was shown in *Mercer v Denne*[4], where it was established that fishermen had the right to dry nets on a privately owned beach. The owner of the beach was restrained from building on the beach because to do so would interfere with the customary rights. If the custom could not have been exercised at some time since 1189, the claim will fail, as in *Simpson v Wells*[5], where the holding of a stall on a highway was shown not to have been authorised before the fourteenth century.

(B) Continuity

The custom must have been continuously in operation but it need not have been exercised throughout the required period as long as the right actually existed. It seems that a customary right cannot be lost by disuse once it is established, but failure to exercise the right may make it more difficult to prove in the first place. In *Wyld v Silver*[6], the rights of people in a parish to hold an annual fair on a specific piece of land were recognised as a custom, even though no such fair had been held within living memory. Consequently, they were able to prevent the landowner from building on the land. Likewise in *New Windsor Corporation v Mellor*[7], mentioned previously, a local authority was prevented from utilising land where it was proved that for many centuries the land had been used for recreational purposes by the local inhabitants, even though such rights had not been exercised in recent times.

(C) Peaceable enjoyment

The basis of a custom is that it is exercised by common consent. If it is exercised with force or in secret there can be no custom (*nec per vim nec clam nec precario*). If the so-called custom is exercised by permission it cannot be as of right, and,

---

[2] *Brocklebank v Thomson* [1903] 2 Ch 344
[3] *New Windsor Corporation v Mellor* [1975] Ch 380
[4] [1905] 2 Ch 538
[5] (1871-2) LR 7 QB 214
[6] [1963] Ch 243
[7] [1975] Ch 380

therefore, it is impossible to establish as a local custom. In *Mills v Colchester Corporation*[8], a claim to a custom entitling the claimant to an annual licence to fish for oysters failed, as the existence of the licence prevented the fishing from being as of right.

(D) Reasonableness and certainty

The courts will not recognise any custom which is unreasonable. On that basis, an attempt to claim the existence of a customary right enabling the Lord of the Manor to excavate on land without paying compensation for the damage to the owners of buildings on that land was deemed to be unreasonable[9]. The custom must also be certain. Those who are to benefit from a customary right must be capable of proper identification. In *Wilson v Wiles*[10], a claim to a local custom to take turf failed because the extent of the *right* could not be identified. The law is reluctant to recognise new customs which have not been previously established. The custom must be consistent with previously established customs and must not conflict with statute law or any basic principle of the common law.

1.6.2   Case law

Case law is the essence of the common law. The greater part of English law consists of rules and principles laid down by judges in courts of law, the more important of which are written down in law reports for future reference. When a judge makes a decision on a particular aspect of the law this will be recorded, and other judges are obliged to follow this decision in subsequent cases. When a judge is considering the facts of a case and applying the relevant law to the facts, it is necessary to look back to previous cases which have involved similar facts in the same area of law to see how those cases have been dealt with.

(A) Law reporting

The importance of case law as a source of law depends upon the existence of law reports. Important cases which establish new principles of law are published in the law reports. The report contains details of the facts of the case together with the decision of the judge (known as the judgment) and the reasons for that decision. By no means are all cases of interest reported. There is no official law report and most court decisions are left unreported. Even so, an unreported case may be taken into account by a judge when coming to a decision in a later case. There is an element of chance as to whether a case is reported or not. The history of law reports goes back to the Year Books. These were manuscripts that referred to cases which had been dealt with in a particular locality. After the demise of the Year Books, the practice grew up in the first part of the sixteenth century, whereby a number of private

---

[8] [1867] LR 2 CP 567
[9] *Wolstanton Ltd v Newcastle Under-Lyme Corp* [1940] AC 860
[10] [1806] 7 East's Term Reports 12

reports were separately published. These were compiled primarily by lawyers for their own personal use and their standard and quality varied greatly. Good examples include those of Coke, Dyer and Burrow, who all established a reputation for reporting cases accurately. All the available reports of the private reporters have been reprinted in what is known as the *English Reports*. These are sometimes referred to by judges in the course of their decisions. There is an index in the English Reports showing in which volume the reports of individual reporters are contained.

Modern law reporting dates from 1865 with the creation of the Council of Law Reporting. In 1870 the Council was incorporated as the Incorporated Council of Law Reporting for England and Wales. The 'Law Reports' comprise four series of reports: Appeal Cases (AC), Queen's Bench (QB), Chancery (Ch) and Family (Fam). These reports are now supplemented by the Weekly Law Reports (WLR), which contain a report of all the decisions which will eventually appear in the more official reports. In addition to these reports there are other transcripts which are published commercially. The best known of these are the All England Law Reports (All ER), which are a general series of reports published weekly that now appear in three or four volumes each year. Although the courts have traditionally preferred to use the more official reports, the importance of the commercially produced reports has increased in recent years. In construction matters and disputes concerning land and buildings it is common to encounter the Local Government Reports (LGR), Property and Compensation Reports (PCR), Building Law Reports (BLR), Housing Law Reports (HLR) and Rydes Rating Cases (RRC) among others. *The Times* newspaper carries daily reports of leading cases while periodicals such as the *Estates Gazette* and *The Journal of Planning and Environmental Law* publish reports of interest to their readers. Many cases are recorded in various reports and reference is made to them in a cross-section of journals. When a case is reported, after the names of the parties involved and the year it was decided, the name of the report is stated and the page where the case is to be found. For example, *Murphy v Brentwood District Council* [1991] 1 AC 398 indicates that the first volume of the Appeal Cases reports for 1991 must be consulted, and on page 398 details of the case are reported.

As part of the modernisation of law reporting, a system of neutral citation of judgments in the Court of Appeal and the Administrative Court was established by two Practice Directions in 2001 and 2002. The House of Lords and the Privy Council also adopted the new system of citation in 2001. Each case is assigned a unique number. There is no page numbering, only sequential paragraph numbering. Referring to part of the judgment of Lord Walker in the House of Lords case of *Stack v Dowden*, the neutral citation would read: *Stack v Dowden* [2007] UKHL 17 at [20]. This was the 17th case heard in the House of Lords in 2007 and the particular part of the judgment cited is in paragraph number 20. Cases in the Court of Appeal are cited as EWCA Civ (Civil Division) and EWCA Crim (Criminal Division); and in the High Court EWHC 1 (Ch) for Chancery Division and EWHC 1 (QB) for Queen's Bench Division (Fam) or (Admin) are substituted to indicate cases heard in the Family Division or the Administrative Court. If a judgment has been reported in more than one series of law reports, the neutral citation must be given first. A good source of guidance on the use of neutral citation (as well as the citing of case law in general) is to be found in *TheOxford Standard for Citation of Legal Authorities* (OSCOLA)[11].

Over recent years developments in information communication technology have led to the introduction of a number of computerised databases that give access to a wide range of cases and law reports. Most reported cases are available through databases such as LexisNexis (a division of Reed Elsevier [UK] Ltd), Westlaw UK and Lawtel (from the legal publishers, Sweet & Maxwell Ltd) or Justis (operated by Justis Publishing Ltd) LexisNexis also stores all unreported judgments of the Court of Appeal, Civil Division delivered since 1980. These databases are available by subscription, but many courts and some reporting services have web pages where cases can be accessed free of charge. House of Lords opinions from 1996 are published on the House of Lords website (very often on the day of release). Many other courts also make full text judgments available online (for example, the European Court of Justice and the Employment Appeal Tribunal).

(B) Judicial precedent

After the reorganisation of the courts implemented by the Judicature Acts (1873–75) and the emergence of good law reporting in the latter part of the nineteenth century, judicial precedent became an integral aspect of case law. By this doctrine of *stare decisis* (to stand upon decisions), whenever a judge reaches a decision on a particular point the rules of law contained in previous decisions which deal with similar issues must be applied. Not every judicial decision makes a precedent, as some courts are more important than others and not every case is important enough to make new law. A distinction is made between the principle forming the decision, called the *ratio decidendi*, and other comments made by a judge which are not strictly relevant to the decision, known as the *obiter dicta*. The *ratio* is the binding precedent which must be followed in future cases. The *dicta*, which is not material to the case, or does not form the basis of the decision, need not be followed in subsequent cases. Even so, *dicta* of an appellate court may carry considerable weight. The doctrine is applied on a hierarchal basis. The rule is that the lower courts are bound by decisions of the higher courts. The County Court and the Magistrates Court, at the bottom of the court hierarchy (inferior courts), are bound by the decisions of the courts above them (superior courts) but are not themselves bound by their own decisions. The High Court is bound by a decision of the Court of Appeal and the House of Lords, while the Court of Appeal is bound by a decision of the House of Lords which is the supreme appeal court in the United Kingdom (including Scotland and Northern Ireland) in both civil and criminal matters. Decisions of this court are binding on all lower courts. Since 1966, the House of Lords has been able to depart from its previous decisions. Instances of this have been rare. The decision in *Murphy v Brentwood DC*[12] is a good example of this process, where the Law Lords overruled the previous decision in *Anns v Merton London Borough Council*[13]. The European Court of Justice (ECJ) (see paragraph

---

[11] http://denning.law.ox.ac.uk/published/oscola.shtml
[12] [1991] 1 AC 398
[13] [1978] AC 728

1.7.1.E.a), whose major jurisdiction is concerned with the Treaties and institutions of the European Union, is not bound by its previous decisions. Questions on the interpretation of European Community Law can be referred by any UK court or tribunal to the ECJ for clarification.

(C) Interpretation of judicial precedent

The importance of a precedent tends to grow with age, but that does not mean that a precedent must be followed regardless of the consequences. Despite the importance of precedent in English law, a court will sometimes refuse to follow an earlier decision. It is the *ratio decidendi* of a case which is binding on subsequent courts, subject to the hierarchy rules. Before the precedent has a binding effect it must be shown to be a decision of a court in the English hierarchy. *Obiter dicta* of a court, particularly the House of Lords, is of weight but need not be followed by a court in subsequent cases. Similar considerations apply to the decisions of Scottish, Irish and particularly Commonwealth cases, which in recent years have been frequently cited in building disputes. Decisions of the Privy Council (see paragraph 1.10) also come into this category. If there are grounds for distinguishing a case from an earlier decision, then the previous decision does not have to be followed. A court may overrule a legal rule in a decision which it considers to be obviously wrong, while the decision of a lower court may be reversed on appeal if the higher court disapproves of the previous case.

(D) The merits of the system

The following are considered to be *advantages* of the system of judicial precedent.

(a) Certainty

It is suggested that precedent gives at least some degree of certainty and consistency to the law so that the probable outcome of a case can be predicted.

(b) Detail

Case law has many detailed rules. The law reports provide full information relating to decided cases and it is argued that a code could never furnish similar precision.

(c) Practical aspects

It is more useful to have a precedent than to argue a case on each occasion that a legal issue arises.

(d) Flexibility

Where appropriate, a court is able to avoid an unsatisfactory precedent by distinguishing or overruling a decision, although the opportunities for this are limited.

The following are put foward as *disadvantages* of the system.

(a) Rigidity

The process gives little scope for manoeuvre (at least in theory). Parliament can, however, bring in legislation to change an unsatisfactory feature of the common law.

(b) Technicalities

The sophisticated methods of avoiding a precedent tend to confuse the law and produce a degree of uncertainty.

(c) Bulk

Because of the volume of cases it is increasingly difficult to refer to every appropriate authority. Sometimes cases go unreported but they still remain as precedents.

1.6.3   Legislation

Although much of English law is derived from case law, governed by the system of judicial precedent, the supremacy of legislation over all other sources of law means that law made by Parliament, or derived from it, is the most important source of law in the United Kingdom today. A statute, or Act of Parliament, is the quickest and clearest method of adding to the law or changing it to meet current social requirements. Such an Act overrules any existing custom, case law or earlier Act with which it is in conflict, and the only external factor which can affect this parliament-made law is a decision of the European Community (see paragraph 1.7). This supremacy of legislation over other sources of law is known as the Sovereignty of Parliament. The effect of this is that Parliament, comprising the House of Commons and the House of Lords together with the reigning monarch, is sovereign and the legality of Parliament to make a specific law cannot be challenged. The courts must apply the Act once it becomes law, although it is a matter for the judges to ascertain what the Acts actually mean.

(A) The making of a statute

In the United Kingdom, Parliament consists of two different legislative institutions known as the House of Commons and the House of Lords. Ideas for new laws are put forward by both the government in power and by private members of Parliament. The former are far more numerous and the latter stand little chance of success unless they are adopted by the government. The idea is put into technical language in a bill. Government bills are prepared by lawyers known as parliamentary draftsmen and they can be introduced by the government in either House of Parliament. The normal practice is to introduce bills in the House of Commons. A bill has to pass through several stages in both the Commons and the Lords before it receives the Royal Assent (the Queen's approval) and becomes an Act. Once a bill becomes an Act it will remain law unless it is repealed. It is presumed not to be retrospective (back-dated) in effect. A statute does not become obsolete simply by the passing of time. There are many Acts on the statute book which are antiquated and of no practical use. As a consequence there are now Statute Law (Repeals) Acts which repeal obsolete enactments on a regular basis. Occasionally an Act is only operative for a limited period, but as a general rule a statute ceases to have effect only when it is repealed by another statute.

(B) Types of legislation

(a) Public Acts

These are Acts which affect the community generally. They are the most common types of Acts which are promulgated (brought into effect).

(b) Private Acts

These do not alter the general law but confer special or local powers. They are often promoted by local authorities.

(c) Consolidating Acts

Such an Act is a statute which gathers together several Acts on one area of the law and re-enacts them so that all the statute law on a particular topic can be found in the same Act. This is periodically done with tax legislation and town planning Acts.

(d) Codifying Acts

A codification takes place when the whole of the law on a particular topic is enacted in one statute. It includes all previous case law, established customs and legislation. The law of most continental European countries is codified but in the United Kingdom and other common law countries there is little codification. The classic example of codification in English law is the *Sale of Goods Act 1893* (now 1979) (see Chapter 2, paragraph 2.5.2.B), which reduced all the law on the subject into a single code.

(C) Delegated legislation

Parliament frequently passes on responsibility for enacting legislation to others. In this way the framework of an Act can be laid down while the delegated body can fill in the detail required. This subordinate legislation appears in the form of rules, regulations and orders, while the legislators range from the government (the Queen in Council) to local authorities. Much of the law relating to building matters and the transfer of land is to be found in this form. Examples include building regulations, and many aspects of planning law and health and safety legislation. Delegated legislation is made by ministerial orders known as statutory instruments, which since 1946 have had to be published or 'laid' before Parliament before they become effective. A statutory instrument can be recognised in that instead of having the word Act at the end of the name of the instrument (document), the order, rules or regulations will be cited (recorded) by reference to year and number with the letters SI indicating its status, e.g. The Home Improvement (Number 2) Regulations, 2007 (SI 2007/1667). Two other forms of delegated legislation are by-laws and the regulations of professional bodies and trade unions. By-laws are local laws which regulate aspects of life. So-called *autonomic* legislation regulates the conduct of the members of professional associations such as the Royal Institution of Chartered Surveyors and The Royal Institute of British Architects, and provides for sanctions where appropriate.

(D) Control of delegated legislation

Control over delegated legislation is exercised by Parliament and the courts.

(a) Parliament

Committees of the House of Commons review statutory instruments and decide which of them should be brought to the attention of Parliament. The enabling Act (the individual Act which grants power to make particular regulations) sometimes itself requires that the instrument be brought to the notice of Parliament. Appropriate government ministers are answerable to Parliament in respect of regulations made by their own departments, while by-laws must be confirmed by a government department before they become law. Parliament also has the overall safeguard in that it may withdraw the delegated power if it so wishes.

(b) The courts

Although the courts cannot challenge the validity of an Act of Parliament, they can challenge delegated legislation on the basis that the sub-legislator has exceeded the powers which Parliament has conferred upon him. In this case, the statutory instrument will be held to be *ultra vires* (beyond the power) and the rules rendered void. Many statutes, those dealing with compulsory purchase of land and planning law for example, contain provisions whereby delegated legislation can be challenged on the basis that it is *ultra vires*. Also, before certain types of delegated legislation are effected, a public enquiry is held so that the views of the public may be made known on the particular issues.

(E) The advantages of delegated legislation

(a) Speed

In an emergency, Parliament may not have time to deal with every problem which arises.

(b) Volume

It reduces the volume of work for Parliament if it deals with general aspects of policy and then delegates the detail to the sub-legislators.

(c) Flexibility

A flexible legislative process confers obvious advantages. The rules can be quickly altered and amended as necessary.

(d) Technicality

Modern day statute law, such as environmental and safety legislation, is highly technical in nature and better dealt with by experts than by members of Parliament.

(F) The disadvantages of delegated legislation

(a) Bulk

Over 3000 statutory instruments come into force each year, creating new law.

(b) Consultation and control

With the widespread use of delegated legislation, law-making moves out of the control of elected representatives of the people and more into the hands of civil servants. Because this type of legislation need not be mentioned in Parliament, there is a danger of insufficient publicity and consultation with interested parties.

(G) Statutory interpretation

Although the courts are denied the opportunity of challenging the supremacy of Parliament, because of the concept of parliamentary sovereignty, it is a matter for the courts to determine the meaning of a particular section of an Act or statutory instrument and to attempt to discover Parliament's intentions from the language used in the provision. The rule is that judges must not imply words into a statute but must interpret the provision from what the enactment says. It is not possible, as in the case of most systems of law in Europe, to look at extrinsic material such as debates in Parliament to help interpret the provision. Rules have been formulated to deal with the interpretation of statutes by the courts. Many Acts contain an interpretation section dealing with the words and phrases used in it. A good example of this is section 205 of the Law of Property Act 1925. Parliament has also helped the courts, to some extent, by passing the Interpretation Act 1978 which defines many expressions used in legislation unless a contrary intention is apparent. The task of the courts is to 'interpret the will of Parliament' as expressed in the statute. To help the judges in that task of interpretation the courts have developed a number of rules. It is for the judge to decide which is the appropriate rule in a particular case.

(a) The literal rule

The basis of this rule is that if the words of the statute are clear and unambiguous they will be applied as they stand.

(b) The golden rule

Where application of the literal rule results in an absurdity or is inconsistent, the meaning to be given is that which expresses best the intention of Parliament from reading the Act in full.

(c) The mischief rule

Here the court attempts to find out the mischief that the Act is attempting to remedy and interprets the Act accordingly[14].

These issues do not tend to arise in continental European systems of law or in the interpretation of European Union legislation (see paragraph 1.7). In Civil systems of law the overall intention or purpose of the legislation is paramount. The background to the legislation is considered as an essential part of the process. Legislation must be interpreted *purposively* (in other words, looking at its purpose) to give effect to the broad intentions of Parliament[15].

1.6.4   Law reform and the Law Commission

It is important that any legal system should be continually assessed in order that its principles do not become out of date. Statute law is the principal method by which the law is changed, but there are also pressure groups who inquire into the state of the law and where appropriate make proposals for amendment. In addition to professional bodies such as the Law Society and the Bar Council, external associations such as the National Council for Civil Liberties and the lawyers' political groups (for instance, the Society of Labour Lawyers and its Conservative equivalent) seek to influence the present state of the legal system. There are also a number of standing committees of lawyers who advise on matters of law reform. At times the Government appoints a Royal Commission to research a particular topic. The Beeching Commission[16], which led to the Courts Act 1971 bringing about a fundamental change in the system of courts, is a good example.

The Law Commission Act 1965 established the Law Commission. This is a permanent organisation consisting of full time Commissioners, who are lawyers appointed by the Lord Chancellor and the Secretary of State for Justice to recommend changes which should be made to the law. It is an advisory body given the task of modernising the legal system. Its recommendations only become

---

[14] *Heydon's Case* (1584) 3 Co Rep 7a; *Gorris v Scott* (1873-74) LR Ex 125
[15] *Litster v Forth Dry Dock & Engineering Co Ltd* [1990] AC 546; *H P Bulmer Ltd v J Bollinger SA (No 2)* [1974] FSR 263; *Pickstone v Freemans Plc* [1987] 3 WLR 811
[16] The Report of the Royal Commission on Assizes and Quarter Sessions (The Beeching Committee Report), Cmnd 4153, 1969

law if they are adopted by Parliament. It can claim considerable success in bringing about law reform, particularly changes in the criminal law. A good example of the Law Commission's work is the Latent Defects Act 1985, which attempts to clarify the law on limitation periods (the length of time a claimant has in which to bring a case against a defendant). In 1993, Sir Michael Latham was commissioned by the Department of the Environment and other bodies connected with the construction industry to suggest a number of mechanisms for improving co-operation and productivity. The Housing Grants, Construction and Regeneration Act 1996 (see Chapter 2, paragraph 2.14.10) was passed as a result of the Latham Report 'Constructing the Team'[17]. This Act, which provides for a new system of dispute adjudication and the outlawing of 'pay when paid' contracts, is a good example of a report leading to the enactment of legislation.

1.7 European Community law

The European Economic Community (EEC) was set up by the first Treaty of Rome in 1957. Its aim was to merge the interests of its member states into a common market of Europe whereby persons, goods, capital and services could circulate freely in order to create stability among its members and improve standards of living. After the merger of the EEC with the European Coal and Steel Community (ECSC) and the European Atomic Energy Authority (EURATOM) these three bodies became known as the European Community or 'EC'. The Treaty of Rome was concerned with attempting to harmonise the economic policies of the member states through common policies in matters such as employment, fair competition, transport, social issues, agriculture and fisheries. In 1973, the United Kingdom became a full member of the Community, thereby agreeing to dilute its sovereign powers. Since then, many other countries have joined the Community and this process is continuing. The original three treaties have been supplemented over the years by the Single European Act, the Treaty on European Union (the Maastricht Treaty), the Treaty of Amsterdam and some provisions of the Treaty of Nice and the Treaty of Athens. The most recent revision was made by the Treaty of Lisbon, which amended the EC Treaty (now named the Treaty on the Functioning of the European Union) and the Treaty on European Union and renamed the Community as the Union. These latter two instruments now constitute the Treaties on which the Union is founded. The Treaties are directly applicable in the United Kingdom, with no need for further legislation by Parliament. This is achieved by way of the European Communities Act 1972, s.2 (1).

1.7.1 Union institutions

There are now seven institutions that provide the Union with its institutional framework. These include those listed below in addition to the European Central Bank.

---

[17] Constructing the team – 'The Latham Report': Final report of the government/industry review of procurement and contractual arrangements in the UK construction industry, 1994, HMSO

(A) The Commission

This is the executive body of the Union. It initiates and drafts Union legislation. It also acts as the guardian of the Treaties and has a duty to investigate any infringements of EU law. Currently each member state is represented on the Commission. Commissioners must act independently of their national status. The President holds office for a renewable term of two years.

(B) The European Council

This body was formally recognized as a Union institution by amendments made in the Treaty of Lisbon. Its role is a political one and it does not have a legislative function. There is an elected president for a term of two and a half years (renewable once). The President cannot hold a national office at the same time.

(C) The Council

The Council is made up of representatives from the governments of each member state. It meets in different configurations depending on the subject matter under consideration. All configurations, other than the Foreign Affairs Council, will be presided over by one of the Council's Member State representatives, on the basis of a system of equal rotation, determined by the European Council. The Council is a political body which reflects the national interests of member states in legislative matters. Although the final decision on any legislative proposal rests with the Council (often in a joint decision-making procedure with the European Paraliament), it usually acts on proposals put foward by the Commission.

(D) The Parliament

Originally referred to as the Assembly, this body is based in Strasbourg in France. Since 1979, members have been elected from member states (MEPs). Representation varies depending upon the size of the member state. Members vote on a personal basis and do not receive any voting mandate from their home state. Parliament has three main roles. It has significant powers over the EU budget, it exercises a supervisory role over the Commission and it has a legislative function. In most Treaty areas, it acts with the Council in a joint legislative procedure.

(E) The Court of Justice of the European Union

(a) The Court of Justice (ECJ)

Based in Luxembourg, and not to be confused with the European Court of Human Rights (see paragraph 1.11), the Court of Justice is charged with ensuring that Union law is enforced and to provide a forum for the resolution of disputes between member states and the EC. It is also concerned with disputes between the institutions of the Union and protecting rights of the individual. Judges are appointed from member states and one of them acts as President for a three-year term. The judges are assisted by Advocate Generals whose role is to help the court by presenting reasoned submissions on the facts and also recommendations for a decision. These are purely objective in nature and are not binding on the judges. Procedures are derived from continental European systems of law, with much greater emphasis on written submissions and pleadings. The Court does not operate a formal doctrine of precedent but it does normally follow its own previous decisions. Dissenting judgments are not expressed and there is no right of appeal.

(b) The General Court

In 1989, a court of first instance (CFI) was established to ease the workload of the Court of Justice. The work of the CFI was originally limited to disputes between the EC and its staff, competition issues and certain matters relating to the ECSM and EURATOM. Since 1993, the CFI has heard all cases brought by individuals or undertakings and under the Treaty of Nice it was given jurisdiction to hear certain other cases at first instance. The Treaty of Lisbon renamed the court of first instance the General Court. There is a right of appeal to the ECJ.

(F) The Court of Auditors

This court was established in 1975 and became a full institution under the Treaty of Maastricht. It carries out audits of all revenue and expenditure of the Union. It has to provide the Council and the Parliament with a statement that transactions have been legally made and that the accounts are accurate.

1.7.2   The sources of European Community Law

(A) The Treaties

A Treaty is a written agreement concluded between two or more states. In a way it is like a Public Act of Parliament made between nation states, but instead of having effect in one particular country it applies to all the parties to the treaty. Treaties are the primary source of EU law and take priority over subsidiary treaties and provisions contained in secondary legislation. Major examples include the two Treaties of Rome (1957), the Single European Act 1986, the Maastrict Treaty (Treaty of European Union 1992), The Treaty of Amsterdam, the Treaty of Nice and the Treaty of Lisbon. Subsidiary treaties or conventions may also be a source of EU law. Trading agreements between the Union and other states come into this category.

(B) Union legislation

Article 288 of the Treaty on the Functioning of the European Union gives the Council and the Commission powers to make secondary legislation in the following forms:

(a) Regulations

These are of general application in all member states. They are binding and directly applicable, and take effect without further enactment.

(b) Decisions

A decision is addressed either to a specific state or individual and is legally binding on the addressee.

(c) Directives

Directives may be addressed to one or more member states. They are binding upon member states as to the objectives to be achieved. Member states have a discretion as to how to achieve the objectives. Normally national provisions are put into place to implement a directive.

1.7.3   Direct applicability and direct effect

If a provision is directly applicable it means that it can take effect in the legal system of a member state without any further enactment. As mentioned above, regulations are directly applicable.

Other provisions of primary (Treaty) law and secondary legislation can have 'direct effect' in certain circumstances. This means that individuals can rely on the provisions of EU law in their national courts, whether or not they have been implemented into national law by the particular member state. In the United Kingdom, this is made possible by s.2 of the European Communities Act 1972. A provision of EU law is capable of having direct effect so long as it is clear and unambiguous, is unconditional in nature and able to take effect without further action by the EU or member states. In the early case of *Van Gend En Loos*[18], a private firm sought to rely on EU law against the Netherlands customs authorities in proceedings before a Netherlands tribunal. The Court of Justice held that the appropiate provision (Article 12 of the Treaty prohibiting member states from introducing new customs duties between themselves) was directly effective and could be relied upon before the Netherlands courts.

Regulations, directives and decisions are also capable of being directly effective if the conditions outlined above are satisfied. In the case of *Van Duyn v Home Office*[19] a Netherlands national who was refused entry to the United Kingdom to take up a job with the Church of Scientology was entitled to rely on a directive even though the UK had not implemented it, in circumstances where the ECJ was satisfied that the time for implementation had passed. A distinction is made between horizontal and vertical direct effect. The ECJ has held[20] that *directives* are only capable of

---

[18] 26/62 [1963] ECR 1
[19] 41/74 [1975] ECR 1337
[20] *Marshall v Southampton and South West Hampshire Area Health Authority* 152/84 [1986] QB 401

having vertical direct effect. That is, they can only be relied upon against the state and organs of the state and not against specific individuals. In cases before the ECJ it has been held that the concept of direct effect can be relied upon where the claim is against an organisation or body providing a public service which is subject to the control and authority of the state. This has included The Royal Ulster Constabulary[21] and British Gas[22].

1.7.4 State liability

The rule that directives have vertical but not horizontal direct effect can lead to injustice. A claimant against a private sector defendant is in a less favourable position than one against a public sector one. The ECJ sought to eliminate this injustice by developing what has become known as the *Francovich* doctrine, the principle of state liability for failing to implement directives. The cases of *Francovich and Bonfaci v Italy*[23] arose out of Italy's failure to implement Directive 80/987 on the protection of workers on the insolvency of their employer. Francovich and Bonfaci brought claims for their losses against the Italian government. The ECJ held that a state would be liable in damages for failure to implement a directive if three conditions were met; the directive must confer rights on individuals, the content of those rights must be identifiable from the directive and there must be a causal link between failure to implement and the loss suffered by the claimant. In subsequent decisions, the ECJ has also added the condition that the breach of EC law must be 'sufficiently serious'[24].

1.7.5 Conflicts between EU law and UK law

In areas of law in which the EU has competence, EU law prevails over UK law if there is a conflict between the two. The *Factortame* series of cases made this clear. The dispute in *R v Secretary of State for Transport, ex parte Factortame*[25] (Factortame 1) arose out of the introduction by the UK government of the Merchant Shipping Act 1988. The statute imposed restrictions on companies operating fishing vessels in British waters, contrary to EU law. Ultimately, the ECJ ruled that national courts are under a duty to give effect to EU law even if this is in conflict with national law and that a national law should be set aside where it prevents the granting of interim relief in a dispute governed by EU law. The House of Lords took the unprecedented step of issuing an injunction which suspended the effect of the offending Act.

---

[21] *Johnston v Chief Constable of the Royal Ulster Constabulary* 222/84 [1986] ECR 1651
[22] *Foster v British Gas* 188/89 [1990] ECR 1 – 3313
[23] 6,9/90 [1991] ECR 1 – 5357
[24] *Brasserie du Pecheur v Federal Republic of Germany* and *R v Secretary of State for Transport, ex parte Factortame* (Factortame 4) 46/93 and 48/93 [1996] ECR 1 – 1029; *R v Minister of Fisheries and Food, ex parte Hedley Lomas* 5/94 [1996] ECR 1 – 2553
[25] 213/89 [1990] ECR 1 - 2433

1.8   The court system in England and Wales

The court system in England is still based on that which was put into place by the Judicature Acts 1873–75 although, of necessity, changes have been made since in an attempt to reflect contemporary needs. Although some courts have both civil and criminal jurisdiction, it is better to consider the jurisdictions separately. The system is essentially a hierarchical one and as a rule it is possible to appeal from a lower court to a higher court.

1.8.1   The Criminal Courts

(A) Magistrates' Courts

The vast majority of criminal cases start off in Magistrates' Courts and over ninety-five per cent finish there as well. Every town of any size has at least one Magistrates' Court and there are approximately 600 such courts in England and Wales. The court is comprised of Lay Magistrates, sometimes known as Justices of the Peace (JP). These are part-time judges, not formally trained in the law, who in criminal matters decide the innocence or guilt of the defendant on the facts put before them. Such judges are unpaid but receive an attendance allowance and payment for loss of earnings. There are about 30 000 Lay Magistrates. Following the Constitutional Reform Act 2005, Local Advisory Committees make recommendations for appointment of magistrates, which go to the Lord Chief Justice for approval. The Lord Chancellor makes the appointment after consultation. All newly appointed magistrates have to undergo some initial training. On matters of law, procedure and sentencing, they are advised by the Clerk to the Magistrates who is legally qualified. The retiring age is seventy. In London, and some of the larger cities in the provinces, 139 District Judges (Magistrates' Courts) supplement the work of Justices. These are paid full-time magistrates, being either solicitors or barristers, who have had considerable experience of practising as lawyers in the criminal courts. They are allocated to the busier courts where the volume of work is greater and more complex. A Magistrates' Court is comprised of three Lay Magistrates although two justices will sometimes suffice. A District Judge (Magistrates' Courts) sits alone and has the powers equivalent to a bench of Lay Magistrates. In court a magistrate is addressed as 'your worship'.

Criminal offences fall into two main categories. These are classified as either summary or indictable offences. In the case of summary offences the magistrates decide the verdict and the sentence. This will also be the case if an offence is triable either summarily or on indictment and the defendant consents to it being heard in the Magistrates' Court. The maximum fine where a case is dealt with summarily is £5000 although higher fines of up to £20 000 are available in cases relating to health and safety and pollution. The maximum custodial sentence which magistrates may impose for any offence is in most cases twelve months' imprisonment. This can be slightly extended if the defendant has been convicted of two or more offences at the same time. The Magistrates' Court can, in certain circumstances, commit defendants to the Crown Court for sentence if, in their opinion, the offence or offences are so serious that the Crown Court should have the power to pass sentence. Indictable offences are so called because they may only be tried *on indictment*, which means by the Crown Court before judge and jury (see below). In such cases the court must proceed with transfer for trial proceedings to remove the case to the Crown Court.

Special conditions apply where the accused is under the age of eighteen. For this purpose the magistrates sit as a Youth Court. Proceedings must take place separately from the adult court and the public are not admitted. Reporting restrictions are also enforced. Magistrates dealing with these cases must have had training in dealing with young offenders and the panel must include at least one woman.

In addition to the actual hearing of cases, the preliminaries relating to them and sentencing, magistrates have extensive powers in respect of granting bail to the defendant or remanding to prison to await trial. Where a defendant is not represented by a lawyer, local solicitors attend on a rota basis to advise the accused. This is known as the duty solicitor system. Since the enactment of the Police and Criminal Evidence Act 1984, persons held in custody at a police station have an automatic right of access to legal advice.

Appeals from the Magistrates' Court

(i) *The Crown Court*: The accused may appeal against sentence or conviction as appropriate.
(ii) *The Divisional Court of the Queen's Bench Division*: Any party to the proceedings (including the prosecution) may appeal on a point of law by way of 'case stated'. The Divisional Court also deals with applications for Judicial Review (see Chapter 6, paragraph 6.2) where there is a defect in the decision which the court has reached.

(B) The Crown Court

The Courts Act 1971 abolished the Courts of Assize and Quarter Sessions and established the Crown Court as the single first instance criminal court above the Magistrates Court. The Central Criminal Court (The 'Old Bailey') is where the Crown Court sits in the City of London area. Although most cities and large towns are near to a Crown Court centre, they are not all of the same importance. There are three levels of courts. The first-tier courts deal with the most important criminal offences. The judges in first-tier courts are High Court Judges, sometimes known as Puisne Judges, and also Circuit Judges (see paragraph 1.15). The first-tier courts act also as regional centres for dealing with High Court civil actions as well as criminal cases. The second- and third-tier courts deal only with criminal cases. Circuit Judges or Recorders (part-time judges) hear cases in these courts but High Court Judges can hear cases in the second-tier courts. In addition to the classification of courts, Crown Court offences are also categorised into three groups according to the seriousness of the offence, indicating the level of judge who may try the particular case. Lay Magistrates are entitled to sit with the judge in the Crown Court. In fact they must form part of the Crown Court where it hears appeals from the Magistrates' Court and when sentencing defendants who have pleaded guilty in the Magistrates' Court and have come to the Crown Court for sentence.

Appeals from the Crown Court

(i) *The Court of Appeal (Criminal Division)*: the accused may appeal against sentence or conviction where appropriate.
(ii) *The Divisional Court of the Queen's Bench Division*: an appeal by way of 'case stated' may be made from the Crown Court to this court.

(C) The Court of Appeal (Criminal Divisions)

This court will be considered with The Court of Appeal (Civil Division) – see paragraph 1.8.2.E.

1.8.2   The Civil Courts

(A) Magistrates' Courts

Although essentially a criminal court, this court has some civil jurisdiction, primarily in family proceedings. This includes applications for custody of children, maintenence orders, and separation and adoption matters. As in the case of Youth Courts, the public is excluded from the proceedings, there are rules as to the composition of the 'bench' and strict limitations are imposed on press reports. There is no power to hear divorce cases. Magistrates are responsible for the granting or refusal of licences required for businesses which sell alcohol to the public, and those for betting shops and casinos where these are still required. There is also jurisdiction to recover unpaid council tax from debtors.

Appeals from the Magistrates' Court

(i) *The Crown Court*: this is appropriate in licensing and debt collecting matters.
(ii) *The Divisional Court of the Queen's Bench Division*: where appropriate, the 'case stated' procedure will apply on a point of law.
(iii) *The Divisional Court of the Family Division*: this will apply in the case of family proceedings.

(B) County Courts

County courts were established in 1846 to deal with minor civil matters cheaply and on a local basis. County courts are the major first-instance courts in civil matters and their jurisdiction is exclusively civil. In recent years claimants have been encouraged to use these courts when initiating proceedings, in an attempt to cut costs. County courts are presided over by Circuit Judges who are either solicitors or barristers. In the major cities more than one judge is allocated to each court. Where appropriate, deputy Circuit Judges may be appointed to reduce delays in the system. Much of the routine work involved in the county courts is undertaken by District Judges. Like Circuit Judges, they are appointed after selection by the Judicial Appointments Commission. There are around 220 county courts across England and Wales. They deal with the lower value and/or less complex civil cases. In practice, this will consist of all small claims track cases, most fast track cases and straightforward multi-track cases (see paragraph 1.18.5.A).

(a) Jurisdiction

The jurisdiction of the county courts is laid down in statute. The general jurisdiction of the county courts is set out in the County Courts Act 1984 (as amended) but there are many other statutes that also confer jurisdiction upon the county courts. The County Courts Act gives general jurisdiction for claims founded on contract or tort, or for money due under a statute. The allocation of business between the county courts and the High Court is subject to change by government. Currently, claims that include a claim for damages for personal injuries (contract and tort) are commenced in a county court if the value of the claim is less than £50 000. Claims over this value can be transferred from the High Court to a county court if this is a more suitable place of trial. County courts cannot hear claims for the tort of defamation (libel or slander) unless the parties agree and the High Court transfers the case.

(b) Appeals from the county courts

 (i) *The Circuit Judge*: There is a right of appeal against the finding of a District Judge to the Circuit Judge.
 (ii) *The Court of Appeal*: Either party can appeal against a county court decision directly to the Court of Appeal.
 (iii) *The Divisional Court of the Chancery Division*: where the county court has bankruptcy jurisdiction, appeal lies to a High Court judge.

(C) The High Court of Justice

The High Court was established by the Judicature Acts 1873–75, replacing the Common Law and Chancery Courts that existed previously. The work of the High Court is divided into three divisions, each of which has a separate jurisdiction. The court is staffed by High Court Judges and their role is to try civil cases which involve some complexity and/or considerable sums of money. High Court Judges are selected by the Judicial Appointments Commission in consultation with the Lord Chancellor and appointments are made by the Queen on their recommendation. Administrative matters in the High Court are dealt with by officials known as Masters who carry out the same types of tasks as District Judges in the county courts. In London, cases are dealt with at the Royal Courts of Justice situated in the Strand. High Court civil cases in the provinces are heard at first-tier Crown Court centres. The majority of chancery matters are dealt with in London, but there are eight other regional centres where such matters can be dealt with. High Court civil cases can be started off in the provinces without the need to go to London. This is done by filing the appropriate documents at District Registries which exist in the larger cities in England and Wales (often in premises used primarily as county courts). When this takes place, the District Judges are given the powers of Masters of the High Court. The jurisdiction of the High Court is principally civil in nature and is virtually unlimited.

(a) The Queen's Bench Division

This is by far the largest of the three divisions and it has the residual task of dealing with all matters not covered by the other divisions. It is presided over by a President and staffed by High Court Judges. A large number of judges are required because the division also staffs the Crown Courts at those first-tier centres where serious criminal cases and High Court civil cases are heard. The majority of actions brought are claims in contract and tort outside the limits of the county courts. The judge generally hears the case alone without a jury. Where a person's character is in dispute, a jury is empanelled (formed) to sit with the judge. Two highly regarded specialist courts, The Commercial Court and the Admiralty Court, sit within this division. The Queen's Bench Division also administers the Technology and Construction Court, which deals with disputes relating to building matters (see paragraph 1.9).

One increasingly important aspect of the jurisdiction of the Queen's Bench Division is its supervisory jurisdiction. This is a process whereby the court has powers to declare unlawful the decision of an inferior court, tribunal or other public body such as a local authority if it is acting in a judicial manner. This process is known as Judicial Review and is concerned only with the way in which the original decision of the court or public body was made and not the actual substantive merits of the case (see Chapter 6, paragraph 6.2).

(b) Chancery Division

This is the successor to the Court of Chancery, which dealt with the administration of equity and is the smallest of the three divisions. The President of the Chancery Division is the Chancellor of the High Court. The President is assisted by a number of other High Court Judges. Most Chancery cases are heard in London, but High Court Chancery proceedings can also be dealt with in the major cities of the provinces. As well as dealing with matters previously dealt with by the Court of Chancery, the jurisdiction of the Chancery Division covers all causes and matters relating to the sale of land, mortgages, trusts, wills, bankruptcy and company law matters.

(c) Family Division

Established in 1970, this is the most modern of the three divisions and deals with all aspects of family law. The division is headed by the President of the Family Division (also Head of Family Justice). The President is assisted by a number of High Court

Judges. The jurisdiction of the division includes all defended divorce petitions, family property disputes, matters relating to children, adoption, gender recognition and civil partnerships.

(d) Appeals from the High Court

Either party can appeal against a High Court decision to the Court of Appeal (Civil Division). If there is a point of law of general public importance, either party can appeal directly to the House of Lords if the decision is on an appeal by way of case stated from the Magistrates' Court or Crown Court (see above) or by using the 'leapfrog procedure'. For an appeal to go directly to the House of Lords, the parties must agree, the court must certify that the case is appropriate and the House of Lords has to grant leave to appeal.

(D) Divisional Courts

Each of the three divisions of the High Court have Divisional Courts which hear appeals from inferior courts. In the Queen's Bench Division, historically the court heard 'case stated' appeals on points of law from the Magistrates' Court or Crown Court, applications for a writ of habeas corpus and contempt of court applications, together with exercising supervisory jurisdiction over tribunals and inferior courts. However, these functions are these days mostly carried out by a single judge and claims for judicial review are now dealt with in the Administrative Court. In the Chancery Division, the Divisional Court hears bankruptcy appeals from county courts, while in the Family Division the Divisional Court hears appeals from Magistrates' Courts in family proceedings.

(E) The Court of Appeal

Appeals from the Crown Court, the High Court and the county courts are heard in this court. The appeal may be on a question of law or fact from a lower court and certain tribunals. The court is divided into a criminal and a civil division. It is staffed by Lords Justices and Lady Justices of Appeal (see paragraph 1.15.11). The president of the civil division is the Master of the Rolls, while the head of the criminal division is the Lord Chief Justice (see paragraph 1.15). In practice, most appeals are heard by three judges. The Court of Appeal can sit anywhere in England and Wales, but generally it sits in London.

(a) Appeals from the Court of Appeal

Either party can appeal to the House of Lords on a point of law of general public importance. This must be certified by the Court of Appeal and the House of Lords must grant leave to appeal.

(F) The Supreme Court

In 2009, The Supreme Court became the highest court in the UK. It took over the role and functions of the Appellate Committee of the House of Lords. The Supreme Court is the final appeal court for England and Wales and Northern Ireland in civil and criminal cases and for Scotland in civil cases. The Court has twelve judges, known as 'Justices of the Supreme Court' and it is headed by a President and a Deputy President. The Supreme Court sits in panels of an uneven number with a minimum of three judges. Cases are normally heard by five judges. As well as its appellate jurisdiction, the Supreme Court also has devolution jurisdiction. It has the power in this latter respect to determine whether the devolved executive and legislative authorities in Scotland, Wales and Northern Ireland have acted within their powers or failed to comply with any duty imposed on them. The Supreme Court hears appeals from the Court of Appeal (civil and criminal divisions), the Court of Session in Scotland and the Court of Appeal in Northern Ireland. In some limited cases it also hears appeals from the High Court (see above). Most appeals come from the Court of Appeal in England. In order for an appeal to come to the Supreme Court, leave must be given by either the Court of Appeal or the Supreme Court itself. In criminal cases, there is the additional requirement that a point of law of general public importance must be involved.

1.9 The Technology and Construction Court (TCC)

The TCC is a specialist court, led by a High Court Judge and staffed by Circuit Judges. The Court deals mainly with technology and construction disputes. These include building or other construction disputes, claims for the enforcement of the decisions of adjudicators under the Housing Grants, Construction and Regeneration Act 1996, claims by and against engineers, architects, surveyors and other specialised advisers, claims by and against local authorities relating to their statutory duties concerning the development of land or the construction of buildings and claims between landlord and tenant for breach of a repairing covenant. The TCC also hears challenges to the decisions of arbitrators in construction and engineering disputes. The court is based in London, but also operates from a number of regional court centres, some of which have full time TCC judges.

1.10 The Judicial Committee of the Privy Council

This is the final court of appeal for the UK overseas territories and Crown dependencies and for the Commonwealth countries that have retained their right of appeal to the UK. It is composed of members of the Privy Council who are senior members of the judiciary. The Judicial Committee sits in London with a minimum number of three judges. As well as its overseas appellate jurisdiction, the Judicial Committee of the Privy Council also hears appeals from a number of disciplinary committees of the professions. Instead of delivering a judgment it tenders advice to the Sovereign. The Committee is not bound by its previous decisions.

1.11   The European Court of Human Rights

This court (not to be confused with the European Court of Justice – see paragraph 1.7) was established in 1959 and is based in Strasbourg. The court is concerned with the interpretation and application of the European Convention on Human Rights and Fundamental Freedoms (ECHR). The United Kingdom is one of the contracting states and has accepted the court's jurisdiction. Individuals can approach the court directly in respect of an allegation of violation of convention rights. Rulings are delivered by a chamber of seven judges with an appeal to a grand chamber of seventeen judges.

1.12   Tribunals

A major characteristic of the English legal system since the end of the second world war has been the growth in importance of tribunals. A noticeable defect of the traditional court system is that it is unsuitable for dealing with the settlement of every type of dispute. Disputes dealing with specialist topics can often be better dealt with by experts instead of by judges. The increasing role of government in economic and social matters has brought about a proliferation of disputes between private individuals and government departments. Acts of Parliament have set up tribunals in an attempt to provide a speedy and cheap method of settling disputes as a supplement to the court system. The areas dealt with by tribunals vary from immigration appeals and employment matters to disputes concerning tenanted farms.

Procedure in the various tribunals and the routes of appeal were very different and the Tribunals Courts and Enforcement Act 2007 brought in a radical reform of the tribunal system. The Act created an Upper Tribunal, a superior court of record, the primary function of which is to deal with adminstrative appeals and a First Tier Tribunal. The pre-existing Employment Tribunal, Employment Appeals Tribunal and Asylum and Immigration Tribunal all remain in place. The First Tier Tribunal and the Upper Tribunal are both divided into a number of chambers. The composition of the new tribunals will be similar to that of existing tribunals in that legally qualified members will sit alongside 'other' members (experts in the field, such as qualified surveyors for valuation matters). However, the legally qualified members of the two new tribunals will be called 'judges'. There is a Senior President of Tribunals presiding over all five tribunals and each chamber also has a president. There is a new Tribunal Procedure Committee responsible for the production of common tribunal procedure rules and an Administrative Justice and Tribunals Council to oversee the system.

Both tiers of the new tribunal system can review and set aside their own decisions. Most decisions of the First Tier Tribunal can be appealed to the Upper

Tribunal and decisions of the Upper Tribunal, on points of law, can be appealed to a court of law.

1.12.1 The Lands Tribunal

This tribunal was established by The Lands Tribunal Act 1949 to settle certain disputes concerning the valuation of land. In 2009, the Lands Tribunal became part of the new two-tier tribunal system as a chamber of the Upper Tribunal. The Tribunal has a Chamber President, a number of judges, specialist members who are chartered surveyors and two registrars (responsible for case management). The Lands Tribunal is based in London but hearings can be carried out anywhere in England and Wales. The Lands Tribunal hears appeals from Valuation Tribunals, Leasehold Valuation Tribunals and Residential Property Tribunals. It also determines disputed compensation in compulsory purchase and certain other types of land compensation cases. The Tribunal hears applications to discharge or modify restrictive covenants on land (see Chapter 4, paragraph 4.9.6.C) and deals with a range of other types of cases under various different Acts of Parliament and statutory instruments, including applications for a certificate to support an application to register a light obstruction notice under the Rights of Light Act 1959.

1.12.2 The Agricultural Land Tribunals

The eight Agricultural Land Tribunals are organised on a regional basis. Each tribunal is staffed by a legally qualified Chairman and two lay members nominated by the Chairman. Agricultural Land Tribunals became courts of first instance under the Agriculture Act 1958. These tribunals nowadays act mainly under the Agricultural Holdings Act 1986 in determining disputes between landlords and tenants, particularly in relation to succession to tenancies. They also have a role under the Land Drainage Act 1991 in settling drainage disputes between neighbours. At the time of writing, the tribunals are expected to be brought into the new tribunal system in 2010.

1.13 Arbitration

Arbitration is a private process for the resolution of disputes between parties to an arbitration agreement. The dispute is referred to an impartial third party or parties (the *arbitrator* or *arbitral tribunal*), which decides the dispute in a judicial manner on the basis of evidence submitted. An award is then published that is legally binding on the parties. The arbitration process is governed by the terms of the arbitration agreement between the parties, the Arbitration Act 1996 (if the agreement is in writing) and the Common Law.

1.13.1 The Arbitration Act 1996

Section 1.1 of the Act requires that its provisions should all be construed according to the following principles:

- The object of arbitration is to obtain the fair resolution of disputes by an impartial tribunal without unnecessary delay or expense.
- The parties should be free to agree how their disputes are resolved, subject only to such safeguards as are necessary in the public interest.
- The court should not intervene except as provided by this [Act].

There is also a general duty of the tribunal laid out in Section 33 (1) that requires it to:

- Act fairly and impartially as between the parties, giving each party a reasonable opportunity of putting their case and dealing with that of his opponent.
- Adopt procedures suitable to the circumstances of the particular case, avoiding unnecessary delay or expense, so as to provide a fair means for the resolution of the matters falling to be determined.

An arbitrator (or his employee or agent) is not liable for anything done or omitted whilst performing his role unless the act or omission is shown to have been in bad faith[26].

1.13.2   The arbitration agreement

Because arbitration is a consensual process there must be a valid agreement by the parties (an arbitration agreement) to refer their dispute to arbitration. In the absence of such an agreement there is no legal basis for the arbitration. Arbitration agreements that are subject to the Arbitration Act 1996 must be in writing[27]. An agreement can be to submit either present or future disputes to arbitration. An arbitration clause within a contract constitutes an arbitration agreement and this kind of clause can still be a valid arbitration agreement even if the contract is found to be invalid.

The arbitration agreement usually defines the categories of disputes that can be referred to arbitration and establishes the composition and method of appointment of the arbitral tribunal. It may also specify the way in which arbitration proceedings are to be commenced (normally by service of a notice of arbitration on the other party) and the procedure to be followed by the tribunal.

An arbitration agreement is a contract to refer disputes to arbitration. Therefore, if a party commences litigation instead of referring the dispute to arbitration, they are in breach of contract. If, however, proceedings are commenced, then a party can apply to the court for a stay of those proceedings. The court must grant such a stay unless it is satisfied that the arbitration agreement is null and void, inoperative, or incapable of being performed.

1.13.3   Arbitration procedures

After appointment of the arbitrator, but before the parties set out their respective cases, a preliminary meeting will normally be called. This meeting enables the

---

[26] Section 29

[27] Section 5

arbitrator to satisfy himself/herself that he/she has jurisdiction to deal with the dispute, to determine any outstanding issues on procedures and timetable and issue an order for directions setting out the timetable and tasks to be completed by each of the parties. The parties are under a duty to comply without delay with any order or directions of the tribunal[28].

An *interlocutory stage* follows the preliminary meeting and during this stage the parties carry out a number of procedural steps laid down in the arbitrator's order for directions. They will exchange details of their case to each other in the forms of *statements of case*, which will generally consist of:

- Statement of Case.
- Statement of Defence and Counterclaim.
- Statement of Reply and Defence to Counterclaim.
- Statement of Reply to Defence to Counterclaim.

Disclosure and *inspection* will follow, whereby each party compiles a list of all the documents that are or may become relevant to the dispute and the other party is then entitled to inspect and obtain copies of all documents that are still in the other party's possession (as long as they are not protected by legal privilege).

The arbitrator has a wide discretion to decide on how the tribunal should establish the facts of the case, including whether strict rules of evidence should be applied and how evidence should be presented. This includes the discretion as to how best to deal with expert evidence. The arbitrator has the power to appoint his own expert or he may permit the parties to use their own experts. Procedural and evidential matters will often be determined in the arbitration agreement but if they are not, it is up to the arbitrator to decide whether to hold a hearing and, if so, the form that it should take. There are three different procedures:

- Full Procedure.
- Short Hearing Procedure.
- Documents Only Procedure.

1.13.4   *Arbitration award*

The arbitral tribunal decides the dispute by publishing its award. The parties can agree on the form of the award, but, to the extent that there is no agreement, it must be in writing and signed by the arbitrator, or by the parties if it is an agreed award. It should contain reasons (unless it is an agreed award) and be served on the parties without delay once it has been made. An arbitration award may, with the leave of the court, be enforced in the same way as a judgment or order of the court to the same effect.

---

[28] Section 40 (2)

The award can be challenged on three grounds:

- Tribunal's lack of jurisdiction[29].
- Serious irregularity affecting the tribunal, the proceedings or the award[30].
- Error of law[31].

The parties have an absolute right to challenge the award due to lack of jurisdiction or serious irregularity, but the right to challenge due to an error of law may be excluded by agreement of the parties. A challenge must be brought within twenty-eight days and cannot be commenced unless any process of appeal provided by the arbitration agreement has first been exhausted.

1.14   Personnel of the law

It is likely that those involved in property and construction matters, during the course of their professional careers, will have to work together with members of the legal profession. Although solicitors now have the potential of playing more of a role in advocacy in the courts, the legal profession still retains a traditional division into two branches with different functions. Generally speaking, solicitors give advice on legal problems to the general public and conduct legal proceedings on their behalf, whereas the primary function of a barrister is to act as an advocate and give advice to solicitors when requested. The expression *lawyer* can be used to denote either a solicitor or a barrister. Apart from working in general practice and as salaried *in house* lawyers, both solicitors and barristers are to be found in commerce, industry, the civil service and educational institutions.

1.14.1   Solicitors

The Law Society is the organisation responsible for the control of the solicitors' profession. In order to practise as such, a person must have been admitted as a solicitor and possess a current practising certificate. This can only be obtained by passing the professional examinations of the Law Society and completing a period of training with an established solicitor. Once qualified, if the solicitor enters general practice, he or she may deal with a wide range of legal work. This may involve giving general advice, conveyancing (transferring the ownership of land), preparing wills, appearing in the Magistrates' Court, county courts or higher courts, dealing with matrimonial disputes or preparing cases for trial. On the other hand, the solicitor may quickly become a specialist dealing only with cases involving one or two areas of law, such as taxation, town planning or construction law. Much depends on the type of practice and its locality. Some solicitors prefer to practise on their own, while others work in partnerships of varying sizes. The Administration of Justice Act 1985 allows solicitors to form incorporated practices. Traditionally, much of the work of solicitors has been involved with property

---

[29] Section 67
[30] Section 68
[31] Section 69

transactions. At one time, only solicitors could undertake the transfer of land/buildings. This is no longer the case (see paragraph 1.14.3 below).

A solicitor will often instruct a barrister (*brief counsel*) by sending written instructions relating to the representation of a client in legal proceedings. These instructions will include a narrative of the facts, copies of any documents, specifications and, where appropriate, plans. A solicitor may take counsel's opinion, whereby the views of a barrister are obtained on the law which applies to the client's case. Under a provision inserted in the Courts and Legal Services Act 1990 by the Access to Justice Act 1999, solicitors may now acquire wider rights of advocacy before the courts. With appropriate experience or training, solicitors are allowed to appear as advocates in the Crown Court, the High Court, the Court of Appeal and the Supreme Court. Solicitors can now be appointed as Queen's Counsel and to the High Court bench and, in due course, to judicial appointments in the higher courts.

The Law Society is responsible for preserving minimum standards of behaviour for solicitors and it operates a complaints system through the Office for the Supervision of Solicitors. A Legal Services Complaints Commissioner oversees the handling of complaints. The Commissioner has the power to investigate, make recommendations and require the Law Society to produce plans to deal with complaints. The Solicitors' Regulatory Authority was set up in 2007 and is now the independent regulatory body of the Law Society. The Authority sets standards for behaviour and professional performance that are contained in a Code of Practice. It can investigate and intervene in cases of professional misconduct and has certain disciplinary powers. The Solicitors' Regulatory Authority can also refer cases of professional misconduct to the Solicitor's Disciplinary Tribunal. In appropriate cases a solicitor's name may be *struck off* the professional roll. Solicitors may also be liable to their clients if they have acted negligently in the conduct of their case.

1.14.2 Legal Executives

Much of the routine work in solicitors' offices is carried out by unadmitted personnel known as Legal Executives. They carry out a considerable amount of work on behalf of their firms and much conveyancing and litigation is undertaken by them. Training and qualifications are governed by the Institute of Legal Executives. The initial qualification is Associate Membership of the Institute; after a further qualifying period and an examination the Associate may become a Fellow. In turn, a Fellow who completes the legal practice course may become admitted as a solicitor. Under the Courts and Legal Services Act 1990 (as amended by the Access to Justice Act 1999), Legal Executives can now acquire wider rights of audience before the courts and conduct pre-trial litigation work.

1.14.3 Licensed Conveyancers

Until the enactment of The Administration of Justice Act 1985, only qualified solicitors had the legal right to engage in conveyancing (the legal process of buying and selling land/buildings). Since then, members of the Council for Licensed Conveyancers have also been able to engage in conveyancing work for profit.

Members of the Council are required to satisfy educational requirements and practice rules. These rules have been supplemented by the creation of a new body known as the Authorised Conveyancing Practitioners Board, which in its role of developing competition in the provision of legal services, is authorised to supervise the activities of those who legally offer conveyancing services. In particular, there are specific rules dealing with 'tied' arrangements relating to inclusive legal services.

1.14.4   Barristers

The Bar has long been considered the senior branch of the legal profession in England and Wales. The main functions of counsel are to act as advocates in the superior courts, to draft the pleadings which indicate the manner in which the case is to be brought, and to give their legal opinion when so required. In order to practise as a barrister, a person must have been called to the Bar by one of the Inns of Court (Lincoln's Inn, Gray's Inn, The Middle Temple or The Inner Temple). After satisfying the appropriate educational requirements and *keeping term*, a newly called barrister who wishes to practise must undergo a period of pupilage for twelve months. By this process an experienced barrister (known as a pupil master) will supervise the new entrant's work. A newly qualified practising barrister will join one of six circuits in England and Wales and, unless working primarily in London, will appear in cases in the circuit area. Practising barristers are self-employed. Partnerships are prohibited but for convenience a number of barristers share offices or chambers, each contributing towards the overheads of the establishment. The majority of sets of chambers are administered by a clerk who deals with solicitors' firms and negotiates fees. Some sets now dispense with the need for a clerk while the previous restrictions on barristers advertising have been reversed. In the regions barristers' work is often varied and common law and crime orientated. The majority of specialists, especially in commercial, company and Chancery matters, are to be found in London.

Most barristers are known as junior counsel. After a period of successful practice a junior may apply to become a Queen's Counsel (QC). If successful, the applicant is said to have taken silk, which entitles the QC to wear a silk gown in court. Leading counsel, as these barristers are called, do not draft pleadings. Instead, their work is confined to appearing as advocates in the more important cases or giving opinions. At one time, whenever a Queen's Counsel appeared in court, the QC had to be accompanied by a junior barrister. Leading counsel may now appear alone in court, without assistance. Unlike solicitors, counsel may not sue for their fees. This rule has been modified by the Courts and Legal Services Act 1990, which allows a barrister to enter into a contract with a client for providing services and paying fees. As advocates, it used to be the case that barristers were immune from claims against them based on professional negligence[32], but this immunity ended with the decision of the House of Lords in *Arthur JS Hall & Co (a firm) v Simons*[33].

---

[32] *Rondel v Worsley* [1969] 1 AC 191
[33] [2002] 1 AC 615

Although generally a lay person only instructs a barrister through a solicitor, thereby incurring two sets of fees, members of certain professions have direct access to a barrister through arrangements referred to as 'licensed access' and may instruct counsel without the requirement of having to contact a solicitor first. Since 2004 it has also been possible for members of the general public to instruct a barrister directly in some areas of work. A barrister is under a duty to pursue his/her case in a proper manner and must inform the court of all relevant statutes and precedents. A barrister must ensure that his/her client has a fair hearing. The *cab-rank* rule requires barristers to act for any client in any field in which they practice.

1.15 Judicial officers

1.15.1 The Lord Chief Justice

Following the changes introduced by the Constitutional Reform Act 2005, The Lord Chief Justice holds the highest place in the legal hierarchy. The Lord Chief Justice is the President of the Courts of England and Wales, Head of Criminal Justice and Head of the Judiciary of England and Wales. He/she has the responsibility of training and deploying judges and is responsible for their welfare. The Lord Chief Justice represents the views of the judiciary to ministers and Parliament.

1.15.2 The Lord Chancellor

Prior to the Constitutional Reform Act 2005, the Lord Chancellor held the principle legal office in the United Kingdom. The Lord Chancellor had the primary role in the selection and appointment of judges, but this has now mostly been transferred to the Lord Chief Justice. The Lord Chancellor also presided over the Chancery Division of the High Court. A new post has now been created and the Chancellor of the High Court is now the president of the Chancery Division. The Lord Chancellor continues to exercise a formal advisory role on some judicial appointments and has sole responsibility for appointing lay justices following consultation. The Lord Chancellor is a government minister. He/she no longer sits as a judge nor chairs debates in the House of Lords (following the appointment of a *Lord Speaker* to the House).

1.15.3 The Attorney General

The Attorney General is the chief law officer of the Crown and head of the English Bar. The appointment is a political one and the holder is a Queen's Counsel and Member of Parliament. The principal tasks of the office are to advise the government on legal matters and to represent the Crown in civil and criminal proceedings. Certain prosecutions may only be commenced with his/her consent. The Attorney General can also sue on behalf of the public to enforce public rights. Examples of this type of action include stopping a public nuisance (see Chapter 3, paragraph 3.7) or enforcing a charitable trust. The Attorney General can lend his/her name to such an action at the request of a private citizen and these proceedings are known as relator proceedings. If he/she refuses to consent to the bringing of an action, his/her refusal cannot be questioned in the courts.

1.15.4   The Solicitor General

The Attorney General's deputy is known as the Solicitor General. The holder of the post is a Member of Parliament and a Queen's Counsel. The duties are in general similar to those of the Attorney General. The junior law officer will often become the Attorney General when that post becomes vacant. The law officers are forbidden to engage in private practice but receive a salary inclusive of fees.

1.15.5   Director of Public Prosecutions and the Crown Prosecution Service

Abbreviated to DPP, the Director of Public Prosecutions is appointed by the Home Secretary but is responsible to the Attorney General for the exercise of his powers. To a large extent the Director controls the prosecution process and initiates and conducts proceedings in complex cases. The Director is also head of the Crown Prosecution Service (CPS) which has prime responsibility for the conduct of criminal prosecutions in England and Wales. The CPS has regional offices throughout the country and its employees (solicitors or barristers) prosecute in criminal cases.

1.15.6   Master of the Rolls

The judge who presides over the Court of Appeal (Civil Division) is known as the Master of the Rolls. He/she decides the composition of the various appellate courts and organises the distribution of work. In addition, he/she admits newly qualified solicitors to the Roll of the Court, thereby enabling them to practise. The Master of the Rolls is also the Head of Civil Justice.

1.15.7   The Chancellor of the High Court

This is a new post created under the Constitutional Reform Act 2005. The Chancellor of the High Court is also the President of the Chancery Division, a role previously fulfilled by the Lord Chancellor.

1.15.8   The President of the Queen's Bench Division

Another post created in the reforms of 2005, the President of the Queen's Bench Division presides over that division in place of the Lord Chief Justice.

1.15.9   The President of the Family Division

The President of the Family Division, as well as presiding over that division, is also the Head of Family Justice.

1.15.10   Justices of the Supreme Court

Justices of the Supreme Court replace *Law Lords* as the most senior members of the judiciary. The twelve former Lords of Appeal in Ordinary took up the positions of

Justices on the foundation of the Supreme Court in 2009. They are headed by a President and a Vice President and are senior members of the judiciary, appointed from the Court of Appeal.

1.15.11   Lord and Lady Justices of Appeal

Abbreviated to LJ, these are the titles given to the judges who hear cases in the Court of Appeal. They are appointed from judges of the High Court. On appointment they are made Privy Councillors. As they hear only appeal cases, their work, like that of the Supreme Court, is mainly confined to London.

1.15.12   High Court Judges

Abbreviated to J after the surname of the judge in question, High Court or Puisne Judges are appointed by the Crown on the recommendation of the Lord Chancellor after selection by the Judicial Appointments Commission. Appointments are generally made from the ranks of practising Queen's Counsel although solicitors have been appointed to the High Court by promotion from Circuit Judge and even directly from practice. On appointment the judge will be knighted and assigned to one of the three divisions of the High Court. The Queen's Bench Division accounts for approximately two-thirds of the judges.

1.15.13   Circuit Judges

Circuit Judges are referred to as Judge followed by their surnames. Most trials which are heard in the Crown Court or county courts are dealt with by Circuit Judges. Such judges are appointed by the Crown on the recommendation of the Lord Chancellor after selection by the Judicial Appointments Commission. Circuit judges are normally barristers but it is possible for a suitably experienced solicitor to be appointed directly to the circuit bench. Judges are allocated to one of the circuits and hear cases in a group of centres. In court, Circuit Judges are addressed as *your honour*. Mention should also be made here of the office of Recorder. Recorders are part-time judges who hear cases in the Crown Court to supplement the Circuit Judges. Recorders are under an obligation to make themselves available on a number of occasions to hear cases.

1.15.14   Masters

Procedural matters in the High Court are the responsibility of Masters assigned to the Queen's Bench and Chancery divisions of the court.

1.15.15   District Judges

Referred to previously in connection with county courts (see paragraph 1.8.2.B), District Judges have an extensive range of administrative and judicial roles. District Judges are generally drawn from the solicitors' profession, despite the fact that barristers are also eligible. These judges are responsible for maintaining the records of the court and ensuring that documents have been served where appropriate. Moreover, they have responsibility for money which has been paid into court. As far as judicial tasks are concerned these judges deal with interlocutory (procedural) matters, taxation of costs and actions involving relatively small amounts of money.

1.16   Juries

One feature of common-law based legal systems is trial by jury. A jury is a body of persons selected to give a verdict in a particular case. Although seldom used in civil actions today (except in defamation cases) they are always used in criminal trials held on indictment at the Crown Court where the accused pleads not guilty. A jury will consist of twelve men or women who have been randomly selected. In general the jury decides facts and it is left to the judge to decide questions of law. Juries have no place in the appeal courts. Any person on the electoral register aged between eighteen and seventy who has been resident in the United Kingdom for at least five years since the age of thirteen is eligible. A person suffering from a mental health disorder may not sit on a jury and there are certain people who are disqualified from jury service by reason of prior conviction of a criminal offence or being subject to bail in criminal proceedings. The deliberations of a jury are held in secret and investigations into their workings are treated as a contempt of court. At one time the verdict of a jury had to be unanimous but, if certain conditions are met, the court will accept a majority verdict where there is a majority of ten.

1.17   Court procedure

This is governed by the nature of the dispute. There is a considerable difference between criminal and civil proceedings. In the criminal courts much depends on whether the accused is being tried on indictment or is subject to summary proceedings. Choice of court on the civil side is determined primarily by the complexity of the issues involved and the sums of money in dispute. One fundamental distinction lies in the obligation of proving facts. This is the so-called burden of proof. In a civil case it is the responsibility of the claimant to prove the factual issues on the balance of probabilities. A more stringent test applies in criminal cases in that the prosecution must prove the facts at issue beyond all reasonable doubt. Another factor characteristic of court proceedings in the UK, and other common law jurisdictions, is the so-called accusatorial or adversarial system. This means that the parties to a dispute or criminal proceedings have primary responsibility for finding and presenting evidence. The judge does not investigate the facts as such but listens to the case as it is presented by each of the adversaries. This is to be contrasted with the inquisitorial system in force in many continental European countries, whereby the judge searches for facts, listens to witnesses, examines documents and orders that evidence be taken, after which he makes further investigations if he considers them necessary.

1.18   Procedure in civil actions

Although it is possible for those involved in the construction process or in the landed property professions to incur criminal liability, it is more likely that any legal dispute in which they become involved will be of a civil nature. Where the parties to a civil dispute proceed to litigation rather than subjecting their grievance to one of the forms of alternative dispute resolution, they will either commence proceedings in the county courts or the High Court. The landscape of civil procedure has altered drastically over recent years following the adoption of the 'Woolf Reforms' (see below).

1.18.1   The 'Access to Justice' Reports

In 1994, the Lord Chancellor appointed the then Master of the Rolls, Lord Woolf, to undertake a major review of the entire civil justice system. This followed widespread criticism of procedure in the civil courts, particularly in terms of cost and delay. The review culminated in the publication of the *Access to Justice* or *Woolf* reports, which recommended far-reaching changes to the civil justice system. Many of the changes proposed were designed to provide quicker and cheaper access to justice by breaking down the adversarial nature of the pre-existing system.

Lord Woolf's final report[34] proposed a new landscape for civil justice with the following features:

- Avoidance of litigation wherever possible.
- Less adversarial and more co-operative litigation.
- Less complex litigation.
- Shorter and more certain timescales for litigation.
- More affordable litigation.
- Equality between disputants.
- A court structure which meets the needs of litigants.
- Case management by judges rather than by the litigants' legal advisors.

His interim report[35] foresaw a formal role for alternative dispute resolution (ADR) as an integral part of the new civil justice system. In this respect, Lord Woolf recommended:

- That courts should encourage the use of ADR.
- That parties should acknowledge at case management conferences and pre-trial reviews whether or not the parties had discussed the issue of ADR.
- That judges should take into account a litigant's unreasonable refusal to attempt ADR when considering the future conduct of a case.

---

[34] Access to Justice: Final Report to the Lord Chancellor on the civil justice system in England and Wales, Lord Chancellor's Department, July 1996
[35] Access to Justice: Interim Report to the Lord Chancellor on the civil justice system in England and Wales, Lord Chancellor's Department, July 1995

Lord Woolf's proposals were incorporated in the government's 1998 white paper on the future of the legal system[36] and the first stage of the reforms were implemented with the introduction of the new Civil Procedure Rules (CPR) 1998, which came into force in 1999 and now regulate the procedures of the High Court and county courts in England and Wales.

1.18.2 The Civil Procedure Rules (CPR)

Part 1 of the Rules places an obligation (the overriding objective) on the courts (and on the parties to assist the courts) 'to deal with cases justly'[37]. In line with the earlier recommendations in the Woolf reports, dealing with cases justly includes[38]:

- Ensuring that the parties are on an equal footing.
- Saving expense.
- Dealing with cases in a way which is proportionate to their value and complexity.
- Ensuring that cases are dealt with expeditiously and fairly.
- Making efficient use of the court's resources when allocating these to the various cases.

Courts are required to further the overriding objective by 'actively managing cases'. This includes a number of practical activities affecting the ongoing progress of the case through the courts and in the context of ADR it specifically includes[39]:

- Encouraging the parties to co-operate with each other in the conduct of the proceedings.
- Encouraging the parties to use ADR, and facilitating the use of such procedure, if the court considers it appropriate.
- Helping the parties to settle the whole or part of their case.

1.18.3 Alternative dispute resolution (ADR)

There are three main alternative procedures to a claim before a court of law. Arbitration has already been discussed (see paragraph 1.13 above). There is also the possibility of a structured settlement procedure (often referred to as a mini-trial). A neutral chairman sits with representatives appointed by the parties. This tribunal considers the submissions of the parties and agrees a solution. The third key alternative to litigation is ADR. This process seeks to resolve disputes by the use of an independent third party. The third party cannot impose a solution upon the parties, rather they must reach their own resolution of the issues in dispute. The ADR procedure is not appropriate when an injunction is being sought, where there

---

[36] Modernising Justice: The Government's plans for reforming legal services and the courts, December 1998, Cm 4155
[37] Rules 1.1, 1.2, 1.3
[38] Rule 1.2
[39] Rule 1.4

is no dispute between the parties (for example in cases of non-payment), nor when there is a point of law that needs to be ruled upon by a court. There can be a contractual agreement to pursue ADR before going to court and this can be tied in with an arbitration clause in the contract. The contract could, for example, provide that ADR be pursued before proceeding to arbitration. In the case of *Cable & Wireless Plc v IBM United Kingdom Ltd*[40], it was held that an agreement to use ADR is binding and enforceable by the courts. The claimant argued that an agreement to refer disputes to ADR was simply an agreement to negotiate. The court, however, rejected this argument and recognized no distinction between an agreement to refer to ADR and an agreement to arbitrate.

(A) Mediation

Mediation is the most commonly used form of ADR. It is also sometimes referred to as conciliation. The parties appoint a third party mediator who receives their written statements. The case is then discussed with each of the parties individually on a confidential basis. The discussions are conducted *without prejudice* and thus cannot be subsequently raised in court. The desired outcome is that the parties reach a mutually satisfactory solution without having recourse to litigation.

(B) Mediation-arbitration

Under this process the parties agree to refer the matter to arbitration if the mediation is unsuccessful.

(C) Costs and unreasonable refusal to submit to ADR

As noted above, the Civil Procedure Rules require that courts actively encourage parties to resolve disputes through ADR. The court may refuse a successful party costs if he/she has unreasonably refused to pursue the ADR route. The case of *Dunnett v Railtrack Plc*[41] saw the first example of costs penalties being imposed on a successful litigant because of unreasonable refusal to mediate. The case concerned horses straying onto a railway line and being hit by a train. Dunnett (the horse owner) failed in her claim for the value of the horses and nervous shock (post-traumatic stress disorder) in the first instance and applied for leave to appeal to the Court of Appeal. Leave was granted but the court recommended that the parties should explore the possibilities of resolving their dispute by ADR. Dunnett contacted Railtrack suggesting that the matter be referred to ADR. Railtrack refused without any consideration and instead made an offer in full and final settlement of the claim. The case proceeded to the Court of Appeal and Dunnett's appeal was dismissed. Dunnett, the unsuccesful party, would normally have had to pay Railtrack's costs. The Court of Appeal drew attention to the duty of the parties under CPR to fully consider ADR, especially where the court had suggested it. To merely flatly turn down the possibility was to risk adverse consequences in costs. It was held that costs should not be awarded to

---

[40] [2002] EWHC 2059 (Comm)
[41] [2002] EWCA Civ 303

Railtrack, given their refusal to contemplate ADR at a stage before the costs of the appeal started to flow. Subsequent case law has explored what is and is not reasonable in this context and laid down guidance[42].

1.18.4 Commencement of proceedings

Proceedings are started by the completion of a claim form, which is then lodged at the relevant office of the county courts designated as civil trial centres (fifty-eight across England and Wales) or one of the feeder county courts. Basic details of the claim are required, including its value, in order for the allocation of the case at a later stage and the calculation of the fee payable on the issue of the claim form. Particulars of the claim are to be given on the back of the claim form. This is a brief statement of the facts on which the claimant relies. The particulars conclude with a signed statement of truth by the claimant or his/her solicitor.

The claim form can be served on the defendant or their solicitor either by the court or by the claimant. The defendant will also receive a response pack detailing how the claim form can be dealt with. There are five alternatives:

- Acknowledgement of service – Acknowledgement must be made within fourteen days of service.
- Filing of a defence – If the recipient wants to defend the claim then they must file a defence within fourteen days of service (twenty-eight days if it has been acknowledged as above). The time period for filing a defence can be extended by agreement of both parties. The claimant does not have to respond to the defence, but the usual reply is by way of counterclaim (see below).
- Filing of an admission – This can be for the full amount of the claim or for part of it. If the admission is accepted either for the full or part claim, the claimant asks the court for judgment. Admission or part admission must be made within fourteen days of service.
- No response – If the defendant fails to acknowledge service or to file a defence or an admission within the time limits, in most cases, the claimant can apply to the court for a judgment in default. A defendant can apply to the court to have the default judgment set aside.
- Counterclaim – The defendant may feel that they have a claim against the claimant in which case they can file a counterclaim with the defence. This must be prepared in exactly the same way as a statement of case (see above). A counterclaim can be filed subsequently, but only with the permission of the court. No acknowledgement of the counterclaim is required, but the claimant must file any defence to it within fourteen days (again this can be extended by agreement of the parties).

If further information is required by either party, then they can make a request under Rule 18 of the Civil Procedure Rules, 1998. This is made in writing to the other party. If the information is not received, then a party can apply to the court for an order.

---

[42] *Halsey v Milton Keynes NHS Trust; Steel v Joy and Halliday* [2004] EWCA Civ 576

1.18.5 Case management

Designated *civil trial centres* are responsible for case management. These centres are county courts and they also try multi-track cases and some fast track cases (see below). Other county courts act as feeder centres and they refer cases to civil trial centres after allocating a track. Under Rule 3 of the Civil Procedure Rules 1998, it is possible for the court to *strike out* a claim, or a defence, rather than allocate it for trial. This would occur if no reasonable grounds for bringing or defending the claim were revealed.

(A) Case allocation

Where a defendant has filed a defence, the court will decide whether to stay the proceedings (see below) or to allocate the case to one of the following three tracks:

- Small claims track (generally for claims of not more than £5 000). The case will normally be heard in the county courts by a district judge.
- Fast track (generally for claims between £5 000 and £15 000). Cases will normally be heard in the county courts.
- Multi-track (for claims which are not suitable for either the small claims or fast track). Multi-track cases of significant value (a claim of £50 000 or more) will generally be heard in the High Court.

To assist in allocating the case, the court will first require each of the parties to complete and return an allocation questionnaire (or a *case management information sheet* in the Technology and Construction Court). The first section of the questionnaire informs the parties that CPR require them to make every effort to settle their case before a hearing and that the court will want to know what steps they have made in this regard. A series of questions are asked in respect of settlement and ADR and the parties are reminded that the answers will be considered when deciding costs.

(B) Stay to allow for settlement of the case

A party may, when filing the completed allocation questionnaire, make a written request for the proceedings to be stayed while the parties try to settle the case by ADR or other means. This can be done either when all the parties request a stay or where the court considers that a stay would be appropriate. The stay will be for one month or a period considered appropriate by the court. This can be extended by the court.

(C) Case management conference and pre-trial review

In most cases, the court gives directions on case management and sets a pre-trial schedule and a date for the trial. If the case has been allocated to the multi-track, the court can call for a case management conference or a pre-trial review or both. At a case management conference, questions on disclosure of documents and expert evidence are addressed and a trial date is fixed. If the case is a very complex one, a pre-trial review will be necessary. The judge then looks at cost estimates and sets a budget and a programme for the trial.

(D) Pre-action protocols

Most claims are settled without starting proceedings at all and, even where proceedings are commenced, most cases are settled by negotiation before they come to trial.

The CPR introduced a number of pre-action protocols for particular types of disputes, which aim to assist the parties in the process of settlement. They each describe a procedure and a timetable for the parties to follow before proceedings are issued. In particular they require the parties to exchange information about the case at an early stage so that they have a clear picture of the relative merits of each party's case. This can increase the chances of settlement without the necessity of issuing proceedings. Even where litigation cannot be avoided the early exchange of information ensures that cases coming before the courts are much better prepared.

There are currently pre-action protocols in place for:

- Defamation.
- Personal Injury Claims.
- Resolution of Clinical Disputes.
- Professional Negligence.
- Judicial Review.
- Disease and Illness Claims.
- Housing Disrepair Cases.
- Possession claims based on Rent Arrears.
- Possession claims based on Mortgage or Home Purchase Plan Arrears in Respect of Residential Property.
- Construction and Engineering Disputes.

The pre-action protocol for *Construction and Engineering Disputes* includes professional negligence claims against architects, engineers and quantity surveyors. This protocol requires claimants to send a letter of claim to potential defendants in advance of issuing proceedings. This must set out full details of the claim and provide the names of expert witnesses on whose evidence the claimant wishes to rely. The defendant must then acknowledge receipt within fourteen days and provide a detailed response to the letter of claim within a further fourteen days (twenty-eight days from the letter of claim). The response must fully respond to the letter of claim and provide the names of the defendant's expert witnesses.

Twenty-eight days after the claimant receives the defendant's response, the parties should then meet to discuss the issues between them. Paragraph 5.4 of the protocol contains a requirement that, during this meeting, the parties should consider whether ADR might be more appropriate than litigation. The CPR Practice Direction on Pre-action Protocols (paragraph 4.7) also emphasises the parties' obligation to consider the possibility of ADR.

There is a draft pre-action protocol in place for *Claims for Damages in Relation to the Physical State of Commercial Property at the Termination of a Tenancy* (the Dilapidations Protocol). This has been produced by the Property Litigation Association. The objectives of the protocol are to:

- Encourage the exchange of early and full information about the prospective legal claim.
- Enable parties to avoid litigation by agreeing a settlement of the claim before the commencement of proceedings.
- Support the efficient management of proceedings where litigation cannot be avoided.

This protocol requires that a landlord should generally serve a schedule setting out what he/she consider the breaches to be and the works required to remedy these, together with costings. The tenant must respond to the claim within a reasonable time. The landlord and tenant are encouraged to meet to instigate negotiations and both parties are encouraged to consider ADR.

(E) Timetables

As previously mentioned, the court will set a timetable for the various stages to be completed before trial and a date for the trial (within thirty weeks in fast track cases). The courts have taken a strict view with regards to adhering to timetables. In the case of *Linda Rollinson v Kimberley Clark Ltd*[43], the defendant sought to alter the trial date because one of her expert witnesses was not available on the date set in the timetable. The application was dismissed. In the case of *Matthews v Tarmac Bricks and Tiles Ltd*[44], the defendant failed to give details of when expert witnesses would be available. The trial date was set regardless and the Court of Appeal dismissed a subsequent appeal by the defendant. These cases emphasise the point that the professional expert witness owes an overriding duty to the court and not merely to his/her client and thus experts should be prepared to arrange or rearrange their affairs to meet the courts' requirements.

1.18.6 Expert witnesses

Restrictions on the use of expert evidence were introduced by the CPR (Part 35). Such evidence is restricted to that which is reasonably required to resolve the proceedings. Expert witnesses cannot be called without the permission of the court and the court may limit the amount of the expert's fees, which can be recovered from the other party. The duties of an expert witness are also outlined in Part 35. It is the duty of an expert to help the court on the matters within his expertise and this duty overrides any obligation to the person from whom he/she has received instructions or by whom he/she is paid.

---

[43] [2000] CP Rep. 85
[44] [1999] CPLR 463

The form and content of the expert witness report are set out in a CPR Practice Direction. The report should be addressed to the court (rather than to the instructing party) and the report should contain details of the expert's qualification, state the basis on which the expert has reached his/her opinions and, where there is a range of opinion on matters dealt with in the report, it should summarise the range and give reasons for the expert's own opinion. The report should also contain a summary of the conclusions reached. The report concludes with a statement of truth, a statement with regards to the duty to the court, a declaration regarding the RICS Practice Statement and a declaration regarding relevant facts.

Within twenty-eight days of the service of an expert's report, either party can put written questions to the expert about their report. The expert's answers are treated as part of their report. If an expert fails to answer, the court can order that the expert's evidence is inadmissible or that the expert's fees cannot be recovered from the other party. There is a requirement under the CPR that the parties act reasonably in exchanging information and this extends to expert evidence. A number of the pre-action protocols require meetings between experts. In addition, the court has the power to direct a discussion between experts with a view to identifying relevant issues and, where possible, reaching agreement.

Under CPR, the court now has the power to direct that expert evidence be given by a single joint expert rather than each party appointing an expert. The single expert is instructed jointly by the parties or appointed by the court if they are unable to agree. The amount of the single expert's fee can be limited by the court and the parties can be ordered to pay this amount into court. Each party may give instructions to the single joint expert, sending a copy to the other party at the same time.

1.19   The Human Rights Act (HRA)

Following many years of calls for the enactment of a bill of rights in the UK, the Human Rights Act 1998 entered into force in October 2000. The Act does not have the fundamental features of a bill of rights. It does not require special procedures to alter it, nor can measures that contravene its provisions be struck down by the courts. It does not, therefore, jeopardise the supremacy of parliament. The Human Rights Act brought into UK law many of the key provisions of the European Convention of Fundamental Rights and Freedoms (ECHR). It has had a far-reaching impact upon all areas of UK law.

1.19.1   ECHR

The ECHR was based on the Universal Declaration of Human Rights, passed by the UN General Assembly in 1948. It was signed by the members of the Council of Europe (not to be confused with the Council of the European Union) in 1950 and it committed them to protecting a range of human rights. A number of subsequent additions and amendments have been made to the Convention in the form of *Protocols*. The Convention was ratified by the UK in 1951 and came into force in 1953. Until the enactment of the Human Rights Act in 1998, however, none of its provisions were incorporated into UK law. The European Court of

Human Rights (ECtHR) was established in Strasbourg in 1959 to deal with violations of the Convention (see paragraph 1.11). It still remains the case that provided all domestic remedies have been exhausted, a victim of a human rights violation can bring an action against the state in Strasbourg.

1.19.2 The Provisions of the Human Rights Act

As well as introducing a range of Convention rights into UK law, the Act makes these rights directly enforceable in the courts. The Convention rights are defined in section 1 of the Act as the rights and fundamental freedoms set out in Articles 2 to 12 and 14 of the Convention, together with those in Articles 1 to 3 of its First Protocol and Articles 1 and 2 of its Sixth Protocol. The full text of these rights is to be found in Schedule 1 of the Act but they can be summarised as follows:

THE CONVENTION RIGHTS (HRA 1998, Schedule 1)

Part I: The Convention Rights and Freedoms

Article 2	Right to life
Article 3	Prohibition of torture
Article 4	Prohibition of slavery and forced labour
Article 5	Right to liberty and security
Article 6	Right to a fair trial
Article 7	No punishment without law
Article 8	Right to respect for private and family life
Article 9	Freedom of thought, conscience and religion
Article 10	Freedom of expression
Article 11	Freedom of assembly and association
Article 12	Right to marry
Article 14	Prohibition of discrimination

Part II: The First Protocol

Article 1	Protection of property
Article 2	Right to education
Article 3	Right to free elections

Part III: The Sixth Protocol

| Article 1 | Abolition of the death penalty |
| Article 2 | Death penalty in time of war |

(A) Compatibility (s.19)

The minister in charge of a parliamentary bill is required to either make a statement of compatibility with the Convention rights before its second reading stage or, if he/she is unable to do this, make a statement that the government nevertheless wishes Parliament to proceed with the bill.

(B) Duty of interpretation (s.3)

So far as it is possible to do so, existing legislation must be read and given effect to in a way that is compatible with the Convention rights. This obligation applies to everyone when interpreting statutes (not just courts and tribunals). If it is not possible to interpret a statute in line with the Convention, it continues to have legal effect and the courts must still enforce it.

(C) Declarations of incompatibility (s.4)

If a court (of High Court level and above) is satisfied that a piece of legislation is incompatible with Convention rights, it may make a declaration of incompatibility. This has no effect on the validity of the statutory provision, or on the parties to the case. It simply notifies Parliament that the measure has been found to be incompatible.

(D) Duty on courts and tribunals (s.2)

A court or tribunal, in determining any question relating to a Convention right, must *take into account* the relevant ECtHR case law on the subject. The case law in question is not binding on the UK courts. A tribunal, for the purposes of s.2 is 'any tribunal in which legal proceedings may be brought'. An adjudicator under the Construction Act has been held not to fall within this definition. (*Austin Hall Building Ltd v Buckland Securities Ltd*[45]).

(E) Duty on public authorities (s.6)

It is unlawful for a public authority to act in a way that is incompatible with Convention rights. A public authority is anyone who performs functions of a public nature. This includes courts and tribunals but excludes both Houses of Parliament. A victim of such an unlawful act may bring proceedings against the public authority in an appropriate court or tribunal. If it is found that the public authority has behaved unlawfully then the court or tribunal can grant such relief or remedy or make such order within its powers as it considers just and appropriate. This includes an order for damages or the payment of compensation (s.8).

---

[45] [2001] BLR 272

1.19.3 Case law

There is a growing body of case law flowing from the Human Rights Act. Some examples are given below under the relevant ECHR article number:

(A) Right to Life (Article 2)

In the case *of NHS Trust A v M; NHS Trust B v H*[46], the court applied a precedent established before the Human Rights Act in the case of *Airedale NHS Trust v Bland*[47] that lawful withdrawal of treatment to a patient in a permanent vegetative state does not infringe the right to life. In another case heard in the same year, concerning a terminally ill person's wish to end their life, the court held that the right to life does not embrace the right to die[48].

(B) Torture and Degrading Treatment (Article 3)

There have not been many cases brought in the UK under this Convention right. Those that have generally relate to prison sentences. In *R v Drew*[49], a life sentence handed down to a mentally ill offender was held not to breach Article 3 because of the danger posed by the offender to the public. The court was of the view that the alternative (a hospital order) would not have offered sufficient protection to the public.

(C) The Right to Liberty (Article 5)

As with Article 3 above, case law on the right to liberty has tended to relate to sentencing. In the case of *R v Offen*[50], for example, the Court of Appeal held that an automatic life sentence imposed on an offender who had committed two prior serious offences did not infringe Article 5 as the offender was a significant risk to the public.

(D) The Right to a Fair Trial (Article 6)

There has been a good deal of case law generated by this Article. The approach taken by the courts in the UK mirrors that taken by the ECtHR. The courts consider the general fairness of procedure rather than the detail. In the case of *R (Anderson) v Secretary of State for the Home Department*[51], the House of Lords made a declaration under s4, HRA that s29 of the Crime Sentences Act 1997 (which conferred on the Home Secretary control of the release of mandatory life sentence prisoners) was incompatible with Article 6, which requires that a

---

[46] [2001] Fam 348
[47] [1993] AC 789
[48] *R (Pretty) v DPP* [2001] UKHL 61; (2002) EHRR 1
[49] [2003] UKHL 25
[50] [2001] 1 WLR 253
[51] [2002] UKHL 46

sentence is imposed by an independent and impartial tribunal. The decision followed on from similar ECtHR decisions in the cases of *Stafford v UK*[52] and *Benjamin and Wilson v UK*[53].

(E) Retrospective Application of the Law (Article 7)

Several cases look at old offences committed many years in the past, but where offenders are subject to a penalty at a later stage when there has been an intervening change in the law. For example, in *R v C*[54], the defendant had raped his wife in 1970. He was convicted in 2002. The Court held that there was no problem in convicting for an offence that was committed prior to the change of the law on marital rape which had been introduced in 1992 by the House of Lords in the case of *R v R*[55].

(F) Right to Privacy (Article 8)

The case of *R v Secretary of State for the Home Department ex p. Mellor*[56] concerned the right to privacy and the exercise of conjugal rights. The Court of Appeal ruled that imprisonment was incompatible with the exercise of conjugal rights. The court applied the proportionality test in not allowing the rights to be exercised. It did indicate, however, that exceptional circumstances might lead to a decision the other way.

(G) Freedom of Religion (Article 9)

There have been very few cases relating to the Article 9 Convention right in this country. An interesting case was that of *R v Taylor (Paul Simon)*[57]. It was claimed that cannabis was being supplied for use in acts of religious worship (Rastafarianism). The Court held that Article 9 was not violated by the Misuse of Drugs Act 1971, which prohibits the use and supply of cannabis. The House of Lords also ruled that there was no violation of Article 9 in a school's policy that prohibited the wearing of a jilbab[58]. Their Lordships noted that the school was sensitive to the needs of its pupils and provided them with a choice of uniforms.

(H) Freedom of Expression (Article 10)

There have been a number of cases relating to the protection of journalistic sources, and the courts in these were required to balance the freedom of the press

---

[52] [2002] 35 EHRR 32
[53] [2002] ECHR Application No. 28212/95, 25 September 2002
[54] [2004] EWCA Crim 292
[55] [1991] 4 All ER 481, HL
[56] [2001] EWCA Civ 472
[57] [2000] EWCA Crim 2263
[58] *R (Shabina Begum) v Denbigh High School* [2006] UKHL 15

(and the protection of sources) and the public interest. In *Ashworth Security Hospital v MGN Ltd*[59], the *Mirror* newspaper had published information from hospital records about a convicted murderer. The hospital had been unable to find out the identity of the employee who had leaked the information and called for Mirror Group Newspapers (MGN) to disclose the source. MGN argued that this was contrary to Article 10. The Court of Appeal ruled that unless the person was identified and dismissed, further confidential material might be sold. The House of Lords affirmed the decision in *Ashworth* in the case of *Interbrew SA v Financial Times*[60]. In this case it was held that the 'public interest in protecting the source of a leak was not sufficient to withstand the countervailing public interest in letting Interbrew seek justice in the courts against the source'. The leaked documents in the case were partly forged. In other cases the importance of protecting journalistic sources has prevailed. This was so in *Mersey Care NHS Trust v Acroyd*[61]. In this case, an opposite conclusion was reached to that in *Ashworth*. The High Court ruled that, in balancing conflicting rights (the right to privacy and the right to freedom of expression), it was necessary to apply the guidelines set out in *Campbell v Mirror Group Newspapers plc*[62]; this meant looking at the proportionality of disclosure. In the *Mersey Care* case the court held that it would not be proportionate for the hospital to seek redress against the source, given 'the vital public interest in the protection of a journalist's source'.

(I) Freedom of Association (Article 11)

The case of *RSPCA v AG*[63] related to the RSPCA's exclusion of current members and denial of membership to those who did not support its policy against hunting with dogs. The court ruled that the Association could exclude members and applicants who they thought (in good faith) would damage their objectives. However, such applicants should have the opportunity to make representations.

(J) The Right to Marry (Article 12)

Following the *Goodwin v UK*[64] case in the ECtHR, the House of Lords ruled in *Bellinger v Bellinger*[65] that the English law which prevented transsexuals from entering a valid marriage was incompatible with the Convention. The Court did rule that the marriage was void, but the law was subsequently changed by the Gender Recognition Act 2004.

---

[59] [2002] UKHL 29
[60] [2002] EWCA Civ 274
[61] [2006] EWHC 107 (QB)
[62] [2005] UKHL 61
[63] [2002] 1 WLR 448
[64] [2002] ECHR Application No 28957/95 11 July 2002
[65] [2003] 2 AC 467

2 The Law of Contract

2.1 General principles

The law of contract is frequently the first 'case law' subject to which students are introduced when they commence their legal studies. The main reason for this is that contracts affect the general public more than most areas of law and arise daily in business and commercial life. The contract is the most important stage in the process when land or buildings are transferred and when building projects are undertaken. The 'golden age' of the law of contract was in the nineteenth century when its major principles were evolved on free market ideologies. Many of the cases referred to in this chapter date from this ground breaking period. The case illustrations used are not limited to this period, however, and the case law referred to in this chapter ranges from the very old to the very modern.

A contract is a legally binding agreement. It is a bargain and each side, or party to the contract, must contribute something to it for it to be valid. Not every agreement is a contract nor is it intended to be so. The legally binding element must be present before a valid contract can emerge. In other words the parties must be able to demonstrate their intention to adhere to the agreement made. The protection afforded by entering into a contract is that if it is broken by one party to it, the other party must be able to take the contract-breaker to court if desired.

A distinction is made between the situation where the parties exchange mutual promises, known as a bilateral contract, and a unilateral contract where one party promises to do something in return for the other party carrying out some task. When the task is completed the promise made in a unilateral contract becomes enforceable.

2.2 Formalities

A contract may be made in any form that the parties wish. This is the case regardless of the sums involved or the complexity of the agreement. There are advantages in having the contract formally drafted if a large sum of money is involved or the matter is complicated. There is no essential requirement in English law that a contract should be in writing and as a general rule the parties to a contract may insert whatever provisions they wish into the agreement.

Law and the Built Environment   by Douglas Wood, Paul Chynoweth, Julie Adshead and Jim Mason
© 2011 Douglas Wood, Paul Chynoweth, Julie Adshead and Jim Mason

However, it became clear as the nineteenth century progressed, that complete freedom to contract could lead to problems. The courts recognised that there were situations in which a 'hands off' approach to allow the parties to do as they wish could lead to injustice. However, it is only in relatively recent times that the law has placed restrictions on a statutory footing. The most obvious example is the limits placed on the extent to which contracting parties may exclude their responsibility for their liabilities (see the Unfair Contract Terms Act 1977 in section 2.8).

2.2.1 Simple contracts

These are contracts made by word of mouth or in writing or a combination of both. No particular form is required.

2.2.2 Deeds

A contract made by deed is known as a Specialty Contract. Until 1990, certain contracts had to be made 'under seal' and delivered up 'as a deed'. The sealing of a contract referred to a more elaborate execution of a written contract than a mere signature. Typically it could involve an impression made by a signature ring or company motif set in wax dripped onto the document. A seal is no longer necessary but, to be valid, a deed must now comply with the requirements set out in section 2 of the Law of Property (Miscellaneous Provisions) Act 1989 (see Chapter 4, paragraph 4.4.2).

The distinctive features of a contract signed as a deed rather than as a simple contract include the rule that no consideration is necessary for a deed to be valid. Another practical advantage of a contract being made by deed is that the limitation period governing such contracts is twelve years, as opposed to six years in the case of a simple contract.

2.2.3 Contracts which must be made in writing or evidenced in writing

Certain types of contract cannot be enforced or are invalid unless they are in writing although they do not have to be made in the form of a deed. This applies to consumer credit and hire agreements governed by the Consumer Credit Act 1974 (as amended by the Consumer Credit Act 2006). These Acts require that the relevant agreements are 'not properly executed' unless in the form prescribed. Failing to comply with the requirement has the effect of rendering the contract unenforceable.

The requirement that a contract be in writing also applies to the sale or other disposition of an interest in land[1] whilst contracts of guarantee need to be evidenced in writing pursuant to the Statute of Frauds 1677.

---

[1] The Law of Property (Miscellaneous Provisions) Act 1989 section 2 repealed the Law of Property Act 1925 section 40 which required such contracts merely to be evidenced in writing

2.3   Standard form contracts

Certain transactions are governed entirely by standard terms which are pre-determined. An example is where one of the parties enjoys a monopolist position or particular types of business are in relatively few hands. Where this arises the customer is often not in a position to negotiate over the terms of the contract. Instead the person requiring the goods or the services contracts on a standard form prepared in advance by the dominant organisation. Such a contract makes a mockery of the concept of freedom of contract whereby a person is free to contract or not and the selection of subject matter, terms and parties are a matter of choice. This form of contract is known as an adhesion standard form contract, whereby no opportunity exists for any negotiations and the weaker contracting party must 'take it' or 'leave it'.

The type of standard form of contract which is commonplace in construction and land transactions is much fairer. Standard clauses have been settled over the years by negotiation between the various stakeholders in the relevant industries. The purpose of these forms is to facilitate the conduct of trade and a fair allocation of risk between the parties. These are the types of contract invariably used in large scale construction works. The Joint Contracts Tribunal (JCT) Standard Form of Building Contract and the Institution of Civil Engineers (ICE) form of engineering contract tend to govern major works, while other contracts such as the New Engineering Contract have come to play significant roles. These forms of contract are considered separately in paragraph 2.15.

2.4   The essential elements of a valid contract

A simple contract has three essential elements:

- Agreement (or at least the outward appearance of agreement).
- Consideration.
- The intention to create legal relations.

2.4.1   Agreement

It is accepted that before a formal agreement can be reached there must be a valid offer made by the *offeror* and a valid acceptance of that offer by the *offeree*. It may be possible to ascertain with relative ease whether or not a valid agreement has come into being if a contract is entered into solely on the basis of what is agreed in a standard form of contract. It may be considerably more difficult to ascertain whether or not an offer and acceptance have been made where, for instance, a contract is alleged to have come into being by a combination of statements made orally together with documents in writing. The real test is whether the parties have accepted obligations to one another. If that can be established then a valid agreement may be inferred from the conduct of the parties.

In the case of *Trentham (G Percy) Ltd v Archital Luxfer Ltd*[2] a building sub-contract was held to have come into existence even though the parties had not reached full agreement when the sub-contractor began the work. During the progress of the works outstanding matters were resolved by further negotiations. The judge was satisfied in this case that there was sufficient evidence to conclude that there was a binding contract; the parties had clearly intended to create a legal relationship between each other.

Notwithstanding this case the general rule is that arrangements which are too vague, uncertain or are conditional will not take effect. The following are the major rules which attempt to ensure that before an agreement can exist there must be a clear and formal offer and an unequivocal acceptance of that offer. These rules surrounding the formation of an agreement can be compared to the rules of a game such as chess, or the steps in a dance routine.

(A) Rules as to offers

(a) An offer must be distinguished from an invitation to treat

An invitation to treat is a preliminary stage in proceedings which may or may not result in an offer being made. It is not possible to accept an invitation to treat and thereby create a valid agreement. Marked prices on articles for sale will amount to invitations to treat rather than offers to sell. In the case of *Fisher v Bell*[3] a flick-knife was displayed in a shop window with a price tag attached. The seller was prosecuted under the now repealed Restriction of Offensive Weapons Act 1961, which made it an offence to offer to sell such items. The seller was acquitted on the basis that under the ordinary law of contract the display of the article in the shop window was merely an invitation to treat.

A similar situation arose in the case of *Pharmaceutical Society of Great Britain v Boots Cash Chemists (Southern) Ltd*[4]. This case involved the display of prescription drugs on a shelf in Boots chemist shop. The display of the goods was challenged as being in contravention of the Pharmacy and Poisons Act 1933 which required such drugs to be sold only in the presence of a qualified pharmacist. The claimants alleged that the point of sale was when the customer helped themselves from the shelf to the drugs and that therefore the sales were illegal. Finding for the defendants, the judge found that the display of goods in this way did not constitute an offer. The offer for sale was not made when the customer selected the goods, but when the goods were presented to the cashier. The court was satisfied that the cashier was supervised as required by the Act and that no contravention of the law had actually taken place.

Difficulties of classification can arise in connection with advertisements. It is a question of intention which decides whether these are offers or invitations to treat. An advertisement promising a reward was considered to be an offer in the leading case of *Carlill v Carbolic Smokeball Co*[5].

---

[2] [1993] 1 Lloyd's Rep 25
[3] [1961] 1QB 394
[4] [1952] 2 All ER 456
[5] (1893) 1 QB 256

Mrs Carlill contracted influenza (a common cold or flu) after using the defendant's smokeball – a popular preventative medicine of its time administered by inhaling fumes from a handheld device. The defendant had placed an advert in a national newspaper stating their confidence in the device and offering a reward for anyone contracting influenza after using the smokeball in the manner prescribed. Mrs Carlill challenged the defendant to make good on their offer of a reward which they refused to do, claiming the advertisement was an invitation to treat not an offer. Finding for Mrs Carlill, the judge held that the defendants had made an offer and referred to their statement in the advertisement alleging that the defendants had deposited money on account with a well-known bank. The judge found that this demonstrated their intention to be bound by their offer and their willingness to enter into a unilateral contract upon the purchase of the device.

Advertisements in trade magazines or periodicals offering goods for sale are likely to be treated as a formal offer only if the advertiser intends no further negotiations to take place, and all that is required of the other party is to send a cheque for the goods or give a credit card number. In the construction industry context, an invitation to tender to carry out works or supply goods is an invitation to treat. The submitted tender is a formal offer which may or may not be accepted by the employer. Unusually, there have been situations where 'invitations' to tender have given rise to an enforceable contract where the facts have shown a clear intention to create contractual obligations. One case where this happened was *Blackpool and Fylde Aero Club Ltd v Blackpool Borough Council*[6]. The Council failed to consider the claimant's correctly submitted tender for services. Consequently the claimant had no chance of being successful in the tender competition. This failure was found to have invalidated the tender competition and entitled the disgruntled tenderer to claim for damages. A similar result occurred in the case of *J & A Developments Ltd v Edina Manufacturing, Armoura Ltd*[7]. In this case the three lowest tenderers were invited to take part in a further lowest bid reverse auction to win the work. The claimant, one of the three lowest original tenderers, successfully challenged the further round of bidding and was awarded damages compensating the business for the costs of preparing the tender.

(b) Inquiries and replies to inquiries are not offers

Statements of price or rates on their own are not formal offers. Most of the relevant case law is concerned with the purchase of land or buildings where enquiries are made but agreements never actually made. In *Gibson v Manchester City Council*[8] it was decided that a statement made in a letter by the defendants that the council 'may be prepared to sell' and inviting the other party 'to make a formal application to buy' a house was an invitation to treat rather than an offer.

---

[6] [1990] 3 All ER 25
[7] [2006] NIQB 85
[8] [1979] 1 All ER 972

(c) Communication of the offer

It is essential that there is communication of the offer to give the offeree an opportunity to accept or reject it. Only the offeree can accept. This rule is illustrated by the case of *Boulton v Jones*[9], which involved an unincorporated business. The business changed hands between offer and the acceptance of the offer. The agreement failed as the offer had not been made to the offeree purporting to accept it. However, if the offer is made to the world at large as in *Carlill v Carbolic Smokeball Co* (see above), then any person with notice of the offer may accept it.

(d) An offer may be revoked (withdrawn) any time before acceptance

Once a valid acceptance has been made, the offeror is bound by the terms of the offer. In an auction sale, each individual bid is an offer which can be accepted or rejected at any time before the auctioneer signals (usually by bringing down his hammer or gavel) his acceptance of the offer he wants. Auctions have introduced some interesting developments in the law of offer and acceptance. In the case of *Barry v Heathcote Ball & Co (Commercial Auctions) Limited*[10] the auctioneer failed to accept the claimant's bid for machinery notwithstanding the latter's offer was the highest during the auction and no reserve had been set for the items in question. The auctioneer was found to be liable to the claimant for the market value of the machinery involved, less the value of the claimant's bid.

Similar rules apply to arrangements known as options to purchase. An offeror can be obliged to keep an offer open for a specific period provided the offeree has given consideration to have the offer kept open. In such circumstances there will be a breach of contract if there is an attempt to revoke the offer within that period. Revocation of an offer only becomes effective when it is communicated to the offeree. In the case of *Byrne v Van Tinenhoven*[11] the defendant sought to withdraw his written offer by sending a second letter revoking the first. The first offer had already been accepted (as evidenced by a telegram from the claimant) and the second letter was not able to amount to a revocation. Valid communication of revocation may be indirect if from a 'reliable source' such as a mutual friend.

A difficult area arises where an offer requires a certain act to be carried out but the offer is revoked after the act has been commenced but before it has been completed. The problem arises in the case of unilateral contracts and reward cases are a good example. In *Errington v Errington and Woods*[12] it was decided that the offer could not be revoked once the appropriate party had begun the actual performance of the conduct required by the offer. In this case a father bought a house for his son and daughter-in-law. He told the daughter-in-law that if she paid off the mortgage then the house would be hers. He later changed his mind but the offer was deemed to be sufficient to create a unilateral contract once the couple started making mortgage payments.

---

[9] (1857) 6 WR 107
[10] (2000) The Times, 31 August (CA)
[11] (1880) C P D 344
[12] [1952] 1 All ER 149

(e) An offer remains open until it is accepted, revoked, rejected or lapses

Only proper acceptance of an offer will result in a valid agreement. No contract can be formed if there is a valid revocation of an offer or a rejection of that offer by the offeree. An offer may also lapse and become incapable of acceptance by passage of time. This occurs where there is a time limit within which acceptance may be made and that time has passed. It also occurs where no time limit is specified and there has been no acceptance within a reasonable period. The length of time is dependent upon the circumstances of the case and the question of reasonableness may vary depending upon the nature of the contract. For example, an offer to sell perishable goods such as fruit would lapse after a relatively short time.

In order for a revocation to be effective it must be communicated to the offeree. This communication need not necessarily be made by the offeror but must involve a reliable third party as opposed to a mere rumour or suggestion that the offer has been withdrawn. The case quoted in this context is *Dickinson v Dodds*[13] where a third party successfully communicated the revocation of the offer to the offeree on the offeror's behalf.

(B) Rules as to acceptance

Once the existence of an offer has been proved the courts must be satisfied that a valid acceptance of that offer has taken place. It is often difficult to ascertain the exact moment when the contract was formed where contracts arise as the result of long and complicated negotiations. In such cases the conduct of the parties and all their actions and statements will be considered to see whether or not the parties intended to contract and whether or not they were successful. Many of these rules are centred on the proposition that the acceptance must be clear and comply exactly with the terms of the offer.

(a) The acceptance must be in response to an offer and must correspond precisely with the terms of the offer

In *Peter Lind Ltd v Mersey Docks and Harbour Board*[14] alternative tenders were submitted for the construction of a freight terminal. The offeree accepted 'your tender' without specifying which one. Consequently there was no contract between the two parties.

In the case of *Pickfords Ltd v Celestica Ltd*[15] the defendant sought to assert that a contract had been formed where the claimant's offer was accepted subject to a proviso that the claimant's costs for moving should not exceed £100 000. It was held that this limitation on the claimant's offer was not an acceptance and amounted instead to a counter offer.

---

[13] (1876) 2 Ch D 463
[14] [1972] 2 Lloyd's Rep 234
[15] [2003] EWCA Civ 1741

(b) Counter offers

Rather than amounting to a valid acceptance the insertion of new terms into a proposed agreement amounts to a counter offer by the person who makes it. In *Hyde v Wrench*[16] an offer was made to sell a farm for £1000. A counter offer of £950 was made and refused, whereupon the buyer tried to accept the original offer of £1000. It was decided that the original offer had been 'killed' by the counter offer and was no longer capable of being accepted. In these circumstances it is possible for the original offeror to accept the counter offer and the terms of that offer become the terms of the contract. In this situation the parties have 'changed hats' – the offeror becomes the offeree and vice versa. The parties may change hats several times during the course of a negotiation before arriving at mutually acceptable terms of contract.

It might be the case that no final agreement is made as to which offer should be accepted. Both parties may have their own preferred terms of business and seek to impose their written terms on the other using the offer and counter offer approach outlined above. This situation is known as 'the battle of the forms' a term which first came to light in the case of *Butler Machine Tool Co Ltd v ExCell-O Corporation (England) Ltd*[17]. It has been established that the winner of 'the battle of the forms' is the person who last submits the counter offer which is accepted by the other party.

A counter offer must be contrasted with an inquiry or a request for information from the offeree which will not vary the terms of the original offer. The offer can be said to survive the inquiry. In the case of *Stevenson v McClean*[18] the offeree enquired whether a delivery of iron could be staggered over a two month period. The answer was in the negative but the offeree still wanted to go ahead with the contract. The offeror was obliged to accommodate this.

(c) The nature and time of acceptance

Silence will not amount to a valid acceptance, neither will an attempt to force the issue such as was made in the case of *Felthouse v Bindley*[19] by using words such as 'If I hear no more from you on the subject I will assume acceptance'. A contract takes effect from the time that acceptance is communicated to the offeror. Where an offeror insists on a particular method of acceptance that method must be adopted and the offeror can refuse to recognise an acceptance made in any other manner. The defendant was entitled to insist on written notice to a specified address in the case of *Manchester Diocesan Council for Education v Commercial and General Investments Ltd*[20]. In the case of a unilateral contract, the offeror may dispense with the need to communicate acceptance because of the terms of the offer (*Carlill v Carbolic Smokeball Co* – see above). In such circumstances the necessary performance by the offeree will be sufficient acceptance.

---

[16] (1840) 3 Beav 334
[17] [1979] 1 All ER 965
[18] (1880) 5 QB 346
[19] (1863) 1 New Rep 401
[20] [1969] 3 All ER 1593

It is possible for an offer to be accepted by conduct if that conduct unequivocally relates to the offer. In the case of *Brogden v Metropolitan Rly Co*[21] the parties acted in accordance with a draft agreement for the supply of coal. The draft was held to be binding even though it was never formally executed. A contract can come into existence during performance even if it cannot be precisely analysed in terms of offer and acceptance (*Trentham (G Percy) Ltd v Archital Luxfer Ltd* – see above). A postal acceptance is effective when it is posted even if it is late or is never actually delivered, so long as there is proof of posting. The rationale for this is that the postal service is the agent of both the parties and has authority to act on their behalf in the contract formulation. If the offeror specifies that acceptance must actually be communicated and that posting is not enough in itself, the rule does not apply. The post rule will not apply if it would give rise to 'manifest inconvenience or absurdity' as contemplated in the case of *Hollwell Securities v Hughes*[22] where a letter seeking to exercise an option to purchase was lost in the post. However, the situation is different where letters are delayed in the post, particularly, as in the case of *Adams v Lindsell*[23], where the offer letter was wrongly addressed. In this case the acceptance was binding notwithstanding the sale of the goods in question to a third party in the intervening period. The result was that the defendant was liable for breach of the contract formed upon the posting of the acceptance.

(C) Instantaneous communication

An oral acceptance needs to be communicated to the offeror. The same rule applies to faxes and emails. These forms of communication are treated as being instantaneous and take effect, in terms of acceptance, when received. The issue of where the contract was made was important in the case of *Entores v Miles Far East Corporation*[24]. The offeree was based in the Netherlands and the offeror in London. The acceptance was sent back by facsimile from the Netherlands and was received in the London office. The issue of where the contract was made was important as this would dictate which country's laws would govern the operation of the contract. It was held that the contract was subject to English law - the key event being the receipt of the facsimile, not its sending.

The case of *Mondial Shipping and Chartering BV v Astarte Shipping Ltd*[25] considered a related topic concerning the status of transmissions made outside normal working hours. Here a telex message was sent at 23.41. The issue was whether this was 'sent' on the actual day or deemed to be sent on the next day. The court found that the effective communication had happened on the next working day and decided the issues in the case accordingly.

Emails and mobile telephone text messages are widely used as a means of communicating offers and counter offers, acceptances and rejections. On the face

---

[21] [1877] 2 App Cas 666
[22] [1973] 2 All ER 476
[23] (1818) 1 B & Ald 681
[24] [1955] 2 All ER 493
[25] [1995] CLC 1011

of it, the approach in the *Entores* case seems to apply equally well in relation to email – the acceptance is binding from the time the email is received by the recipient's server and is available to be read. One difference is that the sender might not know of the failure of the message to arrive until sometime after the email has been sent. Further, the email may not be read by the recipient until the account is checked at some future time. However, similar shortcomings can be experienced with other means of communication and the basic rules of offer and acceptance can be said to apply to emails.

The European Union has recognised the importance of electronic commerce in the single market and has sought to regulate the applicable laws in this area. The Electronic Commerce (EC Directive) Regulations 2002 created the basic legal framework. However, the Regulations do not help in defining when exactly invitations to treat, offer and acceptances are made in the context of making contracts through websites; a subject also covered by the Consumer Protection (Distance Selling) Regulations 2000. The latter require the supplier to provide the consumer with certain information prior to the conclusion of the contract. The information includes the identity of the supplier, price, description, delivery costs and minimum duration for any services provided. These Regulations are useful in removing obstacles to cross-border online services in the European Union and provides a uniform set of rules for business and citizens alike.

(D) Letters of intent and pre-contractual work

Letters of intent are indications by a potential party to a contract of an intention to contract at a future date. The status of these letters depends on their wording but where appropriate they can constitute a valid acceptance of an offer. Such letters may make provision for goods to be delivered or rendered before the actual formation of the contract. When the contract is eventually signed it will 'relate back' so as to apply to what was done previously as was the case in *Trollope & Colls Ltd v Atomic Powers Constructions Ltd*[26]. This case involved a particularly complicated tendering and quotation arrangement which was not finally resolved by entering into a contract until some time after work had started. The claimant was entitled to payment for work carried out even though the work done was ultimately of no use to the other party. This point was established by the case of *British Steel Corpn v Cleveland Bridge and Engineering Co Ltd*[27]. The case involved the manufacture of steelwork nodes for a bank development in Saudi Arabia. When the nodes were not subsequently used, the question arose as to whether the defendant was able to counterclaim for a breach of contract. They were not permitted to do so as no contract had ever been entered into. However, the defendant was under an obligation in law to pay a reasonable sum for such work as had been done pursuant to its request contained within the letter of intent. The entitlement was on the *quantum meruit* basis. Quantum meruit describes the situation where a judge allows a claim in circumstances where the claimant is entitled to be recompensed by the defendant by receiving a reasonable price or

---

[26] [1963] 1 WLR 119
[27] [1984] 1 All ER 504

remuneration. This entitlement can be found notwithstanding any deficiency in the parties contractual arrangements as in the present case.

A last question to consider in this section is whether a course of dealings between two businesses can amount to a binding agreement that future work will be awarded on similar terms. This question is relevant to the construction industry where partnering and framework agreements are popular. The case which explored the question is *Baird Textiles Holdings Ltd v Marks and Spencer plc*[28]. The claimant had supplied garments to the defendants for a period of thirty years on a series of individual orders. In October 1999 the defendant terminated all supply arrangements without warning. The claimant sought damages based on the previous dealings and claimed entitlement to a notice period and further orders. The court found that the claimant was not so entitled. The relationship between the parties was only as good as the last order and the defendant had, by its actions, clearly not intended for there to be any commitment beyond this basic arrangement.

2.4.2 *Consideration*

Unless a contract is made by deed it must be supported by consideration otherwise it will be unenforceable. The party who wishes to enforce a contract must show that consideration has been provided for the obligation which is sought to be enforced. The classic definition of consideration comes from the case of *Currie v Misa*[29]: 'some right, interest, profit or benefit accruing to one party, or some forbearance, detriment, loss or responsibility given, suffered or undertaken by the other.'

Consideration can be described as 'contractual glue'; something that binds the offer and acceptance together. In its absence the agreement falls apart. A bare promise without consideration is not binding. A contract is essentially a bargain requiring reciprocal obligations between the parties. Sometimes consideration is known as value. Examples of consideration include the payment of money, the provision of goods, the performance of services or the transfer of land. A distinction is made between executed consideration, where the price is paid for the other party's act, and executory consideration, where the parties exchange promises to carry out obligations in the future.

(a) **Consideration must have some value but need not be adequate**

This means that the consideration must have some worth but the courts will not interfere with a bargain which has been made between the parties in the absence of fraud or other underhand dealings. In *Mountford v Scott*[30] a token payment of £1 securing an option to purchase a house for £10 000 was adequate consideration, while in *Chappell Co Ltd v Nestle Ltd Co*[31] the wrappers from bars of chocolate

---

[28] [2001] EWCA Civ 274
[29] (1875) LR 10 Ex 153
[30] [1975] 1 All ER 198
[31] [1987] AC 87

were held to constitute good consideration when capable of being exchanged in part payment for goods. Token consideration of this nature is quite common on land transactions where the land is in effect gifted. It also appears in such agreements as collateral warranties. Forbearance to sue (agreeing not to pursue a claim in return for a promise by the other party) may be adequate consideration. In the *Carlill v Carbolic Smokeball* case paying for and using the smokeball was deemed to be adequate consideration.

(b) Performance of an existing contractual duty is not good consideration

It will not amount to consideration where a party performs an act which is simply a discharge of an existing obligation owed by contract. A similar rule applies where the existing duty is owed by the general law. In *Collins v Godefroy*[32] the defendant agreed to pay the claimant a sum of money if he gave evidence at a criminal trial. A claim for the sum promised failed because the claimant had an obligation imposed by law to give such evidence. It will amount to good consideration if the obligation is a contractual one only if a party does more than he was bound to do under the terms of the contract. Two examples of this rule in practice are the decisions in *Stilk v Myrick*[33] and *Hartley v Ponsonby*[34]. Both cases involve claims by seamen relating to work carried out under their contracts. In the former case, a claim relating to extra work carried out under a contract was dismissed because the crew were contractually bound to carry out any extra work by the terms of their contracts. In the latter case, any extra work involved in the voyage was an addition to the crew's contractual obligations and a successful claim could be made in respect of the additional work which had been carried out.

In *Williams v Roffey Bros Ltd*[35] the defendants were contractors responsible for the refurbishment of a block of flats for the benefit of the Employer. Mr Williams, a joiner, contracted to carry out joinery work on the flats for the sum of £20 000. The contract contained a provision that if the work was not completed by a specific date then damages would be payable by the defendants as liquidated damages to the Employer. The claimant had contracted at a sum which was unprofitable to him and was in no hurry to complete the contract. Somewhat concerned that the contract might not be finalised on time, the defendant promised to pay the claimant, by word of mouth, an extra £10 300 in respect of the flats so long as the work was completed according to schedule. The joiner carried out the work and claimed the extra sums. The Court of Appeal decided that these amounts were payable notwithstanding the terms of the original agreement. Consideration had been given for the contractor's promise to make the additional payment. The contract had been completed, the damages payable to the Employer in respect of late completion had been avoided and it had not been necessary to employ others to finish off the joinery work.

---

[32] (1831) 1 Dowl 326
[33] (1809) 2 Camp 317
[34] (1857) 7 E & B 872
[35] [1990] 1 All ER 512

(c) Consideration must not be past

An act is regarded as past consideration if one party performs an act before any promise of reward is made by the other party. The practical effect of this rule is that it is not possible to develop a social arrangement into a contract by making a promise of consideration after the arrangement has been carried out. In *Re McArdle*[36], alterations and improvements to a house were carried out and paid for before the other parties to the contract agreed to reimburse the cost. The consideration was past.

(d) Exceptions to the rule

- Consideration will not be said to past where there is an implied promise to pay. It is common practice to pay for certain transactions after completion of the event, such as a taxi journey or a meal in a restaurant.
- Similarly cheques are frequently paid in connection with goods and services received in the past. Section 27 Bills of Exchange Act 1882 established that the cheque will nevertheless be honoured in respect of antecedent debts.

(e) Payment of a lesser sum under a contract than the amount which is due will not discharge the debt for a greater sum

The debtor is not discharged from the obligation to pay the balance where a debtor pays a lesser sum to his creditor than that which is due. The established law was that a creditor can go back on the agreement and sue for the balance as happened in the case of *Foakes v Beer*[37]. The issue at stake was whether the interest on a judgment debt could be claimed by the claimant who had agreed to allow the defendant to pay in stages. It could – the defendant had given nothing of value for the claimant's promise not to enforce. There is an important exception to this waiver rule and it arises if, at the creditor's request, some new element is introduced into the arrangement such as payment at a different time or place. Appropriate compliance with this request will amount to consideration for the waiver and the creditor will have no further claim. This is known as the rule in *Pinnel's Case*[38].

However, in this situation there must be a true accord. This was lacking in the case of *D & C Builders Ltd v Rees*[39] where impecunious builders felt they had no choice but to accept a lower sum from their client. It was decided by Lord Denning, that there was no reason in law or equity why the claimant should not enforce the full amount of the debt.

---

[36] [1951] Ch 669
[37] (1884) 9 App Cas 605
[38] (1602) 5 Co Rep 117a
[39] [1965] 3 All ER 837

Both these decisions appear to be at odds with a 2007 case heard in the Court of Appeal. The judgment in *Collier v Wright*[40] has effectively nullified the rule that part payment can never be sufficient by expanding the doctrine of promissory estoppel to come to the aid of the debtor in all such cases. In this case the creditor voluntarily accepted part payment of a debt. The debtor relied on this acceptance and paid the amount agreed. The creditor was then estopped (see (g) below) from going back on his promise to accept less notwithstanding the lack of consideration for such an agreement.

(f) Consideration must move from the promisee

Only a party who gives consideration under a contract (or his agent) can sue in the event of a breach of contract. This rule is similar to but must be distinguished from the privity rule (see paragraph 2.9).

(g) Promissory estoppel

This describes the equitable remedy available in certain circumstances where a party has waived rights under a contract and the other party has relied upon the promise not to enforce those rights. The promisor is estopped (prevented) from going back on the promise even though no consideration has been given for the waiver if certain conditions are fulfilled. The doctrine has its roots in the nineteenth century and in particular the case of *Hughes v Metropolitan Rlw Co*[41]. This case involved a request by a landlord to the tenant to carry out repairs on a rented property. The request was followed by a negotiation between the parties on a new lease during which time the tenant delayed the repairs. The negotiations did not come to anything and the landlord cited the tenant's failure to carry out repairs as grounds for terminating the lease. The court did not agree – the landlord was estopped from pursuing the course of action because the tenant had relied on the landlord's implied waiver of the requirement to repair during the course of the negotiations.

The modern development of the doctrine dates from the 'High Trees' case or to give it its proper name *Central London Property Trust Ltd v High Trees House Ltd*[42]. This case concerns the lease of a block of flats in London which turned out to be unprofitable because of the threat of enemy bombing in the Second World War. The landlord made a written promise to reduce the rent for the duration of the war. In 1945, when circumstances had changed, the landlord changed his mind and started to charge the full rent. It was decided that he could do so for the future, but the full rent could not be obtained for the period between making the promise and the end of the war since the tenants had relied on his previous promise. Before the doctrine can come into being there must be an agreement between the parties, an unequivocal promise by one party to the other and, at least for the time being, an indication that those rights will be waived. The defendant must have given no consideration for the promise but acted upon that promise by relying upon it. The

---

[40] [2007] EWCA Civ 1329
[41] (1877) 2 App Cas 439
[42] [1947] KB 130

promisor is then estopped from altering his position under the contract if to do so would cause harm to the other party.

Estoppel can only be used as a defence to a claim and not as a cause of action. Whether or not promissory estoppel merely suspends an obligation or discharges it completely is the subject of debate. In the case of *Tool Metal Manufacturing Co Ltd vTungsten Electric Co Ltd*[43] contractual rights to a patent were capable of being resumed by a party who had been estopped from claiming them upon reasonable notice being given.

2.4.3 The intention to create legal relations

A contract is a legally binding agreement. The parties must intend that their agreement should be regulated and have the protection of the law for it to become a contract. Where no such intention can be shown there is no contract. Many agreements are never intended to be legally binding whilst in others the presumption will exist that the parties intended to be so bound.

(A) Business agreements

In business and commercial agreements it is presumed that the parties intend to create legal relations. This includes an agreement to build or to transfer land or buildings. This presumption can be challenged (rebutted) if there is evidence to the contrary, or as in the case of *Milner & Son v Percy Bilton Ltd*[44] the words used were too vague to amount to a definite commitment to sell land. There must be strong evidence from the agreement that the parties do not intend to create legal relations. The parties are not bound where the agreement is expressed to be 'binding in honour only' or something similar. This area is akin to the gentlemen's agreement; the problem being that if one or other of the parties no longer wishes to behave in whatever fashion a gentleman should, they can consider themselves no longer bound. A common occurrence in conveyancing transactions and correspondence is the use of the phrase 'subject to contract'. The phrase is often seen on letters sent to the parties in a conveyance by estate agents. The purpose of the letter is often to record the agreement made on price and to signal that both parties must now complete the other formalities of agreement required to bring about the transaction with the assistance of their legal advisors. The use of this phrase is sufficient to prevent any agreement being reached even if the words in the letter itself create the opposite impression.

(B) Social and domestic agreements

In agreements of this type it is presumed that the parties do not intend legal relations to arise. This was the finding in the case of *Balfour v Balfour*[45] where an agreement to pay maintenance before divorce proceedings were commenced was

---

[43] [1955] 2 All ER 657
[44] [1966] 2 All ER 284
[45] [1919] 2 KB 571

found to be not binding. This principle may also be rebutted. An agreement which appears on the face of it to be simply a domestic agreement may be enforceable between the parties. This happened in the case of *Simpkins v Pays*[46] which involved an agreement to share the winnings from a lottery syndicate. The agreement was binding notwithstanding its domestic setting. Again, the presumption that legal relations were not intended will depend on the formality of the agreement, whether consideration has passed between the parties and the language used. In *Spelling v John Spelling Ltd*[47], mutual promises between co-directors, who were brothers, that they would not withdraw money from a family business were deemed to be binding. Similar problems have arisen in cases concerning proposals to share houses with relatives. In *Parker v Clark*[48], a married couple gave up their house in order to look after a family relative in her property. This was in return for an assurance that the property would be left to them by will. It was not. The assurance was deemed to be legally binding and the couple were entitled to recover damages.

2.5   Terms of a contract

The terms of a contract are its contents. Representations are pre-contractual statements and should not be confused with contractual terms. The two can be distinguished – a representation is a statement of fact which acts as an inducement to enter into a contract. A false representation may give a potential claimant a right to claim on the basis of misrepresentation. If the misrepresentation is actionable the remedies are governed by the Misrepresentation Act 1967 and not by the rules relating to remedies for breach of contract. The intentions of the parties and what they understood the representation to mean are relevant to deciding whether a misrepresentation has taken place (see paragraph 2.6.3). If these enquiries are inconclusive the test used by the judge will be to consider what an intelligent bystander would infer from the words and behaviour of the parties at the time the representation was made.

Contractual terms, on the other hand, may be express or implied. Express terms are stated either orally or in writing – the parties are said to have 'expressed themselves' on any particular subject which is thereby included into their contract. Implied terms arise in other ways.

2.5.1   Express terms

The meaning of the terms is a question of fact where the contract has been made on a wholly oral basis. The court must decide the issue from the evidence which is given to it. The 'parol evidence' rule applies where contracts have been recorded in writing. The rule prevents oral or other extrinsic evidence to be admitted to vary

---

[46] [1955] 3 All ER 10
[47] [1973] QB 87
[48] [1960] 1 All ER 93

or contradict the terms of the written agreement. There are some exceptions to this rule, among the most important being:

- to prove a trade custom or usage;
- to indicate the existence of a vitiating factor (see paragraph 2.6);
- where the written contract is not the whole contract.

2.5.2   Implied terms

A contract may contain terms which are not express but which are implied by custom, the courts or by statute. A term will not be implied by custom if the express wording of the contract shows that the parties had a contrary intention. Where appropriate a term will be implied by the custom of a particular geographical area as was the case in *Hutton v Warren*[49]. The claimant was a tenant of a farm and was given notice by the landlord to quit before the crops (which the claimant had planted) were harvested. Local custom dictated that the tenant was allowed to recover a fair allowance for seeds and labour involved in the planting of a crop where a tenant was prevented from harvesting the crop. A term was therefore implied into the lease to this effect. Other than by custom, terms can be implied in one of two ways.

(A) The courts

The courts will imply a term in the following sets of circumstances.

(a) Where such a term is a necessary incident of the type of contract in question

The reasonableness of the term and the nature of the subject matter are important in this context. In contracts to build where a builder constructs a house there is a term implied that the dwelling will be reasonably fit for habitation when completed. Similar terms are implied in respect of the quality of work and the time in which the contract will be completed. Likewise, on the employer's part, it is implied that the contractor will be given possession of the site on which the building works are to take place and that a reasonable sum shall be payable for the work. These terms may be rebutted where there are express terms dealing with these matters to the contrary.

(b) To give the contract 'business efficacy'

Business efficacy involves the notion of making a contract into a workable agreement in such a manner as the parties would clearly have done if they had applied their minds to the matter arising. From this the court creates the common implied intention of the parties. It may be necessary to fill a gap in the contract and the term(s) must be formulated with a sufficient degree of precision. There must be no express term dealing with the same matter, while the stipulations to be implied must be so obvious that they go without saying. The

---

[49] (1836) 1 M&W 466

principle comes from *The Moorcock*[50], where a vessel was damaged unloading a cargo owing to the unevenness of the river bed which became exposed at low tide and which had not been maintained properly. It was decided that there was an implied term in the contract that the owners of the wharf had impliedly contracted to take reasonable care to see that ships unloading their cargos were safe and would not be damaged on the river bed. The case of *Liverpool City Council v Irwin*[51] shows the application of the procedure within a built environment context. The Council let flats in a tower block to the tenants. There were no obligations on the Council stated in the lease as to the maintenance of the building. The flats were poorly maintained by the Council with broken lifts and rubbish strewn walkways. The defendant withheld his rent in protest at the condition of the premises arguing that the Council were in breach of an implied term of the lease that they should adequately maintain the buildings. The House of Lords agreed and implied such a term into the lease using the common implied intention rule.

(c) Where a term is implied by the previous course of dealings between the parties

Terms will be implied into a contract of a similar kind where the parties have previously entered into contracts of the same particular variety containing express terms. This will only occur in the absence of express stipulation to the contrary.

(B) Statute

In some instances, statute will imply terms into a contract. Examples are the Sale of Goods Acts 1979 and the Supply of Goods and Services Act 1982 (as amended by the Sale and Supply of Goods to Consumer Regulations 2002).

The Sale of Goods Act 1979

(a) Terminology

A contract for the sale of goods is one whereby the seller transfers or agrees to transfer the property in goods for a money consideration called the price. 'Goods' includes all personal chattels (basically a person's belongings other than money) and choses in action (intangible personal property confering a right to sue on the owner, for example a policy of insurance or a bond).

(b) Terms implied by the Act

The Sale of Goods Act 1979 implies terms into contracts for the sale of goods as follows:

---

[50] (1889) 14 PD 164
[51] [1976] 2 All ER 39

(i) Title (section 12)

In every such contract there is an implied condition on the part of the seller that he has the right to sell the goods or that he will have the right at the time when the property is to pass. If this condition is broken the buyer may treat the contract as at an end even though he has done some act which would otherwise have amounted to acceptance. Section 12 also provides that there is an implied warranty that the goods are free and will remain free from any encumbrances not known to the buyer before the contract is made.

(ii) Description (section 13)

The vast majority of sales are by description (i.e. the goods are not physically examined by the buyer before purchase) and in such a case there is an implied condition that the goods will correspond with that description. This provision also applies to private sales. It extends to matters such as measurements, quantity and methods of packing as in the case of *Moore & Co v Landaur & Co*[52]. The claimants were entitled to reject imported goods merely because they were packed in boxes of twenty-four rather than thirty as agreed.

(iii) Satisfactory quality (section 14)

The following provisions only apply where the goods are sold in the course of a business. By section 14(2) there is an implied condition of satisfactory quality except as regards defects specifically drawn to the buyer's attention before the contract is made or where the buyer examines the goods before the contract as regards defects which the examination ought to reveal. 'Satisfactory quality' means that the goods meet the standard that a reasonable person would regard as satisfactory having regard, *inter alia*, to their description and price. The Sale and Supply of Goods to Consumers Regulations 2002 have improved the position of the consumer further by adjusting the burden of proof. Goods returned by the consumer within the first six months from the date of sale requesting a repair are assumed to have been faulty at the date of purchase unless the retailer can establish otherwise.

Section 14(3) relates to fitness. The implied condition is that the goods are reasonably fit for any purpose which the buyer makes known to the seller. This purpose will normally be implied but if goods have a number of purposes, the buyer must indicate the one required.

(iv) Sample (section 15)

Certain items such as tiles, carpets and wallpaper are bought on the basis of a sample inspected before the sale takes place. In such circumstances the following conditions are implied:

---

[52] [1921] 2 KB 519

- that the bulk will correspond with the sample in quality;
- that the buyer will have a reasonable opportunity of comparing the bulk with the sample;
- that the goods shall be free from any defects rendering them unsatisfactory which would not be apparent on reasonable examination of the sample.

The Supply of Goods and Services Act 1982

A contract for the sale of goods must be distinguished from a contract for the supply of services where goods are also being sold under the contract. A contract for work done and materials supplied comes into this category. The sale aspect of the contract is governed by sections 2–5 of the 1982 Act which contains implied terms similar to the Sale of Goods Act 1979 (sections 12–15). The works aspects are governed by Part 2 of the Act which imply terms relating to reasonable skill and care, reasonable time for completion, and reasonable charges for services where no price has been fixed at the outset. The supplier must be acting in the course of a business for the terms to apply.

The Late Payment of Commercial Debts (Interest) Act 1998

This Act was introduced to improve the position of small businesses being kept out of money owing to them by larger businesses. The Act implies terms into contracts between qualifying businesses that simple interest calculated at the appropriate rate can be claimed in the event of late payment.

2.5.3   Conditions and warranties

Conditions and warranties are two different types of contractual term and the rules governing them apply equally whether the term is express or implied. This distinction is important because there are different remedies if there is a breach of contract and things go wrong. There is no special test to determine into which category a term falls. Each situation has to be decided on its own merits.

(A) Conditions

These are the more important terms of contract. These are terms of the contract but for which the injured party would not have entered the contract. A breach of condition (known as a repudiatory breach) allows the injured party to treat the contract as finished whereupon he will be discharged from his obligations under the contract. In addition, the other party can be sued for damages. The contract is voidable which means the innocent party has a choice between treating the contract as having been irreparably damaged by the breach of condition (this is known as rescission), or continuing with the contract notwithstanding the breach. The choice is based around the fact that the innocent party should be entitled to keep the benefit of the contract if he so wishes. In either case it is open to the innocent party to pursue a claim for damages.

(B) Warranties

These are terms which are secondary or ancillary to the main purpose of the contract. A breach of warranty allows the injured party to claim damages but not to repudiate the contract. The contract is not voidable. The contract survives the breach of a minor term whilst preserving the right to damages for the innocent party. It is for a court and not for the parties to determine the category of term.

The difference between conditions and warranties and the practical consequences of the difference are evident from a comparison of the cases of *Poussard v Spiers and Pond*[53] and *Bettini v Gye*[54]. It was a coincidence that two cases involving singers should be reported in the press in the same year. Both cases involved singers who were late for their performances at theatres and were told that the agreements to hire them had been fundamentally breached by reason of their lateness. In Poussard's case the court agreed. The singer had missed the all important opening night and her absence amounted to a breach of condition. Bettini, however, had only missed rehearsals and the producers were not entitled to terminate the contract. The producers were able to sue in damages for the breach of warranty.

A problem which has arisen is that a stipulation in a contract may be classified as a term but is neither a condition nor a warranty. The difficulty which arises is then to determine whether or not the injured party can rescind (avoid) the contract. Such provisions have become known as intermediate or innominate terms. The consequences of the breach are important here. Unless the contract makes it clear that the parties intended that no breach of the contract should entitle them to terminate the contract, the term will be classified as an intermediate term. The question is whether or not the nature and effect of the breach are to deprive the injured party of substantially the benefit which it is intended they should obtain under the contract. If so, the injured party is entitled to terminate the contract as well as claiming damages. This was the question considered in the case of *The Hansa Nord*[55]. The question here was whether an innominate term of the contract that 'shipment be made in good condition 'should be treated as a condition or a warranty. The claimant sought to reject the contract based on a small percentage of the goods being sub-standard. The defendant suspected that the real reason for the rejection was a reduction in the market value which rendered the cargo much less profitable. The court did not view the partial unsoundness of the cargo to be a ground for total rejection and treated the breach as a warranty entitling the claimant to damages only.

2.6 Vitiating factors

These are factors which affect the validity of a contract. A contract may be challenged notwithstanding the appearance that it has been properly formed with the essential three ingredients of offer/acceptance, consideration and intention

---

[53] (1876) 1 QBD 410
[54] (1876) 1 QBD 183
[55] [1975] 3 All ER 739

to create legal relations being present. A state of affairs may have arisen which may make the contract no longer enforceable. Depending upon the circumstances a vitiating factor will make the contract either:

- Void (no contract).
- Voidable (the contract exists but can be avoided at the election of the innocent party).
- Binding (an enforceable contract exists).

2.6.1 Capacity of the parties

The first challenge to an agreement is based around the notion of incapacity. The central premise is that, regardless of any assertion to the contrary, a person may lack capacity to enter into a contract. A distinction is made in English law between natural persons and artificial persons. Natural persons have full capacity to enter contracts. There are exceptions to this rule in the case of minors (those under the age of eighteen) and, to a certain extent, in respect of those suffering from a mental disorder and drunks. Drunks lack capacity to enter into contracts whilst so intoxicated as to not know what they are doing and without their intoxication being obvious to the other party. In these circumstances a contract is voidable, but may be ratified by the drunk on becoming sober.

As a general rule, contracts are not binding on minors. A practical exception to this rule is to be found in respect of contracts of employment which are beneficial to the minor. An example of this would be a contract with a newsagent to deliver newspapers to the local neighbourhood. Another exception involves contracts for necessaries. The notion here is that minors are obliged to pay for goods or services they need. The rather bizarre corollary is that minors do not need to pay for goods or services they do not need. This was demonstrated in the case of *Nash v Inman*[56]. A Saville Row tailor attempted to recover £122 16s 6d for items including eleven fancy waistcoats supplied to an undergraduate. The action failed as the minor could demonstrate that he was already adequately supplied with clothes and those supplied by the tailor did not amount to necessaries.

Artificial persons are corporations, local authorities and companies registered under the Companies Acts (see paragraph 2.14.4). The ability of artificial persons to enter into contracts may, in certain circumstances, be limited by their incorporation and internal administration documentation.

2.6.2 Mistake

A mistake arises where the parties make an error as to a term of the contract such as to prevent there being *consensus ad idem* (or meeting of the minds). Mistake does not affect the validity of a contract unless the mistake is a fundamental one. This is known as an operative mistake. Such a mistake will render the contract void. In a limited set of circumstances the contract will be voidable (this may be the position

---

[56] [1908] 2 KB 1

where these is a mistake as to the identity of the person contracted with). Special rules apply to documents. The contract is binding where a person signs a document and by so doing enters a contract. This is so even if the signatory has not read the document nor understands it. The principle of *caveat emptor* – let the buyer beware- applies here. There is a very limited defence based on *Non Est Factum* (it is not my deed), where a person is induced by a fraud or a trick to sign a document. In practice, the defence is difficult to rely on because the signatory must show:

- That all reasonable precautions were taken when signing the document.and;
- The document signed was radically different from the one the person thought they were signing, or;
- The person signing the document was under some legal disability, such as being illiterate, blind or senile.

An example the third point above occurred in *Lloyds Bank v Waterhouse*[57] where an illiterate person failed to inform the bank that she could not read. She nevertheless signed a bank guarantee but in doing so relied on the bank's misrepresentation as to its nature. She was able to avoid a claim based on the guarantee by reason of the operative mistake.

There are some circumstances where the equitable jurisdiction of the English legal system will intervene where the mistake is a non-operative one. This includes rescission of the contract and possible rectification of a contract if it does not accurately express the agreement reached between the parties. In such circumstances, equity will rectify the agreement so as to make it conform to the original agreement. In *Craddock Bros v Hunt*[58] there was an oral agreement to sell land. This was put into writing but, by mistake, the document missed out any reference to part of the land which had been paid for. It was held that the agreement would be rectified. The rule does not apply if there is simply a mistake by one of the parties in expressing intention. In *W Higgins Ltd v Northampton Corporation*[59] the claimant stated an incorrect price for work in connection with a tender relating to the building of houses. The error was due to incorrect estimating on the claimant's part. The tender was accepted by the local authority without realising a mistake had been made but the contract could not be rectified. In this instance the principle was *caveat venditor* – let the seller beware. The claimant found itself in the position that it could not now avoid a contract where they had legitimately (but erroneously) offered to carry out the work for the price stated.

2.6.3 *Misrepresentation*

Misrepresentation is concerned with the effect of statements which are made before a contract is formed. A representation is a statement of fact and not a statement of opinion which is made by one person to another with the object of persuading the other party to enter into a contract. Where that party relies upon the statement, a contract is formed and the statement turns out to be incorrect, a

---

[57] [1991] 10 Trading LR 161
[58] [1923] All ER 394
[59] [1927] 1 Ch 128

remedy may be provided by the law of misrepresentation. An example of an opinion rather than a fact comes from the case of *Bisset vWilkinson*[60] where the vendor of a farm in New Zealand expressed an opinion that the farm would support 2000 sheep. In fact, the farm had never held any sheep. The claimant's sheep farming business failed but they were unable to sue for misrepresentation based on what was an honestly given opinion.

Remedies are governed by the Misrepresentation Act 1967 and the tort of deceit. A misrepresentation can be fraudulent, innocent or negligent. A claimant in such circumstances will be able to claim damages and/or rescind the contract. The court has power to refuse rescission and to award damages instead in the case of a non-fraudulent misrepresentation. A delay in applying for rescission may also be fatal to such a claim. This occurred in the case of *Zanzibar v British Aerospace (Lancaster House) Ltd*[61] where problems experienced with a private jet aeroplane were not reported until several years after the alleged problems first arose.

2.6.4 *Duress, undue influence and inequality of bargaining power*

There are grounds upon which to challenge an agreement where the parties have not given their free consent to be bound by the terms of the agreement. Coercion or actual threats or undue pressure can vitiate a contract. Mere inequality of bargaining power is, as a general rule, insufficient in seeking to set aside agreements. Statutory interventions such as the Unfair Contract Terms Act 1977 and Unfair Terms in Consumer Contracts Regulations 1999 go someway towards protecting consumers in commercially vulnerable positions. The Consumer Credit Act 2006 allows the court to adjust a credit agreement if the court decides that the relationship between lender and borrower is unfair.

2.6.5 *Illegality*

A contract containing an illegal element is void. The illegal aspect may be the contravention of a statute or it may be against public policy to allow certain types of contract to be enforced. Examples include defrauding the Inland Revenue or contracts involving the commission of a crime. The contract price will not be recoverable where a building contractor enters a contract knowingly in contravention of a law. In *Stevens v Gourley*[62] statutory provisions required buildings to be made of incombustible materials. The contract was found to be illegal when the builder erected a wooden building upon wooden foundations. A different situation applies when the contract appears to be perfectly valid at the outset and only becomes illegal while in the process of performance. The contractor may be able to recover the price for the work depending upon the circumstances. In *Townshend Builders Ltd v Cinema News*[63] specifications for temporary work to be undertaken were in contravention of a statutory provision but the completed work was not.

---

[60] [1927] AC 177
[61] (2000) The Times, 23 March
[62] (1859) 7 CB NS 99
[63] [1959] 1 WLR 119

Payment could be claimed as the contract was not fundamentally illegal and the builder was unaware of the contravention until the work was well advanced.

2.7   Privity of contract

One fundamental aspect of the common law is the principle that no person can sue or be sued on a contract unless a party to it. This can cause particular problems in the construction industry where many parties are involved in a building project. Some of the participants will have privity of contract between themselves while others will not. The rule means that a stranger (or third party) to a contract cannot sue under a contract to which they are not a party even if the terms of the contract express that the third party should so benefit. The general aspects of the principle are illustrated by *Tweddle v Atkinson*[64] where a couple were about to marry. The bridegroom's father and the bride's father agreed between themselves that each would make payments to the couple. The husband sought to enforce the contract when the bride's father refused to pay. It was held that there was no privity of contract between the parties and that therefore the claim could not be enforced. There are a number of exceptions to the rule.

Examples of exceptions include third party insurance policies and the agency relationship where a principal can sue and be sued in respect of a contract made by an agent. Tripartite arrangements known as trusts are similarly excepted (see Chapter 4, paragraph 4.6.2.B). The privity rule has been criticised by the higher courts. A successful attack was made on the rule with the enactment of the Landlord and Tenant (Covenants) Act 1995 which abolished the rule between a landlord and the assignee of an original tenant in a leasehold transaction.

It has become standard practice in large scale construction projects for those who finance the transactions to insist that all the parties involved enter into contractual warranties with each other. The reason for this is because of the difficulties which claimants have in being able to successfully sue a defendant in the tort of negligence for financial losses. The collateral warranty is a way of ensuring that in the event of default an injured party will have a potential defendant to sue and claim damages.

This tendency to insist on the use of collateral warranties has so far continued notwithstanding the change in the law brought about by the Contracts (Rights of Third Parties) Act 1999. This non-mandatory Act allows a third party to sue on a contract to which he is not a party but which purports to transfer a benefit on him. The effect of these provisions, when used, is to circumvent the privity of contract rule. Standard forms of building contract were initially slow to embrace this statutory change. However, the most recent edition of the Joint Contracts Tribunal standard form of building contract (see paragraph 2.14.1) gives parties the option of having a third party schedule of rights either alongside or as an alternative to collateral warranties.

---

[64] (1861) 1 Best & Smith 393

2.8   Exemption clauses

2.8.1   Common law

A common practice in contract formation is for a party to insert a clause which in the event of their breach will either exclude liability completely under the contract or limits that liability to a specific amount of money. The former type of clause is an exemption clause whilst the latter is known as a limitation clause. Such clauses are used by suppliers of goods and services in respect of potential problems such as defective materials and unsatisfactory work. The courts have always disliked exemption/limitation clauses and tend to decide against them if there is any ambiguity in what the clause may mean or whether it has been incorporated properly in any given situation. At common law an exemption clause is valid so long as certain basic requirements are satisfied. In *L'Estrange v Graucob*[65] such a clause was upheld notwithstanding that it was written in 'legible but regrettably small print' in a sales agreement. The claimant failed to read the document before signing it but had the opportunity of so doing. A person seeking to rely on such a clause must show that it is a term of the contract and that as a matter of construction it covers the damage in question. The case of *Chappleton v Barry UDC*[66] involved a claimant injured by a hired deckchair which collapsed on him. At the time of hiring the deckchair no notice was given of the exclusion clause on which the Council sought to rely. The clause was contained in a receipt given to the claimant at which he only glanced. The judge held it was unreasonable to communicate conditions by means of a mere receipt. The exclusion will not therefore be effective if the clause or the notice is contained in a document which the average person would not assume to contain contractual terms.

The clause will only be a contractual term if adequate notice is given of it or such a term is implied by a clause having been incorporated into documents where there has been a previous course of dealings between the parties. A common practice is to print exemption clauses on order forms or on a notice. Notice of the clause must be given before, or at the time of the contract. Belated notice of an exclusion clause was given in the case of *Olley v Marlborough Court*[67]. A contract for the hire of a hotel room was made over the telephone. Mrs Olley's fur coat was stolen from the hotel room during their absence. The hotel sought to rely on a notice avoiding liability from theft displayed in the hotel's lobby. The judge deemed that this notice was not adequate as the contract for the hire of the room had been made over the telephone and this unilateral attempt to introduce new terms once the contract had been completed would not be successful. Where exclusion clauses are properly incorporated the position is that liability can only be limited or excluded by clear words. The purpose of the exemption clause is another factor for the court to consider in deciding whether or not it is reasonable as demonstrated by the case of *O'Brien v Mirror Group Newspaper Limited*[68]. This case involved scratch cards distributed with a British newspaper. Due to an error

---

[65] [1934] 2 KB 394
[66] [1949] 1 KB 532
[67] [1949]1 All ER 127
[68] [2001] EWCA Civ 1279

on the cards 1472 people were told they had won a sum of £50 000 each. The claimant attempted to hold the defendant to their promise to pay. The latter relied on its terms and conditions in seeking to avoid liability. The judge allowed the defendant to rely on its exclusion clause notwithstanding the fact that the terms and conditions were not printed in the edition of the paper the claimant purchased. The effect of the exclusion clause here was not to exclude liability altogether but merely to prevent a windfall for the claimant.

2.8.2 *Statute*

The principal statutory provisions regulating unfair reliance on exemption clauses is the Unfair Contract Terms Act 1977 (UCTA) and the Unfair Terms in Consumer Contracts Regulations 1999. A draft bill Unfair Terms in Contracts was laid before Parliament in 2004 to unify the provisions of these two regimes but this has not yet become law. The Act covers liability in respect of a breach of contract and in respect of the tort of negligence. The Act only has application in respect of 'business liability' where the other party deals as a consumer. 'Business liability' relates to a transaction which emanates from business activities while the other party makes the contract in a domestic capacity. Any provision in a contract excluding or restricting liability for death or personal injury is void. In other cases based on negligence, liability can only be excluded or limited if it is fair and reasonable to do so. The reasonableness provision also applies in contractual cases. The fair and reasonable provision will also apply where a party to a contract deals as a consumer or contracts on the other party's standard business terms. The Act does not apply to contracts of insurance and to contracts which contain a foreign element. This provision was considered by the House of Lords in *Smith v Eric S Bush*[69], where a firm of general practice surveyors inserted an exemption clause into a valuation report for mortgage purposes which had been prepared for a building society. The report was shown to the purchasers. The Law Lords concluded that it would not in the circumstances be fair and reasonable to rely on the disclaimer. The factors to be considered when deciding whether a purported exclusion is fair and reasonable include:

- The practical consequences of exclusion – in particular, the cost and availability of insurance cover.
- Equality of bargaining power between the parties.
- Whether it is practicable for the relevant party (or parties) to seek advice from an alternative source.
- An exclusion could well be reasonable if the task is unusual or dangerous.

Similar provisions have been developed in connection with purported exclusions of liability in respect of contracts governed by the Sale of Goods Act 1979 and the Supply of Goods and Services Act 1982. Sections 6 and 7 of UCTA deal with these matters. Any of the terms implied by the Act may be excluded or varied subject

---

[69] [1990] 1 AC 831; see also Chapter 3, paragraph 3.6.10

to UCTA. The Act states that any clause purporting to exclude section 12 of the Act (title) is void. In a consumer sale, any term excluding sections 13, 14 or 15 (description, quality/fitness and sample) shall also be void. A consumer sale arises where:

- The seller is making a sale in the course of business.
- The goods are of a type ordinarily bought for private use or consumption.
- The buyer does not purchase the goods in the course of a business.

A seller may exclude liability under sections 13–15 in a non-consumer sale which is made in the course of business if it can be shown that it is fair and reasonable to do so. The majority of sales in a construction context will be non-consumer in nature. UCTA lays down guidelines as to the factors to be taken into account when applying the reasonableness test. The principal ones are as follows:

- The relative strength of the bargaining position of the parties taking into account the availability of suitable alternative products and sources of supply.
- Whether the buyer received an inducement to agree to the term.
- Whether the buyer knew or ought reasonably to have known of the existence and extent of the term.
- The extent to which the goods were manufactured, processed or adapted to the special order of the buyer (UCTA 1977 s11).

In the case of *Rees-Haugh Limited v Redland Reinforced Plastics Limited*[70] the judge decided it was not fair and reasonable for the defendant to rely on an exclusion clause in their terms and conditions of sale. They sold pipes to the claimant which were not fit for purpose for which the defendant knew they were required. Following this case it is difficult to see how a party can escape liability for supplying defective goods. Similarly, in the case of *Feldaroll Foundry plc v Hermes Leasing (London) Ltd*[71] liability for a Lamborghini Diablo motor car bought for £64 995 but sold with a serious and dangerous steering defect could not avoided by the defendants.

An auction sale or a sale by tender is not a consumer sale. An exemption clause may be valid subject to the reasonableness test if a private buyer buys at auction. It is presumed that a sale is a consumer sale, but once the seller has proved it is a non-consumer sale it is for the buyer to show that it would not be fair and reasonable to rely on the term.

The Unfair Terms in Consumer Contracts Regulations 1999 introduce an important additional criterion for assessing whether a contract term is unfair to consumers. The key provision in the Regulations is '*A contractual term which has not been individually negotiated shall be regarded as unfair if, contrary to the requirement of good faith, it causes a significant imbalance in the parties' rights and obligations arising under the contract, to the detriment of the consumer.*' The Regulations operate alongside UCTA and give the consumer an additional resource with which to challenge a seemingly unfair contract term. The fairness test was illustrated in the

---

[70] [1984]Cons.I.L.L. 84
[71] [2004] EWCA Civ 747

case of *Director General of Fair Trading v First National Bank*[72]. The claimant is tasked by the government to consider any complaint made to him that any contract drawn up for general use in unfair and to take any appropriate action to rectify the situation. In this case the interest provision for late payment of a loan was considered to be unfair within the definition set.

2.9   Discharge of a contract

Where a contract is at an end it is said to be discharged. The rule is that on discharge the parties are freed from their obligations. Contracts do not end automatically and discharge must come about by an act of the parties. It can come about in one of four ways:

- Performance.
- Agreement.
- Frustration.
- Breach of an appropriate term of the contract.

2.9.1   Performance

Each party must perform precisely and completely what he has bargained to do. A person who claims to be discharged from obligations on the basis of performance must show that the work has been completed in full, the goods supplied or the land transferred as appropriate. A building or engineering contract will be discharged by performance when the contractor has completed all the work and the employer has paid all sums due. The contract has not been performed if there are hidden defects. This common law rule is enshrined in *Cutter v Powell*[73], where the defendant agreed to pay Cutter a sum of money for performing duties as a seaman on a ship during a ten-week voyage. Cutter died seven weeks after the commencement of the voyage. His widow attempted to recover wages under the contract. The claim failed because the ten-week contract had not been performed. Similarly in *Sumpter v Hedges*[74] the claimant builder contracted to construct two buildings on the defendant's land for an agreed price. The buildings were half finished when the project was abandoned because of lack of funds. The claimant was unable to recover any money in respect of the work carried out. The courts have recognised certain exceptions where a person may claim a reasonable sum for the work carried out on the basis of a *quantum meruit* application in order to avoid possible injustice and to prevent unfair manipulation of the common law rule. *Quantum meruit* means, 'as much as it is worth'.

---

[72] [2001] 3 WLR 1297 (HL)
[73] (1795) 6 Term 320
[74] [1895] 1 QB 673

The exceptions are as listed below.

(A) Severable contracts

Payment can be claimed for work done on completion of each stage where a contract is severable, sometimes described as divisible. On the other hand, if the contract is an entire one the work must be completed in full before the other party becomes liable to pay. The terms of the contract are important in this context and much will depend on the intention of the parties. The courts tend to lean against finding a contract entire. A severable contract will arise where payments are due from time to time (such as interim or stage payments in construction contracts) and the other party's obligations are rendered in return.

(B) Substantial performance

This arises where performance under a contract, although not complete, is virtually exact. In such a case a claim may be made for the work completed subject to any counterclaim in respect of work remaining unperformed. The contract price can be claimed subject to a deduction equal to the cost of remedying any omissions or defects. In essence, the defects must be of a trifling nature before the exception can be claimed. In *Hoening v Isaacs*[75] the doctrine was applied where the cost of remedying the defects amounted to £56 on a contract worth £750. In *Dakin v Lee Ltd*[76] the court stated that if a builder has done work under an entire contract, but the work has not been completed in accordance with the contract, a claim can be made on a *quantum meruit* unless the customer received no benefit from the work, the work was entirely different from that which was contracted for, or the contractor had abandoned the work. The exception will not apply if the contract has not been substantially completed. The actual cost of remedying the defects in relation to the contract price is a relevant factor. In *Bolton v Mahedeva*[77] a contract was entered into to install a central heating system for £560. The system performed very poorly and the remedial work would have involved a further cost of £174. The judge held that there had not been substantial performance and that the claimant was entitled to nothing for the work done.

(C) Prevention of performance

A claim for damages can be made on a *quantum meruit* for work carried out if a party to a contract is prevented from performing what he has agreed to do by the other party. In *Roberts v Bury Improvement Commissioners*[78] a contractor was not in default where an architect neglected to supply him with necessary plans which prevented the contractor from completing the work by the contract date. The contractor was entitled to be paid for the work performed.

---

[75] [1952] 2 All ER 176
[76] [1916] 1 KB 566
[77] [1972] 2 All ER 1322
[78] (1870) LR 5 CP 10

2.9.2 *Agreement*

It is logical that where contracts are created by agreement they may also be discharged in the same manner. Another contract must therefore be entered into if the parties agree to waive their obligations under an existing contract. This will be appropriate where neither of the parties has completed their obligations due under the contract. Where one of the parties has completed obligations due under the contract but the other party has not, the party to whom the obligation is owed may agree with the other party to accept something different in place of the former obligation. This is known as the doctrine of accord and satisfaction. The subsequent agreement represents the accord, and the new consideration which has been given being termed the satisfaction. Alternatively, an obligation under a contract may be discharged by the operation of one of the terms of the contract itself. Contracts of employment often contain provisions whereby the contract can be determined by either party giving a period of notice to the other. In building and engineering contracts it is common to find provisions whereby the contract can be determined before completion on the happening of specific events. The serious default or insolvency of the other party is a common example.

2.9.3 *Frustration*

'Frustration' in the context of contract law means impossibility. As a rule, contractual obligations are absolute in that a contract is not discharged simply because it is more difficult or expensive than expected to carry it out. Modern-day examples of building contracts that have been frustrated are rare, and to succeed a claimant must show that the circumstances have changed to such an extent that the performance of the contractual obligation has become fundamentally different.

(A) Specific examples of frustration

(a) Destruction of the subject matter

If the subject matter is destroyed and its existence is crucial to the performance of the contract then the contract will be frustrated. In *Taylor v Caldwell*[79], a building which was to be used for a series of concerts was destroyed by fire.

(b) Changes in the law

The doctrine of frustration will apply if a change in the law makes the contract impossible to carry out. The case of *Denny Mott and Dickson Ltd v James B Fraser & Co Ltd*[80] provides an example. War-time regulations banned the sale of timber so a contract attempting to sell the same between the parties was deemed to have been frustrated.

---

[79] (1863) 3 Best & Smith 826
[80] [1944]AC 265

(c) Inability to achieve the main object of the contract

The contract will be frustrated if the basis on which both parties entered the contract has been destroyed. To succeed on this basis there has to be a complete non-occurrence. Comparing the cases of *Krell v Henry*[81] and *Herne Bay Steam Boat Co v Hutton*[82] illustrates how this point of law operates in practice. Both cases involve the coronation of Edward VII. The first contract was for the hire of a hotel room with a view of the coronation procession route. The second case involved a contract for the hire of a boat to watch/take part in a royal regatta. The King cancelled his appearance at both events due to ill health. Both claimants alleged that their contracts had been frustrated by this occurrence as the main object of the contract – namely seeing the monarch - would not now be possible to achieve. The cases were decided differently. In the first case it was held that the contract had been frustrated whilst in the second no frustration was found. The key difference that the judge found in the second case was that the regatta went ahead as planned and the King's appearance was only of minor importance to the enjoyment of the day itself.

(d) Death, personal incapacity or illness

Death or permanent incapacity will frustrate a contract for personal services. There is a similar effect where a party is likely to be ill or incapacitated for a considerable period of time. These events are sufficient to make the contract fundamentally different from that originally envisaged and it will be discharged. This occurred in the case of *Morgan v Manser*[83] where a comedian, working under the name Charlie Chester, was called up to serve in the armed forces during the duration of the Second World War. The disruption caused by the six-year war to a ten-year management contract was sufficient for the parties to treat the contract as having been frustrated. Cancellation of one or a number of performances by a person who later provides the service required will not amount to a frustrating event.

(B) Specific examples of where frustration will not apply

(a) The contract becoming more onerous to perform or less financially rewarding

The fact that a contract proves more difficult or expensive to perform will not frustrate the contract unless the difficulty arises from some fundamental change of circumstances. In *Tsakiroglou v Noblee Thorl GmbH*[84] a contract to ship ground nuts from the Mediterranean to India was not frustrated by the temporary closure of the Suez Canal. The cargo would have to be sent around the Cape of Good Hope instead which was at least twice as far as the standard route. This did not amount

---

[81] [1903] 2 KB 740
[82] [1903] 2 KB 683
[83] [1948] 1 KB 184
[84] [1961] 2 All ER 179

to frustration. In *Davis Contractors Ltd v Fareham UDC*[85] builders agreed to erect seventy-eight houses in six months. The period extended to twenty-two months owing mainly to a lack of skilled labour and a shortage of materials. Building costs in that period had risen considerably and the builders contended that they should be entitled to claim on a *quantum meruit*. The House of Lords decided that the contract was not frustrated as it was simply more difficult to carry out. In the case of *Amalgamated Investment and Property Co v John Walker*[86] the claimants attempted to frustrate a contract when after exchange of contracts, but before completion of the purchase of industrial premises, the Department of the Environment listed the property which was the subject of the sale. The Court of Appeal held, rejecting the appeal, that listing was an inherent risk in all property transactions relating to buildings of historical and architectural interest and the transaction after listing was not radically different than it was previously.

(b) Self-induced frustration

A frustrating event must not have been one which the parties could have contemplated when making the contract. The courts will give effect to the intention of the parties where express provision has been made in the contract for the contingency in question. The event causing the frustration must not have been due to the conduct of the parties.

(C) Effect of frustration

A frustrating event only operates to discharge the contract from the time of the frustrating event. It does not frustrate it from the outset (*ab initio*). Where the common law rules still apply (mainly insurance and shipping contracts), it is not possible to recover money which has been paid before the frustrating event takes place unless there has been a total failure of consideration (the other party failing to perform their part of the contract). Other contracts than those stated above are governed by the Law Reform (Frustrated Contracts) Act 1943 which allows:

- Money that has been transferred before the frustrating event to be recovered, and money due is no longer due.
- Expenses incurred prior to the frustrating event may be deducted from money due to be returned.
- A party who has carried out work or services prior to the frustrating event may claim compensation on a *quantum meruit* basis.

2.9.4 Breach of an appropriate term of the contract

Any failure by a party who contracts to fulfil obligations under the contract amounts to a breach. Whenever a party to a contract is in breach this gives rise to

---

[85] [1956] AC 696
[86] [1977] 1 WLR 164

an obligation on his part to pay damages to the person who has suffered loss, subject to a valid exemption clause to the contrary. The obligations of the parties to perform the contract remain unchanged unless the breach can be classified as a repudiatory breach. In each case the issue as to whether the breach is to be taken as a repudiation depends upon the importance of the breach in relation to the contract as a whole. Repudiation will assert itself in a building contract where execution of the works is so unsatisfactory as to affect the very basis of the contract. The injured party has the option either to terminate the contract or to affirm it in the case of a repudiatory breach. The appropriate test to ascertain whether or not a party has repudiated the contract is whether or not a reasonable person would believe that the other party did not intend to be bound by the contract. If the test is satisfied the injured party may treat the contract as at an end and is released from further performance. The claimant may rescind the contract but must act without delay to do so (the normal rules as to seeking equitable remedies will apply – see paragraph 2.12). Unjustified rescission of a contract does not always amount to a repudiation.

The injured party need not wait for the date set for performance where he knows that a breach will take place. A right of action exists immediately as if there were a breach, and the claimant may sue for breach of contract. In the case of *Lovelock v Franklyn*[87] the defendant committed such a breach when he sold an item he had contracted to sell to the claimant to a third party instead. The claimant knew of the sale to the third party and was able to seek damages before the envisaged sale between the parties was due to take place.

2.10   Damages

2.10.1   *Unliquidated damages*

The claim is for unliquidated damages where the parties to a contract make no pre-assessment of any damages payable in the event of a breach. The object of such a claim is to put the injured party in the same position as if the contract had been performed. Any loss suffered as a consequence of the breach, whether physical or financial in nature, can be claimed by a successful claimant. It is against public policy to allow compensation for every consequence which might logically result from the defendant's breach. The potential liability of the defendant in this situation could be unlimited.

(A) Remoteness and causation

The rule in *Hadley v Baxendale*[88] states that the only losses which are recoverable are those which may fairly and reasonably be considered as arising naturally from the breach of the contract, or losses which may reasonably be supposed to have been in the contemplation of both parties at the time they made the contract in the event of a breach. The facts in the case involve the repair of a shaft used in a mill. An

---

[87] (1846) 8 KB 371
[88] (1854) 9 Ex 341

example of the rules as to the recoverability of damages under what became known as the *Hadley v Baxendale* tests came from the decision in *Victoria Laundry Ltd v Newman Industries Ltd*[89]. The claimants ordered a new boiler for their business which arrived late. The claimants were entitled to recover damages for normal loss of profits by applying the first part of the Hadley *v* Baxendale test. The boiler supplier should have anticipated the lost profits. The contentious item was whether the claimant was entitled to recover further losses due to the demise of a profitable government contract. The defendants were unaware of the existence of the government contract and it could not therefore be said to be within the parties' reasonable contemplation as envisaged in the second part of the Hadley *v* Baxendale test.

This narrow approach to the remoteness of contractual damages was upheld by the House of Lords in the case of *Transfield Shipping Inc v Mercator Shipping Inc (The Achilleas)*[90]. The claimant chartered a ship from the defendants for a seven-month period. The claimant was late in returning the ship, causing losses to the defendant who had arranged for a third party to re-charter the ship on its return. The claimant was content to pay damages based on the normal market rate of charter rates but the defendant insisted on additional damages caused by the volatility in the market being experienced at that time. Their lordships decided that only the damages based on a normal market rather than an exceptionally high market rate could be claimed from the defaulting party. Another case involving chartered ships is *Golden Strait Corporation v Nippon Yusen Kubishka Kaisha*[91]. This case raised the issue of the effect upon a repudiated contract of an event which would have cancelled the contract in the normal chain of events. In this case the outbreak of the Iraq war in 2003 would have triggered rescission had the contract still been live. The House of Lords decided that the actual outbreak of the war limited the scope for damages to be recovered under the contract from the defaulting party.

In *Quinn v Burch Bros Ltd*[92] the defendants failed, in breach of contract, to supply the claimant plasterer with a step ladder. As an alternative he used a trestle table which slipped, causing injury to the claimant. The Court of Appeal took the view that the injury was the claimant's own fault and that the defendant's breach of contract did not cause the injury. The breach of contract had merely given the claimant the opportunity to injure himself – it was impossible to say the defendant had caused the injury in law.

(B) Classification of damages

(a) General damages

The measure of damages awarded is usually the actual monetary loss. The cost of reinstatement will constitute general damages in cases of defective building work.

---

[89] [1949] 1 All ER 997
[90] [2008] 2 Lloyd's Rep. 275
[91] [2007] 2 WLR 691
[92] [1966] 2 QB 370

This occurred in the case of *East Ham Corporation v Bernard Sunley & Sons*[93]. If this formula is incapable of representing the actual loss to the claimant then the damages will amount to the decrease in the value of the property.

(b) Consequential loss damage

These are additional losses suffered as a consequence of the defendant's breach of contract and can be awarded as a further 'head' of damages.

(c) Damages for mental distress

The traditional rule was that damages for breach of contract should not take account of any mental distress and inconvenience suffered by the claimant. This rule is illustrated in the case of *Addis v Gramophone Co Ltd*[94] where a company wrongfully dismissed its manager in a way that was 'harsh and humiliating.' The claimant received damages for loss of salary and commission, but nothing for his injured feelings. Deviation was made from that position in *Jarvis v Swan Tours Ltd*[95], where the Court of Appeal decided that in an appropriate case such damages could be an additional element in the sum awarded. This case involved a holiday to which the claimant was looking forward to immensely. In the event he had a thoroughly miserable time due mainly to events advertised in the holiday brochure either not occurring at all or being sub-standard. The claimant was awarded damages for loss of enjoyment on the holiday. The damages awarded amounted to twice the original price of the holiday itself.

From this last case the principle emerged that damages may be awarded where the object of the contract is to give pleasure, relaxation, peace of mind or freedom from molestation. The case of *Farley v Skinner*[96] extended this principle further to apply to contracts which were not solely for pleasure, relaxation and peace of mind. The claimant had asked his surveyor to consider in his report the issue of aircraft noise above a property he was considering buying near Gatwick Airport in London. The surveyor reported that the property was unlikely to suffer greatly from such noise. Unbeknown to the surveyor the property was close to a navigation beacon over which the aircraft 'stacked up' in busy periods. The claimant was entitled to recover damages from the surveyor for loss of enjoyment due to regular noise pollution suffered.

Damages for loss of enjoyment are not usually permitted on commercial contracts. However, damages were awarded in the case of *Watts v Morrow*[97] in respect of the physical discomfort and mental distress resulting to the claimant from the repairs necessitated to remedy defects a surveyor had failed to notice during his work.

---

[93] [1966] AC 406
[94] [1909] AC 488
[95] [1973] 1 All ER 71
[96] [2001] 4 All ER 801
[97] [1991] 4 All ER 937

2.10.2   *Liquidated damages*

In some cases the parties to a contract make an attempt in the contract to assess in advance the damages which will be payable in the event of a breach. This provision for liquidated damages will be valid if it is a genuine attempt to pre-estimate the likely loss suffered as a consequence of the breach. There can be no inquiry into the actual loss suffered. If the clause is a valid liquidated damages clause, the sum stipulated is recoverable upon that breach even though the loss is less or even nil. Such a provision must be distinguished from a penalty clause. This is a stipulation which is inserted to frighten the potential defaulter and to compel performance of the contract. A penalty clause is invalid but the injured party may recover any actual loss on the Hadley and Baxendale principles set out above in relation to unliquidated damages.

It is common practice in construction and engineering contracts to find a liquidated damages clause for delay alongside an extension of time clause, giving the contractor the right to extra time if he is delayed by matters outside the control of either party or due to the default of the employer and/or his agents. Relevant matters would include industrial action, bad weather, or the employer delaying the execution of the works by failing to supply necessary plans or give possession of the site. Any claim to liquidated damages will be lost if any delay in the performance of the contract is caused by the employer. The question as to whether a clause is a penalty or liquidated damages depends upon its construction and the surrounding circumstances at the time of making the contract.

The leading case in this area is *Dunlop Pneumatic Tyre Co Ltd v New Garage Ltd*[98]. The contract between the parties provided that the defendant would have to pay £5 for every tyre it sold under the list price provided by the claimant. In this instance the courts were satisfied that this not a penalty and was an honest attempt to quantify the effects of a breach of the contract and it was therefore upheld. A number of propositions were put forward to determine whether a provision is a liquidated damages clause or a penalty:

- The name which the parties give to the clause is not conclusive and it is the task of the court to decide the category.
- The essence of liquidated damages is that the sum stated is a genuine pre-estimate of the probable loss, while the essence of a penalty is that it is a threat to carry out the contract.
- It is presumed to be a penalty clause if the sum stated is extravagant compared with the greatest possible loss.
- It is a penalty if the breach consists only in not paying a sum of money by a certain date and the sum fixed is greater than the sum which was originally to be paid. For example, X agrees to pay Y £5000 on January 1 and if he fails to pay at the contract time Y must pay £10 000 as 'liquidated damages'.

There is a presumption that where a single sum is made payable on the happening of one or more events, some of which are serious and some of which are of little consequence, the sum is likely to be a penalty. There is a likelihood of greater losses

---

[98] [1915] AC 79

emanating from a major breach than from a minor one. In *Law v Redditch Local Board*[99] the sum stated in the relevant clause was to be paid on the happening of a single event only. Therefore, it was deemed to be a valid pre-estimate of likely loss and was considered to be a liquidated damages clause.

2.10.3   Mitigation of loss

The injured party has a duty to mitigate any losses suffered. This means that reasonable steps must be taken to minimise damage. An employee who is wrongly dismissed must attempt to find alternative employment while a buyer of goods which are not delivered must try to buy as cheaply elsewhere. Failure to do so will be taken into account when assessing damages. Only reasonable steps to mitigate need be taken. The claimant is not expected to incur great expenditure or undertake great risks.

2.11   Limitation of actions

Limitation periods are the time periods within which a claimant must commence an action for damages. It is recognised that a claimant must pursue a claim with due diligence while potential defendants should not have the threat of litigation pending indefinitely. Specific time periods are laid down by statute within which actions for damages must be brought. The reliability of evidence diminishes over time as memories fade. Claims that have been in circulation for a considerable period of time make bad law and the eventual outcome of a case unreliable.

(A) Limitation in contract

The law is statute based and governed by the Limitation Act 1980. Section 5 of the Act states that if a claim for breach of contract is based on a simple contract the action must be brought before the expiration of six years from the date on which the cause of action accrued. Section 8 deals with the case of a deed stipulating that the action must be brought within twelve years from the date the cause of action accrued. The claim is statute-barred and cannot be pursued if it is not commenced within these time limits. The date when the cause of action accrued is the date when the breach of contract occurred. If the breach is a continuing one a claimant can choose the last date that the defendant was in breach before the time period begins to run.

(B) Fraud or concealment

Limitation periods have to provide for the possibility of a defendant acting fraudulently or concealing the true state of affairs from a potential claimant. The current provisions are to be found in sections 31 and 32 of the 1980 Act.

---

[99] (1892) 1 QB 127

Section 32 covers the situation where the claimant is unaware of the true state of affairs because of the defendant's fraud or deliberate concealment of a breach of contract. The limitation period does not begin to run until the claimant has discovered the fraud or concealment or could with reasonable diligence have discovered it. An example of the rule is *Clark v Woor*[100], where the claimant commissioned the defendant builder to construct a bungalow. The claimant specified the materials to be used and gave detailed instructions. The defendant knowingly used inferior facing bricks from those specified and concealed the true state of affairs from the claimant. No supervising architect or surveyor was involved in the contract. The claimant became aware of the defects some eight years after construction of the bungalow. The claim was held, by the Court of Appeal, not to be statute-barred. Cases concerning defective foundations have been covered by sections 31 and 32 of the 1980 Act. In *Applegate v Moss*[101] the defendant builders agreed in 1957 to build houses on a raft foundation supported by specified steel network. Cracks appeared beneath the houses eight years after their completion. On inspection it was revealed that there was no raft and the reinforcement was inferior to that specified. The claimants succeeded in their action by taking advantage of the concealment provisions. A similar result was reached in *King v Victor Parsons and Co*[102], where the defendants concealed the fact that a house had been built on a tip that had been filled in and did not have any proper foundations. The claimant's claim was not deemed to be statute-barred when cracks appeared outside the limitation period.

2.12   Equitable remedies

These may be available to an injured party where the common law remedy of damages is inadequate or inappropriate. They comprise the remedies which before the Judicature Acts 1873–75 were only available in the courts of equity. The courts of equity and common law were fused by these Acts and the resultant position is that any civil court is able to grant these remedies, if thought appropriate. They are discretionary and not automatically available in the event of winning a case. Certain principles apply generally to the grant of equitable remedies while others apply, in addition, to individual remedies. In all cases the conduct of the parties is taken into account. No equitable remedy will be available if damages are considered to be an adequate remedy in the circumstances of the case. Limitation periods are not relevant to equitable remedies. Time is of the essence in such circumstances and each equitable remedy must be sought with reasonable promptness.

2.12.1   *Specific performance*

Specific performance is a court order directing the defendant to carry out a promise according to the terms of the contract. It is appropriate where the subject

---

[100] [1965] 2 All ER 353; see also Chapter 3, paragraph 3.13.4
[101] [1971] 1 QB 406
[102] [1973] 1 WLR 29

matter of the contract is not freely available, such as a rare painting or antique. In such cases the payment of a sum of money would not be adequate compensation in the event of a breach of contract. It is mainly used as a threatened remedy where contracts for the sale or lettings of land are broken (see Chapter 4, paragraph 4.6.1.C). The normal conditions required before equitable remedies will be granted apply. Specific performance will not be awarded to enforce a contract for personal services or where the contract requires supervision to ensure that it is being enforced properly. This was the case in *Wolverhampton Corpn v Emmons*[103] where the defendant owned the land on which the claimant sought an order compelling specific performance of a building contract. The court refused to grant the order in these circumstances. A claim for damages was more appropriate in the circumstances. Specific performance of a building contract may be awarded where:

- The building work to be carried out is clearly specified in the contract.
- The claimant has a special interest in having the work done which cannot be satisfied by an award of damages.
- The builder is in possession of the land, so it is not practicable to employ another builder.

2.12.2   Injunction

This equitable remedy restrains a person from continuing a wrong or alternatively can be used to order a party to do something to remedy a breach of contract. Unlike specific performance it can apply to contracts containing a personal services element. The usual rules as to equitable remedies apply and an injunction will not be granted if damages are an adequate remedy. It has been held to be appropriate to restrain a contractor from continuing work after a breach of contract has taken place. Similarly in the case of *Bath and NE Somerset District Council v Mowlem plc*[104] it was decided that contractual provision for liquidated and ascertained damages would not prevent the council from obtaining an injunction to restrain the contractor's refusal of access to the site to replacement contractors.

Failure to obey an injunction is a contempt of court and may result in the imposition of a fine or imprisonment.

2.13   Agency

The agency relationship is of vital importance in commercial and business life. An agent is a person who acts on behalf of another who is known as a principal. Such an agent may conduct the principal's affairs in many ways but the primary function is to create a contractual relationship between the principal and a third party. Where the agent contracts with such a party he does so on behalf of the principal.

---

[103] [1901] KB 515
[104] [2004] BLR 153 and 100 Con LR 1 CA

The effect of this arrangement is to create an enforceable contract between principal and third party with the agent dropping out of the transaction. This relationship is a familiar characteristic of business life. Companies will often contract through their directors and managers, while partners will act on behalf of their firms (see paragraph 2.14.2). The self-employed and employees can act in this capacity. Auctioneers, estate agents, architects and engineers are all examples of agents.

2.13.1 Creation

(A) Express authority

The agent may be expressly appointed by word of mouth or in writing. Familiar appointments include estate agents to find prospective purchasers for residential and commercial properties, an engineer appointed to administer a contract on behalf of an employer, site agents acting as an employer's agent on site, and a sales representative selling goods on behalf of a company. No particular form of appointment is required unless the agent is empowered to execute deeds, in which case the authority must be given by power of attorney.

(B) Implied authority

The relationship of principal and agent will be inferred if, by their conduct, the parties have acted in such a manner so that it may be deemed to exist. This may occur where one party receives a commission, accepts goods, or pays for items ordered by another person. In *Ryan v Pilkington*[105] an estate agent was instructed by owners of property to find a purchaser. The estate agent accepted a deposit from a prospective purchaser 'as agent' of the owners. He was deemed to have acted as an agent although he had not been expressly authorised to accept deposits. The owner was liable for the deposit when it was misappropriated by the estate agent.

(C) Necessity

An agency of necessity arises in an emergency where a carrier of goods needs to take immediate action to protect them. This may occur when the carrier cannot obtain instructions from the person on behalf of whom the goods are being carried. The carrier may deal with the goods as is considered appropriate either by sale or by storage in order to preserve them. The agent must act in good faith and in the interests of the parties concerned. The implication of an agency of necessity will result in the carrier being able to claim payment in respect of his efforts to preserve the goods.

---

[105] [1959] 1 WLR 402

2.13.2   *Ratification*

The principal is not bound if an agent has no authority to act on his principal's behalf or the agent exceeds his authority. As an exception to this rule the principal has the option of confirming transactions which were made without his authority. If this option is exercised the agent's acts are legitimised from the outset. The principal can adopt the transaction so as to obtain the benefit and undertake the obligations agreed. The agent is personally liable if the principal does not ratify the transaction. Certain conditions apply:

- The principal must have existed and the third party must have been informed by the agent that the agent was acting on behalf of the principal.
- The principal must have had capacity to contract when the agent acted.
- Ratification must take place within a reasonable time.
- The contract must be capable of ratification.

2.13.3   *Estoppel*

If a principal by conduct or acquiescence allows third parties to believe that somebody is acting as their authorised agent the principal will be estopped from denying the existence of the agency where the third party relies on such conduct or representation to their detriment. This is the case even though the principal had no intention of creating the principal/agent relationship or the agent has no authority of any sort. Where a principal becomes aware of the likelihood of this problem arising he should inform appropriate third parties with whom the agent has been dealing. If this occurs the principal will not be bound by the agent's acts. Such an agency will only apply if the person dealing with the alleged agent has no notice of the lack of authority.

2.13.4   *The scope of an agent's authority*

To a large extent the agent's authority will depend on what has been agreed between the principal and agent. The actual authority that has been specifically granted to an agent can be implied by the nature of the job, task or particular business. In some cases an agent acquires status from the authority and powers which third parties assume an agent to possess. This is known as the ostensible or apparent authority of an agent. A principal will be liable in respect of those acts which are usually undertaken by an agent in respect of a particular job. An engineer, architect or site agent will bind the principal when carrying out the normal tasks associated with these professions under a contract even though the specific individuals do not have express authority to act in a particular way. Any agent signing a cheque or a contract on behalf of a principal should make it abundantly clear that the transaction is being carried out on behalf of the principal and should qualify any signature as such. Failure to do so will make the agent personally liable on the cheque or contract. A person who is not an agent but holds themselves out to be so is personally liable on a contract. A problem which can arise is that of the undisclosed principal. It may be that an agent, when dealing with a third party, fails to disclose the nature of his position and the third party takes the agent to be a principal. In such circumstances the third party may elect to sue the agent or the principal on the contract so long as the principal can be identified. The agent will not be liable on the contract where the agent discloses his position but refuses to identify the principal. Another factor is the extent of the agent's implied authority to the third party so far as his power to contract is concerned. An auctioneer has implied authority to make statements relevant to individual properties. An estate agent has no implied authority to give a warranty that premises can be used for a specific purpose. In *Hill v Harris*[106], such an agent was deemed to have no authority to warrant that premises used for boot and shoe making could be occupied for a confectionery and tobacco business and was held personally liable. A similar finding was made in the case of *Nimmo v Habton Farms*[107] where a bloodstock agent went beyond his authority in agreeing terms for the purchase of a racehorse which subsequently had to be destroyed.

2.13.5 *The agency relationship*

The existence of the relationship of principal and agent imposes certain duties and obligations upon both parties. The concept is primarily based on contract. Agency is a major exception to the privity rule as a principal may sue on a contract made by an agent. In addition to the contractual aspects there is also a fiduciary element of trust underlying the obligations between the parties.

(A) Duties of an agent

(a) Skill and care

An agent must exercise skill and care in the performance of his duties. The standard expected is that of a reasonably experienced member of whichever profession to which the agent belongs. Where an agent holds himself out as having special skills he must be able to apply them. There is a duty to obtain the best price possible if an agent is employed to sell. In *Keppel v Webster*[108] estate agents were liable when they omitted to inform their client that they had received a higher offer for his property.

(b) Accounts

An agent must account to his principal in respect of all transactions connected with the agency. Accounts should be rendered to the principal when requested. All sums received on the principal's behalf should be handed over even if the agreement under which the money was received was illegal. The agent must not mix up the principal's property with his own.

---

[106] [1965] 2 WLR 133
[107] [2003] 1 All ER 1136 (CA)
[108] [1927] 1 KB 527

(c) Delegation

An agent cannot further delegate duties to another except in the usual course of business by employing assistants and secretarial staff unless it is standard practice in a particular type of agency to delegate duties. Some delegation may be required for the proper performance of work. It is not normal in the construction industry for delegation to be allowed unless there is express authority to that effect.

(d) Obedience

The agent is under a duty to obey the lawful instructions of the principal unless they are illegal. If not, the agent could well be in breach of contract.

(e) Good faith

This is the very essence of the agency relationship as an agent must disclose anything which might affect the principal's position under the contract. An agent must not act for both sides in a transaction. In *Fullwood v Hurley*[109] an agent acted for both sides in the purchase of a hotel without the knowledge of the respective parties. He was only entitled to commission from the vendor who instructed him. The agent must not take a secret profit from his position nor must he take bribes. Instead the agent is entitled to commission or other agreed remuneration. In *Mahesan v Malaysia Officers Housing Association*[110], both the amount of the bribe and the secret profit were recovered by the principal where the agent had accepted money allowing a third party to make a secret profit. The agent is accountable to his principal in respect of any benefit received from the unauthorised use of his position. If the obligation is broken the principal may dismiss the agent without notice and recover the secret profit and withhold any commission payable. In the event of bribery both the agent and the person paying the bribe may be guilty of a criminal offence.

(B) Duties of the principal

(a) Payment

Any agreed amount of commission may be claimed by the agent. Payment can only be effectively claimed if there is an express or implied provision to that effect. The amount depends upon the contract or the custom in a particular trade or business.

(b) Indemnity

The agent must be reimbursed for expenses properly incurred in carrying out his duties. Entitlement may be lost if the agent acts beyond the authority given to him or he performs his duties negligently.

---

[109] [1928] 1 KB 498
[110] [1970] 1 WLR 241

(c) Lien

Any agent has a right to retain possession of goods where the principal has not paid his proper remuneration or reimbursed him.

2.13.6   Termination of agency

The agency relationship may be determined by an act of the parties themselves or by operation of law. A professional person will cease, in the ordinary course of events, to act as an agent on completion of the contract which he was engaged upon. Appointment as an agent may be limited to one or various stages of the work in construction projects. If the contract is for a fixed term the relationship may terminate by expiration of time. However, a principal may revoke an agency at any time for good reason but will be subject to a claim for damages by the agent if the revocation was not justified. Death or insanity of either of the parties will terminate the relationship. Bankruptcy of either party will also bring the agency to an end.

2.13.7   The Commercial Agents (Council Directive) Regulations 1993

These regulations came into force on 1 January 1994 and extend the common law rights of commercial agents against their principals. Where the Regulations apply they include provisions for the remuneration of the agent where the agreement is silent on the issue. The Regulations provide for the agent's entitlement to commission both during and after the agency agreement has been terminated. Compensation following termination of the agency agreement is also included.

2.14   Business organisations

There are three main methods of carrying on a business in England and Wales:

- As a sole trader.
- As a partnership.
- As a limited company.

2.14.1   Sole trader

A sole trading situation exists where only one person is entitled to receive the profits from a business organisation. This may arise in an enterprise run entirely by one person, or where the proprietor of a business employs a number of people. Those who carry on business in this manner will normally do so because of personal preference. Indeed, its principal advantage is almost certainly that of control. A sole trader will have virtually complete control over the organisation, subject only to the rights of creditors and the Inland Revenue. As well as being entitled to all the profits, the sole trader will also be subject to few legal formalities and will therefore be able to run their business with a considerable degree of privacy. On the other hand, if the business does incur losses there is nobody else to bear these apart from the sole proprietor who will be personally liable for all the debts of the business. Equally, it can be difficult for this form of business organisation to raise capital for investment in the business. In the context of professional practices (for example surveyors, solicitors and accountants) it is now extremely difficult for a sole practitioner to find the time to carry out the work to earn fees, combine that work with management of a practice and also to undertake continuing professional development. The high premiums required for professional indemnity insurance also act as a barrier to sole practice. As a consequence many sole practitioners have tried to build niche practices in their respective areas of expertise, or have ended up amalgamating with others as described below.

2.14.2   Partnerships

A partnership exists where a number of individuals agree to jointly carry on business in circumstances where they collectively own the business (and any profits generated) but where they do not form a separate company to do so. In order to distinguish this arrangement from a company (which requires a process of incorporation to bring it into existence) partnerships are sometimes referred to as *unincorporated associations*.

Traditionally, partnerships were chosen as a method of carrying on business if there was a restriction on forming a company, as was the case in many professions. The central notion here was that professionals should be prepared to stand by their advice and services rendered. Thus, by trading as a partnership, they remain personally liable for any debts and errors, and ultimately risk loss of home and even bankruptcy, as there is no limit on such liability. This was considered to be more appropriate than allowing professional advisors to hide behind the so-called 'veil of incorporation' of a limited company whereby the liability of individual owners (shareholders) is limited to the value of their shareholding. In recent years these restrictions have been lifted to a large extent, but even so, many professional practices appear to prefer to keep partnership status unless they are of considerable size. The advent of limited liability partnerships has changed the landscape further. Business partnerships, as opposed to those in the professions, are rare because there is seldom any advantage in forming a commercially based firm instead of a limited company.

(A) Law and form

The law is governed by the Partnership Act 1890. The major characteristic of a partnership is that there is in existence the common intention between the partners to carry on a business with a view to making a profit. It will not arise simply because the parties are co-owners of property. A partnership is valid even though entered into by word of mouth with no formalities. However, for practical reasons, partners often choose to enter into a written partnership agreement. This will deal with matters such as the nature of the business, capital, profit and losses, partnership property, holding of meetings, etc. The most important aspect of the agreement is that it overrides certain provisions in the Partnership 1890 Act which would otherwise operate to imply certain basic terms. A partnership agreement also has the flexibility of being able to cover the position of each individual partner. This agreement is not open to public inspection, nor are the accounts of the firm.

(B) Relationship with other partners

Each partner owes a duty of good faith to the other partners. Partnerships operate on an agency basis (see paragraph 2.13). Each partner therefore has implied authority to bind the firm by transactions entered into in the ordinary course of business. Each partner is entitled to take part in the management of the firm and is entitled to inspect the partnership books. Decisions are made on a show of hands in the majority of cases, but unanimity is generally required in the case of major changes such as the admission of a new partner. Partners are said to be *jointly and severally liable* for partnership debts. This means that the firm may be sued *en bloc* or individual partners may have proceedings brought against them for the entire amount owed by the firm (rather than simply their share of the debt). Retired partners (and the estates of deceased partners) are also liable for debts incurred by the firm during the period when they were partners. The partnership relationship can be brought to an end by dissolution of the firm. This may be effected without a court order and usually by mutual agreement.

(C) Limited liability partnerships

The Limited Liability Partnership Act 2000 created this new form of organisation for businesses – a hybrid between the partnership and the limited liability company. A limited liability partnership (LLP) has a separate legal identity to that of its members in the same way as a company. The LLP is therefore capable of entering into contracts and owning property. The formalities required to set up and run an LLP are less onerous than those associated with setting up and running a company. In the absence of a partnership agreement the standing arrangement will be that profits, losses and capital are shared equally and all members have an equal right to manage the LLP. The LLP has more in common with a limited company in terms of managing its affairs.

2.14.3 Limited companies

A company is an incorporated body which exists as a legal 'person' which is quite distinct from its members. Its assets therefore belong to the company and not to its members. Unlike a partnership, it has perpetual succession which means that its continuing existence is unaffected by changes in its membership, or alterations to its structure. Companies are creatures of statute and the current law is to be found in the Companies Act 2006. The vast majority of companies are limited liability companies. As discussed above (see paragraph 2.14.2) this means that where the company is limited by shares (the main type) the liability of its shareholders is limited to the extent of their individual shareholding. The shareholders cannot therefore be pursued by the creditors for anything more than the value of their shareholding. The benefit to the shareholder of this arrangement is that their maximum financial exposure through the business is predetermined – something which, as we have seen, is not the case for partners or sole traders. Private companies can be identified by the word 'Limited' at the end of the company name or the abbreviation 'Ltd'. If the company is a public one (see 2.14.3.A), its limited liability is indicated by the letters 'plc' at the end of the company name. Non-profit-making companies sometimes form themselves as companies limited by guarantee, while a handful of companies operate on the basis of unlimited liability - primarily because they are not obliged to file accounts.

(A) Operating the company

Most businesses operate as private companies. Upon formation of the company the business owners become its first members by purchasing shares in it. Private companies tend to have a nominal share capital which is issued by dividing the sum collectively invested into shares of £1 each or similar. This nominal capital may have little relationship to the actual financial state of the business. Private companies are often family businesses. They tend to be small- to medium-sized organisations, although there are instances of large family businesses remaining as private (as opposed to public) companies to enable the owners to retain as much control as possible. The members of a private company will also generally be its managers. If the articles (discussed below) so provide, there may be restrictions on the rights of members of private companies to transfer shares and on the number of members that the company can have. A public company has no such limitations on its membership and transfer of shares but must have a minimum share capital of £50 000. Shares of public companies are bought and sold on the stock exchange and are freely transferable. Professional managers are invariably recruited to act as managers and directors of public companies.

A company is formed by lodging a number of documents with the Registrar of Companies (based in Cardiff). These include the Memorandum of Association and the Articles of Association. The Memorandum lists the original members of the company, records their intention to form the company, and their agreement to take at least one share in it. The Articles contain the company's internal constitution. They describe the company's management structure and set out the rules that all members will be subject to as a matter of contract law. Once formed, a Certificate of Incorporation is issued to the company which signifies its birth. After it has been created it will continue to exist despite changes in its organisation until it is wound up. A company may borrow money like any other person in addition to raising capital by issuing more shares. In the case of small companies this is often in the form of loans made in return for personal guarantees given by the major shareholders. A loan may be secured by a debenture which is a charge over the company's property. This is more likely to be an option for companies with substantial fixed assets.

Companies operate through the decisions of their boards of directors and through the wishes of their members at general meetings. Directors have historically been subject to a number of equitable and common law duties and these (and others) have now been codified by the Companies Act 2006. Sections 171 to 177 of the Act therefore now impose the following statutory duties on directors:

- Duty to comply with the company's constitution.
- Duty to promote the success of the company.
- Duty to exercise independent judgement.
- Duty to exercise reasonable care, skill and diligence.
- Duty to avoid conflicts of interest.
- Duty not to accept benefits from third parties.
- Duty to declare an interest in a proposed transaction or arrangement.

Public companies must hold an annual general meeting to discuss matters such as the accounts and payment of a dividend. Private companies can do so if they chose to do so and must do so if required by their articles. The dividend is a periodic income paid to a shareholder by the company which usually reflects the financial buoyancy of the company. Decisions at meetings are made in the form of resolutions. Certain resolutions require a simple majority decision (fifty-one per cent) whilst others deemed 'special resolutions' require a larger proportion of the vote (usually seventy-four per cent) for a motion to be passed.

Following a European directive from 1989 regulations were passed in the United Kingdom in 1992 permitting the formation of a private company by one person. The single member is able to act as sole director and shareholder. The Companies Act 2006 now extends this to public companies as well.

(B) Liquidation of companies

If a company is to be dissolved it is said to be wound up or put into liquidation. Most winding ups are voluntary operations decided upon by the directors, but the process can also come about by court order where a creditor has presented a winding up petition to the court. If the company has financial problems it may be able to save itself by making voluntary arrangements as an alternative to going into full liquidation. Directors of the company make a proposal for such an arrangement. This may amount to a composition of the company's debts or a scheme of arrangement of the company's affairs. The insolvency practitioner appointed under the Insolvency Act 1986 (normally Chartered Accountants) will be appointed to act as supervisor. If the company is unlikely to be able to pay its debts, an alternative may be an Administration Order. This is made through the court system and the order will be made either because it is considered that the company's future can be secured or to give time for the organisation to make a voluntary arrangement. While the order is in force there can be no order made for liquidation. The Enterprise Act 2002 has made it possible to seek an out of court appointment of an administrator.

Where liquidation of the company becomes necessary the liquidator takes control of the company's property. The powers of the board are taken over and the liquidator is required to call in all assets, realise them, and distribute the proceeds to the appropriate creditors so far as is possible. The liquidator will be particularly concerned with transactions of the company made immediately before liquidation to try to ensure that any disposals made with the intent of defeating creditors are traced. If so, they could well be rendered void. Once the liquidator has paid the costs and expenses of the liquidation, he must pay off the creditors who have submitted formal proof of their debt. If there are surplus funds after distribution to the creditors, these are distributed to the members of the company according to their interests and rights.

(C) The capacity of the company

Paragraph 2.6.1 examined the question of capacity in terms of the freedom of certain persons (including artificial persons) to enter into contractual arrangements. Before the enactment of the Companies Act 2006 companies were required to define the extent of their powers to enter into contracts by setting out the objects of the company in their memorandum of association. If a company subsequently entered into a contract that fell outside these objects it was said to be acting *ultra vires* ('beyond the powers') and the contract would be void.

The leading case in this area is *Ashbury Railway Carriage Ltd v Riche*[111] where a company had been formed with the object of carrying on the business of making and selling rolling stock. The company entered into a contract with Riche to construct a railway in Belgium but defaulted on their obligations. When Riche sued for breach of contract his claim failed as the construction of a railway (rather than rolling stock) was *ultra vires* and the contract was therefore void.

The fiction underpinning the decision in the above case was that before entering into a business transaction every company should enquire into the authority of the other to enter into the proposed contract by examining its memorandum of association. Such a state of affairs was clearly not in the interests of open trade and revisions were made to the legislation to rectify the situation. The Companies Act 2006 now completely removes the *ultra vires* rule. As we have seen there is no longer any requirement for the objects of the company to be stated in its memorandum. Furthermore, section 39(1) now provides that the validity of an act done by the company shall not be called into question on the grounds of lack of capacity by reason of anything in the company's constitution.

2.15 Forms of contract in the construction industry

As mentioned at the beginning of this chapter it is a widespread practice in contemporary commercial life to use standard forms of contract. Contracts involving the sale of land and buildings are notable examples. In the construction and engineering context there are a plethora of standard forms. In 1964, the Banwell Committee recommended the use of one single standard form of contract

---

[111] (1875) LR 7 HL 653

in the construction industry. This call for a single standard form has been repeated on several occasions through the decades. However, the reality has been an upsurge in the varying types of forms used. Although not essential it is more convenient and safer to use a standard form where the contract is complex and expensive. In many cases a contracting party has little option other than to be a party to such an arrangement. Such a form does give the professional and industry parties to a contract a degree of certainty as to their likely obligations under the contract. Constant use in practice means that its users should be well versed in the form's application and how it distributes risk among those contracting. Moreover, it is open to the parties to agree among themselves to modify the forms where appropriate. Simply because a standard form of contract is used does not mean that the ordinary rules of contract law can be avoided. All of the standard forms of contract discussed here and used in the United Kingdom have been amended to ensure compliance with the Housing Grants, Construction and Regeneration Act 1996 (see below).

The popularity of the various forms of contract is analysed bi-annually by a survey carried out by the Royal Institute of Chartered Surveyors in collaboration with David Langdon, a leading firm of consultants to the construction industry. The Joint Contracts Tribunal (JCT) forms have remained by far and away the most popular forms over the course of the surveys. The latest survey looking at contracts in use in 2007 records around eighty per cent by number of the sample taken used JCT with the New Engineering Contract being used in fifteen per cent of those contracts sampled by value.

2.15.1   *The Standard Form of Building Contract, JCT 05*

In 1931 the JCT was set up, consisting of representatives from the construction industry and the professions involved in major building works. The best known form of contract issued by the JCT is the JCT 05 Standard Form of Building Contract. This form is for building work procured using the traditional method. It is intended for use in connection with all types of building works. This form comes in three versions, with or without reference to bills of quantities, and also for use with approximate quantities. The latest edition was published in 2005 with amendments made in 2007 and 2009. The 2005 form consists of three sections. These are the articles of agreement, the contract conditions and the schedules.

The articles are primarily concerned with definitions. Apart from setting out the names of the employer (the client) and the contractor (the builder) they deal with the contractor's obligations, the contract price and the identity of the architect. The appointment of an architect or 'contract administrator' is a fundamental feature of this traditional method of procurement. The architect is responsible for supervision of the works. It is normal practice to name the quantity surveyor engaged by the employer. Such a person has responsibility for the valuation of work and reports to the architect/contract administrator. The contract conditions together with the contract bills and drawings form the substance of the contract. The conditions are divided into nine sections where related topics are grouped together.

A common feature of the traditional method of executing building works is for the main contractor to appoint independent sub-contractors to carry out specialist tasks, designs or supply materials. The sub-contractor is liable to the main contractor in the event of any default. The conditions deal at length with matters such as the contractor's obligations and the architect's powers, particularly in respect of ordering variations, provisions for certification and payment, and the methods of dealing with any disputes. Fluctuations are a further area covered. This clause is concerned with any changes which have come about in the amounts paid for labour and in the price of materials since the contract was entered into.

2.15.2 Institute of Civil Engineers' Conditions of Contract

Dating from 1999, the 7th edition of the Institution of Civil Engineers'(ICE) Contract is the current established contract for use in connection with major civil engineering construction works. The form dates from 1945 and the same form is used by private and public employers. Under the ICE contract the engineer has extensive powers of supervision and control. The engineer is not, as such, a party to the contract. The contract is made between the promoter/employer and the contractor. The engineer acts as an agent of the employer and in accordance with normal agency rules must act in the best interests of the employer. The engineer will have a contract with the employer based on the appropriate conditions of engagement. In contrast to JCT 05 the contractor is not paid on the basis of a 'contract sum'. Instead the contractor is paid on a 'measure and value' basis calculated on the basis of contract rates for the actual work carried out. This is sometimes known as 'admeasurement' or a 'remeasurement' contract. The basis of the contract will be found in the tender which has been accepted by the promoter. The conditions envisage that the contract will be accompanied by drawings, together with a specification describing the proposed works and appropriate bills of quantities, measuring and costing the works in question. The main provisions of the contract cover the engineer's control of the works, the obligations of the contractor, the powers of the promoter and the engineer, certification and payment, and mechanisms for dispute resolution. Where a contract for civil engineering works is of less that six months' duration and the contract price is less than £150 000, the ICE Minor Works Contract based on ICE conditions may be an appropriate option.

2.15.3 Other JCT forms

The JCT publishes a contract for use in connection with minor and intermediate works in a similar fashion to the ICE. Although based on the main JCT form, the small works document is somewhat basic and is not appropriate in respect of contracts involving more than £150 000. The Intermediate form is a popular contract and is reasonably flexible in operation. It can be used in both the public and private sectors and allows sub-contract work to be placed with a 'named person', This procedure of nominating sub-contractors has disappeared from JCT SBC 05 due to reports of the difficulties experienced with operating the nomination provisions in practice.

2.15.4   Other forms of main contract

(A) FIDIC International Conditions

Since 1956, civil engineering contracts containing an international element have been able to take advantage of this form which is based on ICE conditions. The national law governing the contract must be stated in part 2. The engineer is appointed to act as representative and agent for the client. The contract contains the normal provisions to be found in standard forms relating to building works and provides for resolution of disputes by arbitration under the International Chamber of Commerce rules (ICC).

(B) GC/Works/1

These are encountered on government based projects. A major characteristic of this form is the extensive powers of the employer, who is referred to as 'the authority'. The form provides for the appointment of a project manager who has similar powers to those of the engineer under the ICE conditions. This contract has some interesting provisions including the authority being able to order the contractor to accelerate their work and to make payment by reference to a cash flow 'S' curve rather than by reference to the measured work performed.

2.15.5   Sub-contracts

Sub-contracting is a major feature of the UK construction industry, with a considerable proportion of the work undertaken being carried out by specialists responsible for certain aspects of the contract. The practice of the employer making individual agreements with sub-contractors is not common in England and Wales and the standard procedure is for the work to be originally let out 'en bloc' to the main contractor who then sub-lets aspects of it but is responsible for the overall work completed. Standard forms are available to cover the situation where the sub-contractor is 'domestic', in which case the employer plays no part in selection other than to be in a position to veto any appointment to which the employer objects. Domestic sub-contractors are now covered by a procedure laid down in clause 3.7-3.9 of JCT 05. The JCT 05 does not require the use of any particular standard form of sub-contract conditions although there are now JCT forms of sub-contract available known as SBC Sub 05.

2.15.6   Management contracts

The essence of a management contract is that the main contractor does not physically undertake any of the building work involved. Instead, the actual physical work is carried out by 'works contractors' (sub-contractors) and the main contractor manages the operations. The advantage to the management contractor is that contractual liability is diminished because, as a general course, the management contractor is only liable if the sub-contractor can also be held responsible.

There are indirect economies of scale in that the main contractor can reduce operating costs by not having to keep a large workforce, with appropriate reductions in equipment and plant. In 2008 the Joint Contracts Tribunal issued the JCT Standard Form of Management Contract (MC 05). Management contracts should not be confused with construction management, where there is no main contractor in the scenario and where individual contracts are made directly between the developer and the works contractors. A JCT form exists for this procurement approach and is known as the JCT Standard Form for Construction Management Contract (CM 05).

2.15.7   Design and build contracts

In a traditional construction contract the task of design is essentially a matter for the design team comprising the architect/engineer as appropriate. It is becoming increasingly common to find contracts where the contractor has partial or complete responsibility for design matters. A number of design and build contracts in standard form are now available. Probably the best known of these 'package deal' or 'turnkey' contracts is the JCT DB 05 Design and Build Contract. The procedure for determining the design in such contracts is made up of the 'Employer's Requirements' and the 'Contractor's Proposals' which will become incorporated into the contract. An employer who enters a design and build project on the basis of lowest costs might find difficulties if he wishes to vary it at a later stage because these types of package deal tend to allow the contractor to object to a variation which will affect his responsibility for design. It is common practice for design and build contracts to provide for sub-contracting of design elements.

2.15.8   NHBC schemes

The National Housebuilding Council (NHBC) has been in existence since 1936 and now operates under the trademark of 'Buildmark'. This body was established by leading builders on a voluntary basis to encourage consistent high standards in house building. The system operates by the maintenance of a register of builders and developers whose work adheres to the standards prescribed by the Council. Those builders on the register enter into a standard form agreement with the first purchaser and with the NHBC. After stating that he is a party to the scheme, the builder warrants that the property has been built properly and that it complies with the Council's requirements. By registration on the scheme, the builder authorises the building council to issue the appropriate Buildmark documents. An insurance system operates to cover any defects arising in dwellings covered by the scheme.

In order to be covered by the scheme the defects must become apparent and be notified to the council within the first ten years of construction. It is only in the 'initial guarantee period' of two years that full cover is given to the purchaser by the builder. During the remaining eight year 'structural guarantee period', the NHBC (rather than the builder themselves) agrees to cover defects but is limited to major damage covered by structural defects or settlement/subsidence problems. Subsequent purchasers may also obtain the benefit of the scheme for the remaining unexpired term of the guarantee. The Council employs officers to inspect work completed and in the event of non-compliance a builder may be removed from the register. The contract specifies the obligations of the Council to satisfy any judgement obtained by the purchaser against the builder relating to defects in the construction of a dwelling. In practice, disputes are dealt with by conciliation and arbitration. The NHBC is one of the few regular users of the 'approved inspector' system in the building regulation process (see Chapter 5, paragraph 5.6).

2.15.9 NEC 3 Engineering and Construction Contract

The original version of this form, the New Engineering Contract (NEC) was published in 1993 by the Institution of Civil Engineers. The NEC was praised in the Latham Report as being a means of responding to growing discontent within the industry to long winded contractual procedures and adversarial attitudes. The NEC sought, and has succeeded, in being applicable to both building and engineering projects. A further objective for the NEC was to accommodate all varieties of design responsibilities. This is achieved by the flexibility of using core clauses which can be adapted to various types of projects. Secondary option clauses can also be 'bolted on' to the contract to suit the client's requirements. All the clauses are written in plain English using only common words and written in the present tense.

The over-riding aim of the NEC contracts have been to form a stimulus to good management and a collaborative and co-operative method of working. This approach is not without its doubters who prefer the legal certainty approach embodied by the JCT contracts. Nevertheless, the NEC 3 has been used successfully on some high profile projects including the Channel Tunnel Rail Link, Terminal 5 at Heathrow Airport and most importantly The Olympic Delivery Agency and Office of Government Commerce is procuring all work for the 2012 games using this form of contract. It remains to be seen how the JCT will respond to the NECs assault on its position as the industry's preferred supplier of standard contracts.

2.15.10 Housing Grants, Construction and Regeneration Act 1996 (HGCRA)

Throughout this chapter, case law and statue law have been examined to illustrate principles of contract law as they apply to the Built Environment. There is one statute which is of great importance to the Construction Industry which is worthy of special mention. Construction industry practice was turned on its head by thirteen short clauses buried inside this statute dealing mainly with unconnected provisions. The clauses impacted greatly on payment provisions and the resolution of construction contract disputes. The effect of the terms set out below is to empower those individuals and firms within the construction industry who hitherto found themselves at the mercy of their contractual partners when a dispute situation arose. Armed with the provisions of the Act, a disgruntled party may now know why they have not been paid and, if they do not approve of the reasons given, now have the power to do something about it through the dispute resolution procedure of adjudication. Adjudication has replaced litigation and arbitration as the industry's preferred form of dispute resolution.

(A) Background

This Act was the result of a number of the recommendations made in the Latham Report and subsequent Department of the Environment Consultation papers. It is also consistent with the obvious desire of the Woolf Report to promote Alternative Dispute Resolution as a means of resolving disputes. It received the Royal Assent in July 1996 and applied to all construction contracts entered into after 1 May 1998. Several small amendments were made to the Act following a long consultation with construction industry stakeholders. The stakeholders were generally pleased with how the Act was working. Changes to the Act are to be introduced by the Local Democracy, Economic Development and Construction Act 2009. At the time of writing it is still uncertain when the relevant part of the new legislation will come into force.

The Act can be divided into three main areas:

- Definitions and scope.
- Adjudication.
- Payment.

(a) Definitions and scope

The Act applies to 'Construction Contracts' which are defined as agreements with any person for the carrying out of construction operations. It extends to sub-contracts and management contracts. It also covers agreements for the provision of architectural design or surveying work, and advice on building, engineering, interior work and exterior decoration or landscaping work in relation to construction operations. The contract must be in writing or evidenced in writing. There have been many instances where the courts have been asked to decide whether or not a contract is in, or is evidenced in, writing sufficient for a reference to adjudication to be valid. In the leading case of *RJT Consulting Engineers v DM Engineering*[112] it was held that in order to comply with the Act all the material terms of the oral contract were required to be evidenced in writing. This requirement that contracts be in writing is removed by the new legislation. In practice this means that more matters will be capable of referral to adjudication notwithstanding their lack of having been properly recorded in writing.

(b) Exceptions

The following are not covered by the Act, but may, by agreement between the parties, import the terms of the Act:

- Contracts with residential occupiers.
- Contracts relating to drilling for or the extraction of oil or natural gas.
- Contracts relating to the extraction of minerals and certain nuclear work.

---

[112] [2002] 1 WLR 2344

- Contracts relating to the manufacture or delivery of building or engineering components, materials or plant (if there is an installation of these items, that aspect will be covered).
- Purely artistic work.

(c) Adjudication

Section 108 of the Act provides that a Construction Contract must contain certain provisions relating to adjudication otherwise the provisions of the 'Scheme' will apply. The 'Scheme' is the crucial aspect in this legislation and is effectively the default position with which contracts draftsmen must comply. The right to adjudication arises in respect of any difference occurring between the parties to a construction contract.

Construction contracts must contain the following provisions:

- The right of any party to give notice of intention to submit a dispute to adjudication at any time.
- A timetable which provides for an adjudicator to be appointed and the dispute referred within seven days of notice.
- The adjudicator shall reach a decision within twenty-eight days of the matter being referred to him, this period to be extended by mutual consent of the parties.
- The twenty-eight-day period may be extended by another fourteen days with the consent of the party who originally referred the matter.
- The adjudicator has a duty to act impartially.
- The adjudicator must take the initiative in ascertaining the facts and the law.
- The adjudicator's decision will be binding until the dispute is finally determined by arbitration or by a court of law.
- The adjudicator is not liable for acts or omissions in carrying out his functions unless he has acted in bad faith.
- The adjudicator's decision may be regarded by the parties as a final determination of the matter despite the interim nature of his decision.

(d) Payment

The payment sections of the Act (sections 109–112) operate in a similar way to the adjudication provisions. These sections provide for a system of stage payments. A construction contract must deal with payment in a specific way to prevent the provisions of the Act applying by default:

- If a construction contract is at least of forty-five days' duration, any party to the contract is entitled to payments by instalments.
- The parties to the contract are free to agree the amounts of the payments and the stages when payable. If they do not, the provisions of the Scheme will apply.
- An adequate mechanism must be in place to determine what payments are due and the final date for payment must be specified.
- Every construction contract must contain provisions relating to the serving of notices by the payer and payee in respect of making payments and, where

appropriate, notice of an intention to withhold payment. Certain additional protection is given to the payee in the absence of an effective notice of intention to withhold payment.

- When it comes into effect the Local Democracy, Economic Development and Construction Act 2009 will make changes to the terminology and timing of these notices.
- In the event of non-payment by the payer or there is no effective notice of withholding payment, the payee has the right to suspend performance of the contract. This may be effected by a notice to suspend the performance of the contract. The new legislation seeks to allow the unpaid party to suspend that part of the works affected by the non-payment. This right ceases when the amount due is paid in full.

(e) 'Pay when paid' clauses

A further initiative introduced by the Act is the outlawing of conditional payment clauses. Provisions making any payment under a construction contract conditional upon the payer receiving payment from a third party are ineffective. The intention here was to outlaw the sometimes nefarious practice of main contractors to deny sub-contractors money properly owing under their sub-contracts because they themselves had not been paid by the Employer. The performance of the sub-contract was completely removed from any main contract arrangement and these clauses have been consigned to history. The only exceptions arise in situations of insolvency. The new legislation seeks to widen the definition of 'pay when paid clauses' and prevent clauses with a similar effect being used to avoid payment being made where it is due and owing.

3 The Law of Tort

3.1 The nature of tort

A tort is a civil wrong. The law of tort is part of the civil side of English law and is developed from common law principles. Unlike the law of contract there is no complete body of rules, which apply to all torts, in the way that all contracts are governed by the same general principles which remain fairly static. This is the reason why the subject is sometimes referred to as the law of torts. In civil legal systems (virtually all the other countries in Europe), contract and tort tend to be grouped together as the law of obligations. Tort is a more modern branch of the law than contract. Although a number of torts were established by the end of the nineteenth century, the twentieth century witnessed major developments, which are continuing at a rapid pace in the new century. The expansion of tort has been much influenced by the rise of capitalism and manufacturing together with advances in transport, technology and construction activities.

A claim in tort is concerned with the adjustment of losses between the relevant parties. These are the claimant(s) and the defendant(s). The principal remedy sought is damages (money). The claimant is seeking compensation for loss to property, reputation, money, physical injury or some other interest protected by the law. This may be in the form of an act, omission, or the giving of advice. There can be an overlap between tortious liability and other areas of law while certain factual situations may result in a civil action in tort and also in criminal proceedings. Common examples include road traffic accidents and accidents at work. In such circumstances each set of proceedings is dealt with differently. One aims at compensating the victim while the other aims to punish the wrongdoer. Tortious claims, like contractual claims, are subject to the civil burden of proof where the claimant must prove the case on the balance of probabilities. In criminal cases the case must be proved by the prosecution beyond all reasonable doubt.

Liability in contract is dependent on the existence of an agreement while duties in tort are imposed automatically by the law. The same act may be a tort and a breach of contract. This is known as concurrent liability. As long as there is no contradiction between the positions of the relevant parties the law allows the claimant to

Law and the Built Environment   by Douglas Wood, Paul Chynoweth, Julie Adshead and Jim Mason
© 2011 Douglas Wood, Paul Chynoweth, Julie Adshead and Jim Mason

chose the form of the action (contract or tort)[1]. In such circumstances the law of tort is usually preferred because of its more generous position in respect of limitation periods[2]. Duties in tort, between parties to a contract, may exceed their duties under the contract[3]. If a contract limits the obligations of a specific party a wider duty in tort will not be implied[4]. A person who commits a tort is known as a tortfeasor. Where more than one person is responsible for the commission of the tort, they are known as 'joint' tortfeasors making either or both of the defendants liable for the full extent of the claimant's injuries.

3.2   Liability in tort

This has traditionally depended on fault. It acts as a system of allocating losses which normally requires a claimant to prove that the defendant has deliberately or carelessly caused harm to the claimant. Torts vary in the mental elements required to incur liability on the defendant's behalf. Some torts require the defendant to have intended to do the act which amounts to the tort. As a general rule the law of tort is not concerned with a person's motive but in some circumstances its presence will assist the claimant's case in that it makes a reasonable act unlawful. This is relevant in nuisance and defamation. Sometimes torts are classified as strict liability. This is where the defendant is liable for the consequences of his actions even though he neither desired them nor ought necessarily to have avoided them. State of mind, in such circumstances, is disregarded. Examples of strict liability torts include product liability claims, based on the Consumer Protection Act 1987, and claims based on breach of statutory duty. Loss or damage, represented by an award of damages, is not always a prerequisite of a successful claim. In some circumstances a defendant's conduct may be actionable as a tort even though the claimant has sustained no loss. These torts are said to be actionable *per se*. Where there are repeated trespasses over a person's land, even though the landowner has suffered no loss or damage, an action may be brought in tort to restrain the trespasser from passing over the property.

One issue which needs to be appreciated from the outset is that the vast majority of tortious claims never see the inside of a court of law. In the majority of cases, where a claimant is successful in an action, the damages will be paid by an insurance company. Without the existence of insurance many claimants, probably a majority, would be left without compensation. In motor accident cases insurance is compulsory while many professions make it a condition of practice that their members are insured. Property owners take out insurance policies to cover damage to buildings and/or contents while if premises are let the lease will often contain provisions as to who has responsibility for insurance. Likewise, most of the established forms of building contract require insurance against public liability. In addition to private insurance schemes another source of compensation is the social security system for those who qualify.

---

[1] *Henderson v Merrett Syndicates Ltd* [1995] 2 AC 145
[2] See paragraph 3.13.4
[3] *Holt v Payne Skillington* [1996] PNLR 179
[4] *William Hill Organisation Ltd v Bernard Sunley & Sons Ltd* [1982] 22 BLR 8

3.3   General defences in tort

As we proceed through a consideration of the various torts it will become apparent that if a defendant can raise a successful defence the claimant's action will fail. Often, if the defence is properly raised, it will act as a complete bar to the claim. In some circumstances defences will be partial in nature. Defences are specific in nature where they are only relevant in connection with a specific tort. The main specific defences which can apply to a claim in negligence, volenti and contributory negligence, are broader in nature and can apply to other torts. They will be considered here in more detail.

3.3.1 'Volenti non fit injuria' (consent)

This means consent. Voluntary assumption of risk is a complete bar to a claimant being able to claim successfully in the tort of negligence and prevents the claimant from recovering damages even though the tort is established. It arises where the claimant knows of the risk involved, has the choice to accept the risk, but is prepared to run it. The test is objective. In *Smith v Baker*[5] a workman was injured when rocks fell on him from an overhead crane. No warning was given of when the crane was in use. The claimant was unaware of the danger and did not freely accept the risk involved. He was deemed not to have consented to run the risk. Where the claimant engages in a method of work, through personal choice and not at his employer's will, the defence might succeed[6]. The claimant must be mentally capable of giving consent[7]. In 'rescue' cases where the negligence of the defendant creates an emergency, and the claimant deliberately takes a risk in order to rescue someone in immediate danger, the defence will not apply as there is no genuine freedom of choice[8]. If the risk was taken unnecessarily a different result may apply[9].

3.3.2 Contributory negligence

At common law a person who was partly responsible for any harm they suffered could not recover in tort. The position is now regulated by the Law Reform (Contributory Negligence) Act 1945 which provides that, in such cases, the defence will not fail but the court will make an apportionment between the parties according to the degree of fault. The claimant's damages will be reduced by the extent to which the court considers them to be responsible for their own loss. Frequently the claimant's behaviour will be a contributory factor to the incident which has caused the damage. It can also apply where the claimant's behaviour exacerbates the amount of resulting harm. The defence frequently arises where a person fails to wear a seatbelt in a vehicle with the result that more extensive injuries are suffered than if it had been worn. It can have application in

[5] [1891] AC 325
[6] *ICI v Shatwell* [1965] AC 656
[7] *Kirkham v Chief Constable of Manchester* [1990] 3 All ER 246
[8] *Haynes v Harwood* [1935] 1 KB 146; *Chadwick v British Railways Board* [1967] 1 WLR 912
[9] *Cutler v United Dairies [London] Ltd* [1933] 2 KB 297

economic loss cases. In *Cavendish Funding Ltd v Henry Spencer*[10] the claimant lent money for the purchase of a building based on a valuation made by the defendants. The valuation figure was in excess of £1.5 million. As a safeguard an additional valuation was carried out by another company who valued the property at £1 million. The claimants relied on the defendant's figure. The property was worth £250 000. In subsequent proceedings the claimant's damages were reduced by twenty-five per cent as they should have checked the discrepancy between the two valuations. In these cases the claimant must show that the defendant failed to take reasonable care and contributed to his loss. In *Wheeler v Copas*[11] damages awarded to a bricklayer were reduced by fifty per cent when he was injured on a ladder, which had been lent to him, which broke under his weight.

3.4   Tort and human rights

The Human Rights Act 1998 incorporated the European Convention on Human Rights into United Kingdom law from 2000 onwards. The Convention (Protection of Human Rights and Fundamental Freedoms) was drafted in the period following World War 2 but until 2000 it had little effect on the legal system in the United Kingdom. From 1966 it was possible for British citizens to petition the European Court of Human Rights (ECtHR) based in Strasbourg, in France, to obtain rulings as to whether or not fundamental rights had been breached by activities carried out by the state. As the British government was not bound by decisions of the Strasbourg court these rulings were of little importance. Since the Human Rights Act 1998 became law the major articles of the Convention became binding in the United Kingdom while, as far as it is possible to do so, case law and statute must be applied in a way which is compatible with convention rights. The various Articles enable individuals to seek remedies when public authorities act in a way which is incompatible with Convention rights. The courts have powers to declare that a decision or action is unlawful and to grant appropriate remedies.

The main consequence of the enactment of the Human Rights Act 1998, in tort cases, has been in respect of claims brought against local authorities, and other public bodies, based on the manner in which they have carried out, or failed to carry out, their statutory functions. Moreover, s.3 HRA 1998 requires a court or tribunal to interpret primary and secondary legislation in accordance with 'Convention Rights'. This may well be relevant where neither of the parties is a public authority. As we proceed through the various sections of the chapter, reference will be made to human rights issues where appropriate. In tort, the area which has been most affected by the 1998 Act has been private nuisance[12].

---

[10] [1998] PNLR 122
[11] [1981] 3 All ER 405
[12] See Paragraph 3.7 1

3.5 Vicarious liability

This, as such, is not an independent tort. At times, a person is deemed to be legally responsible for torts committed by others. Liability arises because of the relationship between the parties and is known as vicarious liability. It provides a method of making a person, other than the actual tortfeasor, liable for the commission of the tort. In practice the only relationship which gives rise to this rule, to any degree in English law, is that between employer and employee. The principle is that an employer is liable for any torts committed by employees during the course of their employment. The act complained of by a claimant will normally be based on negligence. This is somewhat ironic in that the fault principle[13], which is a prerequisite to liability in negligence, will not apply in such situations. A more limited form of vicarious liability arises between principal and agent[14] and between partners in a firm[15]. It should be remembered that this principle does not exonerate the employee who committed the tort from liability. The tortfeasor and the employer may both be sued by the claimant. As the employer is obliged to take out public liability insurance any claimant may find that the employer is more likely to be able to pay out on a judgment than the employee who may well be a man of straw. If the employer satisfies the judgment he may be able to claim a contribution from the employee under the Civil Liability (Contribution) Act 1978.

3.5.1 Employees and independent contractors

There can be no liability imposed on the employer unless the person responsible for the tort is an employee. This was traditionally known as the master/servant relationship and is dependent on there being a contract of service between the parties. This has been contrasted with the arrangement where an employer nominates a self-employed independent contractor to carry out work based on a contract for services. In the latter case there will be no vicarious liability incurred as a result of the contractor's acts. Difficulties have always existed in distinguishing between the relationships but in the last twenty years, because of the numerous varieties of working relationships which have developed, the problem is greater than ever. An important factor is the amount of control which the employer has over the worker together with payment of wages and rights of dismissal and suspension[16]. A commonplace arrangement, which has existed in the construction industry, is the use of labour-only sub-contractors who are classified as independent contractors. They agree to work for a lump sum without any tax or insurance contributions being taken into account.

---

[13] See Paragraph 3.6.2
[14] See Chapter 2, section 2.13
[15] See Chapter 2, section 2.14.2
[16] *Viasystems [Tyneside Ltd] v Thermal Transfer [Northern] Ltd* [2005] EWCA 1151

(A) Course of employment

Once it has been determined that the employer/employee relationship exists the courts must be satisfied that the employee was acting in the course of employment before the employer can be held liable in respect of his actions. This is a question of fact that can cover wrongful acts that have been authorised by the employer and acts which were authorised but were carried out in an unauthorised manner. The question is whether the employer has prohibited the act itself, in which case the employee cannot be in the course of employment when performing it, or whether the employer has prohibited a particular method of carrying out the act in which case the employee may be in the course of employment. An employer will not generally be liable where the employee's act is outside the scope of his employment. In *Kooragang Investments Pty Ltd v Richardson & Wrench Ltd*[17] an employed valuer was deemed to have acted outside the course of his employment when carrying out valuations for a client whom his employers had blacklisted. Where an employee is acting on his own account and is involved in an unauthorised escapade he is said to be on a 'frolic of his own' and the employer will not be liable. In *Hilton v Thomas Burton [Rhodes] Ltd*[18] employers were not liable when four workmen left work to go to a café seven miles from the demolition site where they were working. Shortly before reaching the café, they decided to turn back and one of their party was killed due to the negligence of the driver.

(B) Liability for independent contractors

There are a limited number of situations where an employer may be liable for the acts of an independent contractor.

(a) Selection of the contractor

In *Kealey v Heard*[19] the owner of a number of houses, who was in the process of having them converted into flats, was held liable where a plasterer was injured because of faulty scaffolding erected by another (unknown) independent contractor. It was decided that the employer should have supervised the works as he had overall control of the contract.

(b) Contractor employed to carry out the tort

In *Ellis v Sheffield Gas Consumers Co*[20] the defendants hired contractors to dig up a road without having any authority to do so. When the claimant was injured, because of a hole that had been dug, the defendants were liable as the defendants had sanctioned the tort.

---

[17] [1982] AC 462
[18] [1961] 1 WLR 705
[19] [1983] 1 All ER 973
[20] (1853) 2 E & B 767

(c) Non-delegable duties imposed by statute or common law

There are a number of instances (mainly statutory) where there is an obligation imposed on a person to act in a particular manner. In such circumstances, the obligations cannot be delegated to another. Highway operations are a good example[21]. It can arise also on a common law basis[22].

3.6 Negligence

This is the most important independent tort. It covers a wide range of activities resulting in more litigation than all the other aspects of tort put together. Whereas other torts tend to protect specific interests negligence may be invoked in relation to a wide variety of interests. Obvious examples are protection against personal injury and damage to property. In some circumstances the tort offers protection against economic (financial) losses. As an independent tort it is of comparatively recent origin and is concerned with conduct. Although the non lawyer tends to equate negligence with 'lack of attention' or 'carelessness' liability in negligence is dependent upon the claimant being able to prove that:

- The defendant owed the claimant a duty of care.
- The duty was breached (broken) by the defendant.
- The claimant suffered damage as a consequence of the breach.

These three requirements were established in the leading case of *Donoghue v Stevenson*[23]. Two friends visited a café. The claimant was treated, by her companion, to a bottle of ginger beer manufactured by the defendants. Having sampled some of the contents she realised that the bottle contained parts of a decomposed snail. She suffered nervous shock and became physically ill with gastro-enteritis. The claimant had no contract with the café proprietor who sold the items to her friend. She sued the manufacturers of the ginger beer in tort. The House of Lords decided that a manufacturer owes a duty of care to the ultimate consumer of the goods irrespective of whether a contract exists between the relevant parties[24].

3.6.1 Duty of care

This is a matter of law. Before 1932 there were situations where the courts recognised the existence of a legal duty of care. Examples included the relationship between doctor and patient and lawyer and client. The courts were reluctant to deal with the issue of where such a duty should arise. Claimants were required to show that their case came within an existing category of duty or that a new area of duty should be introduced. The issue became more problematical, where contractual duties existed, with the courts tending to avoid holding liability when someone was

---

[21] *Gray v Pullen* (1864) 5 B & S 570
[22] *Honeywill & Stein v Larkin Bros Ltd* [1934] 1 KB 191
[23] [1932] AC 562
[24] *Grant v Australian Knitting Mills* [1936] AC 85

not a party to a contract. There were no firm principles relating to the duty of care until the decision in *'Donoghue'*[25]. Lord Atkin pronounced a general test that a person owes a duty of care to his neighbour. He then defined a neighbour as someone who is 'so closely and directly affected by my acts that I ought reasonably to have them in contemplation as being so affected when I am directing my mind to the acts or omissions which are called in question'[26].

(A) The period of expansion

In the decades after *Donoghue v Stevenson* was decided the courts did not concern themselves greatly with the concept of the duty of care. In the 1970s, and the early 1980s, the higher courts embarked on an expansionist role. In a number of leading cases the courts found a duty of care to exist in situations where they had not previously done so. Examples include *Dutton v Bognor Regis UDC*[27] and *Anns v Merton LBC*[28]. This latter decision created a presumption of the existence of a duty of care which the defendant then had to rebut on policy grounds. The case had a significant effect on construction activities and, in particular, on local authorities when carrying out their inspection and approval activities of new buildings. Liability was imposed in negligence where previously no duty of care was owed. From the mid 1980s onwards the 'retreat from *Anns*' began. In a series of cases[29], culminating in *Murphy v Brentwood DC*[30], the Law Lords became highly critical of the decisions based on *'Dutton'* and *'Anns'*

(B) 'Murphy v Brentwood District Council'

In *'Murphy'* the House of Lords declared that all the cases based on these earlier decisions had been wrongly decided. This case concerned a new semi-detached house which had been built on a concrete raft on a landfill site. The raft was not adequate for the purpose and some eleven years after construction the claimant discovered cracks which appeared when the house subsided. The plans received local authority approval when the house was built. The claimant sold the defective property to a new purchaser for £35 000 less than its value in good condition. The claimant sued the council for negligence in approving the foundations. The House of Lords dismissed the claim on the basis that the damage suffered was purely economic in nature. It was emphasised that a defect which does not render a building an immediate danger to the health and safety of its occupants is purely economic in nature and not foreseeable. Any remedy should be in contract and not in tort in such cases.

---

[25] See Paragraph 3.6
[26] [1932] AC 562 at 577
[27] [1972] 1 All ER 462
[28] [1978] AC 728
[29] *Peabody Donation Fund [Governors] v Sir Lindsay Parkinson & Co Ltd* [1985] AC 210; *Yuen Kun Yeu v A-G of Hong Kong* 1988 [AC] 175; *D & F Estates Ltd v Church Commissioners for England* [1989] AC 177
[30] [1991] AC 398

(C) 'Caparo Industries plc v Dickman'

A significant factor in the '*Murphy*' decision was the decision in *Caparo Industries v Dickman*[31]. In '*Caparo*' Lord Bridge considered there were three criteria for determining the imposition of a duty of care:

- Foreseeability of damage (neighbour test).
- Proximity of relationship.
- Whether it is just and reasonable to impose a duty of care (policy)

This three pronged approach was confirmed in *Marc Rich & Co AG v Bishop Rock Marine Co Ltd and others, The Nicholas H*[32]. Each factor cannot operate independently of the other two. The courts have not closed the categories of negligence but a claimant seeking to establish a new duty situation will have to establish that such an imposition accords with previous analyses of justice and policy. The '*Caparo*' approach was confirmed in *Mitchell [A P] v Glasgow City Council*[33].

(a) Foreseeability

This first requirement confirms that a duty of care is not owed to the world at large. This is the factual aspect of the duty of care and is really a refined version of the 'neighbour' test in *Donoghue v Stevenson*. It means that a claimant must show that, at the time of the defendant's negligent act, it was foreseeable that some damage to that particular claimant was foreseeable. If damage to someone else is foreseeable, but not to the claimant, the action will fail. In *Bourhill v Young*[34], the action failed when the claimant alleged that she had suffered nervous shock after hearing the impact of a crash which resulted in her giving birth to a stillborn child. She was outside the area of foreseeable shock and the claim failed.

(b) Proximity

Foreseeability of harm is an aspect of proximity while whether proximity exists, in a particular set of circumstances, is also influenced by policy considerations. Proximity is not easy to define as it can mean different things in different situations. It probably indicates a relationship between two parties where it is fair and reasonable that one should owe the other a duty of care. In road traffic accident cases the requirement is satisfied by the existence of foreseeability while in negligent misstatement cases[35] the parties will normally have to establish some prior relationship. In psychiatric damage cases, where the claimant is a secondary

---

[31] [1990] 2 AC 605
[32] [1996] AC 211
[33] [2009] UKHL 11
[34] [1943] AC 92
[35] See Paragraph 3.6 10

victim[36], the claimant is required to have 'close ties of love and affection' with the victim. In *Hill v Chief Constable of West Yorkshire*[37], relatives of the victims of a serial killer had no claim against the police where it was alleged that they had failed to use reasonable care to apprehend the murderer. It was held that there was no proximity between specific individuals and the police in the exercise of their duties.

(c) Just and reasonable

The third element of '*Caparo*' confirms that no duty of care will be imposed unless it is just to do so in the circumstances. This is the policy factor where judges have to decide whether there should, or should not be, a duty in the particular circumstances. Numerous issues apply here: whether the parties have insurance cover, the overburdening of particular professions and the 'floodgates' argument where to impose liability would result in too many claims of a particular type being brought before the courts are a few examples. The House of Lords in '*Hill*' confirmed that the police enjoy immunity from actions in negligence but it appears that the courts are not prepared to give public bodies immunity in every situation. The issue has arisen in a human rights context[38]. The immunity enjoyed by public bodies has also been scrutinised in this way[39]. Those involved in the judicial process are immune from any civil proceedings against them during the course of a trial. This would include an action in negligence. Judges, magistrates, witnesses and arbitrators enjoy this privilege. There have been cases where persons appointed to perform some form of professional task have sought the immunity that an arbitrator has from claims in negligence against them. These have been unsuccessful. Examples include certifying that a building contract is progressing satisfactorily[40] and making a valuation of shares[41]. The immunity enjoyed by advocates, while arguing cases in court, appears to have been lost[42].

3.6.2 Breach of duty

Breach of the duty of care depends upon standards of 'reasonableness'.

Negligence is based on fault so the claimant must prove that the defendant has fallen below the standard of care expected of him. This is the reasonable man test which was formulated in *Blythe v Birmingham Waterworks Co*[43]. As a general rule the existence of such a breach is applied by an objective test. The courts have considered whether the standard differs according to the type of person who owes the duty of care. The same standard of care is expected of motorists however old or experienced[44]. Those who continue to drive after feeling unwell may well be

---

[36] See Paragraph 3.6.9
[37] [1992] 2 All ER 625
[38] *Osman v United Kingdom* [1999] Crim LR 82
[39] *X v Bedfordshire County Council* [1995] 3 All ER 353
[40] *Sutcliffe v Thackrah* [1974] AC 727
[41] *Arenson v Casson, Beckman, Rutley & Co* [1977] AC 405
[42] *Hall [Arthur & Co] v Simons* [2000] 3 All ER 673
[43] (1856) 11 Ex 781
[44] *Nettleship v Weston* [1971] 2 QB 691

negligent if they cause subsequent harm[45]. There will be no breach of the duty of care, on the driver's part, if they are unaware they are unfit to drive and an accident occurs as a result[46]. Minors are rarely sued in negligence because of a lack of financial resources. If they are, the child's age will be taken into consideration. In *Mullin v Richards*[47] the claimant and the defendant, who were fifteen-year-old schoolgirls, were fighting with plastic rulers in a classroom. A fragment broke off the defendant's ruler and flew into the claimant's eye causing her to lose her sight in that eye. The Court of Appeal decided that a fifteen-year-old girl could not have foreseen the likelihood of harm as a consequence of her behaviour. In the case of the sick or disabled the standard of care owed is that which would be appropriate in the case of a reasonable man suffering from that ailment or disability. In determining what is appropriate behaviour the courts consider the foreseeable consequences of the defendant's actions. The question is: what would the reasonable man foresee and not what the defendant personally could foresee[48].

(A) The concept of risk

The courts take into account a variety of factors to help determine the appropriate standard of care. In any particular case a judge may be balancing a number of these factors to ascertain where it should lie. The courts evaluate the concept in terms of risk. In *Bolton v Stone*[49] the claimant was hit by a cricket ball. As it was improbable that the ball would be hit out of the ground, or cause injury if it did, the defendant was not liable. A different conclusion was reached in *Hilder v Associated Portland Cement Manufacturers Ltd*[50] where the defendant allowed children to play football on waste ground, which they owned, next to a busy road. Balls frequently went onto the road and one caused the claimant motorist to crash resulting in his death. The seriousness of the injury risked is another factor. In *Paris v Stepney BC*[51] the claimant, who was blind in one eye, was blinded in his other eye during the course of his employment. He contended that his employers were negligent because they had not provided him with goggles. The argument was upheld. The House of Lords emphasised that a higher degree of care is always required when dealing with persons suffering from a mental or physical disability, children (especially young ones) and elderly people. In *Haley v London Electricity Board*[52] the defendants were placed under a higher duty of care in circumstances where they knew of the existence of blind people in the locality and did not take adequate steps when fencing off excavation works on the highway. In *Withers v Perry Chain Co Ltd*[53] the claimant, who was prone to suffer from dermatitis, was given the most grease-free

---

[45] *Roberts v Ramsbottom* [1980] 1 All ER 7
[46] *Mansfield v Weetabix Ltd* [1997] PIQR 526
[47] [1998] 1 All ER 920
[48] *Glasgow Corporation v Muir* [1943] AC 448; *Roe v Minister of Health* [1954] 2 QB 66
[49] [1951] AC 850 HL
[50] [1961] 1 WLR 1434
[51] [1951] AC 367
[52] [1965] AC 778
[53] [1961] 1 WLR 1314

job available by her employers. She, nevertheless, contracted the ailment. As her employers had done everything possible to protect her, the company was not liable. The only other alternative would be to dismiss her. The utility of the defendant's act is also of importance. The risk must be balanced against the end to be achieved[54]. Sometimes, it is appropriate to consider what the cost and difficulty would be in avoiding an identifiable risk. As long as everything reasonable in the circumstances has been done there will be no liability[55].

(B) Professional liability

Where a person engages in an activity for which some measure of professional skill is required, the degree of competence expected is that of the reasonably competent person exercising that skill or profession. This is the so called *'Bolam'* test[56] which has been given judicial approval in many cases. Most of the reported case law refers to medical negligence but the rule applies to any professional person. The courts tend to rely heavily on expert evidence from practitioners and codes of practice. Such experts are usually appointed by the relevant parties but can be appointed by the court. In *Abbey National Mortgages plc v Key Surveyors Nationwide Ltd*[57] appointment of a joint expert by the court, in addition to experts nominated by the relevant parties, was upheld by the Court of Appeal in a case involving negligent mortgage valuations relating to residential properties. In *Samson v Metcalfe Hambleton & Co*[58] it was emphasised that expert witnesses should be from the same profession as the defendant. In this case, which involved cracks in a wall, the Court of Appeal took the view that a structural engineer was not an appropriate expert witness in a case involving alleged negligence by a building surveyor. Although a professional person must be skilful and careful it is not necessary that he or she be correct[59]. An inaccurate valuation of premises, or of the cost of carrying out building works, is not necessarily negligence. Where a valuation is carried out by unorthodox methods, but comes within a 'bracket' of figures that a competent practitioner would arrive at, it is unlikely that there will be a breach of *'Bolam'*[60]. In determining whether a valuer has exercised a reasonable degree of skill and care, various factors have to be considered. These include the scope of the instructions given, knowledge of the law, and adherence to current procedures and practices. It is normally assumed that the inexperienced professional person will seek the advice of those who are more experienced in complicated situations. Where a surveyor is carrying out a valuation for mortgage purposes[61] a limited visual inspection will suffice, unless the circumstances warrant further investigation, in which case the surveyor must obtain the information which it is reasonable

---

[54] *Watt v Hertfordshire County Council* [1954] 2 All ER 368
[55] *Latimer v AEC Ltd* [1952] 1 All ER 1302
[56] *Bolam v Friern Hospital Management Committee* [1957] 2 All ER 118
[57] [1996] EGLR 99 CA
[58] [1998] 2 EGLR 103
[59] *Pritchard Joyce & Hinds v Batcup* [2009] EWCA 3
[60] *Mount Banking Corp Ltd v Brian Cooper & Co* [1992] EGLR 192
[61] See *Yianni v Edwin Evans & Sons* [1982] 2 QB 438; *Smith v Eric S Bush* [1990] 1 AC 831; see also Paragraph 3.6.10 and Chapter 2, section 2.8.2

for him to have before making the valuation[62]. A recent decision[63] has established that duties imposed by a surveyor's retainer are not limited to carrying out an inspection with a reasonable degree of skill and care. In this case a borrower had deliberately led the surveyor to value the 'wrong' property in a development of partly-built residential property. The valuer had signed the valuation certificate and there had been a breach of contract. If a lay person attempts a specialised task, such as 'DIY', the standard expected is the skill of a reasonably competent person exercising that skill. In *Wells v Cooper*[64] the defendant fixed a door handle onto a door. Evidence showed that he did the job as well as an ordinary carpenter. The handle came off in the claimant's hand and he was injured. As the defendant had exercised the skill of a reasonably competent carpenter he was not liable.

3.6.3 *Damage*

Loss is a prerequisite to a successful claim in negligence. The tort is not actionable *per se* and therefore damage must be proved. As a general rule, the law relating to negligence protects a person's interest in their well being and in their landed and personal property. Damages will be awarded in respect of death/personal injury and in respect of damage to property (as long as the other requirements are satisfied). The claimant's loss must come within the scope of the defendant's duty of care[65]. In addition, financial (economic) losses can be claimed where they are a consequence of the physical injury or of damage to property. The most common examples are loss of earnings due to not being able to work and the cost of reinstating damaged property.

3.6.4 *Purely economic losses*

The courts have always been reluctant to allow liability for pure economic losses which arise from negligent acts even if they are foreseeable. This position has been adopted for a number of reasons: liability is potentially unlimited, such losses are not possible to insure against, are usually too remote and are essentially a concept more suited to the law of contract than the law of tort. The leading case is *Cattle v Stockton Water Works*[66]. In this case, the claimant was building a tunnel for a landowner when the defendant company's water main leaked into the area of the works. This delayed the project and reduced the claimant's profit. No cause of action was found to arise as no property had been damaged or personal injury sustained by the claimant. The loss of profit was a purely economic loss. In *Spartan Steel v Martin & Co*[67] the defendants negligently cut an electric power cable resulting in loss of power to the claimants who manufactured steel alloys. A consignment of steel in the claimant's furnace, at the time of the power cut, had to be destroyed to stop it from severely damaging the furnace. The claimants

---

[62] *Roberts v J Hampson & Co* [1989] 2 All ER 504
[63] *Platform Funding Ltd v Bank of Scotland plc* [2008] EWVA 930
[64] [1958] 2 All ER 527
[65] *South Australia Asset Management Corp v York Montague Ltd* [1996] 3 All ER 365
[66] (1875) LR 10 QB 453
[67] [1973] 1 QB 27

succeeded in their claim for physical damage and the loss of profit on the steel in the process of production. The claim for loss of profits on four more consignments of steel, which were planned but not carried out, failed as they were classified as being purely economic in nature. A similar approach was taken in *Weller & Co v Foot and Mouth Disease Research Institute*[68] where a virus escaped from the defendant's premises causing an outbreak of foot and mouth disease. The claimant auctioneers suffered losses when a ban was put on the movement of cattle preventing any sales of livestock taking place. An action for loss of profits failed as they were treated as being purely economic in nature. In *Greater Nottingham Co-operative Society Ltd v Cementation Piling & Foundations Ltd*[69] the claimants sustained purely economic losses due to the negligence of the defendants in carrying out piling work. The contract between the parties contained no provisions relating to this issue and no claim was allowed in the tort of negligence.

3.6.5 Causation and remoteness

These are sometimes referred to as 'causation in fact' and 'causation in law'.

They mean that the defendant's breach of duty of care must have caused the claimant's loss while sometimes damage to the claimant may have been caused by the defendant but as a matter of legal policy no liability should attach to the defendant. As in contract claims the damage must not be too remote[70].

(A) Causation

When determining the cause of an accident it is necessary to eliminate irrelevant material. This requires a factual investigation to be made. The usual method of determining the legal cause of an accident is to use the '*but for*' test. The question to be asked is: can the claimant prove that 'but for' the defendant's negligence he would not have suffered the injuries complained of[71]? In *McWilliams v Sir William Arrol & Co Ltd*[72] the claimant was killed when he fell while not using a safety harness. Statute required that harnesses should be supplied but the defendants avoided liability because they could show that the claimant would not have worn a harness in any case. The test can only be used where a definitive answer can be given. It may be there are a number of possible causes of the claimant's loss. In such cases, of concurrent multiple causes, the courts have tended to take the view that if the defendant's action or inaction has materially increased the risk of injury to the claimant, they will be liable[73]. Sometimes, when the claimant is injured by the

---

[68] [1965] 3 All ER 560

[69] [1988] 2All ER 971

[70] See Chapter 2, section 2.10

[71] *Barnett v Chelsea & Kensington Hospital Management Committee* [1969] 1 QB 428. See also *Environment Agency v Ellis* [2008] EWCA 1117 which highlights the difficulties in applying the test where the damage suffered is attributable to a number of causes.

[72] [1962] 1 WLR 295

[73] *Bonnington Castings v Wardlow* [1956] AC 613; *McGhee v National Coal Board* [1973] 3 All ER 1008; *Fairchild v Glenhaven Funeral Services Ltd* [2002] 3 WLR 89 c/ f *Wilsher v Essex Area Health Authority* [1988] 1 All ER 871

defendant's negligence, but before the case is heard, an unrelated consecutive event occurs that causes the claimant the same loss for which he is suing the defendant. Where two independent events cause the same harm the '*but for*' test is applied so that the defendant will usually escape liability for harm caused by the second event. In *Performance Cars Ltd v Abraham*[74] the defendant negligently drove his vehicle so that it collided with a Rolls Royce car. The Rolls Royce was later negligently struck by another car. The first defendant was liable for the cost of the respray to the car while the second defendant was not liable.

More difficulty arises where a second independent event causes similar but increased harm. Policy issues often apply in these cases with the courts trying to achieve a balance of not over or under compensating claimants[75].

(B) Remoteness of damage

The consequences of a defendant's act can be so far reaching that as a matter of legal policy a limit is put on the defendant's liability. Originally the rule was that a defendant would be liable for anything that was a direct consequence of his act[76]. This rather generous rule, from a claimant's point of view, was replaced by the reasonable foreseeability test which was formulated in a Privy Council case in 1961[77]. It seems that only the general and not the specific type of damage needs to be foreseen[78]. If the type of damage suffered is foreseeable it does not matter that it came about in an unforeseeable manner. In *Hughes v The Lord Advocate*[79] employees carrying out street works left a manhole uncovered inside a tent. A number of lit paraffin lamps were left at the corners of the tent at night. A boy entered the tent with one of the lamps. The lamp fell into the hole, causing an explosion, and the boy was badly burnt. The court held that although this was an unlikely sequence of events some fire-related damage was a foreseeable consequence of leaving the site unattended. A similar approach was taken in *Jolley v London Borough of Sutton*[80] where a teenage boy was seriously injured by an abandoned boat which fell onto him. The House of Lords took the view that some harm was reasonably foreseeable in the circumstances and the local authority was held liable as they should have removed the boat from the area.

3.6.6 The 'thin skull' rule

The principle is that a tortfeasor must take his victim as he finds him. This means that a defendant will be liable for all the damage suffered by the claimant if it is foreseeable that the claimant will suffer the general type of harm that he in fact suffers. This is so even if the claimant, due to some kind of sensitivity,

---

[74] [1962] 1 QB 33
[75] *Baker v Willoughby* [1970] AC 467; *Jobling v Associated Dairies Ltd* [1982] AC 794
[76] *Re Polemis and Furness Withy & Co* [1921] 3 KB 560
[77] *Overseas Tankship [UK] Ltd v Morts Dock & Engineering Co [The Wagon Mound No 1]* [1961] AC 388
[78] *Bradford v Robinson Rentals* [1967] 1 All ER 267
[79] [1967] 1 All ER 267; see also *Corr v IBC Vehicles Ltd* [2008] UKHL 13
[80] [2000] 3 All ER 409

suffers to a greater extent than would normally be foreseen. In *Smith v Leech, Brain & Co*[81] the defendant's employee was negligently splashed on the lip by molten metal. This caused a pre-malignant condition to develop. The claimant later died of cancer and his widow sued. The defendants were liable. Even though the death from cancer was not foreseeable some harm resulting from the negligence was. The rule has been applied to a variety of 'sensitivities' and even where the harm suffered is psychiatric injury[82]. It does not apply where the claimant's initial loss is increased by their lack of financial resources to take steps to minimise their loss[83]. This decision has not been popular with the higher courts[84].

3.6.7 *Intervening acts*

An intervening act (or 'novus actus interveniens') breaks the chain of causation between the claimant and the defendant. The occurrence of such an act, after the defendant's breach of duty has taken place, has the effect of exonerating the defendant for losses suffered by the claimant which occur after the intervening act has taken place. The courts have been somewhat erratic in the application of this doctrine often obscuring legal principles with policy considerations when deciding who should bear the loss in any particular case.

The intervening act can arise in three ways. The cause may be that of a third party in which case a new defendant may be introduced into the scenario. In *Baxhall Securities Ltd v Sheard Walshaw Partnership*[85] the chain of causation was broken when a firm of surveyors, on inspecting a roof, failed to discover defects caused by the negligence of the architects who designed the structure. For the act of the third party to break the chain of causation the defendant must not have any duty to guard against the third party's act and the consequence of the third party's act must be foreseeable. In *Ward v Cannock Chase District Council*[86] the claimants lived next door to a house that the defendants had allowed to fall into a serious state of repair. While the defendants repaired the property next door the claimants were required to move out of their house. In the claimant's absence, vandals broke into the house and caused damage. The court decided that there was no break in the chain of causation as the council had failed to effect the repairs quickly enough. They were liable in negligence. The second way in which an intervening act may come about is where a natural act occurs. This will rarely break the chain of causation but in those situations where the defendant can show that the act is unforeseeable and is independent of his own negligence he may be relieved of liability[87]. Finally, the chain of causation may be broken by an intervening act of the claimant. In this case there is an assertion that the claimant is responsible for their losses. If that is so the defendant is exonerated from any

---

[81] [1962] 2QB 405
[82] *Walker v Northumberland County Council* [1994] 1 All ER 737
[83] *Liesbosch Dredger v SS Edison* [1933] AC 448
[84] See *Dodd Properties [Kent] Ltd v Canterbury City Council* [1980] 1 All ER 928
[85] [2002] BLR 100
[86] [1986] 2 All 537
[87] *Carslogie Steamship Co v Royal Norwegian Government* [1952] AC 292

liability. To succeed it must be shown that the claimant's actions are unreasonable[88].

3.6.8 Proof in negligence cases

The normal burden of proof in civil actions applies here. The claimant must prove the facts relied upon on the balance of probabilities. Once the appropriate standard of care has been established the claimant must prove that the defendant was negligent rather than the other way around. Evidence must be produced to demonstrate how the defendant behaved showing that this was below the required standard. There are two exceptions to this.

(A) Civil evidence act 1968 s.11

Often the facts on which a negligence case is based will result in a prosecution being brought against the defendant as well. This provision provides that a conviction on a criminal charge is admissible as evidence in a civil case based on the same facts. In a negligence case this has the effect of creating a rebuttable presumption of negligence. In other words, it is for the defendant to show that on the balance of probabilities he was not negligent.

(B) Res Ipsa Loquitur

This means literally, 'the thing speaks for himself'. This assists a claimant where there is no known cause of the accident. Its effect is to raise a presumption of negligence on the defendant's part which the defendant must then rebut. The principle was raised in *Scott v London & St Katherine's Docks*[89] where bags of sugar fell on the claimant when he was standing near the door of the defendant's warehouse. At first instance the case failed, in the absence of evidence of negligence, but on appeal the claimant succeeded. Three requirements must be satisfied for the plea to succeed.

(a) The thing causing the damage must have been under the defendant's exclusive control

In *Gee v Metropolitan Railway*[90] the claimant fell out of a train when he leaned on the door as it was moving out of a station. The door had been under the defendant's control just before leaving the station and this raised a rebuttable presumption of negligence. In *Easson v LNER*[91] a boy fell out of a train some seven miles after the last stopping place. The defendant did not have sufficient control over the manually operated door as anyone might have unsecured the door since the last stop.

---

[88] *Wieland v Cyril Lord Carpets Ltd* [1969] 3 All ER 1006
[89] (1865) 3 H & C 596
[90] (1873) LR 8 QB 161
[91] [1944] 1 KB 421

(b) *Res Ipsa Loquitur* cannot be relied upon where the cause of action is known

In *Barkway v South Wales Transport Co*[92] a bus swerved and crashed injuring the claimant. The cause of the accident was a burst tyre. As all the facts were known the doctrine could not be relied upon.

(c) The accident should be of a sort that does not normally happen in the absence of negligence

In *Chaproniere v Mason*[93] a stone was found inside an iced bun. It would not have been there but for the negligence of the defendant.

The traditional view was that where the doctrine applies the burden of proof is shifted to the defendant who must prove that he was not negligent[94]. A different approach was taken in *Ng Chun Pui v Lee Chuen Tat*[95] where it was considered that all a defendant need do to avoid liability is to give an explanation for the accident which is consistent with negligence while there is an absence of negligence on his part. The claimant must then prove that the defendant was negligent.

3.6.9 Psychiatric injury

It may be that when a claimant brings an action based on personal injury the loss suffered by the claimant may not be a physical injury but instead a 'recognised psychiatric illness or disorder'[96]. The courts were originally reluctant to allow claims in nervous shock cases, as they were originally called, because of the problem of fraudulent claims, the difficulty of calculating damages in respect of such actions and the fear that making such incidents actionable would give rise to too much litigation. Initially the courts would only allow such a claim when it was accompanied by physical injury. The law developed when the legal system began to compensate those persons who suffered from psychiatric injury where the claimant feared for their own safety[97]. The principle was taken a step further in *Hambrook v Stokes*[98] where the claimant's wife, fearing that her daughter had been hit by a lorry, suffered nervous shock leading to her death. The claim succeeded as the court considered that a claimant's action could succeed if nervous shock was caused by fear of harm to one's spouse or children. The law was extended to cover the situation where the claimant feared for the safety of their work colleagues[99] and also where the claimant was a rescuer[100]. This expansionist approach reached its peak in *McLoughlin v O'Brian*[101]. The claimant's husband and children were injured in a car crash. The claimant arrived at the hospital about an hour after the

---

[92] [1950] 1 All ER 392
[93] (1905) 21 TLR 633
[94] *Henderson v Henry E Jenkins & Sons* [1970] AC 282
[95] [1988] PIQR 170
[96] Per Lord Bridge in *Attia v British Gas* [1987] 3 All ER 455 at page 462
[97] *Dulieu v White & Sons* [1901] 2 KB 669
[98] *Hambrook v Stokes* [1925] 1 KB 141
[99] *Dooley v Cammell Laird* [1951] 1 Lloyds Rep 271; *Young v Charles Church* [1997] BMLR 146
[100] *Chadwick v British Railways Board* [1967] 1 WLR 912
[101] [1983] AC 410

accident and was informed of the death of one of her children and saw the three other injured members of her family in a very poor condition of health. The claimant, who was a woman of reasonable fortitude, suffered nervous shock and a change of personality. The House of Lords held that since the claimant's relationship with the victims was sufficiently close and the woman was present at the 'immediate aftermath' of the accident she could claim successfully.

(A) The Hillsborough litigation

This concerned a series of events in which one hundred football supporters were crushed to death due to the negligence of the police in failing to control the crowd properly at a soccer match. A number of claims were settled, test cases were brought and the courts took different approaches from first instance to the House of Lords[102]. The House of Lords took the opportunity in '*Alcock*' to lay down a number of control tests which have to be satisfied to establish liability for psychiatric injury or illness where the claimant is a 'secondary victim' who suffers psychiatric injury from seeing, or hearing, of the injury of another.

(a) Relationship between the claimant and the victim

There must be a sufficient degree of proximity between the claimant and the victim. There is a rebuttable presumption that this is present between husband - wife and parent - child. Other claimants have to bring evidence to establish a close tie of love and affection.

(b) Proximity would normally require a claimant to be physically close to the accident in time and space

There can be no liability for 'mere' grief or sorrow[103]. If there is no casual link between the incident and the psychiatric injury there can be no successful claim. In *Taylor v Somerset HA*[104] a woman was told that her husband had died of a heart attack. When she arrived at hospital she was told he was dead. She identified her husband's body about an hour after his death but when she suffered psychiatric depression and claimed against the hospital it was held that the actual purpose of her visit to the hospital was to identify the body. This had nothing to do with the cause of his death. A secondary victim must be a person of normal fortitude to succeed and will not be compensated if they are more susceptible to shock.

(c) The claimant must witness the accident by their own unaided senses

The claimant must witness the accident, or its immediate aftermath, personally. Seeing the accident on television, hearing it on the radio, being told of it by a third

---

[102] *Jones v Wright* [1991] 2 WLR 814 (first instance); *Jones v Wright* [1991] 3 All ER 88 (Court of Appeal); *Alcock v Chief Constable of South Yorkshire Police* [1992] 1 AC 310 (House of Lords)
[103] *Hinz v Berry* [1970] 2 QB 40
[104] [1993] 4 Med LR 34

party or reading about it in the paper will not suffice. In *McFarlane v Caledonia Ltd*[105] the claimant was a bystander who witnessed the '*Piper Alpha*' disaster on a oil rig from a support ship. He was asleep at the time of the explosions which resulted in the death of one hundred and sixty four men. The claimant was not involved personally in any of the rescue work and his claim based on psychiatric injury failed.

(B) Primary victims

A person is a primary victim if they are fearful of physical injury to themselves. Where a person comes into this category, as in *Dulieu v White*[106], the action will succeed where it was foreseeable that physical or psychiatric injury would occur because of the defendant's negligence. In such cases the claimant need not suffer any physical injury and it does not matter that the claimant is more susceptible to shock than the average person. A person who witnesses an accident will not be automatically treated as a primary victim because they are a rescuer or a primary victim. The leading case is *Page v Smith*[107] where the claimant sustained no physical damage because of the defendant's negligence, but had to put up with the recurrence of a psychiatric injury which had arisen some years before. The courts have extended liability for stress-related illness to situations where the defendant has assumed responsibility for the claimant's mental health. An important example is *Walker v Northumberland County Council*[108] where an employee was exposed to stress at work by the negligence of his employers. After a period of absence, due to stress-related problems, he was given additional duties to carry out which exacerbated his mental state and in a subsequent claim he was successful.

3.6.10   Negligent advice

One issue, which the law of negligence has had to address, is whether an action should lie where a claimant has relied on a negligently made statement and consequently suffered financial loss. A major problem is that such losses will often be purely economic in nature and the law of negligence has an antipathy towards such claims[109]. Where the parties are in a contractual position the claimant may be able to take advantage of the provisions laid down in the Misrepresentation Act 1967. The tort of deceit may be applicable to this situation but it only applies to fraudulently made statements[110]. A significant development took place with the decision in *Hedley Byrne v Heller & Partners Ltd*[111]. The claimant advertising agents acted on behalf of a client known as Easipower. As they had not previously worked for the client they asked Easipower's bank for a credit reference. The bank replied that the company was 'good for ordinary business arrangements'. Easipower went

---

[105] [1994] 1 All ER 1
[106] [1901] 2 KB 669 See Paragraph 3.6.9
[107] [1996] 3 All ER 272
[108] [1995] 1 All ER 737. See Paragraph 3.6.5
[109] See Paragraph 3.6.3
[110] *Derry v Peake* (1889) 14 App Cases 337
[111] [1964] AC 465

into liquidation owing the claimants a considerable sum of money. Although the defendants avoided liability by inserting a valid disclaimer with their advice the Law Lords decided that an action could be brought in these circumstances. 'Hedley Byrne' is an important decision as it recognised that a duty of care would arise in certain situations where a person gives negligent advice which results in financial loss. It also decided that the duty can be owed where there is no contractual liability and where the claim is in respect of purely economic losses. In such cases, there is an assumption of responsibility by the party who actually gives the advice.

(A) The pre-requisites of liability

(a) Special relationship between the parties

This is where there is a relationship of trust between the parties and it will arise where the defendant knows, or ought reasonably to foresee, that the claimant will rely on his skill and judgement. As a general rule the advice must be formally given[112]. Many of the reported cases involve claims against accountants and valuers. In *Yianni v Edwin Evans*[113] such a relationship was considered to exist where a surveyor, instructed by a building society to value a house for mortgage purposes, owed a duty to the purchaser of the house where it was foreseeable that the valuation would be relied upon. Although this is a first instance decision it was approved in *Smith v Eric S Bush*[114] on similar facts. If a valuer is appointed by a receiver, no duty of care is owed as the valuer is acting for the receiver and the advice may well have not been acted upon[115]. In *Caparo v Dickman*[116] it was held that where accountants are instructed to audit a company's accounts their duty is owed to the existing investors as a group but not to specific shareholders.

(b) Specialist skill of the person giving the advice

A duty only arises where the defendant is in the business of giving such advice or represents competence to do so[117]. The minority view in 'Evatt' was that a duty to take reasonable care is not the same as a duty to meet a professional standard of competence. In *Tai Hing Cotton Mill Ltd v Liu Chong Hing Bank*[118] the view was taken that silence or inaction could not amount to a misstatement unless there is a duty to disclose[119].

(c) Reliance

The claimant must reasonably rely on the defendant's advice and the reliance must be reasonably foreseeable to the defendant. There is a greater likelihood of liability

---

[112] However, see *Chaudhry v Prabhakar* [1988] 3 All ER 718
[113] [1988] 2 QB 438; see 3.6.3
[114] [1990] 1 AC 831. See also Chapter 2, section 2.8.2
[115] *Raja v Austin Gray* [2003] 13 EG 117
[116] See Paragraph 3.6.4
[117] *Mutual Life & Citizens Assurance Co v Evatt* [1971] AC 793
[118] [1980] AC 80
[119] Per Lord Scarman at page 87

arising where the claimant is a lay person seeking advice from a professional person than where both parties are engaged in professional activities. In *Welton v North Cornwall DC*[120] the claimants undertook alterations to their premises in circumstances where an environmental health officer negligently required them to carry out works which were not required. It was clear that the officer knew that his instructions would be relied upon by the claimants and the officer inspected the alterations as they were being carried out. The test is whether the defendant ought reasonably to be expected to know of the advice given. In *Lambert v West Devon BC*[121] the defendant breached the duty of care, which they owed to the claimant, where a planning officer told the claimant he could proceed with development where the officer did not have the powers to deal with the matter himself.

3.6.11 Occupiers liability

This is negligence liability in respect of defective premises and it is governed primarily by statute. It is concerned with the extent of the liability of an occupier of premises when a person enters those premises and suffers physical loss. The issue of damage to personal property sometimes arises as well. The modern law is to be found in two statutory provisions. The principal Act is the Occupiers Liability Act 1957. The 1957 Act applies only to lawful visitors and provides that an occupier of premises owes a duty of care to see that such visitors will be reasonably safe when using the premises for the purpose(s) for which they are present. Trespassers are not governed by the 1957 Act. The Occupiers Liability Act 1984 provides that in some circumstances an occupier may owe a duty of care to a trespasser.

Both Acts are concerned with defective premises. Premises include any fixed or moveable structure. In addition to land and buildings it has been held to include cranes, scaffolding, ladders, ships and aircraft. Liability rests with the occupier and not beyond in respect of both Acts. An occupier is one who has control over the premises and it is a question of fact in each case as to who has occupation. Premises may have more than one occupier[122]. Where large scale building works are in progress the site owner and the main contractor may be both in occupation[123]. Where a lease is entered into liability rests, in the majority of cases, with the tenant. An empty building may be occupied. In *Harris v Birkenhead Corporation*[124] a local authority failed to block up a derelict house which was subject to a compulsory purchase order. They were liable as occupiers when a four-year-old child gained entry through an unsecured door and fell from a second floor window. Public rights of way [highways] are excluded from both Acts and are governed by the common law.

(A) Lawful visitors

By s.2 [2] of the Occupiers Liability Act 1957 occupiers owe a duty of care to lawful visitors. The Act covers damage to persons and to property. A lawful

---

[120] [1997] JPL 1

[121] [1997] 98 LGR 45

[122] *Wheat v Lacon & Co Ltd* [1966] AC 552

[123] *AMF International v Magnet Bowling Ltd* [1968] 1 WLR 1028

[124] [1976] 1 WLR 279

person is a person who expressly, or by implication, has been given the right to enter premises. This would include those persons who have entry as of right, by authority imposed by law, such as Health and Safety officials, Customs and VAT officers. As far as express permission is concerned this is a question of fact. The courts are reluctant to infer that an implied permission exists and the burden is on the person claiming the permission to prove it. The presence of a path or walkway up to a front door impliedly gives a person permission to enter premises and state their business to the occupier. This licence extends no further than the front door. An occupier may set restrictions or limitations on visitors entering the premises. A guest in an office, or in a hotel, would become a trespasser if they went through a door marked, 'Danger. Staff only' or 'Private'. In *Westwood v The Post Office*[125] an employee who disregarded a notice which said, 'Only the authorised attendant is permitted to enter' was held to be a trespasser when he was killed by falling through a defective trapdoor. An occupier may revoke the right of a lawful visitor to remain on the premises at any time. In such circumstances the visitor must be given a reasonable time in which to leave after which they become a trespasser. A person who starts off as a lawful visitor may become a trespasser if they abuse the purpose for which they are present. Where a person enters premises under a contractual right the obligations under the 1957 Act will be implied into the contract. While the visitor is on the premises the occupier must take care to see that the visitor will be reasonably safe in using the premises for the purpose for which he is invited or permitted to be there. Whether the duty has been breached is a question of fact in each case based on the general law of negligence. It is the visitor and not the premises that has to be made reasonably safe. The duty only extends to the purpose for which the visitor was actually allowed entry. In *Ward v Tesco Stores Ltd*[126] a customer slipped on yoghourt which had spilled onto the floor in the defendant's store. There was evidence to the effect that spillages were not cleaned up effectively after they occurred and the defendants were held to be negligent. In *Fryer v Pearson*[127] there was no breach of duty when a family visitor was injured by a needle when kneeling on the floor. There was no evidence that the occupiers knew the needle was there or that is created any danger.

(B) Some problem areas

The degree of care owed depends upon the status of the visitor. The occupier must be prepared for children not to be as careful as adults. In the case of a child, the test is a subjective one and the premises must be safe for a child of that age. Even if children are lawful visitors they may be attracted by some dangerous object to exceed the scope of their right to be on the premises. This is the concept of 'allurement' which might place a child visitor at risk of harm. In *Glasgow Corporation v Taylor*[128] the local authority was liable when a seven-year-old boy

---

[125] [1973] 1QB 598
[126] [1976] 1 All ER 219
[127] *The Times* April 4th 2000
[128] [1922] 1 AC 44

stole some attractive berries from a botanical gardens, open to the public, and died from poisoning. In *Jolley v London Borough of Sutton*[129] the attraction was an abandoned boat which fell on a fourteen-year-old boy who was trying to lift it off the ground. An occupier can expect very young children to be accompanied by an adult. In *Phipps v Rochester Corporation*[130] a five-year-old boy fell into a trench when collecting blackberries. The defendants were held not to be liable as this was the kind of danger from which a reasonable parent ought to protect his child. Similarly, in *Simkiss v Rhondda BC*[131] a seven-year-old girl was injured when she fell down a steep hill where she was having a picnic opposite the block of flats where she lived. Evidence was submitted to the effect that her father regarded the site as safe so there was no reason for the defendant local authority to consider it to be dangerous.

When tradesmen enter premises to carry out work, the occupier can expect skilled visitors to take any necessary precautions as long as the occupier leaves them free to do so. In *Roles v Nathan*[132] the occupiers were not liable when chimney sweeps were killed by a leak of carbon monoxide gas when sealing a hole in a boiler. They should have been aware of the danger and ensured that the boiler was turned off. In *General Cleaning Contractors v Christmas*[133] the occupier was not liable when a window cleaner sustained injuries where a defective window caused him to fall from his ladder. The cleaner ought to have been aware of the risk. Where a person is injured or killed because of the faulty work of an independent contractor the occupier may be able to exclude liability if he can show that he took care in selecting the contractor and took reasonable steps to ensure that the work had been carried out properly. In *Haseldine v Daw*[134] the claimant was killed when a lift fell to the bottom of the shaft. The maintenance of the lift had been delegated to a reputable firm of specialist contractors and because of the technical nature of the process the occupiers could not be expected to check that the work had been carried out properly. There can be liability if the work is capable of being checked by the occupier with relative ease to ensure that it was satisfactory. There may also be situations where the occupier should check that the independent contractor is adequately insured. In *Kealey v Heard*[135] the owner of a number of houses, who was having them converted into flats, was held liable when a plasterer was injured because of faulty scaffolding erected by another (unknown) independent contractor. The court considered that the employer should have supervised the works as he had overall control of the building activities on the property and he had not discharged his duty by delegating the works to an independent contractor. In large scale construction projects an occupier would be expected to have the contractor's work supervised by a surveyor, engineer or architect as appropriate[136].

---

[129] [2000] 3 All ER 409
[130] [1955] 1 QB 450
[131] [1982] 81 LGR 460
[132] [1963] 1 WLR 1117
[133] [1953] AC 180
[134] [1941] 2KB 343
[135] [1983] 1 WLR 573
[136] See *A M F International v Magnet Bowling* [1968] 1 WLR 1028 and Paragraph 3.13

(C) Warnings and defences under the 1957 Act

A warning may absolve the occupier from liability in which case it discharges any duty of care which might have been owed by the occupier to the visitor. The warning must come from the occupier and it must be adequate in that it specifies the danger clearly so that the visitor can avoid it. The occupier's duty is to render the visitor safe rather than the premises. In *Rae v Mars (UK)*[137], where a surveyor was injured when inspecting a storehouse in a factory, it was suggested that if unusual dangers exist there should be additional warnings indicating the immediacy of the danger together with the possibility of additional safeguards such as barriers if they are appropriate. There is no duty on an occupier to warn of obvious dangers[138] but if the danger is not obvious the warning must be detailed enough for the occupier to put the visitor on guard for their own safety.

The following defences may have application to lawful visitors.

(a) Volenti

Where a visitor voluntarily accepts the risk and choses to enter the premises the defence of consent may be applicable.

(b) Contributory negligence

Visitors who fail to use reasonable care for their own safety may find their damages reduced when an apportionment takes place between the occupier and the visitor.

(c) Exclusion

An occupier may attempt to exclude liability by a notice communicated to a visitor or by a contractual term. Any limitation of liability by the occupier must be read subject to the Unfair Contract Terms Act 1977 in situations where there is 'business liability.' This includes professions and activities undertaken by central and local government. Any attempt to exclude liability for death or personal injury caused by negligence will not be upheld. In the case of property damage the stipulation will not be upheld unless it is reasonable in the circumstances. If lawful visitors have little option other than to enter the premises the occupier will find it difficult to exclude liability.

(D) Trespassers

Trespassers are not governed by the Occupiers Liability Act 1957. Historically, an occupier of premises owed no duty of care to trespassers. A trespasser may be injured by the steps that the occupier has taken to keep him out, by the

---

[137] [1990] 1 EGLR 161
[138] Cotton v Derbyshire Dales District Council [1994] EWCA Civ 17; *The Times* June 20 1994

condition of the premises or by an activity which is taking place on the land. An occupier is entitled to place static deterrents on the property such as broken glass[139] or to place spikes on top of a wall but must not create hidden dangers such as traps or manholes. At common law apart from having a duty not to deliberately inflict damage on trespassers an occupier was not liable for a trespasser's injuries. In *Addie v Dumbreck*[140] the defendant colliery owner was held to owe no duty of care towards a child trespasser who was crushed by haulage gear at a colliery. A significant development took place when the House of Lords introduced the concept of a 'duty of common humanity'. In the case of *British Railways Board v Herrington*[141] a six-year-old boy was electrocuted on a railway line after climbing through a fence which had not been properly maintained. Children regularly played near the line and railway staff were aware of their regular presence on the track. Local inhabitants also crossed the line as a short cut from one side of the railway embankment to the other. It was admitted that the boy was a trespasser but the House of Lords decided that the Board owed a duty to act with 'common humanity' towards child trespassers. They had not done so and were consequently liable. The Law Lords appeared anxious to lay down a standard higher than the common law position but not as high as the duty to take reasonable care owed under the Occupiers Liability Act 1957. Liability would arise if the occupier knew of the danger, and the likelihood of the trespass, in addition to having the ability and resources to prevent the accident. The case was subjected to critical reviews and comments and the problem of the relationship between trespassers and occupiers was referred to the Law Commission. The report of the Commission (No. 75) formed the basis of the Occupiers Liability Act 1984.

(E) The Occupiers Liability Act 1984

The Act applies to all persons other than lawful visitors. In addition to trespassers it will include those using a private right of way. Those using a public highway are specifically excluded. It does not apply to claims in respect of lost or damaged property. The Act does not provide that an occupier automatically owes a duty of care to trespassers. An occupier will only owe a duty of care to a trespasser if s.1 [3] of the 1984 Act is satisfied. For the section to apply the occupier must:

- Be aware of the danger or have reasonable grounds to know it exists.
- Know, or have reasonable grounds to believe, the trespasser is in the vicinity of the danger or is likely to come into the vicinity.
- The risk is one against which he may reasonably be expected to offer to the other person some protection.

The tests centre around the requirement for reasonable behaviour by the occupier and in the few cases that have been dealt with by the courts, s.1 [3] has been

---

[139] *Clayton v Deane* (1817) Taunt 489
[140] [1929] AC 358
[141] [1972] AC 877

interpreted in the context of 'common humanity.' The standard expected of the occupier will vary from case to case. Important factors are the character of the trespass, where it has taken place and the likelihood of injury. The greater the risk, the more precautions the occupier will have to take. Is the trespasser a stranger to the locality who has lost his way or a burglar inspecting a target property? Certain premises, such as railway lines and construction sites, require greater supervision than a private residence.

There are few examples of successful claims based on the Act. A number of cases concern swimming accidents[142]. In 'Tomlinson', the defendant local authority owned a park which included a lake. Warning signs which prohibited swimming were erected by the defendants because of the dangerous condition of the water. It was known that people did swim in the lake so the local authority decided to make the lake inaccessible to the public. The work was delayed due to lack of funds. The claimant, aged eighteen, jumped into the lake and was severely injured when he struck his head. The Law Lords took the view that the claimant had chosen to run the risk of his injuries and, in any case, a reasonable occupier ought not to be obliged to go to the financial cost of avoiding the danger. In *Higgs v* Foster[143] a police officer who trespassed on premises, while on surveillance of suspected criminals, fell into an inspection pit and was seriously injured. He failed in a claim for personal injuries as the occupier could not have suspected his presence or that he would enter the area via the pit.

(F) Warnings and defences under the 1984 Act

s.1 [5] of the 1984 Act covers warnings. Any warning notice will discharge the duty as far as adults are concerned. In the case of children it depends on age as to whether or not they can read or understand it.

The following defences may have application to trespassers.

(a) Volenti

s.1 [6] of the 1984 Act preserves the defence of consent. In *Ratcliffe v McConnell*[144] a trespasser dived into the shallow end of a swimming pool and was injured. He disregarded an appropriate warning notice and was taken to have accepted the risk.

(b) Contributory negligence

Although not specifically referred to in the Occupiers Liability Act 1984 the defence would apply.

---

[142] *Tomlinson v Congleton Borough Council* [2003] 3 WLR 705; *Donoghue v Folkstone Properties* [2003] EWCA Civ 231; *Rhind v Astbury Water Park* [2004] EWCA Civ 756
[143] [2004] EWCA Civ 843
[144] [1999] 1 WLR 670

3.6.12   The Defective Premises Act 1972

Those who instruct construction professionals to carry out building works, relating to residential dwellings, may wish to consider whether this Act can assist them. Frequent problems, in a construction context, are latent defects and faulty workmanship. Where a builder is carrying out work he may incur negligence liability. If the builder is also the owner of the property and transfers the title to a new owner there is no liability. A series of cases from *Dutton v Bognor Regis UDC*[145] attempted to extend the liability of the builder in respect of damage to the building itself but the decision in *Murphy v Brentwood DC*[146] emphasised that such damage would be considered to be purely economic in nature and therefore not recoverable. A claimant may sue for personal injury, or damage to property on account of latent defects, but this is rarely the core issue. Consequently, the provision in s.3 of the 1972 Act which made it possible to bring proceedings, even though the building had been disposed of, is not of great practical importance.

S.1 of the Act imposes the principal obligation to build dwellings properly. Any person involved in construction activities owes a duty to ensure that the work is carried out in a workmanlike manner, and with proper materials, so that the dwelling will be fit for human habitation when completed. The Act applies to a wider range of individuals than the builder. Architects are included but those exercising simply inspection or valuation functions will not be. The enactment is narrow in operation. It only applies to 'dwellings'. Commercial premises are excluded. It excludes those dwellings which are subject to 'approved schemes' such as NHBC. The effect is that virtually all new domestic properties will be excluded. The limitation period is a strict six years from completion, unless alterations are required, in which case time runs from the date when the rectification work is completed. The provision is really only of use in connection with extensions and conversions to existing properties. It seems that where there are a number of defects it is necessary to consider the effects of the defects as a whole and that minor defects will not give rise to liability under the Act unless they render the premises dangerous or unsuitable for habitation[147].

3.6.13   Limitation of actions in negligence

The Limitation Act 1980 governs claims in the law of tort. A claim in negligence is statute-barred unless brought within six years from the date on which the cause of action accrued. As an exception, s.11 of the 1980 Act requires a personal injury action to be brought within three years. One problem is that of hidden or latent damage. This is damage which only manifests itself some time after the limitation period has expired. The modern law on limitation, in negligence cases, dates from *Cartledge v Jopling and Sons Ltd*[148]. This case affirmed the position that a cause of action accrued at the date when the damage or injury took place and not when it was discovered. Shortly after this decision the Limitation Act 1963 was enacted

---

[145] Paragraph 3.6.1
[146] Paragraph 3.6.1
[147] *Bole and another v Huntsbuild and another* [2009] EWHC 483
[148] [1963] AC 758

to allow claimants, in personal injury cases, additional time in which to bring actions. The issue arose in *Sparham-Souter v Town & Country Developments [Essex] Ltd*[149]. This was a defective foundations case which involved claims against the builders of houses and the local authority. The Court of Appeal took the view that the 'reasonable discovery' test was applicable. The cause of action accrued when the damage was discovered by the injured party, or ought to have been, if the claimant had acted with due diligence. These rules were developed in the now discredited decision in *Anns v Merton LBC*[150]. Some years later the decision in *Pirelli General Cable Works v Oscar Faber & Partners*[151] overruled the reasonable discovery test. The case concerned a chimney which developed cracks and had to be replaced. The chimney was built in 1969 and the claimant discovered the damage in 1977.The Law Lords decided that the cause of action accrued when damage occurred to the building regardless of whether it was discoverable at that time. The claim failed and was statute barred. In 1984 the Law Reform Committee published their report titled 'Latent Damage'[152].

(A) The Latent Damage Act 1986

The Act was a compromise between the '*Sparham-Souter*' and '*Pirelli*' positions. The primary limitation period is six years from the date when the cause of action accrued. This is the date when the damage occurred. A claimant who cannot satisfy that provision has an alternative time period in which to bring a claim. The period is three years from the date when the damage was discovered or ought to have been discovered. This secondary limitation period is subject to a longstop provision. It provides that an action for damages for negligence cannot be brought more than fifteen years from the date on which any act or omission alleged to constitute negligence occurred. This provision does not apply to personal injury claims. These limitation rules only apply to claims in respect of damages. If an equitable remedy is sought, such as a claim for an injunction, the maxims of equity will apply and the remedy must be claimed as soon as is reasonably possible.

3.6.14 *Defences to negligence*

In negligence actions, apart from showing that one of the essential elements of the tort is missing, the defendant may allege that the claimant has consented to run the risk of the damage that has been sustained. This acts as a bar to the action. Nowadays, the courts tend to prefer to invoke the defence of contributory negligence, on the defendant's part, where appropriate. Sometimes the unlawful conduct of the claimant will act as a defence. This may arise where the claimant, when injured or killed, was involved in some unlawful activity and it would not be reasonable to impose a duty of care on the defendant.

---

[149] [1976] QB 858
[150] [1978] AC 728; see Paragraph 3.6.1
[151] [1983] 2 AC 1
[152] [Cmnd 9390 November 1984]

(A) 'Volenti non fit injuria' (Consent)

This is a complete defence. It arises where the claimant knows of the risk involved, understands the nature and degree of it and freely accepts it. If the claimant has no option but to accept the risk it will not apply. There must be a genuine free choice. A rescuer does not necessarily accept a risk voluntarily.

In *Haynes v Harwood*[153] a policeman was injured when he attempted to stop a runaway horse. He did not act voluntarily because he was under a duty to try and protect the public by stopping the animal. Volenti was not applicable. This case is contrasted with *Cutler v United Dairies*[154] where a private individual attempted to calm a horse which was unlikely to harm anyone. The claimant was injured but it was held that he had freely consented to run the risk and the defence succeeded.

(B) Contributory negligence

The defence applies where a claimant suffers damage due to their own negligence as well as through the negligence of the defendant. Until 1945 it was a complete defence and no damages were payable if it succeeded. The effect of proving contributory negligence is to reduce the damages awarded to the claimant. In practice, the claimant's damages are reduced to the extent that the court considers him liable for the loss suffered. The defendant must show that the claimant failed to take reasonable care for his own safety and contributed to his own loss. Common practical examples are where passengers in vehicles fail to wear safety belts[155] and motor cyclists fail to wear crash helmets[156]. In *Wheeler v Copas*[157] the claimant bricklayer's damages were reduced by fifty per cent when he was injured by falling off a ladder which he had borrowed. The ladder was very 'flimsy' and not suitable for carrying heavy building materials.

3.7 Nuisance

Nuisance comes in two main forms: private and public. Private nuisance is an established tort while public nuisance is primarily a criminal offence which causes danger or inconvenience to the public at large. When a public nuisance occurs it may also give rise to a claim for civil remedies by a claimant who has suffered 'special damage'. Environmental legislation also gives local authorities powers to proceed quickly when a nuisance situation is likely to affect the health of people in a particular locality. This is known as a statutory nuisance. There is another tort which is concerned with the manner in which land is used which has tended to overlap with private nuisance. This is the rule in the case of *Rylands v Fletcher*[158].

---

[153] [1935] 1 KB 146 Paragraph 3.3
[154] [1933] 2 KB 297 Paragraph 3.3
[155] *Froom v Butcher* [1976] QB 286
[156] *O'Connell v Jackson* [1972] 1 QB 72
[157] [1981] 3 All ER 305; see Paragraph 3.3
[158] (1868) LR 3 HL 330

The decision was traditionally seen as an attempt to impose strict liability on landowners who damage their neighbour's land. In modern times it has become established that to be liable the perpetrator of this tort must be able to foresee the likelihood of its occurrence. Liability for the consequences of allowing it to take place is strict[159].

3.7.1 Private nuisance

A private nuisance is an indirect interference with a person's use or enjoyment of land. It is a tort which protects a person from interference with the land which he occupies. The tort was developed in the nineteenth century in an attempt to give claimants a remedy where their land, or buildings, became affected by the problems which had been exacerbated by the industrial revolution and the growth of manufacturing industry. The law attempts to strike a balance between allowing persons to use their land as they wish and the rights of persons not to be affected by the actions of their neighbours.

(A) The nature of the interference

The nuisance may consist of the defendant allowing some item to enter the claimant's property or, more commonly, by an activity taking place on the defendant's land which affects the claimant on his land. The essence of the tort is a 'state of affairs' that is continuous or recurrent but which is indirect in nature. Dirt, smells and noise are common situations that have been litigated.

Allowing a dilapidated wall to fall on a neighbour's land has constituted a nuisance[160]. Allowing water to flow on to neighbouring land because of a blocked drain has also been actionable[161]. In *Lemmon v Webb*[162] the defendant committed a nuisance where he allowed tree roots to spread to neighbouring land from his own property. In *Laws v Florinplace Ltd*[163] the operation of a sex shop in a residential area was deemed to be a nuisance.

(B) The parties to the action

Private nuisance protects the occupier's use and enjoyment of land. A claimant needs to have an interest in the land affected in order to bring a case. This would enable a freeholder, or leaseholder, to bring an action but not a licensee. The principle was derived from *Malone v Laskey*[164] where the wife of a tenant of premises could not sue in private nuisance where damage was caused by vibrations which emanated from machinery belonging to the defendants. Some doubts as to

---

[159] See *Cambridge Water v Eastern Counties Leather* [1994] 2 WLR 53; *Transco plc v Stockport Metropolitan Council* [2003] UKHL 61
[160] *Brew Brothers v Snax Ltd* [1970] 1 All ER 587
[161] *Sedleigh-Denfield v O'Callaghan* [1940] AC 880
[162] (1894) 3 Ch 1
[163] [1981] 1 All ER 659
[164] [1907] 2KB 141

whether the rule still applied arose in 1993 when *Khorasandijan v Bush*[165] was decided. This case concerned harassment, in the form of telephone calls, brought by a daughter living in her mother's house. An injunction was granted despite the fact that the daughter had no legal interest in the property. The requirement to have a legal interest was revived in *Hunter and Others v Canary Wharf*[166] and applied in *Delaware Mansions Ltd v Westminster City Council*[167]. Courts in the future may find themselves not bound by this rule where it is found to be in conflict with Article 8 of the European Convention on Human Rights[168]. A nuisance may continue over a period of time and its effects can be felt by successive owners or occupiers of the same property. It is established law that an occupier can sue in respect of a private nuisance even though it started before he went into occupation.

There are three potential defendants in an action for private nuisance. The person primarily liable for the nuisance is its creator. In most cases this is the occupier of the land. The defendant need not have an interest in the land where the activity takes place[169]. Liability may be incurred even though actual occupation of the land has ceased and entry onto the land to abate the nuisance is not possible. Most nuisance actions are brought against the occupier of the offending land. This will cover a freeholder and, where appropriate, any tenant in occupation. If the nuisance is due to the activities of an independent contractor the occupier may still be liable if the activity carries with it a special risk that a nuisance may be caused to neighbours[170]. An occupier may also be liable if the nuisance is caused by a trespasser where the occupier adopts the nuisance for his own purposes or knows of its existence but fails to take reasonable steps to abate it. In *Sedleigh-Denfield v O'Callaghan*[171] the defendants were liable because they ought to have known that land had been flooded as a result of a trespasser's acts and taken appropriate steps to get rid of the nuisance. This principle has been extended to cover dangerous states of affairs which arise naturally[172]. If the premises are leased the tenant will primarily be liable. If the landlord creates a nuisance, and then lets the property, or authorises the tenant to commit or continue a nuisance, liability may be incurred by the freeholder. The authorisation may be express or implied or by acquiescence[173].

(C) The loss suffered

Most torts are either actionable *per se* or require harm or damage to have been suffered by the claimant. Private nuisance is different. Where physical damage to

---

[165] [1993] 3 WLR 476
[166] [1997] 2 WLR 684. See also *Crown River Cruises Ltd v Kimbolton Fireworks Ltd* [1996] 2 Lloyds Reports 533
[167] [2001] UKHL 55
[168] See *McKenna v British Aluminium* [2002] Env LR 30
[169] *Esso Petroleum Co Ltd v Southport Corporation* [1956] AC 218; *Hussain v Lancaster City Council* [2000] QB 1
[170] *Honeywill & Stein v Larkin Bros Ltd* [1934] 1 KB 191; *Matania v National Provincial Bank* [1936] 2 All ER 633
[171] [1940] 3 All ER 349
[172] *Goldman v Hargrave* [1966] 2 All ER 989; *Leakey v National Trust* [1980] 1 All ER 17
[173] *Harris v James* (1876) 45LJQB 545; *Mowlan v Wandsworth LBC* [2001] EGCS 4

the land has taken place a fairly minor interference is sufficient to constitute the tort. In the absence of physical damage a claimant may rely on personal discomfort as the basis of the claim. The discomfort must be substantial and that should be judged by 'plain and simple notions'[174]. Where interference with the enjoyment of land is alleged the claim is said to be based on 'amenity damage.' Even if there is no physical damage, a court can award compensation for annoyance and discomfort. In *St Helens Smelting Co v Tipping*[175] the claimant purchased a large estate some distance from the defendant's copper works. The works prospered and became busier. The emission of fumes from the factory left most of the vegetation in the area dead and injured the claimant's livestock. The court, finding in favour of the claimant, made the distinction between actual physical damage to property and interference with the enjoyment of property. It was confirmed that proof of a substantial level of interference is required in the latter case. The law of nuisance does not protect the right to a view[176] or the right to light[177] in the absence of an easement. Moreover, the courts are loathe to protect what they perceive as being purely recreational activities[178].

(D) Ingredients of a successful action

The principal function of the law, in private nuisance cases, is to balance the competing interests of neighbouring occupiers and to decide at what point an interference becomes intolerable and therefore actionable. The law tries to strike a balance between allowing persons to use their land as they wish and the right of persons not to be affected by the actions of their neighbours. Central to the tort are the concepts of indirect interference and reasonableness. Private nuisance is a form of action against unreasonable behaviour. Not every interference constitutes a nuisance. The longer the interference lasts and the greater its extent the more likely that it will constitute a nuisance. In *Southwark LBC v Mills & Others*[179] cases were brought by council tenants who lived in blocks of flats against their landlords complaining of noise from adjoining occupiers. As lack of sound proofing in the flats was the principal cause of the problem, and not the day to day noise caused by individual tenants, the claims failed. The amount of interference is relevant. Where building works of a temporary nature, such as conversions or demolition, are carried out with a reasonable degree of care so as not to cause undue inconvenience to neighbouring properties, no tort is committed. If the interference can be avoided fairly easily the claimant may have a remedy. In *De Keyser's Royal Hotel Ltd v Spicer Bros Ltd*[180] the claimant hotel proprietor successfully applied for an injunction to prevent pile driving operations taking place at night.

---

[174] *Walter v Selfe* (1851) 4 De G & Sm 315 per Lord Knight Bruce VC
[175] (1865) 11 HL Cas 642
[176] *Att-Gen v Doughty* (1752) 2 Ves Sen 453
[177] *Dalton v Angus* (1881) 6 App Cas 740
[178] *Bridlington Relay Ltd v Yorkshire Electricity Board* [1965] Ch 36
[179] [1999] 2 WLR 742
[180] [1914]] 30 TLR 257; see also *Andrae v Selfridge* [1937] 3 All ER 255

When considering whether or not an actionable nuisance has taken place the courts take into account a number of factors.

(a) Foreseeability of harm

In *Cambridge Water Co Ltd v Eastern Counties Leather plc*[181] it was confirmed that foreseeability of harm of the relevant kind is an essential ingredient of the tort of private nuisance. Lord Goff stated that 'foreseeability of harm is indeed a prerequisite of the recovery of damages in......nuisance'[182]. The difficulties involved in proving foreseeability of harm of the 'relevant type' are well illustrated by *Savage v Fairclough*[183] where, in an action based on private nuisance against a pig farmer for alleged contamination of spring water by use of nitrates, the court held that a hypothetical good farmer would not have been able to see that application of fertilizers would have resulted in a real risk of contamination to the water.

(b) Locality

Different standards apply in different localities. Occupiers in urban and industrial areas are expected to put up with more discomfort than those in residential areas while those in agricultural areas are expected to embrace the characteristics of the countryside[184]. In *Sturges v Bridgman* Lord Justice Thesiger remarked 'What would be a nuisance in Belgrave Square would not necessarily be so in Bermondsey'[185]. In practice locality is only relevant in cases of interference with the enjoyment of land where a claim is being made in respect of amenity loss. If there has been actual physical damage to property, the character of the neighbourhood is irrelevant[186].

(c) Duration of the nuisance

The act complained of must have an element of continuity or repetition before it can become actionable. There must be a state of affairs which repeatedly affects the claimant's land. A single escape, or activity, is not sufficient unless the act is evidence of a dangerous situation which results from a continuing state of affairs.

In *Midwood v Corporation & Mayor of Manchester*[187] the claimant recovered in nuisance for losses caused by a single escape of gas. In *Spicer v Smee*[188] defective wiring in the defendant's bungalow caused a fire which spread to the claimant's property. Liability in private nuisance was imposed on the defendant. In *Crown River Cruises Ltd v Kimbolton Fireworks Ltd*[189] the claimant's barge was badly

---

[181] [1994] 2 WLR 53

[182] [1994] 2 WLR at page 72

[183] [2000] Env LR 183

[184] *Halsey v Esso Petroleum Co Ltd* [1961] 2 All ER 145; *Laws v Florinplace Ltd* [1981] 1 All ER 659

[185] (1879) 11 Ch D at page 87

[186] *St Helens Smelting Co v Tipping* (1865) 11 HL Cas 642

[187] [1905] 2 KB 597

[188] [1946] 1 All ER 489

[189] [1996] 2 Lloyds Rep 533

damaged by a fire which had come about as a consequence of the defendant's fireworks display.

(d) Sensitivity

Where land is put to a use which is abnormally sensitive to factors such as heat or vibrations the defendant will escape liability. In *Robinson v Kilvert*[190] the claimant used the ground floor of premises for stacking brown paper which required special methods of storage if it was not to deteriorate. The defendant caused heat from a boiler in the cellar to escape to the ground floor where it damaged the paper. The defendant was not liable as the heat was not unreasonable and it was the nature of the paper which had caused the damage.

The rule also has application where a person is abnormally sensitive to a particular state of affairs. In *Heath v Mayor of Brighton*[191] noise from a power station which disturbed a church minister, when conducting services, was held not to be actionable as it appeared to have no effect on anybody else.

(e) Utility of the defendant's act

It is no defence that the act complained of is for the benefit of the public at large. The courts have to balance private interests against the public benefit. In *Adams v Ursell*[192] the smell from a fried fish shop led to its closure even though it was recognised that it supplied good food in a poor neighbourhood. Likewise, in *Bellew v Cement Co*[193] the only cement factory in Ireland was closed on nuisance grounds. In more modern times there have been some indications that the courts may take social utility into account when deciding whether or not to grant an injunction to stop the offending activity completely or to restrict the times when it can operate[194].

(f) Malice

Improper motive is not an ingredient of private nuisance but its existence may be evidence of unreasonable behaviour. Evidence to show that the defendant is acting from a malicious motive will assist the claimant. In *Christie v Davy*[195] the defendant banged a tray, and other items, on the dividing wall between two semi-detached houses in order to disrupt the claimant who gave music lessons. His malice was held to render the noise actionable as a nuisance. In *Hollywood Silver Fox Farm Ltd v Emmett*[196] the defendant sent his son to fire a shotgun, in the vicinity of the claimant's land, to interfere with the breeding of foxes for the fur trade which was

---

[190] (1889) 41 Ch D 88
[191] (1908) LT 718
[192] [1913] 1 Ch 269
[193] [1948] Ir Rep 61
[194] See *Dunton v Dover District Council* [1977] 76 LGR 87; *Miller v Jackson* [1977] 3 All ER 338; *Kennaway v Thompson* [1980] 3 All ER 329
[195] [1893] 1 Ch 316
[196] [1936] 2KB 468

the claimant's business. This was an actionable nuisance and an injunction was granted to restrain the defendant in the future.

(E) Remedies

(a) Damages

If the defendant is liable the claimant is entitled to claim damages which can include consequential losses as long as they are foreseeable. This includes any losses sustained because of physical damage to the land and any business losses. Any decrease in the value of the land is recoverable. In *Hunter v Canary Wharf Ltd*[197] it was stated that damages should be measured by the effect which the nuisance has on the value of the land. It was also stated, by a majority of judges, that damages for personal injury could not be recovered in private nuisance[198]. Where an injunction is claimed, as in the vast majority of private nuisance actions, the court has a discretion to refuse the injunction and award damages instead. This is an order for damages in lieu of injunction[199].

(b) Injunction

This is the principal remedy claimed, in the majority of cases, and it requires the offending activity to be terminated. It will normally be granted except where the offending activity is slight or irregular in occurrence. It is an equitable remedy and therefore discretionary in nature. An injunction may be perpetual in which case the activity must be stopped completely or it may be partial in which case time limits will be imposed on when the activity can take place. A good example of the latter arose in *Kennaway v Thompson*[200] where the Court of Appeal put a limit on the times when a motor boat club could hold their activities. This case is also a good example of the rule that 'coming to the nuisance' is no defence. Where a claimant is aware of a nuisance, but voluntarily comes to a situation where it exists, that does not provide a sustainable defence to the defendant[201]. In *Dennis v Ministry of Defence*[202] the claimants owned a country house, with adjoining land, in the vicinity of an airbase where pilots were trained to fly jet aircraft. The claimants alleged that the noise involved in these operations amounted to a nuisance and a successful claim was brought for the decrease in the value of the land due to the nuisance.

(c) Abatement

A claimant may stop the nuisance by remedying the cause. This is the process of self-help. Cutting back overhanging branches or foliage are examples. The

---

[197] [1997] 2 All ER 426
[198] See also *Transco plc v Stockport MDC* [2003] UKHL 61
[199] See *Shelfer v City of London Electric Lighting Co* [1895] 1 Ch 287
[200] [1980] 3 WLR 361
[201] See *Sturges v Bridgman* (1879) 11 Ch D 852; *Miller v Jackson* [1977] QB 966
[202] [2003] EWHC 793

claimant must ensure that no unnecessary damaged is caused and no damage is inflicted on an innocent third party. Unless there is an emergency, the offending occupier should be informed and given a reasonable time to remedy the situation. Care should be taken when exercising this remedy as the abator may find that they have become a trespasser or caused a breach of the peace.

(F) Defences

The general defences of 'volenti' and contributory negligence will apply but where the claimant's action is based on the unreasonable use of land by the defendant they are of little relevance.

The following specific defences may have application.

(a) Prescription

Prescription means long use. The continuance of a private nuisance, for at least twenty years, entitles the defendant to exercise the nuisance as long as the claimant was aware of the nuisance before the twenty year period began and an actionable nuisance has existed throughout that time. The leading case is *Sturges v Bridgman*[203] where the claimant doctor built a consulting room at the end of his garden and complained of noise and vibrations from a confectioner who had been in the business of manufacturing sweets for over twenty years. The defendant's argument that he had been pursuing his trade for more than the prescription period failed because the interference did not become actionable, as a nuisance, until the claimant extended his waiting room to be adjacent to the defendant's premises.

(b) Statutory authority

Where the act which gives rise to the nuisance is authorised by statute that authority will give the defendant a defence if it can be shown that the interference with the claimant's rights was permitted, expressly or impliedly, by the statute. What the alleged defendant is authorised to do, or not do, depends on the interpretation of the specific provisions[204].

(c) Planning permission

Where a local authority grants planning permission for development within its area, and authorises a change in the character of land, the consent may act as a defence, in a similar way to statutory authority, but only if it is the consequence of the permission being granted. In *Gillingham BC v Medway [Chatham] Dock Co Ltd*[205] planning permission was granted to operate a busy commercial dock enterprise twenty-four hours each day. Heavy lorries passed through the residential neighbourhood surrounding the commercial dock. The local authority's

---

[203] (1879) 11 Ch D 852
[204] *Allen v Gulf Refining* [1981] AC 1001
[205] [1993] QB 343

attempt to obtain an injunction failed. If the planning permission does not change the character of the neighbourhood a nuisance may arise and it was emphasised in *Wheeler v Saunders Ltd* that as a general rule planning permission does not act as a defence[206]. In *Derek Watson v Promosport Ltd*[207] the claimants brought an action based on nuisance against the defendants who operated a motor racing circuit. The defendants had permission for the designated use subject to conditions. The court took the view that a change in the character of the area would be found if there had been a 'strategic' planning decision affected by considerations of public interest.

3.7.2 Public nuisance

Public nuisance is primarily a criminal offence. It arises where a nuisance-like activity affects a section of the public or where there is an interference with the exercise of public rights. A single act may be sufficient to incur liability. Public nuisance is concerned with interferences with the lives and activities of a community although a private individual may bring an action in tort if they can prove so called 'special damage'. There is no requirement for the public nuisance to have any connection with the actual use of the land. It is not possible to indicate how many people need to be affected before an action can be brought as this is an issue of fact in each case depending upon how any representative cross-section of the population in the particular locality is affected[208]. It may well be that a particular set of circumstances gives rise to claims both in private and public nuisance[209].

(A) Examples

Public nuisance covers a diverse set of activities. By far the most common situation where it arises is in connection with the highway. A temporary obstruction of the highway is unlikely to be actionable unless it can be proved that it is unreasonable. In *Trevett v Lee*[210] the defendant was required to use a hosepipe to connect his premises to the water supply as there was no mains connection. The claimant, who suffered personal injury when tripping over the pipe, failed in his claim as the defendant's conduct was considered to be reasonable. Other highway examples include picketing on the road[211], positioning a tee on a golf course in such a position that golfers hit balls onto a nearby highway[212], and organising a pop festival in such a way that it causes traffic congestion, noise and general inconvenience to the public at large[213]. It is a public nuisance to allow property to fall into such a state that users of the highway are endangered. In such circumstances

---

[206] [1996] Ch 16
[207] [2008] EWHC 759
[208] See *Att-Gen v PYA Quarries* [1957] 1 All ER 894
[209] See *Halsey v Esso Petroleum Co Ltd* [1961] 1 WLR 683
[210] [1955] 1 All ER 406
[211] *Thomas v National Union of Mineworkers* [1985] 2 All ER 1
[212] *Castle v St Augustine's Links* [1922] 38 TLR 615
[213] *Att-Gen of Ontario v Orange Productions Ltd* [1971] DLR 257

liability would appear to be strict[214]. A defendant cannot avoid liability by delegating tasks to independent contractors where danger arises from works being carried out to the highway or from the state of the highway itself. Damage caused by something falling onto a highway can be a public nuisance. An owner of land adjoining a highway is liable for injuries caused by the collapse of a natural projection, such as a tree, if he knew of the defect or ought to have known of it[215]. In the case of an artificial projection, such as a lamp or a hoarding, liability is strict[216]. The sale of food and drinks which are not pure have been deemed to amount to a public nuisance[217]. In *Dollman v Hillman Ltd*[218] a successful claim was made where the claimant suffered injury because of fat left on the pavement outside a butcher's shop. In *R v Johnson*[219] the making of obscene telephone calls to a large number of women constituted public nuisance while in *R v Rimmington*[220] there was no public nuisance committed when the actions of the defendant caused no common injury to a section of the public. In this case over five hundred packages were sent to members of the public containing racially offensive material. The addressees were chosen at random and on an ad hoc basis.

(B) Proving special damage

Unless a claimant can prove special damage there will be no civil cause of action available. This is damage over and above the inconvenience and annoyance suffered by the public at large. If it cannot be established there will only be the possibility of criminal liability on the defendant's part. Before special damage can be proved the loss to the claimant needs to be of a different variety than that suffered by other individuals or there needs to be a significant difference in the extent of the damage. In *Benjamin v Storr*[221] the proprietor of a coffee house was affected by horses and carts, belonging to the defendant, which obstructed the highway outside his premises and blocked out light from all the shops in the row. The claimant could prove special damage, in excess of the other businesses, as customers had difficulty reaching the coffee house and the smell of the horses put customers off visiting the premises. Likewise in *Halsey v Esso Petroleum Co Ltd*[222] smuts from the defendant's oil depot caused actual damage to the claimant's car and the noise from the oil tankers caused him to have sleepless nights. The claimant was able to prove that he had suffered more than other residents who had been affected by the defendant's activities. Special damage may also arise where the nuisance results in the claimant having to incur greater expenditure. In *Rose v Miles*[223] the defendant obstructed a creek thereby trapping the claimant's barges.

---

[214] *Wringe v Cohen* [1940] 1 KB 229
[215] *Noble v Harrison* [1926] 2 KB 332
[216] *Tarry v Ashton* (1876) 1 QB 314
[217] *AB v South West Water Services* [1993] 1 All ER 609
[218] [1941] 1 All ER 355
[219] [1997]] 1 WLR 367
[220] [2006] 1 AC 459
[221] (1874) LR 9 CP 400
[222] [1961] 1 WLR 683
[223] (1815) 4 M & S 101

The claimant was able to recover the cost of unloading the cargoes from the barges and transporting the items by land. Similarly, in *Tate & Lyle Industries v GLC*[224] the defendants received a licence to operate ferry terminals on the River Thames. The claimants had a new jetty constructed by the river from where they loaded sugar onto merchant ships. Because of an abundance of silt on the river bed, caused by the construction of the ferry terminals, the claimants had to spend a considerable amount of money having the riverbed dredged to remove the obstruction. The claimants successfully sued for special damage. In *News Group Newspapers v Society of Graphical Trades etc.*[225] the cost of providing transport and extra security for workers was recoverable as damages in public nuisance.

(C) Remedies

Although public nuisance is primarily a criminal matter it is possible, in some circumstances, for damages to be claimed by an individual. The case is brought in the name of the Attorney General who in such circumstances is acting as the upholder of public rights. The claim for damages is known as a relator action. This enables an injunction to be obtained on behalf of those affected by the nuisance. An alternative is for the local authority to apply for the injunction on behalf of the local community. In *Hunter v Canary Wharf*[226] doubt was raised as to whether damages for personal injury which had resulted from public nuisance could be recovered. In *Corby Group Litigation v Corby BC*[227] the Court of Appeal confirmed that damages for personal injuries can be recovered in public nuisance cases.

(D) Defences

The principal general defences are applicable and the defence of statutory authority. Prescription does not apply to public nuisance.

3.7.3 Nuisance and human rights

As with other areas of the law the Human Rights Act 1998, which invoked the European Convention on Human Rights into English law, has been used to supplement existing domestic rights in the law of tort. In nuisance cases Article 8, which sets out the right to respect for family and private life, is the provision which claimants are likely to rely upon while the First Protocol of Article 1, which entitles every person to the peaceful enjoyment of his possessions, is sometimes relevant as well. In the handful of cases that have been decided, with a human rights element, claimants have not progressed very well. In *Marcic v Thames Water Utilities Ltd*[228] the claimant brought an action against the defendants, in nuisance, in circumstances where the appropriate remedy would have been to seek an enforcement

---

[224] [1983] 2 AC 509
[225] [1987] ICR 181
[226] [1997] 2 All ER 426
[227] [2008] EWCA Civ 463
[228] [2003] UKHL 66

order issued by the water industry regulator against the defendant. Mr Marcic lived in a house which was regularly flooded with foul water from a sewer belonging to the defendants. Because of intensive building in the locality the sewers were no longer adequate to do their job. The House of Lords considered there was no valid claim in private nuisance nor was there any infringement of Article 8. The Law Lords took the view, as in the earlier case of *Hatton v United Kingdom*[229], that there must be a balance struck between the public interest and the rights of claimants, and that in both cases there had been no breach of the claimant's rights. A similar approach was taken in *Dennis v Ministry of Defence*[230] where the claimants successfully pleaded nuisance and an interference with Article 8 rights. Damages were awarded in respect of the decrease in the value of the claimant's land but the court refused to grant an injunction to restrict flight training from RAF Wittering. The public interest in Harrier pilots continuing to be trained at the airbase exceeded the rights of individuals to peaceful enjoyment of their land.

3.7.4 Statutory nuisance

Because the process of bringing actions based on private nuisance is so cumbersome, expensive and slow it was decided that the solution lay in putting the most common examples of nuisance into statutory form. The process dates from Victorian times when it was originally devised to deal with sanitation problems. The object of the law is to provide an expedited method of bringing nuisances to an end where the common law is too slow and where the activity is so serious that the cost should be borne by the local authority. Where a nuisance can be dealt with by this process it is known as a statutory nuisance. The current law is to be found in part 3 of the Environmental Protection Act 1990 (EPA). The system is operated by local authorities via their Environmental Health Officers (EHOS). By s.79 of the 1990 Act every local authority has a duty to inspect its areas for statutory nuisances and to take steps to abate them.

(A) How the system works

S79 Environmental Protection Act 1990 states the circumstances which give rise to a statutory nuisance:

- Premises.
- Smoke from premises.
- Fumes or gases from premises.
- Dust, steam or other effluvia, arising on industrial/business premises.
- Accumulations or deposits.
- Animals.
- Noise emitted from or caused by a vehicle, machinery or equipment in the street (Added by the Noise and Statutory Nuisance Act 1993).
- Any other matter declared by any enactment to be a statutory nuisance.

---

[229] [2003] 37 EHRR 28
[230] [2003] EWHC 793

(B) 'Prejudicial to health or a nuisance'

Before any of the above situations can constitute a statutory nuisance the circumstances complained of must be 'prejudicial to health or a nuisance.' This means that the act complained of must either be a nuisance (public or private), in the common law sense, or an actual threat to the health of persons affected by it[231]. At one time the courts interpreted this as being any personal discomfort or temporary inconvenience[232] but nowadays, if the first limb of the definition is being relied upon, it must be injurious to physical health whether actual or anticipated. In *Coventry City Council v Cartwright*[233] a rubbish dump owned by the local authority, in a residential area, was held not to be a statutory nuisance where there was no likelihood of disease or of vermin being attracted to it to spread disease.

(C) Abatement

If the local authority is considering taking enforcement action Environmental Health Officers will have to evaluate the extent to which the local population are being affected by the alleged statutory nuisance. In particular the nature and location of the activity together with its duration and utility will need to be considered. Any abatement notice must be served on the 'appropriate person'. It should require abatement of the nuisance or restrict its occurrence. It may require works to be carried out or other steps be taken to comply with the notice. The notice should also state the penalties for non-compliance with the notice. Once a person has been served with the notice any contravention of it, without reasonable excuse, renders that person guilty of a criminal offence. An appeal against the notice can be made to a magistrates court within twenty-one days. In limited circumstances it is a defence to show reasonable excuse. The test here is an objective one and is not available where the notice has been contravened deliberately or intentionally. Businesses and trades may put forward the defence of best practicable means in that they did the best they could to prevent or counteract the nuisance. Special defences apply to noise on construction sites.

3.7.5 Rylands v Fletcher

In this case, the defendant mill owner employed independent contractors to construct a reservoir on his land in order to supply water to run the mill. Unknown to the defendant, and the contractors, an old mine shaft lay underneath the land. When the reservoir was filled the water escaped through the unsealed shafts and flooded the claimant's coal mine. Although it was established that the defendant had not been negligent, and that the contractors were competent, the defendant was held to be liable.

---

[231] *National Coal Board v Thorne* [1976] 1 WLR 543
[232] *Betts v Penge UDC* [1942] 2 KB 154
[233] [1975] 1 WLR 845

The reason for the decision was stated as follows:

> 'A person who for his own purposes brings onto his land and collects and keeps there anything likely to do mischief if it escapes, must keep it in at his peril, and if he does not do so, is prima facie answerable for all the damage which is the natural consequence of its escape[234].

The decision, and the reasoning on which it was based, was upheld by the House of Lords[235]. In the higher court a qualification was made by Lord Cairns to the effect that the defendant was only liable if he brought the thing on to his land in the course of a non-natural use of the land. This qualification has been accepted in later cases as an essential part of the rule and, in practice, usually a considerable obstacle towards a successful claim.

It might appear that the courts in this case were developing a new principle of liability. Lord Goff in *Cambridge Water Company v Eastern Counties Leather plc*[236] suggested that the trial judge had not stated any new principle of law. Instead, he had simply extended the law of nuisance to cases of isolated escapes. Lord Goff took the view that 'Rylands' is for all practical purposes a variety of private nuisance and this is the reason why it is limited to protecting rights in and in connection with the enjoyment of land. There are few differences between the torts except that in nuisance it is not necessary to show an accumulation or non-natural use.

(A) Essentials of the tort

(a) Control of the land

The defendant must be in control of the land but need not have an interest in it. A licence is sufficient[237]. This would cover utilities contractors laying pipes, cables or sewers beneath the highway. In contrast, by analogy with the position in private nuisance, the established view is that a claimant must have an estate in land to have the necessary *locus standi* to bring the action.

(b) Accumulation

The item must not be naturally present on the land. The escape of vermin, weeds or rock from the defendant's land will not be actionable[238].

(c) Dangerous things

The defendant must have accumulated on his land an item that he realised would give rise to a high risk of danger or 'mischief' if it escaped. This has included

---

[234] *Rylands v Fletcher* (1866) LR 1 Exch 265 at 279 per Blackburn J
[235] (1868) LR 3HL 330
[236] [1994] 2 WLR at page 58
[237] *Charing Cross Electric Supply Co v Hydraulic Power Co* [1914] 3 KB 772; *Rainham Chemical Works Ltd v Belvedere Fish Guano Co Ltd* [1921] AC 465
[238] *Giles v Walker* (1890) 24 QBD 656; *Pontardawe RDC v Moore-Gwyn* [1929] 1 Ch 656

fire, water, oil, gas and electricity. A falling flagpole[239], fairground chair[240], and a landowner who allowed caravan dwellers to live in his field who 'escaped' and committed minor criminal offences within the locality[241] have come within the definition.

(d) Escape

There must be an escape from the place controlled or occupied by the defendant to other land. In *Read v Lyon*[242] the claimant munitions inspector was killed when a explosion took place in a shell-filling shop. As there was no escape from the premises there was no liability under the tort. Although the escape will normally be accidental the tort may cover intentional releases of dangerous things[243]. It may be that the 'thing' itself does not actually escape but the consequences of the event causes injury. In *Miles v Forest Rock Granite Co Ltd*[244] a blast of explosives on the defendant's land caused rocks to fall onto an adjoining highway resulting in damage.

(e) Non-natural use of land

The courts have traditionally refrained from laying down specific examples of what would be a natural use of land, and conversely what would be a non-natural one, preferring to consider the issue on a case by case basis. Modern courts have increasingly been ready to hold that a use is natural with the result that the defendant escapes liability. The issue was considered in the leading modern cases dealing with the tort[245]. In *Transco*[246] it was indicated that the use, to be non-natural, had to be something which is out of the ordinary in that place and at that time. The judges found that the supply of water for domestic purposes in large pipes did not amount to a non-natural use. A different result was reached in *LMS International v Styrene Packaging and Insulation*[247] where *Transco* was followed. The case concerns an explosion. In the process of manufacturing polystyrene, a spark ignited an inflammable gas at the defendant's factory and caused a fire damaging the claimant's premises. The process was deemed to be non-natural as it involved a high risk of such an incident happening.

(f) Foreseeability and damage

Originally *Rylands v Fletcher* was regarded as a strict liability tort. In practice it never has been because of the need to prove non-natural use and the availability

---

[239] *Shiffman v Order of St John* [1936] 1 All ER 557
[240] *Hale v Jennings* [1938] 1 All ER 679
[241] *Att-Gen v Corke* [1933] Ch 89
[242] [1947] AC 156
[243] *Crown River Cruises Ltd v Kimbolton Fireworks Ltd* [1996] 2 WLR 533
[244] [1918] 34 TLR
[245] *Cambridge Water v Eastern Counties Leather* [1994] 2 WLR 53; *Transco v Stockport MDC* [2003] UKHL
[246] Lord Bingham at page 687
[247] [2006] BLR 30

of specific defences. The case of *Cambridge Water v Eastern Counties Leather*[248] gave the first opportunity to review the law for many years. The case concerns the defendant leather manufacturers who in the process of greasing pelts for tanning purposes used toxic chemical solvents. Over a twenty-year period there were frequent spillages of the chemicals through the concrete floor in their warehouse where the solvents were stored. This had the effect of contaminating the local domestic water supply. When changes in the law required water companies to inspect their water resources the claimants made a routine inspection and discovered the contamination. As a consequence the water authority were forced to move their pumping station and tried to recover the cost of so doing from the defendants. An action was brought which included, inter alia, claims in private nuisance and in *Rylands v Fletcher*. It was stressed by the House of Lords that foreseeability of harm is a necessary requisite of any successful claim in either tort. On that basis the action failed. The case established that a defendant can only be liable for a type of damage which was reasonably foreseeable. If proved, a defendant will be liable for all the damage which is the natural consequence of the escape. Economic losses are not recoverable and the modern view is that damages for personal injuries are not recoverable under the rule[249].

(B) Defences

(a) Volenti

Where there is consent, express or implied, to the defendant bringing the substance or accumulation on to his land this will be a good defence in the absence of negligence. Consent is normally implied where the existence of the item offers some advantage to the claimant. A good example is buildings in multiple occupation where the presence of the item offers some benefit to the occupiers. Water tanks and sprinkler systems to protect buildings from fire have come within this category[250].

(b) Default of the claimant/contributory negligence

If the defendant contributes to the escape of the dangerous thing the claimant's damages will be reduced by an apportionment of liability under the Law Reform (Contributory Negligence) Act 1945. If the escape is entirely the fault of the claimant, or damage occurs because of the sensitivity of the claimant's property, it appears, by analogy with nuisance, that the defendant should not be liable[251].

---

[248] [1994] 2 WLR 53
[249] Lord Bingham in *Transco plc v Stockport MDC* [2003] UKHL at page 66
[250] *Carstairs v Taylor* (1871) LR 6 Exch 217; *Peters v Prince of Wales Theatre Ltd* [1943] KB 73
[251] *Eastern & South Africa Telegraph Co v Cape Town Tramways Co* [1902] AC 381; *Ponting v Noakes* [1894] 2 QB 281

(c) Statutory authority

Whether or not the defence applies is a matter of construction in each case. The issue is normally whether the defendant was acting under a duty. In *Green v Chelsea Waterworks*[252] the defendants were not liable when a water main burst as they were under a statutory duty to maintain a water supply. In *Charing Cross Electricity Co v Hydraulic Co*[253], on similar facts, the defendants were only acting under a power which did not oblige them to provide a water supply so the defence did not apply.

(d) Act of God

If the escape is a natural catastrophe which the defendant could not have foreseen or guarded against the defence might apply. In *Nichols v Marsland*[254] it was successfully pleaded in a destructive storm but in *Greenock Corporation v Caledonian Railway*[255], on similar facts, the court refused to accept the defence.

(e) Act of a stranger

If the escape is caused by the act of a third party over whom the defendant has no control there will be no liability. In practice it will be the actions of a trespasser. In *Box v Jubb*[256] the defence applied where a third party was responsible for causing a flood. A defendant may be liable in negligence if the act of the stranger is foreseeable.

3.8 Trespass

Although often associated with the criminal law trespass is a long established tort. Together with the torts of private nuisance and *Rylands v Fletcher* it protects interests in land. Another role of trespass is to protect a person's interest in their personal property while the rules relating to trespass to the person protect an individual's interest in their personal security. Trespass is the oldest of all the existing torts. All types of trespass are actionable *per se*. It is not necessary for a claimant to prove damage to succeed. Another feature relating to all categories of trespass is that any interference must be direct to be actionable. It is an intentional tort. If a defendant can show that he had no intention of entering upon the land then he has not committed the tort of trespass to land. Although statute has created criminal offences in connection with trespass to land such circumstances are rare[257]. There is a greater overlap with the criminal law in connection with trespass to the person particularly in connection with crimes of assault. Sometimes, other factors have to exist before there can be criminal as well as civil liability. Trespass to goods is a civil matter unless criminal intent can be shown. This section of the chapter will deal primarily with trespass to land.

---

[252] (1894) 70 LT 547
[253] [1914] 3 KB 772
[254] (1876) 2 Ex D 1
[255] [1917] AC 556
[256] (1876) 4 Ex D 76
[257] See Public Order Act 1986. Criminal Justice and Public Order Act 1994

3.8.1 Trespass to land

This tort is a direct interference upon land in the possession of the claimant. It can be contrasted with private nuisance where the interference is indirect. If your neighbour throws dead flowers or tree branches on to your land that is a trespass while if tree roots spread to your land from next door that will amount to nuisance[258].

The interference can occur in a number of ways but the most obvious methods are set out below.

(a) Entry onto the land by the defendant without the claimant's permission

The slightest crossing of the boundary is sufficient but there must be some contact with the fabric of the property.

(b) Directly causing objects to enter onto the claimant's land

Leaning a ladder against a wall on the claimant's land has been held to be a trespass[259]. Placing items on a boundary would be actionable. Throwing stones, dumping rubbish or placing projections over neighbouring land would come into this category. Shared driveways can be a problem. In *Anderson v Bryan*[260] the laying of a driveway over the holes in which fence posts had been placed amounted to a trespass. If there is contact with the claimant's property, that is sufficient to constitute a trespass. Leaning a bicycle against a shop window would be sufficient. It is not necessary to cross the actual boundary of the premises.

(c) Refusing to leave the land when asked to do so or abusing the position for which the visitor is present

A trespass may be intentional at its outset or it may arise where a person's lawful right to remain on land has been revoked. If the permission to be on the land has expired, or the right to be there has been withdrawn, a person will become a trespasser if they do not exit the land within a reasonable period of time. A similar result arises where a person originally enters land lawfully but then abuses the position for which they are there. A person who lawfully enters land to deliver post or goods may become a trespasser if they extend their visit by entering a garage or outhouse. This may have important consequences if they are injured by the state of the premises which they have entered without permission[261]. If the trespass is not an isolated incident, and it continues on a regular basis, it gives rise to a new cause of action from day to day as long as it lasts. This is known as a continuing trespass. It arises where a person fails to remove something which was initially on the land lawfully but has ceased to be so. If a person is given a licence to keep their

---

[258] *Lemmon v Webb* [1894] 3 Ch 1
[259] *Westripp v Baldock* [1939] 1 All ER 279
[260] [2000] Unreported CA
[261] See Occupiers Liability. Paragraph 3.13

caravan on a piece of land but the licensor then revokes the licence it will be a continuing trespass to keep the item there.

(A) The extent of the tort

Possession, not ownership, gives rise to a cause of action in trespass. What actually amounts to possession depends on the type of property. It is usually straightforward in connection with a house or commercial premises but possession of open land may depend on evidence of actual use. A licensee will normally lack the exclusive possession which is necessary to found an action based on trespass[262].A hotel guest or a lodger will not have the *locus standi* to bring a successful action. Possession of land carries with it the right to the soil and things under it together with such amount of airspace as is needed for the normal use and enjoyment of the property[263]. It is long established that trespass can be committed in respect of the subsoil[264]. In *Kelsen v Imperial Tobacco Co Ltd*[265] an advertising sign which extended by a few inches over the claimant's property was actionable as a trespass. Overhead cables have attracted litigation as have crane 'jibs'. In *Woollerton & Wilson Ltd v Costain Ltd*[266] the defendant's crane swung over the claimant's land resulting in a trespass while in *Anchor Brewhouse Developments Ltd v Berkley House [Docklands Developments] Ltd*[267] crane booms were left to swing in the air when unused causing them to pass over neighbouring property. Overflight by aircraft is governed by the Civil Aviation Act 1982 which prevents any claim in trespass or nuisance as long as the flight is at a reasonable height and appropriate flying conditions have been adhered to. Similar rules apply as far as light aircraft, microlights and gliders are concerned. In practice this means adhering to the rules laid down by the Civil Aviation Authority (CAA). Similar rules apply to military aircraft. The 1982 Act imposes strict liability in respect of physical damage to property which arises from an overflight[268].

(B) Remedies

(a) Damages

The object is to restore the claimant to the position they were in before the tort was committed. If no loss has been sustained no damages are recoverable. If damage has occurred the amount of compensation will be the cost of restoring the property to its former condition. If the cost of reinstating the property to its original condition is out of all proportion to the loss suffered, damages should only represent the decrease in the value of the property. In an appropriate situation a claim for the loss of use of the property will be upheld.

---

[262] *Hill v Tupper* (1863) 2 H & C 121; *Manchester Airport plc v Dutton* [2000] QB 133
[263] *Bernstein v Skyviews etc Ltd* [1977] 2 All ER 902
[264] *Cox v Moulsey* (1848) 5 CB 334
[265] [1957] 2 QB 334
[266] [1970] 1 WLR 411
[267] [1987] 38 BLR 82
[268] See s76 [2] Civil Aviation Act 1982 and *Southgate v Commonwealth of Australia* [1987] 13 NSWLR 188

(b) Injunction

Where the trespass is a continuing problem, which is likely to be the case if the claimant has resorted to litigation, an injunction is more likely to be the appropriate remedy. Trespasses over land, or into airspace, are most likely to be dealt with in this manner. In *Costain*[269] the operation of the injunction was suspended when the offending party offered a substantial sum as compensation. An additional factor in the case was that the work was near completion[270]. This tends to be a factor which the courts bear in mind when granting the remedy. Damages can be awarded in lieu of an injunction but only if the requirements laid down in *Shelfer v City of London Electric Lighting Co*[271] are satisfied. These consist of minimal injury to the claimant, which can be estimated in monetary terms, adequate compensation can be made by a small monetary payment and the situation is one where it would be oppressive to grant an injunction.

(c) Action for recovery of the land

If the claimant is not in possession of the land, and has an immediate right to possession, a claim can be made for repossession of the land. At one time there were procedural problems involved in obtaining repossession of the land but nowadays it is possible to enforce the right to possession even if the defendant's identity is not known. A person seeking to recover land in this way will frequently claim for mesne (pronounced 'mean') profits. This is any profit gained by the defendant while in unlawful occupation together with reasonable costs incurred by the claimant in obtaining possession.

(d) Distress damage feasant

Where a chattel is unlawfully on the claimant's land, and has done actual damage to the claimant's property, the claimant may keep the item until the damage has been paid for. Damage caused by cricket and golf balls are good examples. In such circumstances the ball may be lawfully retained until the damage has been paid for. The remedy does not give the claimant the right to use the property or to sell it.

(e) Self help

As an alternative to taking legal action the occupier may use reasonable force to eject a trespasser. As self help is not encouraged by the courts the rightful occupier must act carefully so as not to be in breach of the criminal law[272]. In *Arthur v Anker*[273] the claimant was deemed to have consented to run the risk of having her car clamped where notices on private land prominently displayed the risk of clamping and indicated that a release fee would be payable.

---

[269] See Paragraph 3.23.2
[270] *See Jagger v Sawyer* [1995] 2 All ER 189
[271] [1895] 1 Ch 235
[272] See Criminal Law Act 1977 and Protection from Eviction Act 1977
[273] [1997] QB 564

(C) Defences

(a) Statutory authority

A wide range of officials have powers of entry laid down by statute. Examples include Health and Safety Inspectors, Trading Standards Officers and Environmental Agency officials. If they are acting beyond the scope of their authority they will be trespassers.

(b) Volenti

The consent may be express or implied. If express it is a question of fact depending upon the circumstances. If there is no express consent a visitor has a right to proceed to the front door of premises to state the nature of their business but nothing more. The occupier, in such circumstances, has the option of revoking the visitor's right to be there and if there is non-compliance the visitor will be a trespasser.

(c) Third party rights

A person who enjoys a third party right over an estate in land, such as an easement or a *profit a prendre*, will not be a trespasser. A person who enjoys a customary right over land will also come into this category as will a licensee unless the permission is revoked. Those who exercise their right to pass and repass over the highway, or have the benefit of rights over a private road, will not be liable in trespass[274].

(d) Necessity

The necessity may relate to the preservation of life or property. There must be no negligence on the defendant's part[275].

3.8.2 Trespass to goods

As with other forms of the tort trespass to goods is actionable *per se* and must be direct and intentional to be actionable. The tort is an interference with possession so the owner, or a lawful borrower of the goods, may instigate proceedings except against anybody else who has a better legal title. Examples include a bailee of goods to whom the chattels are entrusted to carry out work, such as a car repairer who has the vehicle in their workshops while carrying out repairs, or a dressmaker who is making alterations to a wedding dress. The tort may not only be committed by taking or destroying the goods but also by simply touching them, although this will rarely arise in practice[276]. Related to the tort of trespass to goods is that of

---

[274] *DPP v Jones* [1999] 2 All ER 257
[275] *Rigby v Chief Constable of Northamptonshire* [1985] 2 All ER 285; *Monsanto plc v Tilly* [2000] Env LR 313
[276] *Kirk v Gregory* (1876) 1 Ex D 55

conversion. This is now governed by the Torts (Interference with Goods) Act 1977 but the common law rules relating to this area of law are still of relevance. Conversion arises where somebody deals with another's property in such a way to act as to be a denial of that person's rights or acts in such as way as to be inconsistent with the rights of the claimant. If goods are found the finder will have a right of possession against everyone except someone with a better title. Case law has assisted the finders of jewellery in this respect[277]. Liability can arise in respect of any act which amounts to a denial of title. Not only does it include taking, disposing or destroying the goods but also where the bailee refuses to restore goods on demand or where goods are wrongfully delivered to a third party. If a person has lawful authority to be in possession of the goods there is no trespass or conversion. It is no defence that the defendant is mistaken as to their rights. The injured party may retake the goods as long as they act with no more force than is necessary in the circumstances. If the defendant is no longer in possession of the goods, damages can be claimed representing their value and possibly consequential damages as well.

3.8.3   Trespass to the person

This is a tort which protects a person's interest in their security and well being. As in the case of the other types of trespass the interference must be direct and physical while the tort is again actionable *per se*. There is an overlap with the criminal law as the conduct of the defendant may also give rise to a criminal offence. There are three main aspects of the tort. The first is assault which arises where a threat is made against somebody else. The second is battery which amounts to the actual use of force against another person. Finally there is false imprisonment where the defendant causes the claimant's freedom to be totally restrained. As far as any assault is concerned the claimant must be in apprehension of an immediate battery before the tort can be committed. If the defendant does not have the capacity to carry out the tort then no assault will have taken place.

The traditional view was that words alone would not constitute an assault but there is now authority from the criminal law that it can be[278]. A battery amounts to a use of force against another person. It must be a direct and intentional act. Self-defence may be a defence to assault and battery as long as it is proportionate. The police may rely on statutory powers in this respect but any force used must be proportionate. Consent is relevant. Where the consent is express that will be a matter of fact and it will be a defence. Consent may also be implied. Where a person has capacity they may consent to, or refuse, medical treatment. In the case of sporting activities consent will only be applicable to activities which come within the rules of the game. Necessity may also be a defence and nowadays it plays a more prominent part in medical cases than implied consent. False imprisonment is concerned with unlawful detention. It arises where the defendant causes the claimant's freedom to be totally restrained. There must be no safe means of escape. It is a strict liability tort and can arise even though

---

[277] *Armory v Delamirie* (1721) 1 Strat 505; *Parker v British Railways Board* [1982] QB 1004
[278] *R v Ireland* [1997] 4 All ER 225

the claimant is unaware of the detention. If the defendant is carrying out a lawful arrest no tort is committed. Where a person is detained under the Mental Health Act 1983, with a mental illness, the tort is not committed. The Protection from Harassment Act 1997 made harassment both a criminal offence and a civil matter. It is widely drafted and the conduct of the defendant can amount to anything which a reasonable person may equate with harassment. There is no requirement to show actual loss.

3.9   Defamation

This tort protects interests in reputation. If the defendant makes a defamatory statement about the claimant, which is published, the claimant will have a right of action against the defendant unless the latter can establish a defence. The major issue for this area of law is to find a compromise between the protection of a person's reputation and the right to freedom of speech. Another related matter is that English law does not recognise a general right to privacy. Defamation has a number of peculiarities. The cases are among the most expensive forms of litigation. They tend to continue for a long time and many go to appeal. Damages are often higher than in personal injury cases. Legal costs take up large proportions of the claim. Cases often involve people in the public eye[279]. An unusual characteristic of these actions is that they are still tried by jury. In practice they are the only type of High Court civil action that is. The use of juries makes the outcome of cases unpredictable. Jurors, in these cases, are notorious for awarding inflated sums by way of damages. It is only in the last twenty years that the Court of Appeal has been able to vary the amount of damages awarded by a jury in defamation actions[280]. There have been attempts to expedite proceedings by introducing a summary process whereby cases can be dealt with by judge alone. In practice the more substantial cases are still dealt with by judges and jury.

In English law, defamation consists of two categories. Defamation in permanent form, usually where the statement is written, is known as libel. Defamation arising from the use of the internet is classified as a libel. Where the defamatory statement occurs in a transient form, such as a spoken statement or a gesture, it is called slander. Libel is actionable *per se* while slander is not. In practice there is little difference between the two because if a slander infers that a person is unfit or incompetent to carry out their job, or that they have committed a criminal offence punishable by imprisonment, the tort will be actionable *per se*. A statement made 'off the cuff' in an abusive manner is unlikely to be defamatory.

3.9.1   *Essentials of a valid claim*

A claimant must prove the following to succeed in a defamation action.

---

[279] *Hamilton v Al Fayed [No 1]* [2000] 2 All ER 224; *Jason Donovan v The Face* [1998] Unreported
[280] Courts & Legal Sevices Act 1990; see *John v Mirror Group Newspapers* [1996] 2 All ER 35 and *Kiam 11 v MGN Ltd* [2002] EWCA Civ 43

(A) Defamatory statement

If the case is being heard by judge and jury this is a matter for the jury. The test, which tends to be used to ascertain whether the statement is defamatory or not, was that laid down by Lord Atkin in *Sim v Stretch*[281]. The judge said that a statement will be defamatory if its effect is to 'lower the claimant in the minds of right-thinking people, or cause them to be shunned or avoided.' A claimant cannot select potentially libellous statements to rely on if the written passage overall is not defamatory[282]. Another relevant issue is that of an innuendo where words do not appear to be defamatory, if taken at face value, but the claimant asserts that they have an inner meaning[283].

(B) Statement must refer to the claimant

If the claimant is named the position is straightforward. It is sufficient that the claimant can show that people think it refers to him or her. This may be so even though a fictional name is used or if two people have the same name[284]. It can also arise if there is nobody named but it is evident in the circumstances that there is a reference to the claimant[285].

(C) Publication to a third party

To be actionable there must be publication to at least one person who is not the defendant's spouse or the claimant. This can be extensive in nature and can include every sale of a newspaper, every lending of a book from a library and each time the statement appears on the internet. Even speaking in a loud voice about the claimant so that people can hear can be actionable[286].

(D) Remedies

(a) Damages

The normal rules relating to damages will apply. The Court and Legal Services Act 1990 allowed the Court of Appeal to review damages awards in defamation cases in circumstances where they considered them inappropriate[287]. There is now a ceiling on general damages of £200 000. Exemplary damages may be awarded in circumstances where the claimant can prove that the defendant knew that the

---

[281] [1936] 52 TLR 669
[282] *Charleston v News Group Newspapers* [1995] 2 All ER 315
[283] *Byrne v Dean* [1937] 1 KB 818
[284] *Newstead v London Express Newspapers Ltd* [1940] 1 KB 377
[285] *Dwek v Macmillan Publishers* [2000] EMLR 284
[286] *McManus v Beckham* [2002] EWCA Civ 939
[287] Paragraph 3.24

tort was being committed or was reckless in that respect. The award of damages will often be accompanied by a suitable apology or correction.

(b) Injunction

An injunction may be granted to prevent publication of a defamatory statement or a statement being repeated. The remedy is an equitable one and the normal rules applicable to such remedies apply.

(E) Defences

There are four main defences to a defamation action together with two additional defences that were refined by the Defamation Act 1996. The general defence of '*Volenti*' may also be relevant.

(a) Justification

This means truth and is a complete defence. It amounts to an assertion that the material is true. The burden of proof is on the defendant to show that is the case. The defence may succeed even though some of the details may be inaccurate.

(b) Fair comment

The so called 'critics defence' protects the right to express opinions. Frequently relied upon by authors and publishers the opinion must be based on the facts and it only applies where the comment is of public interest. The issue is whether or not the opinion is genuinely held and it is for the claimant to show that the opinion is not honestly held. The defence can be defeated by proof of malice or underhand motive.

(c) Absolute privilege

There are some circumstances where freedom of expression is essential. The most important examples are statements made in either of the two Houses of Parliament, statements made in the course of judicial proceedings, including tribunals, and communications made between officers of state. The statement cannot be relied upon in a court of law.

(d) Qualified privilege

This defence is concerned with the nature of the statement itself and not the place where it is made. It arises where a person making a statement has a legal, moral or social duty to make it and the person receiving it has an interest in so doing. If the defence is sustained the statement cannot be used in a court of law. Unlike absolute privilege it can be defeated by malice. The extent of the defence is difficult to categorise but it has covered comments made in a reference and reports of parliamentary proceedings by newspapers. It also includes accurate reports of public meetings[288]. The defence is one which is based on questions of law and not of fact[289].

(e) Unintentional defamation

This is not strictly a defence as the defendant acknowledges that defamation has taken place. This is the 'offer of amends' which allows a person who has published a statement alleged to be defamatory to make an appropriate correction and apology to the defamed person and to pay compensation and/or costs. The process is governed by s.2 of the Defamation Act 1996 which requires the offer to be made before the service of any defence. If accepted it brings an end to the proceedings. Non-acceptance by the aggrieved party may be relied upon in subsequent proceedings as a defence by the defendants.

(f) Innocent dissemination

A printed libel could impose liability not only on the author but also on the publisher and 'secondary publishers' such as newspapers and booksellers. S.1 of the Defamation Act 1996 gives distributors a defence in these circumstances as long as the defendant has taken all reasonable care and has no reason to consider their act may have a defamatory effect. It may extend to publication on the internet where information is provided by a person over whom the internet provider has no control.

(g) Consent

A person who consents to publication cannot complain that it is defamatory.

3.9.2   *The privacy problem and human rights*

English law has never recognised a basic right to privacy. Problems of definition, the likelihood of large amounts of litigation and unreasonable restrictions on the freedom of the press are all given as reasons why it is not desirable to embrace such a concept. So-called 'celebrities' have in recent years been heavily involved in such litigation[290]. The Calcutt Committee, which reported in 1990, considered that privacy could be protected by other means and did not recommend the creation of a new tort of privacy. Examples include the use of the equitable remedy available for breach of confidence, trespass to land, breach of contract and of copyright. A number of statutory provisions also provide protection by regulating the manner in which information may be obtained and stored[291]. Article 8 of the Convention on Human Rights guarantees a right to 'respect for private and family life'. Its

---

[288] *Reynolds v Times Newspapers* [1999] 3 WLR 1010
[289] *Jameel v Wall Street Journal* [2006] 4 All ER 1279
[290] *Campbell v MG Newspapers* [2004] 2 All 99; *Douglas & Others v Hello* [2006] QB 125; *Mosley v News Group Newspapers* [2008] EWHC] 687
[291] Data Protection Act 1998 Freedom of Information Act 2000

application to the law of privacy has been considered by the European Court of Human Right[292].

3.10   Breach of statutory duty

The issue here is where there has been a breach of a statutory provision, resulting in criminal liability, is it possible for a civil action to be brought by the claimant in tort. The majority of statutes are essentially regulatory in nature and the question of civil liability sometimes does not exist or is minimal. Much depends on the intention of the legislature. The operation of this area of law is based on statutory interpretation which often involves policy considerations. The relevant statute must be intended to create civil liability otherwise no claim for damages will exist. Much of the law relating to breach of statutory duty is concerned with accidents at work while the presence of Health and Safety legislation is important in this context. Some Acts specifically exclude civil liability. The Health and Safety at Work etc. Act 1974 states that the Act gives rise to no civil liability but some of the Regulations made under the Act do. The Building Act 1984 does give rise to civil liability. Frequently the statute does not indicate whether it gives rise to a claim for damages or not.

3.10.1   How it works

(A) Conditions

Two major requirements must be satisfied before a claimant can succeed in an action based on breach of statutory duty.

(a) Duty of care owed to the claimant was imposed on the defendant

The claimant must show that the statute was intended by Parliament to confer a civil remedy for its breach and the duty owed by the defendant to the claimant was broken. A duty must be identifiable from the precise wording of the statute[293].

(b) Injury of a kind that the statute was intended to prevent

In *Ginty v Belmont Building Supplies Ltd*[294] statutory regulations required those involved in the roofing business to use crawling boards when at work. The defendants supplied the boards but the claimant, an experienced workman, failed to use them and fell through the roof. Although technically in breach of the statute, the defendants were acquitted as they had done everything that could be expected in the circumstances. The breach of duty must be the cause of the damage which

---

[292] *Peck v UK* [2003] 36 EHRR 41
[293] *Chipchase v British Titan Products Co Ltd* [1956] 1 QB 545
[294] [1959] 1 All ER 414

must not be too remote. In *Young v Charles Church [Southern] Ltd*[295] an electrician succeeded in a claim based on psychiatric damage when a pole on which he and his colleague were standing struck a live wire resulting in the death of the other workman. The defendants were in breach of the relevant construction regulations which contemplated such damage. If the courts consider that an alternative remedy was intended by the relevant statute they will not impose a duty.

Volenti and contributory negligence may be available as defences in claims for breach of statutory duty.

3.11   Employers liability

The liability of employers to those who work for them may arise in a number of ways and is based both on common law, statute and EU law. Where appropriate, an employer may be vicariously liable for a tort committed by an employee during the course of employment. If there has been a breach of statutory duty, and the relevant statute imposes civil liability, the employer may incur liability. An employer owes a non-delegable duty in respect of the health and safety of employees irrespective of any conditions imposed by statute. The leading case is *Wilson & Clyde Coal Co Ltd v English*[296] where four main 'duties' were identified.

3.11.1   Duties

- Provide a safe place of work.
- Provide a safe system of work.
- Provide competent staff.
- Provide safe plant and equipment.

(A) Satisfying the obligations

An employer must take reasonably practicable steps to ensure that the premises are safe[297]. As we have seen earlier an employer can expect that those skilled in a particular calling are aware of the dangers in carrying out that skill and will take appropriate measures to protect themselves from injury[298]. Employers must implement a safe system of work at their premises. In practice, every company is now under a statutory duty to carry out an assessment of risks which are likely to be present in the workplace. It must be carried out by a 'competent person' and it must identify any hazards involved and the likelihood of those hazards causing harm. Steps must be devised to deal with potential hazards. An unsafe practice cannot be relied upon simply because it is a common practice[299]. At common law

---

[295] *The Times* May 1 1997
[296] [1938] AC 57
[297] *Latimer v AEC Ltd* [1953] AC 643
[298] Paragraph 3.13.2
[299] *Re:Herald of Free Enterprise, The Independent* December 18 1987

the employer must take steps to try to ensure that the system which has been installed is known to employees and is complied with.

Employers have a duty to ensure that their employees are competent to carry out the tasks which are entrusted to them. This includes taking the best practicable steps to eliminate unsafe practices and not to condone bad behaviour. Any equipment which is provided must be safe and properly maintained. To avoid misuse of equipment by employees, it is often prudent for employers to give training and updating to their workforce. Employers' obligations have now been extended to cover psychiatric injuries covered by negligent work practices. It seems that a successful claimant must now show that it was reasonably foreseeable that he would suffer a psychiatric illness as a result of the employer's breach of duty[300].

(B) Defences

(a) Volenti

In *Smith v Baker*[301] it was held that volenti would only be relevant if the claimant accepted freely and understood the specific risks involved. There must be no coercion. The defence will not apply where there is a breach of statutory duty.

(b) Contributory negligence

Where appropriate, an apportionment of damages may be made under the Law Reform (Contributory Negligence) Act 1945. If the employee is considered one-hundred per cent responsible for their misfortune there may be a full reduction and no damages will be awarded to them[302].

3.12   Product liability

The modern law of negligence has greatly assisted injured parties who suffer damage where there is no privity of contract between the parties. The difficulties encountered in proving negligence have always been considerable in connection with defective products especially proving fault and causation. The issue was addressed at European Community level in 1985 by Directive 85/374/EEC. Member states were required to comply with the Directive within three years. The result in the United Kingdom is the Consumer Protection Act 1987.

The Act imposes strict liability on producers for harm caused by defective goods. People injured by faulty products can sue for compensation without having to prove negligence provided they can prove the product was defective and the defect in the product was responsible for the harm. Regulations were introduced in 2005 to supplement the Act. The Act and Regulations leave untouched claims in contract against the retailer of the product, any action in negligence and, where appropriate, any claim for breach of statutory duty.

---

[300] *Barber v Somerset County Council* [2004] UKHL 13
[301] *Smith v Baker* (1891) AC 325
[302] *Jayes v IMI [Kynoch] Ltd* [1985] ICR 55

3.12.1 How it works

By s.1[2] of the Act, liability is imposed on the 'Producer'. This will include the manufacturer but will also cover minerals which are 'won or abstracted'. Where a product does not fall within these categories, but the development of the item is attributable to an industrial or related process, it will be covered by the Act. This would cover crop production and those involved in similar processes. Those who brand-name products, import products into the European Community or hold themselves out as being producers are covered by the Act. A supplier will normally not be liable under the Act as long as they do not come under any of the former categories. They do have obligations to name producers in circumstances where consumers suffer damage covered by the Act otherwise they will be personally liable. The products covered by the Act are extensive. All consumer goods and those used in the workplace are included. This includes component parts and certain raw materials. Food is covered. Buildings themselves are not covered by the Act but building materials are included[303].

S.3 of the Act provides that there is a defect in a product if the safety of that product is not as persons generally are entitled to expect. All the circumstances are to be taken into account including packaging and any instructions relating to use. The Act has no application if the item is safe but useless. The Act only provides for claims in relation to death, personal injury and damage to private property. Small claims are excluded (less than £275) while no claim can be made in respect of damage to the respective product itself. Damage to business property and economic losses resulting from defective products are excluded.

A successful claimant must show that the damage was caused wholly or partly by the defect in the product. The limitation period is similar to that in respect of latent defects in negligence claims. Time runs for three years from the date on which the damage was caused by the defective product, or the date on which the damage could have reasonably been discovered. Enforcement of the Act is in the hands of local authority trading standards departments while central government also has enforcement powers. Failure to meet the requirements of the safety regulations, made under the Act, can result in a fine of up to £5000 or a prison sentence of up to six months.

(A) Defences

Defences are covered by s4 of the 1987 Act. If there is no actual defect there is no liability. If the defendant is not a supplier, or is an exempt supplier, there will be no liability. Where the defect is attributable to compliance with any statute or European Community rules prescribing how the product is made there is a defence. More problematical is the 'development risks' defence. Manufacturers who can demonstrate that the state of scientific and technical knowledge, at the time the product was put on the market, was such that they could not be expected to have discovered the relevant defect are exempt from liability.

---

[303] s46

3.13   Remedies and limitation periods

The law of tort provides a number of remedies depending on the category of tort which has been committed by the defendant. Much depends on the nature of the tort and the circumstances in which it has arisen. As a general rule remedies tend to be judicial in nature or extra-judicial. As far as judicial remedies are concerned the main remedies are damages and injunctions.

3.13.1   Damages

Damages are the principal remedy in tort as in contract. They are compensatory in nature and in tort their aim is to put claimants in to the position they would have been in had the wrong not been committed. The claimant should not be worse or better off as a result of the tort being committed. This is the principle of *restitution in integrum*. Damages may be either general or special. General damages include matters such as loss of future earnings, pain and injury suffered, losses which result from the decrease in value of a house because a surveyor negligently failed to recognise defects when carrying out a valuation and loss of the ability to enjoy life as you did before the tort was committed. This is sometimes called amenity loss. General damages are not capable of being precisely quantified. Special damages relate to costs which can be precisely identified such as itemised repair costs.

Also classed as general damages, but non-compensatory in nature, are contemptuous damages. These are awarded where the claimant's rights have been infringed but the court considers that the claimant was wrong to bring the action. Nominal damages are awarded where little damage has been caused but the court considers that the claimant was correct to bring the action. Exemplary damages are awarded where the court disapproves of the defendant's conduct and are awarded to deter others from similar behaviour. Another category, known as aggravated damages, may be awarded to compensate for injury to feelings and distress caused by the defendant's bad behaviour. This last category is compensatory in nature but recognises that the claimant's position has been made worse by the defendant's malice.

Compensatory damages can be divided into pecuniary and non-pecuniary losses. This relates respectively to financial and other losses suffered. In *Farley v Skinner*[304] the defendant surveyor was asked to prepare a report relating to a house which the claimant was buying. The claimant specifically asked the surveyor if the subject property was troubled by noise from aircraft as he wanted a house in a quiet location. The surveyor said that this would not be a problem and the purchase went ahead with the claimant spending a considerable amount of money improving the property. The claimant went into occupation but found that aircraft noise was a major problem. The House of Lords awarded the claimant £10 000 by way of damages. As mentioned earlier[305], the House of Lords has stated that when calculating damages for breach of duty it is necessary to ascertain exactly what the duty consists of. The defendant will only be liable for consequences arising from

[304] [2001] UKHL 49
[305] Paragraph 3.8 and *South Australian Asset Management Corp v York Montague Ltd* [1997] AC 191

the negligent performance of that duty. The *South Australian Assett Management* case concerns the 'classic' situation of claimants lending money for the purchase of property based on valuations made by defendants which turn out to be vastly optimistic. In this case the House of Lords took the view that the defendants did not owe a duty to the claimants to advise whether or not to make the loans but simply to make a valuation of the subject property. Their liability was limited to the consequences of their advice being wrong and not for the overall drop in property prices in the market. There are policy considerations here while the case does not lay down how the courts identify the duty which is being owed.

In the case of compensation in respect of damage to land and buildings a court can take the approach of awarding a sum equal to the decrease in the value of the property or award the cost of reinstating the property to its original condition. The latter has tended to be the approach which the courts have favoured except where the claimant has no intention of repairing the building or where the cost of reinstatement would be out of all proportion to the loss suffered. In addition, a claimant will be entitled to compensation for loss of use during the time that the repairs are being carried out and this will extend to loss of profits in the case of a business. If a property is destroyed the award will be the market value of the property at the time of destruction. There is a duty on the claimant to take reasonable steps to mitigate any tortious losses sustained.

3.13.2   *Injunction*

This is an equitable remedy which prohibits a wrongful act or sometimes requires a defendant to take steps to put matters right[306]. The usual rules relating to equitable remedies apply. It is discretionary in nature and must be appropriate to the circumstances. It is awarded if the court considers it 'just and equitable' in the circumstances. It tends to be used where there is a course of conduct rather than a single act so it is particularly appropriate in trespass and nuisance cases. There are cases where a court may decide to award damages in lieu of an injunction[307] but these rules are stringently applied to prevent wrongdoers with means being able to pay for the injury they inflict. Injunctions are normally perpetual and prohibitory in nature but an injunction may be interlocutory (interim).This is where the order is granted before the case is heard in an attempt to prevent further harm. The grant of such an injunction is not an indication that the claimant has won their case. Increasingly, modern courts try to effect a compromise between the parties in the manner in which the order operates[308]. Failure to obey an injunction is a contempt of court which may result in the imposition of a fine or imprisonment.

3.13.3   *Extrajudicial remedies*

During the course of this chapter it has been shown that the law does allow a certain degree of self-help. The recapture of chattels, abatement of a nuisance and re-entry

---

[306] *Redland Bricks Ltd v Morris* [1970] AC 652
[307] *Shelfer v City of London Electric Lighting* [1895] 1 Ch 287
[308] *Kennaway v Thompson* [1981] QB 88

onto land are good examples. Although tolerated, self-help is not popular with the courts although it is recognised that its use does help to limit potential litigation. The problems associated with it can be illustrated by the decision in *Revill v Newberry*[309].

3.13.4 Limitation periods

Limitation periods are the time periods within which a claimant must commence an action for damages. A claimant must pursue a claim with due diligence while potential defendants should not have the threat of litigation pending indefinitely. The present law is to be found in the Limitation Act 1980 as amended by the Latent Damage Act 1986.

As a general rule claims must be brought within a six-year period unless the claim is based on personal injury in which case it is three years. If a claim is made outside these periods it is said to be statute barred. Time is calculated from the date on which the cause of action accrued. In most cases this will be the date when the event took place or the claimant could, with due diligence, have discovered the problem[310]. Similar cases have arisen in connection with defective foundations[311]. By s.33 Limitation Act 1980 the court has power to override the statutory limit where it considers it equitable to do so. It must be satisfied that it is reasonable to do so taking into account the history of the case, conduct of the parties and the availability of evidence.

As has been shown in the contract chapter, if the defendant acts fraudulently, or conceals the proper state of affairs from the defendant, the limitation period does not begin to run until the claimant has discovered the true position[312].

---

[309] [1996] QB 567
[310] See *Clark v Woor* [1965] 2 All ER 353 [decided on similar previous legislation]
[311] *Applegate v Moss* [1971] 1 QB 406
[312] See s31 and 32 Limitation Act 1980 and Chapter 2, section 2.11B

4 Land Law

4.1 The two types of property

The subject of land law is essentially concerned with the rights that can exist in land. It describes the nature of these rights, and the circumstances in which those who are entitled to them can enforce them against others. Land, of course, is a form of property but most legal systems make a distinction between land and all other forms of property. English law makes a distinction between what it describes as real property and personal property. Real property is comprised of land as well as most of the rights which people can own in land[1]. The term is sometimes abbreviated to 'realty' and is also the origin of the expression 'real estate' which was originally confined to North America but which is now increasingly used throughout the world.

Personal property comprises all other types of property. It includes items of property having a physical existence (tangible property) as well as property rights which are independent of any physical item (intangible property). Intellectual property rights, including patents and copyright, are examples of the latter. The term is sometimes abbreviated to 'personalty'. Although the two concepts are not strictly synonymous with each other, personal property is also sometimes loosely described as 'chattels'.

The origins of the distinction between real property and personal property lie in the approach that the courts historically took to protecting rights in the different types of property. Today the law continues to treat land differently to all other types of property. This is not only reflected in the way it is still treated by the courts but also in terms of the whole body of law which we describe as 'land law' and which is the subject of the present chapter. This, of course, applies only to land and not to all the other forms of property which we describe, collectively, as personal property. Before moving on to examine the rights that people can have in land we should therefore first clarify the nature of the property that, according to the law, actually falls within the meaning of 'land'.

---

[1] For historical reasons leases are strictly personal rather than real property. However, today, they have far more in common with real property and are sometimes described as 'chattels real'

Law and the Built Environment   by Douglas Wood, Paul Chynoweth, Julie Adshead and Jim Mason
© 2011 Douglas Wood, Paul Chynoweth, Julie Adshead and Jim Mason

4.2 What is land?

4.2.1 Some definitions

A dictionary or everyday definition of land would describe it in terms of those parts of the earth's surface that are not covered by water. However, the legal definition, as contained in a variety of common law and statutory sources, is considerably wider than this. For example, the definition in section 132(1) of the Land Registration Act 2002 expressly includes 'land covered with water'. Perhaps the best-known definition appears in section 205(1)(ix) of the Law of Property Act 1925 where land is defined as including 'land. . . .mines and minerals. . . . [and]. . . .buildings or parts of buildings'. Section 132(1) of the Land Registration Act 2002 also confirms that 'other structures' erected on land are also included, as well as buildings.

The inclusion of mines and minerals in the above definition is consistent with the common law position that 'land' includes not simply the surface of the earth within a given plot of land but also the subsoil and minerals below it, the vegetation growing naturally upon it, and the airspace above it. Indeed the concept of a cone of ownership extending infinitely downwards and upwards from the boundaries of one's plot of land is encapsulated in the Latin maxim: *cuius est solum, eius est usque ad caelum et ad inferos* (whoever owns the soil, it is theirs up to Heaven and down to Hell). Because of this, as we saw in Chapter 3, paragraph 3.8.1.A, the invasion of someone's airspace, for example by swinging a crane jib over their land, amounts to a trespass.

Whilst the 'cone of ownership' concept provides a useful starting point to understanding the vertical extent of a given plot of land there are, in practice, a number of limitations to this, both at common law and under statute. In Chapter 3, paragraph 3.8.1.A we saw, for example, in the case of *Bernstein v Skyviews and General Ltd*[2] that an aeroplane flying several hundred feet above land for the purposes of taking photographs may indeed be entitled to do so providing it does not infringe the reasonable enjoyment of the land affected. In a similar vein, section 76(1) of the Civil Aviation Act 1982 provides civil aircraft with immunity from trespass as long as they are flying at a reasonable height above the ground. A number of statutory provisions also limit the 'cone of ownership' in the context of minerals lying beneath the surface. These include provisions relating to the extraction of coal[3] and oil[4].

Finally, the common law also makes a distinction between different categories of things growing on the land. As stated above, naturally occurring vegetation forms part of the land. However, following the sale of land, disputes have sometimes arisen over the ownership of crops and trees which have been planted by the previous owner. If forming part of the land they will obviously be transferred to the new owner automatically at the time of the sale whereas if they retain their status as separate chattels the original owner will retain ownership in them, and therefore be entitled to remove them.

---

[2] [1978] QB 479
[3] Coal Industry Act 1994, ss.1(1) & 7(3)
[4] Petroleum Act 1994, ss.1(a) & 2(1)

The common law resolves this problem by drawing a distinction between what it describes as *fructus naturales* and *fructus industriales*. *Fructus naturales* are things which grow naturally on land (for example vegetation) but also things planted by man which then produce a crop each year without any further human intervention (for example fruit trees). These form part of the land on which they grow and will therefore pass to the new owner on a sale of the land. These items should be distinguished from *fructus industriales* which the law regards as chattels rather than land. These are cultivated crops which require annual human intervention (for example wheat or potatoes). As items of personal property, the owner of the land retains ownership in them and is therefore entitled to remove them before parting with the land to the new owner.

Just as things which grow on the land can potentially become part of the land on which they are situated, so under certain circumstances, can inanimate objects. This brings us to an important area of law which is concerned with what are described as 'fixtures'.

4.2.2 *Fixtures*

A fixture is a chattel which has become (in a legal sense) a part of land by being attached to it. Once again this is important on a sale of land as the basic rule is that fixtures pass with the land but chattels do not. On a transfer of land, chattels may be removed but not fixtures which have become a constituent part of the land. In order to ascertain whether an object is a fixture or a chattel, the courts have traditionally applied two tests.

(A) The degree of annexation test

This is the primary test. Such a test is applied to show how permanently the object has been attached to the land. If something is physically fixed to land (for example by nailing, screwing, being set in concrete or similar) it is presumed to be a fixture and the more firmly it is fixed the stronger the presumption becomes. Conversely, if something is not fixed to land it is presumed to be a chattel. The following cases illustrate the courts' approach in applying the test.

In *Smith v City Petroleum Co Ltd*[5] petrol pumps on a filling station forecourt were deemed to be fixtures in a dispute over their status. Similarly, in *Buckland v Butterfield*[6], a wooden balcony which had been bolted to the side of a house was also held to be a fixture.

Conversely, in *TSB v Botham*[7] where electrical 'white goods' were slotted into standard holes in a fitted kitchen but not fixed in any way, they were held to be chattels. Some quite significant objects have also been held to retain their status as chattels as a result of applying the logic of this test. For example, the case of *Berkley v Poulett*[8] concerned the status of a statue in the grounds of a stately home.

---

[5] [1940] 1 All ER 260
[6] (1820) 2 Brod & Bing 54
[7] [1994] 1 All 3R 272
[8] [1977] 1 EGLR 86

Although weighing approximately half a ton it was not fixed down in any way but was simply secured in position by its own weight. On this basis it was held to be a chattel. The status of an even larger and heavier object was considered in *Royal Bank of Canada v Beyak*[9] where a mobile home was also held to be a chattel.

The degree of annexation test is, however, only a *prima facie* test. It is not conclusive about the status of the particular item under consideration but simply raises a presumption about this. This presumption can sometimes be rebutted by applying the purpose of annexation test.

(B) The purpose of annexation test

This test is used if the first is difficult to apply, as is often the case in such disputes. In the event of a conflict between the two rules, this rule will prevail. Unlike the first test, this test is not concerned with the physical way in which the item has been placed in position. Instead it addresses the intention with which it was placed there. If it was placed with the intention of effecting a permanent improvement of the land or building in question it is a fixture. If, on the other hand, it was placed in position simply for its better enjoyment as a chattel, or for security purposes, then it remains a chattel. Each situation depends very much on its own facts. Is the intention to improve the use of the land or enhance the chattel?

The principle is well illustrated by the comments of Blackburn J in *Holland v Hodgson*[10] where he stated that a pile of stones stacked together in a yard would be considered as chattels but the same set of stones forming a wall would be part of the land.

The way in which the application of the second test can rebut the presumptions generated by the first test can be seen in the following two cases. In *Hulme v Brigham*[11] two printing machines, each weighing twelve tons, were bolted to a workshop floor to prevent vibration when they were in use. Despite the extent of their physical annexation to the building they were nevertheless held to be chattels in view of the purpose of this annexation. The presumption and rebuttal operated in entirely the opposite direction in *D'Eyncourt v Gregory*[12]. In this case some small, free-standing stone statues were placed in niches in the façade of a house. Although they were not physically attached to the building they were held to be fixtures because they were an integral part of the house's architectural design.

In *Elitestone Ltd v Morris*[13] the House of Lords approved the use of this twofold test approach when deciding on the status of certain objects but felt that it was less helpful when deciding on the status of others. In that case the Law Lords had to decide whether a wooden bungalow resting on, but not attached to, concrete pillars was a chattel. If so, the defendant's tenancy of the site could not be one of a dwelling house and he would not enjoy security of tenure under the Rent Act 1977 (see Chapter 5, paragraph 5.16.2). Overruling the Court of Appeal, they took the view

---

[9] (1981) 119 DLR 505
[10] (1872) LR 7 CP 328
[11] [1943] KB 152
[12] (1866) LR 3 Eq 382
[13] [1997] 2 All ER 513

that decisions about the status of a house itself needed to be considered on a more common sense basis rather then being subject to the precise analysis suggested by the twofold approach. It was therefore unnecessary to apply the degree of annexation test at all. The purpose of annexation is the defining question and this is to be determined objectively, according to the facts of the case. In deciding that the bungalow formed part and parcel of the land, the judges were influenced by the fact that a house which was constructed in such a way that it could not be removed except by destruction could not have been intended to remain a chattel but must always have been intended to form part of the land.

The *Elitestone* approach was also followed in *Chelsea Yacht and Boat Club Ltd v Pope*[14] where the status of a houseboat had to be considered. It was argued that the boat had become a fixture and would therefore automatically be transferred on a sale of the land as it had all mains services connected. However, as it could easily be moved to another mooring without causing damage to its fabric, it was held to be a chattel.

4.3   Ownership of land

4.3.1   The nature of 'ownership'

The concept of 'ownership' involves the exclusive right to use, possess, control, destroy or dispose of property within one's ownership. In a theoretical legal sense we might describe ownership as indicating that one has all the rights in a particular item of property that are capable of existing. If, for example, you own a pen (an item of personal property) no one else can stop you using it and you are free to destroy it or give it away if you choose to do so. You own all the rights in it.

In this sense it is not possible to own land in English law. Instead, it is only possible to own *rights* in land. Some of these rights are bundled together to form packages of rights known as *legal estates*. It is therefore possible to own a legal estate in land which will bear a strong resemblance to the familiar concept of ownership of property which applies to personal property. The rights within this package (the so-called natural rights) will include the following:

- Exclusive possession – the right to control and manage the land including the right to exclude everyone else from it.
- Enjoyment – the right to enjoy all the benefits which the land has to offer (this includes the right to draw percolating water from the ground and certain rights over neighbouring land, including a right to support for the soil).
- Alienation – the right of the estate owner to sell or otherwise dispose of the legal estate in the land.

An estate owner is said to hold the land rather than to own it. This concept of holding land in this way has its origins in the Feudal System and is known as *tenure*. Historically there were many different types of legal estate. As a result of section 1

---

[14] [2001] 2 All ER 409

of the Law of Property Act 1925, there are now only two, the freehold and the leasehold.

4.3.2 The freehold estate

The legal term for the freehold legal estate is the 'fee simple absolute in possession'. This rather complicated expression was used to distinguish it from some of the other legal estates that could also exist before the enactment of this legislation. The various parts of the expression have the following meanings:

- Fee – This simply means that the estate can be inherited.
- Simple – Essentially the freeholder can pass the estate to anyone.
- Absolute – This signifies that the grant will continue for ever.
- In possession – Denotes that the person who has the benefit of the estate is entitled to immediate possession of the land or, if the land has been let, is entitled to rent from the land.

Perhaps unsurprisingly the expression is rarely used in full and is often abbreviated to 'fee simple' (or just 'freehold'). The fee simple is characterised by the fact that it is of indefinite duration. Should they choose to do so an owner of a fee simple and his heirs can therefore own it in perpetuity.

4.3.3 The leasehold estate

The legal term for the leasehold legal estate is the term of years absolute. This is a confusing expression as a lease does not have to be for a fixed 'term of years'. Equally, it does not have to be 'absolute' in the sense that it must continue for ever, or even for the originally agreed term if the lease contains some mechanism for premature termination.

A leasehold estate, like the freehold estate, is a package of rights in the land itself. It is, however, characterised by the fact that it is granted by another estate owner who grants these rights for a term of lesser duration than they themselves are entitled to. Because a freeholder's estate is of unlimited duration he may therefore grant a lease for any period he likes and, in practice, one can often encounter leases of 999 years as well as many shorter terms. A leaseholder can only grant a lease (described as a 'sub-lease') for a lesser term than that which has been granted to them. The owner of a 999-year leasehold term therefore has considerable scope to grant leases, for example for five weeks, five months, five years, fifty years or 500 years. The estate owner who grants a leasehold estate to another obviously retains some rights in the land himself, including an entitlement to receive rent and, crucially, for the land to revert back to him at the end of the term. The rights retained by the grantor are therefore collectively referred to as the 'reversion'.

We have seen that the term of the lease does not have to be for a fixed 'term of years' but can be measured by reference to some shorter time interval, for example weeks or months. Equally, it does not have to be what is described as a 'fixed-term tenancy' at all. It can instead take the form of a 'periodic tenancy'.

Under this arrangement the length of the term is not fixed at the outset but continues on a rolling basis until terminated by the service of an agreed period of notice. Periodic tenancies may be described, for example, as weekly tenancies, monthly tenancies, quarterly tenancies or yearly tenancies, depending on the agreed period that has been used to define them. Either party can terminate such a tenancy by serving notice to quit on the other party to expire at the end of the agreed period. If notice is not served, the tenancy simply rolls on from agreed period to agreed period.

In practice the leasehold estate is variously described as a term of years, a lease, a demise or a tenancy. The person who grants a leasehold estate is known as the lessor or landlord. The owner of the estate is known as the lessee or tenant. It is important to understand that the leasehold estate is not necessarily an inferior estate to the freehold estate. The two estates are simply legal vehicles for the economic activities of property management and investment. For example, consider a situation where a freehold owner grants a lease of a property for 999 years at a rent of £50 per annum. Which is the more valuable legal estate? The leasehold estate, and its practical implications for particular types of property, is addressed in greater detail in Chapter 5 which deals with the law of landlord and tenant.

4.3.4 Co-Ownership of land

It is obviously quite common for two or more people (for example, husband and wife, or business partners) to jointly own the same legal estate in land simultaneously. Where this occurs the law describes this as a co-ownership, and the individual estate owners as co-owners. In English law there are two types of co-ownership: the 'joint tenancy' and the 'tenancy in common'.

(A) Joint tenancy

A joint tenancy is said to exist where two or more people collectively own the whole property estate rather than each of them owning a distinct share of its total value. The individual owners are actually treated by the law, not as separate owners at all, but as one single inseparable group owner. All of them would therefore be able to say 'this is ours!' in relation to the whole property but none of them would be able to say 'this is mine!' in the sense of being able to identify a particular share which was exclusively their own.

The two main characteristics of the joint tenancy are the presence of what are known as 'the four unities' and the operation of the 'right of survivorship' on the death of one of the co-owners. Whilst the first of these is a theoretical concept which the law has developed to assist in identifying the existence of a joint tenancy, the second is an entirely practical consequence which all readers should fully understand.

(a) The four unities

The textbook rule is that a joint tenancy can only exist if the four unities are all present. These are:

- Unity of interest – as each co-owner is collectively entitled to the whole, the interest of each of them must, by definition, be identical.
- Unity of possession – the land must not be physically divided up but each co-owner must have a right to possession of the whole.
- Unity of title – there must be a single deed that vests the property in all co-owners.
- Unity of time – the single deed must vest the property in all the co-owners at the same time rather than making provision for some of them to join the group at a later date.

(b) The right of survivorship

Since a joint tenant is not regarded as having a distinct share in the property it would not be possible for them to leave it to anyone on their death. They are not therefore permitted to dispose of their interest by will and even if they make no will (therefore dying 'intestate'), neither will their interest pass to the normal beneficiaries under the rules of intestacy. Instead, the right of survivorship will operate whereby their interest passes automatically to the remaining joint tenant or joint tenants. For this reason, although cohabiting spouses will typically be happy to hold property as joint tenants, it will often be inappropriate for other types of co-owner.

(B) Tenancy in common

In a tenancy in common each co-owner has a recognized share of the property which need not necessarily be the same size as those of other co-owners. It is therefore appropriate where the parties contribute differing amounts of capital to the purchase of the land. There is no right of survivorship and on death an individual share will pass to those entitled to the share by the will of the tenant in common, or if the tenant has died intestate subject to the intestacy rules.

Although each co-owner owns a share of the property it is important to understand that this is a share of its value (or 'beneficial interest') rather than an entitlement to a particular part of the physical building. The property is not, therefore physically divided and, for this reason, the Law of Property Act 1925 refers to the tenancy in common as 'land held in undivided shares'. Although none of the other unities need to be present we can see, therefore, that unity of possession must exist, even in a tenancy in common.

(C) Identifying the type of co-ownership

Normally the intending co-owners will decide, at the time they purchase the property, whether they are to hold it as joint tenants or tenants in common and this will then typically be stated in the deed transferring the property to them. If the deed fails to state the capacity in which the co-owners intend to hold the property the common law presumes a joint tenancy. However, the presumption will be rebutted if there is evidence of a contrary intention. This will be the case where:

- The deed includes words (described as 'words of severance') which indicate that the parties intended to have separate shares in the land. The following examples have been held to be words of severance: 'in equal shares'; 'equally'; 'divided between'; 'amongst'; 'respectively'.
- The co-owners are business partners.
- The co-owners have contributed to the purchase price in unequal shares.

(D) Severance of a joint tenancy

It is possible to convert a joint tenancy into a tenancy in common by a process of severing the joint tenancy. The main practical effect of severance is to defeat the right of survivorship. A husband and wife who hold their matrimonial home as joint tenants might therefore decide to sever the joint tenancy when contemplating divorce. Although other methods of severance are possible the normal way would be through the service of a written notice by one joint owner on all other tenants clearly expressing their intention to sever.

4.4   Proving ownership of land

4.4.1   The two systems of conveyancing

If an owner wishes to sell his land (or, of course, to be strictly accurate, to sell his legal estate in that land) he must first prove to the buyer that he is its rightful owner, and therefore free to sell it. This process of proving ownership is referred to as proving the seller's 'title' to land. This is an important aspect of the whole process of transferring ownership of a legal estate which is itself described as the conveyancing process.

As we will see, for historical reasons there are presently two systems of conveyancing in England and Wales. The first is the traditional unregistered system, which currently still applies to approximately 20% of all titles to land. The second is the newer land registration system which accounts for the remaining 80%, and which will eventually replace the unregistered system entirely. Before examining these systems we should first introduce the nature and role of deeds in this process in view of their importance within each of the two systems.

4.4.2   The nature and role of deeds

Deeds are documents which comply with certain legal formalities in order to ensure that their authenticity can be more easily proved than would be the case with an ordinary written document. They are used in many legal and business situations but have a particular role within land law. The reason for this is that in almost all cases the only way that a legal estate or legal interest (one of the third party rights in land – see paragraph 4.6.1) can be created or transferred is by deed[15].

---

[15] Law of Property Act 1925, s. 52(1)

The traditional common law formalities required that a deed had to be signed, sealed and delivered to be valid. This meant that the person to be bound by the deed had first to sign the document, then to add their personal seal to it in sealing wax, and finally that they had to personally and formally hand it over to the other party. In practice deeds were also signed by a witness to the parties' signature although this was not strictly required for a deed to be valid. Over time some of these formalities, notably the requirement for a wax seal, were relaxed. There was briefly a period when a small self-adhesive red sticker was used instead of sealing wax. Eventually even this was dispensed with and documents simply included a small pre-printed circle containing the letters 'LS' (*locus sigilli* or 'the place of the seal') alongside the parties' signatures.

The formalities for the creation of a deed are now contained in section 1 of the Law of Property (Miscellaneous Provisions) Act 1989. This no longer requires a document to be sealed in order to be a valid deed but does set out three additional requirements. Firstly the face of the document must make it clear that it is intended to be a deed. This will typically be achieved by the document describing itself as a deed or expressing itself to be executed or signed as a deed. Secondly, the document must be signed by the person to be bound by it in the presence of a witness who must then also sign. Finally, the document must be delivered to the person who can rely upon it although this need not be done formally and can take place by post or by someone on behalf of the person who is to be bound by it.

Deeds can take many forms, according to the purpose for which they are created. In the context of the creation or transfer of a legal estate the following would be the most common:

- Conveyance – transferring a freehold estate on sale.
- Deed of Gift – transferring a freehold estate where there is no consideration.
- Assent – transferring a legal estate to a beneficiary by the personal representatives of a deceased estate owner.
- Mortgage Deed – granting a mortgage to a lender over a legal estate in return for a loan.
- Lease – granting a new leasehold estate.
- Deed of Assignment – transferring an existing leasehold estate.

4.4.3 The traditional unregistered system

When someone acquires a legal estate in land all the old deeds relating to the property are handed to them, together with a new deed (for example, a conveyance) by which the previous owner transfers the estate to them. Traditionally, the way in which someone proved ownership of a legal estate was therefore simply by being able to produce the deed transferring the estate to them, and also some of the old deeds that proved that the previous owners also had good title at the time that they transferred the estate in the past. The process is referred to as deducing title and is illustrated by the following simple example.

In the year 2010 Helen wishes to purchase the freehold in Blackacre from George. George has a large bundle of old deeds relating to the property including the following:

- Conveyance from Charles to David dated 1930.
- Conveyance from David to Elaine dated 1957.
- Conveyance from Elaine to Fiona dated 1985.
- Conveyance from Fiona to George dated 1989.

George can therefore prove his ownership of the freehold to Blackacre by producing the 1989 conveyance to him and also some of the earlier deeds which prove that Fiona was entitled to transfer the estate to him, and that the earlier estate owners were similarly entitled to effect the transfers which they made. George deduces title in this way by demonstrating an unbroken chain of ownership stretching back into the past.

The earliest deed which an estate owner produces in the chain of ownership is referred to as the root of title and a question arises about how far back in time it is reasonable to go in order to certain that the current owner is indeed the rightful owner of the estate. This is actually a matter for the parties to agree but, in the absence of contrary agreement, section 23 of the Law of Property Act 1969 provides that it should be fifteen years. In practice this means that one should go back to the first document in the chain that is older than this minimum period. In the above example, if we go back fifteen years, we reach the date 1995. The first document which is older than this is the 1989 conveyance from Fiona to George. Therefore, in this example, because George has owned the property for so long, he only has to produce this single conveyance to Helen as evidence of his title.

In practice, the estate owner will not want to part with the original deeds until a purchaser is actually ready to hand over the purchase price to him so he initially deduces his title by producing copies of the relevant documents. Before the invention of photocopiers these had to be typed or handwritten in the form of summaries of various documents called 'abstracts of title'. Because of the laborious nature of this process the clerks who produced them did so using an abbreviated form of language bearing a striking similarity to modern day text speak. In later years photocopies of the documents attached to a schedule (called an 'epitome of title') replaced the use of abstracts. However produced, these copy documents are mailed to the purchaser (or their legal advisor) at some point in advance of the completion of the transfer.

4.4.4   *The land registration system*

(A) Principles of registration

The traditional unregistered system was extremely inefficient. It relied on bundles of title deeds that could easily become lost or stolen. It was also unnecessarily time consuming as title had to be investigated on the occasion of every transaction affecting the title.

The Land Registration Act 1925 therefore introduced a system of land registration with the aim of simplifying the conveyancing process. It established the Land Registry with the intention that all titles should eventually be registered in a series of district registries. The current legislation is now contained in the Land Registration Act 2002. Today, as we have seen, the majority of titles are now registered but the process is still not complete. The Land Registry currently has ambitious plans to complete the process by 2012.

The estates which are capable of registration at the Land Registry (the 'registerable estates') are freeholds and leaseholds granted for more than seven years. Their owners are free to register them voluntarily but registration is now compulsory on the first occasion that the estate is sold, or is subject to certain other transactions. On application for first registration the estate owner must deduce their title to the Land Registry in the same way that they would do for a purchaser of unregistered land. If satisfied, the Land Registry will prepare a register for the estate which will mirror the legal situation disclosed by the pre-registration deeds and will allocate a unique title number to it. From this point onwards the deeds cease to have any significance and the register, rather than the deeds, provides conclusive evidence of the ownership of the estate. As the state guarantees the accuracy of the register there are provisions for the payment of compensation to those who suffer loss as a result of any errors within it.

(B) The form of the register

The registers exist in electronic format and are public documents. On payment of a small fee anyone can obtain a copy of the register for a particular title, either by post, or online through the Land Registry website. The register comprises three parts.

(a) Property register

This part of the register contains the description of the property. It states whether the title is freehold or leasehold and describes the property by reference to its postal address, and to a plan filed at the registry showing the extent of the property edged in red. If the property has the benefits of any rights over neighbouring properties (for example a right of way) this will also be recorded in this part of the register.

(b) Proprietorship register

The proprietorship register contains three types of information. Firstly it includes the names and addresses of the estate owners (who are described as the 'registered proprietors'). Secondly it states the class of title that the registry has awarded to the estate, according to the strength of the application for first registration or subsequent upgrading. The following four possible classes of title can be awarded:

- Title Absolute – As its name suggests, this is the strongest class of title and indicates that the state is willing to provide an absolute guarantee to the registered proprietor's title to the estate.
- Good Leasehold Title – This indicates that the state is prepared to guarantee the leasehold title but not the superior title from which it is derived. This might be,

for example, because the freehold title is unregistered and insufficient evidence of that title was available on registration.

- Possessory Title – These titles are extremely rare and indicate only that the registered proprietor is in occupation of the land but without any other evidence of his entitlement. This might occur where the deeds have been lost or where the registered proprietor is in occupation through adverse possession (see paragraph 4.5).
- Qualified Title – One is unlikely to come across this form of title. However, it might be awarded if the state wished to exclude some significant impediment in the registered proprietor's title from the terms of the guarantee being provided by the act of registration.

Finally, the proprietorship register also contains details of any restrictions that have been placed on the way in which the registered proprietor is free to dispose of the property in order to protect the interests of certain third parties who have rights in the property, for example those of beneficiaries under a trust (see paragraphs 4.6.2.B and 4.10.2.C).

(c) Charges register

The charges register contains notices of certain third party rights to which the estate is subject and which will bind a purchaser. These are discussed further in paragraph 4.10.2.A.

(C) Subsequent dealings

Once an estate has been registered, subsequent sales and other dealings are dealt with according to the requirements of the Land Registration Act 2002. As previously stated there is therefore no requirement to deduce title to a purchaser in the manner described above for unregistered title. The register now provides conclusive evidence of title so all that is required is to provide an official Land Registry copy of it to the purchaser in advance of the sale.

The way in which a transfer of the legal estate takes effect is also slightly different for a registered title. The document giving effect to the transfer is still a deed but (in the case of a freehold estate) is referred to as deed of transfer rather than a conveyance. In fact, this may often be printed on a standard form downloaded from the Land Registry website and its appearance will therefore lack the solemnity we perhaps associate with deeds. Once the deed has been executed, unlike the situation with unregistered title, the transfer of the estate is not immediately effective. Section 27(1) of the Land Registration Act 2002 provides that dispositions of registered land only become effective once they are registered. Following a completion of their purchase the purchaser must therefore lodge the deed of transfer with the registry and apply for the name of the registered proprietor to be amended in the proprietorship register. There is a strong incentive to do so as a failure to complete the registration within two months results in the legal title reverting to the former owner.

4.4.5 *Electronic conveyancing*

Despite recent advances in technology the conveyancing process remains a largely paper-based process. Contracts, transfers of estates and their subsequent registration at the Land Registry all still have to take place by the creation and postage of written documentation. However, a joint report by the Land Registry and the Law Commission (*Land Registration for the Twenty-First Century: A Conveyancing Revolution*, 2001, Law Com No. 271) sets out bold plans for the introduction of e-conveyancing. It envisages the use of wholly electronic documents and deeds, executed by electronic signatures with immediate and secure electronic links between the Land Registry and a network of conveyancers and financial institutions. This would facilitate the instant creation and transfer of legal rights and a consequent reduction in the time and uncertainty involved in the conveyancing process.

This is no mere pipe dream. One of the stated purposes of the Land Registration Act 2002 was to create the legal framework in which registered conveyancing can be conducted electronically and this is now effectively in place. Since the introduction of the Act the Land Registry has also made significant changes to its procedures with the aim of facilitating the introduction of e-conveyancing. As already noted, electronic copies of the register are now available online. Significantly, the Land Registry has also now introduced the secure online portal which will be used by institutional subscribers to access its fully electronic conveyancing services in the future and some of these are now in place. At the time of writing a limited system is already in operation by which lenders can register the discharge of mortgages electronically. A pilot scheme is also being trialled for the fully electronic granting and registration of mortgages involving the first ever electronic deed, incorporating its electronic signature by the borrower. The Land Registry has also declared its intention of introducing a facility for the electronic transfer of legal estates themselves by the end of 2010.

4.5 Acquiring ownership by adverse possession

4.5.1 *The nature of adverse possession*

Adverse possession is a mechanism which allows a trespasser to acquire title to land after being in possession of it for a certain amount of time, and thus to displace the rights of the real (or 'paper') owner. The concept is sometimes known as squatters' rights. Although capable of producing some harsh results for those who are deprived of their land it can nevertheless be justified on grounds of public policy. It provides a mechanism for encouraging the efficient use of society's available land resources in circumstances where affected land has been neglected, or perhaps abandoned, by its paper owner for a considerable period of time.

The mechanisms, and the relevant time periods, for the acquisition of title by adverse possession have traditionally been very similar for all types of land, whether registered or unregistered. This traditional approach continues for unregistered land but adverse possession of registered land has been treated entirely differently since the enactment of the Land Registration Act 2002. We will examine each of these approaches in turn, before moving on to consider the requirements which the law says must be satisfied before a trespasser can successfully claim adverse possession under either system.

(A) Unregistered land

Adverse possession has traditionally been based on the principle of limitation of actions whereby an action in the courts becomes 'statute-barred' after a certain period of time. This continues to be the case with unregistered land. The limitation period for actions for the recovery of land is twelve years (Limitation Act 1980, s.15). Thus, once a trespasser has been in possession of land for twelve years, the paper owner is statute-barred from recovering possession. From this moment the trespasser, as the person in possession of the land, has a better right to the land than the paper owner. Additionally, once the twelve-year period has elapsed, the paper owner's title is actually extinguished (Limitation Act 1980, s.17). The courts will therefore enforce the trespasser's right to remain in possession of the land – even against the paper owner who now has no title to the land.

The time period starts to run from the moment that a trespasser takes adverse possession of the paper owner's land. The paper owner is then regarded as having been 'dispossessed' or as having 'discontinued his possession' (Limitation Act 1980, schedule 1, paragraphs 1 & 8). It is not necessary for the same person to be in adverse possession for the whole twelve-year period. A trespasser may transfer his uncompleted right to adverse possession to another trespasser who would then be entitled to rely on the combined periods of adverse possession.

Once the twelve-year period has started to run paper owners often seek ways of 'stopping the clock' in order to prevent the trespasser acquiring title once the full twelve years has elapsed. Mere assertions of their legal rights by the paper owner, or requests that the trespasser leaves the property, are not sufficient. However, the following mechanisms may be effective.

(a) Action for possession

If the paper owner brings an action for possession, and is ultimately successful in removing the trespasser, this will clearly bring the adverse possession to an end. However, if the paper owner is not seeking an immediate end to the trespasser's possession but simply wishes to preserve his own title to the land the following two alternative options are available.

(b) Written acknowledgement of the paper owner's title

A written acknowledgement, by the trespasser, of the paper owner's title will stop the clock and start the twelve-year limitation period running afresh (Limitation Act 1980, ss.29 & 30). Such an acknowledgement may be express or may be implied from some other written statement. For example, in *Lambeth LBC v Bigden*[16], the

---

[16] (2000) 33 HLR 478

trespasser was held to have provided such an acknowledgement when he wrote to the paper owner requesting them not to sell the property. Thus, a paper owner may protect his position by retaining, or obtaining, appropriate written acknowledgements from the trespasser.

(c) Unilateral licence

As we will see below (paragraph 4.5.2.B) possession cannot be 'adverse' if it is lawful, for example if the paper owner has granted permission for the trespasser to remain on the land. The Court of Appeal's decision in *BP Properties Ltd v Buckler*[17] suggests that the paper owner may be able to prevent time running in favour of a trespasser simply by granting him a unilateral licence ('permission' - see paragraph 4.7.5.A) to occupy the property.

The facts of the case were that Buckler lived in a farmhouse with his elderly mother. She had formerly had a tenancy of the house but this had long ago expired and the family had continued in possession as trespassers. In 1974 BP (who owned the freehold) attempted to gain possession of the house before the expiry of the twelve year limitation period. Because of local hostility to them they withdrew the action and wrote to the old lady telling her that she could live in the house rent-free for the rest of her life.

On her death, twelve years later, BP sought possession from Buckler who then himself claimed title by adverse possession. The Court of Appeal granted possession. Old Mrs Buckler had been in possession by virtue of the licence granted in 1974 and this had stopped time running. Consequently, Buckler had only himself been in adverse possession from the date of his mother's death and BP were not therefore statute-barred from bringing the action against him.

The decision has been criticised as allowing paper owners to prevent time running against them by a unilateral act of giving permission, without having to incur the expense of court proceedings. However, in *Buckler* the old lady had made no response to BP's letters. If she had expressly rejected the offer of the licence the adverse possession would, presumably, not have been interrupted.

(B) Registered land

Since the enactment of the Land Registration Act 2002 it has become more difficult to acquire title to registered land by adverse possession. Title can only now be acquired by following a two-stage procedure laid down in the Act rather than by acquiring it automatically after twelve years' adverse possession.

Under section 96 of the new Act the twelve year limitation period in section 15 of the Limitation Act 1980 no longer applies to registered land. Hence, a trespasser can have been in adverse possession for considerably more than twelve years without the paper owner's right to possession becoming statute-barred.

However, if a trespasser has been in adverse possession of land for the last ten years, he can apply to be registered as proprietor of the relevant title (schedule 6).

---

[17] (1987) 55 P & CR 337

His application triggers a notification, by the Land Registry, to the registered proprietor who then has three months in which to object.

If he fails to object to the application within the required time period, the trespasser will automatically be registered as the new proprietor. If he does object within the three-month time limit the trespasser's application will automatically be rejected (unless one of the three special circumstances considered below exist). If rejected, he must wait a further two years before making a further application and, if the paper owner is serious about recovering possession, he will bring an action for possession within this period. At the end of this two-year period, if the trespasser is still in possession, he may make his second application and this will automatically be successful.

The three circumstances, referred to above, where the trespasser's first application will not be rejected automatically on receipt of an objection from the paper owner, relate to complicated matters of law. If the trespasser alleges that one of these applies then the matter would be determined by the Adjudicator (an independent judicial officer created by the Land Registration Act 2002 with responsibility for determining contested land registration applications). The three circumstances are listed below.

(a) Estoppel

The trespasser may be registered as the new registered proprietor in circumstances where the doctrine of estoppel applies. This will be the case where he has acted to his detriment in the belief, encouraged or acquiesced in by the paper owner, that he owned the land in question. For example, if he has built a garage on land which he believes to be his own with the acquiescence of the paper owner, the paper owner will then be estopped from denying his entitlement to the land.

(b) Some other entitlement to be registered

The trespasser may be registered if, irrespective of his adverse possession, he is entitled to be registered as proprietor for some other reason. These cases are likely to be rare but will include situations:

- Where the trespasser is entitled to the land under a will but is in possession of the land without the consent of the deceased's executors.
- Where the trespasser has contracted to buy the land and has paid the purchase price, but where the legal estate has not been transferred to him.

(c) Reasonable mistake as to boundary

Where the physical boundaries between two properties have not been fixed by the Land Registry, this ground provides a mechanism for correcting the register through the mechanism of adverse possession. If the trespasser has reasonably believed, for at least ten years, that the land to which his application relates has belonged to him then he may be registered as the proprietor. If he has knowingly encroached on the registered proprietor's land then it is unlikely that the test of reasonable belief would be satisfied. Claims are therefore more likely to be successful where the encroachment was by the trespasser's predecessor in title, or where fences were inaccurately placed on the initial development of the land.

4.5.2 Requirements for adverse possession

A trespasser cannot acquire title by adverse possession, either to registered or unregistered land, unless he can show that he has *adversely possessed* the paper owner's land for the required time period. The reported cases demonstrate that the following three requirements must all be present for adverse possession to exist.

(A) Factual possession

The trespasser must, as a matter of fact, be 'in possession' of the land. This concept is synonymous with the concept of exclusive possession – the trespasser must have control of the land to the exclusion of all other persons, including the paper owner. In *Powell v McFarlane*[18] Lord Justice Slade articulates this notion, that only one person can be in possession at any one time, in the following terms:

> 'Factual possession signifies an appropriate degree of physical control. It must be a single and [exclusive] possession....Thus an owner of land and a person intruding on that land without his consent cannot both be in possession of the land at the same time. The question what acts constitute a sufficient degree of exclusive physical control must depend on the circumstances, in particular the nature of the land and the manner in which land of that nature is commonly used or enjoyed.'

Generally, clear evidence of exclusion of other persons is required and any continued use by the paper owner will usually defeat the trespasser's claim. A mere trespass is not sufficient – for example the occasional walking over the land could not amount to adverse possession. In *Powell v McFarlane* grazing a cow, coupled with making hay and limited repairs to fencing, did not suffice. Enclosing the land by erecting a new fence[19] or fitting new locks to doors[20] are generally the types of actions that will be required.

Where land is suitable for very limited uses it will be easier to demonstrate the required degree of physical control. In *Red House Farms (Thornton) Ltd v Catchpole*[21] a small island had been formed when a river changed course. The island was unsuitable for any significant agricultural purpose. In these circumstances a trespasser was able to establish adverse possession by regularly using it for shooting.

---

[18] (1977) 38 P & CR 452 at 470–471
[19] *Buckinghamshire County Council v Moran* [1989] 2 All ER 225
[20] *Lambeth LBC v Blackburn* (2001) 82 P & CR 494
[21] [1977] 2 EGLR 125

(B) Adverse to the rights of the paper owner

The whole notion of adverse possession is that possession must be inconsistent with and contrary to the rights of the paper owner. This does not mean that possession must necessarily cause an inconvenience or annoyance to the paper owner[22]. There is not even a requirement that the paper owner should be aware that the trespasser is in possession[23]. However, if the possession is enjoyed by virtue of some legal entitlement then it cannot be adverse. Hence, the existence of a lease or licence will defeat a claim as the possession, even if exclusive, is by the agreement of the paper owner.

(C) The intention to possess

There can be no adverse possession unless the trespasser also has an intention to possess the land (*animus possidendi*). The trespasser's attitude to *ownership* is irrelevant. He may know that the land belongs to someone else or he may mistakenly believe that it is his. Alternatively, he may never have thought about the question of ownership but simply treated the land as his because it was there and it suited his purposes. Whatever the trespasser's understanding about the *ownership* of the land, he must intend to *exclusively possess* it – in other words he must intend to take control of it as if it were his own and to exclude everyone else from it. Once again, this is clear from Lord Justice Slade judgment in *Powell v McFarlane*[24]

> '. . . . the *animus possidendi* involves the intention, in one's own name and on one's own behalf, to exclude the world at large, including the owner with the paper title if he be not himself the possessor, so far as is reasonably practicable and so far as the processes of the law will allow.'

It will always be a question of evidence as to whether the trespasser had the necessary *animus possidendi*. In many circumstances this will be inferred from his acts of factual possession – for example, enclosing land by erecting a new fence or fitting new locks to doors will usually be taken as convincing evidence that the trespasser intends to establish exclusive possession.

Many adverse possession cases arise where land is vacant and awaiting future development and a trespasser takes up possession in the interim. It is now clear that the trespasser will have the necessary *animus possidendi* in these circumstances even if he takes up possession with the understanding that the paper owner may wish to use the land in the future – he does not have to have the intention to exclude the paper owner in all future circumstances. Lord Justice Slade emphasises this in *Buckinghamshire County Council v Moran*[25]:

---

[22] *Treloar v Nute* [1976] 1 WLR 1295
[23] *Rains v Buxton* (1880) 14 ChD 537
[24] (1977) 38 P & CR 452 at 471–472
[25] [1989] 2 All ER 225

'What is required for this purpose is not an intention to own or even an intention to acquire ownership but an intention to possess, that is to say an intention for the time being to possess the land to the exclusion of all other persons, including the owner with the paper title.'

4.5.3   Adverse possession and human rights

As we saw in Chapter 1, paragraph 1.11, the United Kingdom is a signatory to the European Convention on Human Rights and Fundamental Freedoms (ECHR). The rights within the Convention have also now been enacted into English law by the Human Rights Act 1998, and are therefore directly enforceable in the English courts. Article 1 of Protocol 1 to the Convention contains an entitlement to the protection of property and, for several years, there was much debate as to whether the law of adverse possession was incompatible with this.

The debate centred on the case of *J.A. Pye (Oxford) Ltd v Graham*[26]. In that case the claimants were property developers who owned some fields adjacent to the defendants' farm. The claimants' long-term aim was to develop the fields but, in the meantime, had allowed the defendants to use them for grazing. The fields were totally enclosed and access to them was gained through a padlocked gate for which only the defendants had a key. The parties had originally entered into a formal licence agreement for the use of the fields but when this expired in 1984 the defendants continued to use the fields for a further thirteen years. During this time they had made a number of requests for the formal licence to be renewed and had been willing to pay for the use of the fields but their requests were all ignored.

In 1997 the defendants' therefore sought to formalise their rights to adverse possession by registering a caution against the claimants' title at the Land Registry (the relevant procedure for registered land before the enactment of the Land Registration Act 2002). As a response to this the claimants commenced the current proceedings for possession of the fields, arguing that the defendants' lacked the necessary intention to possess. The House of Lords eventually ruled in favour of the defendants, holding that they had been in adverse possession of the land for the requisite twelve years. There was no requirement that they should have had an intention to acquire ownership of the land but simply to use it for their own benefit. In the circumstances they had demonstrated the necessary a*nimus possidendi* and their willingness to pay for the use of the land if so requested was irrelevant.

Following the loss of the case in the English courts the claimants then commenced proceedings against the UK government in the European Court of Human Rights (ECtHR) in Strasbourg. They alleged that, by depriving them of their property, the law of adverse possession violated Article 1 of Protocol 1 to the ECHR. The case was finally decided by the Grand Chamber of the ECtHR which ruled that the law of adverse possession was, in fact, entirely compatible with Article 1[27]. The reasoning of the Grand Chamber is more easily understood if one first refers to the wording of Article 1 (italics and separate paragraphs added):

---

[26] [2003] 1 AC 419
[27] *J.A. Pye (Oxford) Ltd v United Kingdom* [2007] ECHR 700

'Every. . . . . .person is entitled to the peaceful enjoyment of his possessions. No one shall be *deprived of his possessions* except in the public interest and subject to the conditions provided for by law and by the general principles of international law.

The preceding provisions shall not, however, in any way impair the right of a State to enforce such laws as it deems necessary to *control the use of property* in accordance with the *general interest. . . . . .*'

Within the wording of the Article the Grand Chamber took the view that the law of adverse possession was not actually a mechanism for depriving a person of his possessions. In common with similar provisions in other European countries its purpose was instead to control the use of property via the limitation period. The resulting deprivation of possessions was simply a consequence of this. This could be justified as being in the general interest under Article 1 if the adverse possession mechanisms were 'proportionate', in the sense of achieving a fair balance between the general interest and the rights of the paper owner. The Grand Chamber was satisfied that the law was proportionate as:

- The law had been in force for many years so the paper owner would have been aware of the limitation period.
- The limitation period was not excessively short.
- Relatively little action would have been required by the paper owner to have 'stopped the clock' from running against him.

4.6   Third party rights in land

Up until this point in the chapter we have been largely concerned with the two legal estates, the freehold and the leasehold. Because of their similarity to the concept of ownership we could perhaps refer to these as the 'ownership rights' in land. The other category of rights which can exist in land are what we will describe as 'third party rights'. These are rights, not in land which one controls and enjoys, but in land controlled and enjoyed by someone else. The third party rights are described as 'interests' in land rather than estates. They can exist either as legal interests or as equitable interests.

4.6.1   Legal interests

Section 1 of the Law of Property Act 1925 provides that only five legal interests are capable of existing. Only two are of any practical significance for our purposes and these will be considered in detail below. They are:

- Easements – see paragraph 4.7
- Mortgages – see paragraph 4.8

4.6.2   Equitable interests

As discussed in Chapter 1, paragraph 1.5, equity developed because of the deficiencies of the common law. As a consequence of this, a set of separate and rival courts grew up alongside the common law courts, granting different remedies such as injunctions and specific performance. Equity was more flexible and recognized the existence of certain rights which the common law would not. These are the rights which, in a land law context, we refer to as 'equitable interests'.

The classification of a right as being either a legal or an equitable interest has little significance in terms of its substance. However, the distinction has traditionally been crucial in determining the extent to which a right is binding on future owners of the land. Although the situation is now complicated by the introduction of land registration, the basic rule is:

- Legal interests – will always be binding on a purchaser of the land.
- Equitable interests – will only be binding on a purchaser of the land providing certain requirements have been complied with.

These issues are primarily the responsibility of lawyers rather than built environment professionals but will briefly be dealt with in paragraph 4.10. There are a large number of equitable interests but the following are of particular importance.

(A) Restrictive covenants – see paragraph 4.9

(B) Trusts

The defining characteristic of a trust is the separation of the title to property from the right to enjoy its benefits. The person holding the title (for example the freehold estate) is known as the trustee. The person who is entitled to enjoy the benefits (for example, to occupy it, or to receive the rent from it) is known as the beneficiary.

Historically, the common law did not recognize this distinction. It would only protect the rights of a person holding title to property, even where they had agreed to hold the property for the benefit of someone else (the beneficiary). If the title owner subsequently failed to honour his obligations under such an arrangement the beneficiary was consequently unable to obtain redress from the common law courts. The law of equity therefore intervened to protect the interests of the beneficiary through the device of the trust. For this reason a trust is an equitable interest rather than a legal one. The rights which the beneficiary owns in the property are variously described as the 'equitable interest, the 'beneficial interest' or simply the 'equity'. Trusts can be created expressly, by implication, or by statute.

(a) Express trusts

An express trust will arise where the legal estate is transferred to someone on terms that he is to hold it on trust for a third party. Alternatively, an existing owner of a legal estate can expressly declare that he holds it on trust for a third party. In either case the declaration of trust should generally be in writing (Law of Property Act 1925, s.53(1)(b)).

(b) Implied trusts

Implied trusts will typically arise where a third party contributes to the purchase price of a property being bought by a purchaser. In such circumstances, although the legal estate will be transferred into the name of the purchaser, he will generally hold the land on trust for himself and the third party in the proportions in which they contributed to the purchase price. The same principles would operate where a property is bought in joint names but the parties contribute unequal shares of the purchase price.

(c) Statutory trusts

Although beyond the scope of this chapter, readers should be aware that statutes often use trusts in hidden ways to achieve particular legal outcomes. For example, although few would be aware of it, all co-owners of land (see paragraph 4.3.4) are actually joint tenants of the legal estate, holding the beneficial interest in the property on trust for themselves, either as joint tenants, or as tenants in common (Law of Property Act 1925, ss.34(2) & 36(1)).

(C) Contractual rights in land

Section 2 of the Law of Property (Miscellaneous Provision) Act 1989 requires a contract to create or transfer a legal estate or interest to be in writing, and to be signed by the parties. Providing these formalities have been complied with the contract is binding as a matter of contract law. If one party fails to honour the contract the other will therefore be entitled to damages in respect of their losses.

However, as the law regards every piece of land as unique, these types of contract will normally be enforceable by the equitable remedy of specific performance (see Chapter 1, paragraph 1.5 and Chapter 2, paragraph 2.12.1). Where this is the case, under the principle that 'equity regards as done that which ought to be done' the purchaser of the legal estate or interest acquires an equitable interest in the land from the moment that the contract is entered into. On the signing of a contract for the creation or transfer of a legal estate the purchaser is therefore said to acquire an 'estate contract' in the land. In the same way, where the transaction relates to a legal interest (for example an easement or a mortgage) an 'equitable easement' or an 'equitable mortgage' would come into existence.

Providing the requirements of section 2 of the Law of Property (Miscellaneous Provision) Act 1989 have been satisfied the same principles can also operate to create equitable interests where there is some deficiency in the parties' attempts to create or transfer legal rights. This might arise if, for example, a deed has been improperly executed (see paragraph 4.4.2) or, where the land is registered, upon a failure to effect registration of a transaction at the Land Registry (see paragraph 4.4.4.C). Once again, depending on the substance of the transaction, the following equitable interests are capable of being created in this way:

- Estate contract.
- Equitable easement.
- Equitable mortgage.

4.7   Easements

4.7.1   *The nature of easements*

An easement can exist as a legal interest in land. It is a right enjoyed by the owner of one piece of land over a piece of land owned by someone else. All sorts of rights have been recognised as easements although it is helpful to categorize them as being either positive or negative in their effect.

(A) Positive easements

Positive easements are a class of rights that entitle the owner of the right to perform some positive act on the other piece of land. The best known example is a right of way over a neighbour's land.

(B) Negative easements

In contrast, negative easements are rights which entitle their owner to stop the owner of the other land from behaving in a particular way on their own land. The classic example of a negative easement is a right to light. This is a right for one owner to receive light through his windows. The effect of this would be to prevent his neighbour from building on his land in such a way as to restrict the flow of light to these windows.

Although we can categorise easements in this way, and can list particular examples of rights that have been held to be easements, one of the leading land law textbooks for law students[28] notes that 'easements are rather like elephants: easy to recognise but very difficult to define'. For this reason, the courts do not actually attempt to define them. Instead, they decide if a particular right is capable of existing as an easement by asking if it satisfies certain essential characteristics.

4.7.2   *Essential characteristics of an easement*

The essential characteristics of an easement were first described in the case of *Re Ellenborough Park*[29]. The case concerned a park in Weston-super-Mare. Its original owners also owned the surrounding land which they later sold off in individual plots for building purposes. At the time of the sales they granted the purchaser of each plot the right to use the park for recreational purposes. They subsequently sold the park itself to a developer who planned to build upon it. The owners of the surrounding plots claimed that their rights to use the park were

---

[28] Judith-Anne MacKenzie and Mary Phillips, *Textbook on Land Law*, 12th Edition, Oxford University Press, 2008, p. 501
[29] [1956] Ch 131

binding on him and that he was therefore prevented from building on it. The court had to decide whether these rights were easements, and therefore binding, or simply personal rights which the developer could ignore. The Court of Appeal identified four essential characteristics of an easement. As these all existed in the present case it held that the plot purchasers' rights to use the park were easements, and therefore binding on the developer. The four essential characteristics were identified as follows.

(A) There must be a dominant and a servient tenement

This means that there must be a piece of land which benefits from the easement (the dominant tenement) and another area of land which has the burden of the interest over it (the servient tenement). Although the two properties must be near to each other, they need not necessarily be adjacent to each other.

(B) An easement must accommodate the dominant tenement

The right must improve the usefulness or amenity of the dominant tenement rather than simply conferring a personal benefit on its owner. The test is whether any possible owner of the dominant tenement would regard the right as a benefit and therefore if it has the effect of increasing the value and saleability of the land.

In *Hill v Tupper*[30] the owner of a canal which adjoined Hill's land granted him a right to let out pleasure boats on it. The court in that case held that this was not a right that was capable of existing as an easement. It was not a benefit to Hill's land but simply conferred a commercial benefit on him as an individual. This case can be contrasted with *Moody v Steggles*[31] where the owner of a public house had a right to place an advertisement for the business on neighbouring land. The public house had existed on the plot for hundreds of years so the land and the business carried on there had become intertwined. In these circumstances the court held that the right was capable of existing as an easement.

(C) The dominant and servient owners must be different persons

Even if the previous two characteristics are present any right benefitting the dominant tenement cannot be an easement during any period when the two tenements are owned by the same person. The reason for this is that one cannot have rights against oneself. During such periods any such right falls into abeyance and is referred to as a 'quasi-easement', ready to spring into life in certain circumstances under the rule in *Wheeldon v Burrows*[32] if the two tenements subsequently become owned by different persons (see paragraph 4.7.3.B.c).

---

[30] (1863) 2 H&C 121
[31] (1879) 12 Ch D 261
[32] (1879) 12 Ch D 31

(D) The right claimed must be capable of forming the subject matter of a grant

This final characteristic means that the right must be one which the law recognises as capable of being granted by deed. This embraces a number of practical and policy requirements, including the following.

(a) It must be specific and capable of precise definition

If the nature of a right is too vague to be clearly described in a deed then it cannot be an easement. The following examples illustrate the approach taken by the courts in this context.

- Rights of way – A right of way is capable of existing as an easement as it is possible to define the right with precision. The location of the affected road or path can be clearly described (for example by reference to a plan). Any restrictions on the extent of the right (for example limiting it to passage on foot or at certain times of the day) are also capable of being identified in a deed. However, in *Chaffe v Kingsley*[33], the Court of Appeal considered that a reference in a deed to a right of way over an 'intended road' which was not yet in existence was not sufficiently precise to be recognised as an easement.
- Rights of drainage – Rights of drainage are also a common form of easement, the location of which are typically marked on deed plans.
- Rights to light – Rights to light are capable of existing as easements. However, an easement of light cannot exist for the benefit of land with no buildings on it[34] but only in respect of a window or other aperture in a building which is primarily designed to admit light[35].
- Rights to air – Under the same principle there can be no general easement to the flow of air over one's property, for example for the benefit of a windmill[36], but only one capable of definition by reference to some defined channel or ventilation shaft[37].
- Rights of support – Although an estate owner is entitled to a natural right of support from the soil of neighbouring property for his land in its natural state there is no such right for the benefit of buildings which have been built upon it. Nevertheless, such a right is capable of existing as an easement[38] and is extremely common in the case of terraced or semi-detached properties.
- Rights to use facilities – The rights to use facilities on neighbouring property are capable of existing as easements, including a right to use a toilet[39].

---

[33] (2000) 79 P & CR 404
[34] *Roberts v Macord* (1832) 1 Mood & R 230
[35] *Levet v Gas Light & Coke Co Ltd* [1919] 1 Ch 24
[36] *Webb v Bird* (1861) 10 CBNS 268
[37] *Wong v Beaumont Property Trust Ltd* [1965] 1 QB 173
[38] *Dalton v Angus* (1881) 6 App Cas 740
[39] *Miller v Emcer Products Ltd* [1956] Ch 304

- Rights of storage – In *Wright v Macadam*[40] the court held that a right to store coal on a neighbour's land is capable of existing as an easement. Although easements of storage are capable of existing in respect of all types of goods and materials there are important limitations to this which will be discussed in paragraph 4.7.2.D.b.
- Rights to a pleasant view – It is well-established that there can be no easement to enjoy a pleasant view over neighbouring property because it is incapable of precise definition[41]. Similar principles would also prevent the existence of an easement of privacy[42].

(b) It must not amount to exclusive possession of the servient tenement

Rights which would have the effect of excluding the servient owner from possession of his land cannot exist as easements. The assertion of such rights is more akin to a claim to the servient owner's estate itself than to the more limited rights associated with an easement. In *Copeland v Greenhalf*[43] a wheelwright claimed to be entitled to an easement to store vehicles on a 150 foot long strip of land belonging to his neighbour. The court rejected his claim on the basis that it amounted virtually to a claim to possession, or at any rate to one for the joint use of the land.

If storage on the servient land is seen as ousting its owner from possession it is difficult to reconcile the above decision with that in *Wright v Macadam*[44] where, as we have seen, a right to store coal on a neighbour's land was held to be an easement. The courts have sought to reconcile the apparent contradiction in a series of cases relating to car parking. Since *London & Blenheim Ltd v Ladbroke Parks Ltd*[45] it has been established that a right to park a car is capable of existing as an easement, at least where the right does not amount to a claim to the possession of a defined parking space. However, that case also established that it will always be a question of degree as to whether the nature of the right claimed is so extensive as to leave the servient owner without any reasonable use of his land.

The *London & Blenheim* test was applied in *Hair v Gillman*[46] where a right to park a single car on a forecourt that could accommodate four cars was held to be an easement. In contrast, the Court of Appeal came to a different conclusion when applying the same test in *Batchelor v Marlow*[47]. In that case a right to park up to six cars on Mondays to Fridays for the whole of the working day was held to be incapable of being an easement as it so deprived the servient owner of the use

---

[40] [1949] 2 KB 744
[41] *William Aldred's Case* (1610) 9 Co Rep 57b
[42] *Browne v Flower* [1911] 1Ch 219
[43] [1952] Ch 488
[44] [1949] 2 KB 744
[45] [1992] 1 WLR 1278
[46] (2000) 80 P & CR 108
[47] [2003] 1 WLR 764

of his land that it rendered his ownership 'illusory'. More recently, the House of Lords has cast doubt on the *London & Blenheim* test in the case of *Moncrieff v Jamieson*[48]. Although their Lordships' comments in that case were made *obiter*, they suggested that the correct test should not be about the extent to which the servient owner retains *use* of the land, but about the extent to which he retains *possession* and therefore *control*. If this approach is followed in subsequent cases it suggests that the courts may tolerate a much greater level of interference in the servient land than has hitherto been the case.

(c) It must not involve the servient owner in expenditure

An easement is a right to do something (a positive easement) or a right to prevent something being done (a negative easement). It is not a right to have something done so the law will not recognize a right as an easement if it requires any positive action, and therefore the expenditure of money, on the part of the servient owner. Therefore in *Regis Property Co Ltd v Redman*[49] the court rejected a claim that a right to receive hot water amounted to an easement.

(d) It must not amount to the creation of a new negative easement

Rights to light and rights of support are negative easements as they prevent the use of the servient land in certain ways. However, the courts are extremely reluctant to recognise any further negative easements because of their effect in restricting development of the land affected. In *Phipps v Pears*[50] the court therefore rejected a claim to an easement of weather protection following the demolition of a building which had previously sheltered another from the elements.

4.7.3 Acquisition of easements

A right does not automatically come into existence as an easement simply because the law recognises that it is capable of so existing. Easements must also be acquired by the owner of the dominant land, either by 'grant' or 'reservation'. A grant takes place where a landowner grants an easement over his land to the owner of other land. This will typically occur where the landowner sells part of his land and he grants easements to the purchaser over the part he retains. A reservation only ever takes place on a sale of part. Here, the landowner reserves easements over the part being sold for the benefit of the land he is retaining.

(A) Express grant or reservation

This arises where the grant or reservation is expressly stated in a deed, typically the deed transferring a part of the landowner's land to a purchaser.

---

[48] [2007] 1 WLR 2620
[49] [1956] 2 QB 612
[50] [1965] 1 QB 76

(B) Implied grant or reservation

In certain circumstances where a landowner transfers part of his land to a purchaser but the deed is silent about the question of easements the law will impliedly grant or reserve them. Both implied grant and reservation are possible although, as we will see, the latter is less common. Easements can be implied in four different ways.

(a) Easements of necessity – grant or reservation

The courts will readily imply an easement where transferred or retained land would otherwise be completely unusable. In *Nickerson v Barraclough*[51] the court therefore held that a right of way had been impliedly granted in respect of a 'landlocked' piece of land that had no access to the road otherwise than across neighbouring land.

(b) Intended easements – grant or reservation

Where the parties obviously intend that the transferred or retained land should have some specific use, the law will give effect to the presumed intention of the parties and will imply an intended easement. In *Wong v Beaumont Property Trust Ltd*[52] a lease was granted for the use of a cellar as a restaurant. However, for health and safety reasons, the cellar could not be used in this way without the installation of a ventilation duct over land retained by the landlord. In order to give effect to the parties' shared intentions the court held that an easement had been impliedly granted permitting its installation.

(c) The rule in *Wheeldon v Burrows* [1879] 12 ch 131 – grant only

Under this rule, where a person sells part of his land, the purchaser will obtain the benefit of any rights (the so-called 'quasi-easements') which the seller was enjoying over the land at the time of sale. The right must be necessary for the reasonable enjoyment of the land and also be continuous and apparent, which means that the right must be of a permanent nature and discoverable with relative ease. Where the rule applies it converts any existing quasi-easements into easements for the benefit of the land being transferred.

(d) Section 62 Law of Property Act 1925 – grant only

This provision was included in the Law of Property Act 1925 as a word-saving provision so that, on the sale of a property, all existing easements would automatically be transferred to the purchaser without the need to specifically refer to them in the conveyance. However, the courts have interpreted it as actually granting new easements in certain circumstances by converting existing licences

---

[51] [1981] Ch 426
[52] [1965] 1 QB 173

('permissions' - see paragraph 4.7.5.A) into easements. The case of *Wright v Macadam*[53] which we have previously considered illustrates the operation of this rule. During the course of a lease the landlord had informally agreed that his tenant could store coal in a shed on neighbouring land. When the lease expired a new lease was granted which, like the first one, made no mention of any right to store coal. The court held that the grant of the new lease converted the existing licence to store coal into an easement under section 62.

(C) Prescription (presumed grant)

(a) General rules

Where a landowner can demonstrate, in effect, that he has continuously exercised an easement over other land for a minimum period of time (typically twenty years) the law will presume that such an easement has been granted at some point in the past, notwithstanding the absence of any evidence to this effect (for example in a deed).

In order to demonstrate that his enjoyment of the land in question arises from his entitlement to an easement he must demonstrate that he has behaved as if he has an absolute right to such enjoyment rather than, for example, having to do so by force, under cover of darkness or with the consent of the landowner. The law describes this as proving that his enjoyment was 'as of right' and this requires him to demonstrate that such enjoyment was *nec vi, nec clam, nec precario* (without force, without secrecy, without permission).

The usual way of acquiring an easement by prescription is under the Prescription Act 1832. Under section 2 a period of twenty years' uninterrupted enjoyment as of right immediately prior to bringing an action in court will be sufficient to establish an easement. Although the enjoyment must be 'uninterrupted' section 4 provides that nothing shall be deemed to be an interruption unless 'submitted to or acquiesced in for one year' by the dominant owner. Thus, in practice, it is sometimes said that enjoyment as of right for nineteen years and one day is sufficient to establish the easement.

> Other mechanisms exist for acquiring an easement by prescription including a 40 year period under section 2 which operates in a slightly different way to that described above. It is also possible to rely on common law prescription or the doctrine of lost modern grant, both of which, in practice, provide alternative ways for calculating a 20 year period.

(b) Rights to light

Although an easement of light can also be acquired by prescription in any of the ways described above, section 3 of the Prescription Act 1832 provides an additional mechanism which, in practice, is the most frequently used. This provides that twenty years' uninterrupted enjoyment of light immediately prior to action will automatically result in an easement being acquired unless it has been enjoyed on

---

[53] [1949] 2 KB 744

the basis of a written agreement. The significance of this provision is that the dominant owner need not demonstrate that enjoyment has been 'as of right' and only the existence of a written agreement will defeat a claim after an uninterrupted period of twenty years.

The rules previously discussed as to the nature of an interruption also apply to the acquisition of easements under section 3. Previously the only way to interrupt the acquisition of an easement of light was to physically obstruct the light to the affected window. Historically, this took the form of erecting a hoarding adjacent to the window although this would now be difficult due to the requirement to obtain planning permission. The Rights of Light Act 1959 therefore now provides that the registration of a light obstruction notice will have the same effect.

4.7.4 Extinguishment of easements

Once acquired, easements become permanent rights in land, capable of binding successive purchasers of the servient tenement. However, there are a number of ways in which they can be extinguished.

(A) Express release

This arises where the dominant owner expressly gives up his right to the easement by deed.

(B) Implied release (abandonment)

Release may also be implied from the circumstances. However, mere non-use of the easement is not sufficient. The circumstances must be such that these demonstrate a clear intention by the dominant owner to permanently abandon the easement. In *Stokoe v Singers*[54] the owner of an easement of light had bricked up the affected windows for over twenty years. Nevertheless, the infill had not been bonded into the surrounding wall and the iron bars on the outside of the window were left in place. The appearance of the window therefore remained and the court held that these circumstances did not amount to abandonment. In contrast, an easement of light was held to have been abandoned in *Moore v Rawson*[55] where the wall containing the windows was demolished and replaced with a new wall containing no windows.

(C) Unity of seisin

If the dominant and servient tenements ever come into the ownership and possession of the same person any easement is extinguished. As we saw in paragraph 4.7.2.C this is because one cannot have rights against oneself and one

---

[54] (1857) 8 EL&BL 31
[55] [1824] 3 B&C 332

of the essential characteristics of an easement is that the dominant and servient tenements must be owned by different persons.

(D) Statute

In contrast to the situation with restrictive covenants (see paragraph 4.9.6.C) there is no general statutory mechanism for extinguishing an easement. However, a number of statutes do make provision for the extinguishment of easements in particular circumstances, for example the Town and Country Planning Act 1990 and the Commons Registration Act 1965.

4.7.5 Easements distinguished from certain other rights

A number of other rights have similarities with easements and some of these are described below.

(A) Licences

A licence is simply a permission to do something which would otherwise amount to a trespass, for example to walk across someone else's land, or to occupy their land in some way. Unlike an easement it is a purely personal right rather than a right in land. It therefore exists only between the original parties and will not be binding on a purchaser of the land.

(B) Natural rights

Natural rights are the package of rights that the owner of a legal estate is entitled to exercise. Unlike easements they arise automatically and do not have to be separately acquired. Whilst estate owners are entitled to a natural right of support for the soil on their land they have no right of support for the buildings erected upon it unless this has been acquired as an easement.

(C) Public rights, customary rights and town or village greens

Easements are private rights which can only be exercised by the owner of a dominant tenement. Certain other rights can exist which benefit groups of people and which do not require the existence of a dominant tenement. Public rights are one such category and the most frequently encountered is the public right of way. This can exist at common law or under statute and entitles members of the public to use roads, footpaths and certain other land. This now includes the so-called 'right to roam' under the Countryside and Rights of Way Act 2000. Customary rights exist for the benefit of the inhabitants of a particular locality rather than the public at large whilst rights can also exist for the public to use land as a town or village green if registered under the Commons Act 2006.

(D) Profits à prendre

Like easements profits à prendre are private property rights. However, unlike them, they entitle their owner to take some item from the land of another. A right to cut and take timber or to catch fish comes into this category. They can be acquired in similar ways to easements and have traditionally been treated as forming part of the same area of law. They were of great significance historically but are much less so today following the industrial revolution and change from a rural to an urban society.

(E) Party Wall etc. Act 1996

The Party Wall etc. Act 1996 was enacted in order to facilitate certain categories of construction operations in the vicinity of property boundaries. It achieves this by enabling the most appropriate construction solutions to be employed on affected structures irrespective of their location in relation to the boundary or to any common law rights affecting them. Subject to compliance with a procedure described in the Act building owners are given a statutory right to undertake construction work at the boundary and this replaces any previous common law right to do so.

The Act's procedures apply to construction operations in three different situations. They are most frequently encountered where works ('party wall works') are carried out to a party wall or other shared boundary structure. They also apply to the erection of a new boundary structure ('line of junction works') and to excavations which have the potential to interfere with the stability of an adjacent building or structure ('adjacent excavations').

There are minor differences between the procedures in each of these three situations. However, they all commence with the service of an originating notice by a building owner wishing to undertake construction work on an adjoining owner whose property will be affected by it. The adjoining owner can respond in a number of different ways but in most cases a dispute will arise between the parties within the meaning of the legislation. Although there is then scope for this to be resolved by a single agreed surveyor, the parties will usually each appoint a surveyor and the two surveyors will publish a joint award which will regulate the conduct of the works. Providing the building owner undertakes the work in accordance with the terms of the award this will be lawful, notwithstanding the fact that it involves interference with property owned by the adjoining owner.

(F) Access to Neighbouring Land Act 1992

Landowners have no general common law right of entry onto adjoining land to carry out maintenance to their own property. The Access to Neighbouring Land Act 1992 therefore provides a mechanism for an owner to obtain a court order granting access in these circumstances. The right of access is limited to the carrying out of 'basic preservation works' and does not apply to alteration or improvement work.

4.8   Mortgages

4.8.1   The nature of mortgages

In common parlance a mortgage is simply a loan which is secured on land. Rather confusingly the legal definition is entirely the opposite. The mortgage, in a legal sense, is not the money that is loaned but the rights created in the land in order to provide the security. It is therefore the borrower ('mortgagor') who grants the mortgage to the lender ('mortgagee') rather than the other way round. Like the easement, the mortgage can exist as a legal interest in land. Mortgages are created by deed and are often described as a 'legal charge' on the land affected.

Mortgage deeds will contain a large number of terms in addition to the one which actually charges the property to the lender. One of these will specify a date for the repayment of the loan and this is known as the legal date for redemption (sometimes also described as the contractual date for redemption). We will see that this has a particular legal significance. In modern day domestic mortgages, whatever the actual length of the mortgage term, the legal date for redemption might typically be six months after the date that the mortgage was granted. This is not as alarming as it sounds for, as we will see, the borrower is protected from the literal effects of this provision as long as they are not otherwise in breach of the mortgage.

4.8.2   Borrower's rights

For historical reasons the borrower's continuing rights in the property are collectively referred to as the equity of redemption. (Although this is no longer the case mortgages used to be created by transferring the legal estate to the lender for the term of the loan and the borrower's remaining rights therefore existed only in equity.) Thus, even today, we refer to 'the equity' in a property, meaning the value of the property to the estate owner after payment of all monies owed under a loan secured by a mortgage.

(A) The equitable right to redeem

The most important aspect of the equity of redemption is the equitable right to redeem the mortgage. At common law the borrower only had a right to redeem on the legal date for redemption. If he failed to do so the right to redeem was lost forever. The lender was entitled to keep the property and the borrower remained liable to repay the loan. These harsh rules were exacerbated by the fact that some lenders would reputedly go into hiding on the legal date for redemption making it impossible for borrowers to repay on the due date.

Not surprisingly equity intervened to modify the harsh common law rules. It recognised that the lender's interest was simply a security for a loan and that the borrower retained rights in the land (the equity of redemption). It applied the maxim 'once a mortgage, always a mortgage' and permitted redemption at any time after the legal date for redemption had passed.

Because of the importance it placed on the right to redeem, equity also took the view that the terms of the mortgage, including any related business transactions, should not prevent or impede the borrower's right to do so. There should, in the words of equity, be 'no clogs on the equity of redemption'.

(B) Freedom from clogs on the equity of redemption

If, after scrutinising a particular transaction, any 'clogs' are identified they will therefore be struck out. Options for the lender to purchase the mortgaged land have been treated in this way as the exercise of the option effectively prevents the borrower from ever redeeming the mortgage. In *Jones v Morgan*[56] the Court of Appeal therefore struck out just such a clause where the lender was given an option to purchase one half of the mortgaged land.

For the same reason the courts are also wary of clauses which purport to postpone the legal date for redemption as illustrated by the decision in *Fairclough v Swan Brewery Co Ltd*[57]. Fairclough had a twenty-year lease of a hotel. He subsequently borrowed money from the brewery which he secured by mortgaging the hotel to them. The mortgage deed contained a clause requiring him to purchase beer only from the brewery and a further term postponing the contractual date for redemption until the final six weeks of the lease. Three years into the mortgage Fairclough wished to purchase beer elsewhere. He therefore sought to pay off the loan and to redeem the mortgage early but the brewery refused. The Privy Council struck out the clause postponing redemption as it prohibited discharge of the mortgage until the lease was virtually valueless and redemption, at that point, was simply not worth having. Despite the brewery's objections he was therefore free to redeem early.

This decision should be contrasted with that in *Knightsbridge Estates Trust Ltd v Byrne*[58] where the mortgage of several freehold properties contained a clause postponing the contractual date for redemption for forty years. In that case, where the two parties were both large companies with equal bargaining strength, the Court of Appeal held that the clause was valid.

(C) Freedom from ongoing collateral advantages

The courts are also suspicious of terms in a mortgage which purport to provide the lender with some collateral advantage over and above the repayment of the principal and interest under the loan. *Solus* agreements, where a business agrees to obtain all its supplies from a particular wholesaler, are a particular example of this and are common between breweries and publicans. We saw an example of this in *Fairclough v Swan Brewery Co Ltd*.

The courts have traditionally struck out such agreements where the advantage is designed to last beyond the time when the mortgage will be redeemed. In *Noakes & Co v Rice*[59] a publican's obligation to buy beer from the brewery was to continue until the end of his lease, even if the mortgage was redeemed at an earlier

---

[56] [2002] 1 EGLR 125
[57] [1912] AC 565
[58] [1939] Ch 441
[59] [1902] AC 24

date. The House of Lords held that the agreement was unenforceable as the publican would otherwise only recover a tied property on redemption in place of the untied property which he had mortgaged. However, as occurred in the case of *Biggs v Hoddinott*[60], the courts will generally be unwilling to strike out collateral advantages which terminate on redemption as long as they are not otherwise oppressive or unconscionable.

(D) Freedom from oppressive or unconscionable terms

The courts will also strike out other terms which they consider to be particularly unfair to borrowers. This occurred in *Cityland & Property (Holdings) Ltd v Dabrah*[61] where the mortgage secured a loan of £2900. There was no provision for payment of interest but simply a requirement to repay a total sum of £4553 by regular instalments over the six year term of the mortgage. The mortgage also contained the usual clause that the whole of the capital sum would become due if the borrower defaulted on the repayments. The borrower experienced financial difficulties within the first year and went into arrears with his repayments. The lender therefore demanded immediate payment of the £4553. This represented 157% of the loan and an annual interest rate of 38%. The court held that this requirement was unfair and substituted an interest rate of 7%.

A different outcome occurred in *Multiservice Bookbinding Ltd v Marden*[62] where the mortgage repayments were calculated in Swiss francs. Due to a massive devaluation of the pound there was a dramatic increase in the amount payable under the mortgage. This equated to an interest rate of 33% over the ten year term of the mortgage – significantly more than the 38% over a single year in *Cityland*. Nevertheless, the court upheld the relevant clause in the mortgage. The transaction was a commercial one between businessmen of equal bargaining power who were each legally represented with no evidence that the lender had taken an unfair advantage over the borrower. Although the transaction might be seen as unreasonable this was not sufficient for the court to set it aside. This should only occur in situations where the mortgage terms are 'oppressive or unconscionable', meaning that the lender has behaved in a 'morally reprehensible manner'.

(E) Statutory protection

Borrowers also have statutory protection against extortionate charges in mortgages. Most first mortgages of residential property will be regulated by the Financial Services Authority under the Financial Services and Markets Act 2002. Other mortgages are protected under the Consumer Credit Act 2006.

---

[60] [1898] 2 Ch 307
[61] [1968] Ch 166
[62] [1979] Ch 84

4.8.3 Lender's rights

The lender has a number of rights in the property to enable him to enforce payment of the monies due to him in the event of the borrower's default. These are discussed below.

(A) Possession

A lender might wish to seek possession in order to sell a defaulter's property with vacant possession, or perhaps to let it out if the current state of the market is such that a sale would not realise the full value of the loan.

In theory, possession can be obtained by the lender from the moment that the mortgage has been entered into, and without any fault on the borrower's part[63]. In practice, this right will usually be restricted by a term in the mortgage stating that it can only be exercised in the event of the borrower's default.

The right can be exercised without a court order if it does not involve the use of force. However, to prevent misunderstandings, and to avoid the possibility of criminal liability under the Criminal Law Act 1977, it is advisable to obtain a court order, at least where the property is still occupied.

Section 36 of the Administration of Justice Act 1970 gives the court a discretionary power to adjourn or postpone proceedings for possession of a dwelling house. It can, however, only do so if it considers that the borrower is likely to be able to pay off the arrears within a reasonable period.

(B) Sale

The lender has a statutory power of sale and it is not therefore necessary for this to be provided for in the mortgage. To be entirely effective it is said that the power of sale must have *arisen* and it must also have become *exercisable*. Once a power of sale arises the lender is generally capable of giving a good title to a purchaser. However, if it is not also exercisable, he may have to pay damages to anyone who suffers loss as a result of his actions.

Under section 101 of the Law of Property Act 1925 the power of sale arises as soon as the legal date for redemption has passed (see paragraph 4.8.1). Section 103 then provides that it will not be exercisable until:

- There has been three months' default following the service of a notice requiring payment, or;
- Two months' interest is in arrears, or;
- There has been a breach of some other term in the mortgage deed.

The sale may be by auction or by private treaty. There is, however, an obligation on the lender to obtain the true market value of the property as at the date of sale. In *Cuckmere Brick Co Ltd v Mutual Finance Ltd*[64] a lender was held to be in breach of

---

[63] *Four-Maids Ltd v Dudley Marshall (Properties) Ltd* [1957] Ch 317
[64] [1971] Ch 949

this duty of care for failing to advertise before an auction that the land had planning permission for 100 flats. The land sold for £44 000 whereas its true market value with planning permission would have been around £65 000.

Once the land has been sold the lender holds the proceeds of sale on trust. He must then apply them in the order described in section 105 of the Law of Property Act 1925:

1. Discharge of any prior mortgages.
2. Expenses of the sale.
3. Discharge of the lender's mortgage.
4. Discharge of any subsequent mortgages.
5. Balance to the borrower.

(C) To appoint a receiver

A receiver is a person who is appointed to manage the property and to receive its income on the lender's behalf. The power to appoint a receiver arises and becomes exercisable in exactly the same circumstances as the power of sale. The lender may wish to appoint a receiver to recover mortgage arrears instead of selling the property where it is income producing. This might occur where, for example, it is a business and is producing a profit, or where it is tenanted and therefore producing rent.

(D) Foreclosure

Foreclosure is a draconian remedy and is rarely used. It allows a lender to apply to the court for a foreclosure order. If granted the effect is to extinguish all the borrower's rights in the property. It therefore puts an end to the equity of redemption. Title passes to the lender who becomes the new owner. The lender is therefore free to sell the property but no monies are then due to the borrower, even if there is a surplus on the sale. There is, however, little point from a lender's point of view, in seeking a foreclosure order as:

*   Under section 91(2) of the Law of Property Act 1925 the court has discretion to order a sale instead of a foreclosure. Wherever there is positive equity in the property it is likely to do so.
*   The process takes longer than a sale. Unlike the situation with a sale it is necessary to obtain a court order to be able to foreclose. Even if successful a final order is not made immediately. An order nisi is first made, giving the borrower six months to pay the arrears and this period can be extended. The order will not be made absolute until this period has expired and the borrower has still failed to pay.

(E) To sue for breach of contract

This becomes relevant in a negative equity situation where there is insufficient money from the proceeds of sale to pay off the lender's debt. The mortgage deed contains a contract between the borrower and the lender. Irrespective of whether a sale has taken place a breach of this contract entitles the injured party to sue the other for breach of contract. If the borrower has failed to pay all monies owed to the lender then he is in breach of contract and can be sued. A sale of the property will not, therefore, wipe out the borrower's indebtedness.

4.8.4 Further mortgages

It is possible for a single legal estate to be subject to more than one mortgage at the same time. If the borrower defaults and one of the lenders sells the property there may be insufficient proceeds of sale to repay all the loans. If this occurs, rather than sharing the available proceeds equally between all lenders, money is paid according to a pecking order described in rules for the priority of mortgages.

All mortgages of registered land are required to be registered in the charges register of the affected title. The priority of mortgages is therefore simply governed by the order in which they were entered on the register. Mortgages of unregistered land are now rare. However, where this occurs a first mortgage is protected by the lender taking possession of the title deeds and this will always have priority over all other mortgages. Subsequent mortgages have to be registered as a land charge (see paragraph 4.10.1.B) and their priority is governed according to the order in which they were registered.

4.9 Restrictive covenants

4.9.1 The nature of covenants

A covenant is simply a legally binding promise contained in a deed. The person making the promise is referred to as the 'covenantor' whilst the person to whom it is made is known as the 'covenantee'. Covenants can take many different forms. However, in a land law context, there are essentially two broad types. The first relates to the covenants made between the landlord and the tenant in leasehold property and these will be considered in Chapter 5. The other type, which we are concerned with here, consists of those covenants which are made between the owners of neighbouring land, whether they hold that land under a freehold or a leasehold estate.

These types of covenants are generally entered into when an estate owner is selling off part of his land and he wishes to exercise some control over the way in which the part being sold will be used following the sale. They are therefore sometimes referred to as 'vendor and purchaser covenants' or (to distinguish them from the covenants that we will consider in Chapter 5) 'freehold covenants'. The purchaser may be required to enter into covenants restricting the way in which he can use the land in the future ('restrictive covenants') or promising to perform some positive act in respect of it ('positive covenants'). By way of example, restrictive covenants might limit the extent to which the land can be built upon, or limit the height of fences that can be erected upon it. In contrast, positive covenants might require the purchaser to maintain the property in a good state of repair, or to erect and maintain a fence. For reasons which will become clear only restrictive covenants can exist as rights in land and fall into the category of equitable interests. As with easements (see paragraph 4.7.2.A), a restrictive covenant can only exist where there is both dominant and servient land.

4.9.2   Enforceability of covenants

A contractual relationship exists between the covenantor and the covenantee. As a matter of contract law a covenant will therefore always be enforceable between the original parties to the deed in which it appears. Hence, if a purchaser of land covenants to maintain a boundary fence but then fails to do so he will be in breach of contract. This will entitle the covenantee to sue him, and to obtain damages or an injunction on normal contract law principles. In theory, because there is privity of contract between them, the covenant continues to be enforceable between the original parties even after each of them has sold their respective pieces of land.

The more difficult question, and the one which is governed by land law, is whether the covenant is enforceable between subsequent owners of the dominant and servient land, possibly many years after the original owners have sold their land. In seeking to answer this question the law asks whether the burden and benefit of the covenant are capable of 'running with the land'. If the burden runs with the land this means that a purchaser of the land takes subject to the covenant and the covenant can therefore be enforced against him even though the promise was not made by him. Similarly, if the benefit runs with the land, a purchaser receives an entitlement to require someone else to comply with the covenant and is entitled to take them to court if they fail to do so. Let us therefore consider the extent to which the burden and benefits of covenants can run with the land.

4.9.3   Does the burden run with the land?

(A) At common law

At common law the burden of the covenant does not run with the land, and a purchaser of the servient land is not, therefore, bound by it. This principle was established in *Austerberry v Oldham Corporation*[65]. In that case Austerberry had sold some of his land to a company to build a road. The company covenanted in the conveyance that they would build the road and then keep it in repair. Following construction of the road they sold it to Oldham Corporation. When the road later required maintenance Austerberry sued the Corporation for breach of the covenant. The Court of Appeal rejected the claim, holding that the burden of a covenant does not run with the land.

(B) In equity

Equity has intervened to alleviate the harshness of the common law position in certain situations and recognises that the burden of a covenant can run with the

---

[65] (1885) 29 Ch D 750

land providing that certain conditions are satisfied. This position has its origins in the case of *Tulk v Moxhay*[66] which concerned land in Leicester Square.

Tulk owned houses and vacant land in the square. He sold the land to Elms but retained the houses. In the conveyance of the land Elms covenanted that he would not build upon it (a restrictive covenant). However, he subsequently sold the land to Moxhay. There was no covenant against building in the conveyance from Elms to Moxhay but Moxhay was aware of the existence of the earlier covenant that Elms had made. He nevertheless proposed to erect buildings on the land so Tulk issued injunction proceedings against him to prevent this. The court granted the injunction on the basis that Moxhay was subject to the covenant as he had notice of it. The case therefore established that, at least in equity, the burden of a covenant could run with the land in certain circumstances (and therefore could exist as an equitable interest in land). The necessary conditions for this were subsequently developed in later cases and may be stated as follows.

(a) The covenant must be negative (restrictive) in substance

This condition was articulated in *Haywood v Brunswick Permanent Benefit Building Society*[67] where a covenant to repair some houses had been entered into. The servient land was then sold and subsequently mortgaged to the building society by the purchaser. The purchaser defaulted on the mortgage and the building society, which had notice of the repairing covenant, took possession of the property. The question for the court was whether the building society was bound by the covenant. The Court of Appeal held that it was not. The rule in *Tulk v Moxhay* only applied to covenants that were negative in substance, meaning that they must not require the expenditure of money in order to be complied with. This is therefore the origin of the rule that only the burden of a restrictive covenant (but not a positive covenant) can run with the land in equity.

(b) The covenant must have been imposed for the benefit of land retained by the original covenantee

This relates to the requirement that, as with easements, there must be both dominant and servient land. The concept, in the law of easements, of 'accommodating' the dominant tenement is expressed in this context as a requirement for the covenant to 'touch and concern' the dominant land. As with the law of easements this means that the covenant must provide an actual benefit to the land rather than merely a personal benefit for the original covenantee. The leading case establishing the requirement for the covenantee to retain land which is benefitted by the covenant is *London County Council v Allen*[68].

In that case the LCC sold a large plot of land to a builder who covenanted that he would not build upon part of the land which had been designated for use as a road. The builder subsequently sold the plot to Allen. Although Allen had notice of the covenant she nevertheless started to build some houses on it. The LCC applied

---

[66] (1848) 2 Ph 774
[67] (1881) 8 QBD 403
[68] [1914] 3 KB 642

for an injunction to restrain the work. The Court of Appeal refused the injunction as the LCC had not retained any land capable of benefiting from the covenant which was therefore not binding on Allen when she purchased the plot, even though she had notice of it. The rationale for the rule in *Tulk v Moxhay* had been to provide protection for landowners who chose to sell part of their land. The existence of the retained land was therefore an essential condition for the operation of the rule.

(c) The original parties must have intended the burden of the covenant to run with the land

This will usually be apparent from the wording of the covenant in the deed which will typically be expressed to be made by the covenantor 'on behalf of himself and his successors in title'. In the absence of such express wording section 79 of the Law of Property Act 1925 provides that the parties are deemed to have so intended unless they express some contrary intention.

(d) The purchaser of the servient land must have notice of the covenant

This was central to the decision in *Tulk v Moxhay* but, as we will see in paragraph 4.10, this requirement will today more usually be satisfied by registration.

4.9.4   Does the benefit run with the land?

(A) At common law

We have seen that, under ordinary contract law principles, the covenant will continue to be enforceable against the original covenantor whether the covenant was positive or restrictive. However, if the original covenantee has sold the dominant land, the question arises as to whether his entitlement to enforce the covenant against the original covenantor passes to his successors in title. The law says that it will, as long as (a) the covenant 'touches and concerns' the dominant land and (b) the parties intended the benefit to run with the land (and this requirement is now implied by section 78 of the Law of Property Act 1925). In most cases where a covenant has genuinely been made for the benefit of other land a successor in title to the original covenantee will, therefore, be able to enforce against the original covenantor.

(B) In equity

We have seen that in certain circumstances the burden of a restrictive covenant (but not of a positive covenant) can run with the land in equity under the rule in *Tulk v Moxhay* and that the covenant will then also be enforceable against a successor in title to the original covenantor. Under these rules the original covenatee will always be able to enforce the covenant against the covenantor's successors in title. However, for this entitlement to pass to the original covenantee's successors in title, they must themselves demonstrate that the *benefit* of the covenant has passed to them *in equity*. As long as the covenant 'touches and concerns' the dominant land this will almost always be the situation following the case of *Federated Homes Ltd v Mill Lodge Properties Ltd*[69]. Contrary to what had previously been thought, the Court of Appeal held in that case that the benefit of a covenant is automatically annexed to dominant land by section 78 of the Law of Property Act 1925 without the need for any additional evidence or formality.

4.9.5 Building schemes

Building schemes (also sometimes known as 'schemes of development') are housing estate developments where a developer imposes identical restrictive covenants on each plot in order to maintain the quality of the estate. Where the legal requirements of a building scheme are satisfied the benefits and burdens of all the covenants automatically pass to the purchasers of each of the plots, and to their successors in title. This means that, at any time in the future, every plot owner is always entitled to enforce any of the covenants against any other owner who fails to comply with them. Significantly therefore, there is no requirement for the developer to have retained dominant land capable of being benefited by the covenants as each of the plots has the benefit of them.

Although the situation has been refined by subsequent cases the traditional legal requirements for the existence of a building scheme were set out in *Elliston v Reacher*[70]. In that case a building society sold off a large number of plots. It imposed identical restrictive covenants on each purchaser but did not, itself, retain any land once the last plot had been sold. One of the covenants prevented the houses on the estate being used for the purposes of a hotel. Almost fifty years later two of the plot owners on the estate were Elliston and Reacher. Reacher owned two plots which he used for a hotel business. Elliston therefore brought injunction proceedings against him to enforce the restrictive covenant. The Court of Appeal awarded the injunction, holding that both the benefit and the burden of the covenant had run with the land due to the existence of a building scheme. The following legal requirements for a building scheme were identified:

- All the plots must derive their title from a single seller.
- Before any of the sales took place, the seller must have laid out the land as separate plots.
- The seller must have imposed identical restrictions on the purchasers of each of the plots with the intention that these were to be for the benefit of all the other plots.
- The original purchasers must have acquired their plots on the understanding that there were common restrictions on all the plots, and that they were intended to be mutually enforceable.

---

[69] [1980] 1 WLR 594
[70] [1908] 2 Ch 374

4.9.6 Discharge and modification of restrictive covenants

Because the burden of restrictive covenants can run in equity they are capable of preventing an owner from making effective use of their land. It is, however, possible for restrictive covenants to be discharged in a number of ways, including the following.

(A) By agreement

Owners of the dominant and servient land can agree to discharge the covenant, They would give effect to this by entering into a deed of discharge.

(B) By extinguishment

A covenant will automatically be extinguished where the dominant and servient land come into the same ownership. This does not, of course, apply to the plots in a building scheme.

(C) By the lands tribunal

The role of the Lands Tribunal was introduced in Chapter 1, paragraph 1.12.1. Under section 84 of the Law of Property Act 1925 an application can be made to the Tribunal to discharge or modify a restrictive covenant. In order to be successful the applicant must establish one of the following four statutory grounds.

- The covenant has become obsolete due to changes in the character of the property or the neighbourhood.
- The covenant impedes some reasonable use of the land and:
  - o it does not provide any practical benefit of substantial value to anyone, or;
  - o it is contrary to the public interest, and in each case;
  - o that money will be an adequate compensation for anyone suffering loss as a result of its discharge or modification.
- The parties have expressly or impliedly agreed to its removal.
- The discharge or modification will not injure anyone entitled to the benefit of the covenant.

If the Tribunal orders the discharge or modification of a covenant it may also require the servient owner to pay compensation to the dominant owner. The Tribunal is required to take the current planning policies of the relevant local authority into account when deciding whether to discharge or modify a covenant.

4.10 The enforceability of third party rights

Third party rights in land were introduced in paragraph 4.6. We saw how these consist of 'legal interests' (including easements and mortgages) and 'equitable interests' (including restrictive covenants, trusts, estate contracts, equitable easements and equitable mortgages). In addition to legal and equitable interests a leasehold 'legal estate' will, of course, also be a third party right in terms of its relationship with the freehold estate (or any superior leasehold estate) in the same piece of land.

In this paragraph we are concerned with the circumstances in which a third party right will be binding on a purchaser of the land to which it relates, and therefore enforceable against him. This depends on whether the land is registered or unregistered.

4.10.1 Unregistered land

(A) The traditional system

Under the traditional system the enforceability of third party rights depended on whether they were legal or equitable. If they were legal they were always enforceable against a purchaser. If they were equitable enforceability depended on what is known as the 'doctrine of notice'.

Under this doctrine equitable interests were binding on a purchaser *unless* he is what is known as a 'bona fide purchaser for value without notice'. This refers to someone who is acting in good faith who buys the legal estate and, crucially, does so without having any knowledge of the existence of the equitable interest. Such a purchaser would take the land free from the equitable interest which would then cease to exist. The doctrine of notice resulted in great uncertainty as to whether equitable interests were binding in a particular situation, and therefore carried risks both for their owners and for purchasers.

(B) The post 1925 system

Parliament intervened in 1925 to introduce a greater degree of certainty into the situation. The distinction between legal and equitable interests remained. The rules relating to the enforceability of legal rights remained substantially unchanged. However, in the context of equitable interests, the doctrine of notice was largely replaced by two entirely new procedures.

Firstly, under the Law of Property Act 1925, the interests of beneficiaries under a trust in the land were said to be 'overreached'. This means that, as long as he generally pays the purchase monies to at least two trustees, the purchaser would take the land free from the beneficiary's interest. However, this interest would not be destroyed but would instead be transferred to the proceeds of sale. Following the sale the trustees would therefore hold the proceeds of sale, rather than the land itself, on trust for the beneficiary.

Secondly, the Land Charges Act 1925 (now replaced by the Land Charges Act 1972) introduced a system of 'land charges registration'. Land charges largely correspond to the equitable interests. The legislation provided a facility for those with an entitlement to an equitable interest to register them at a central land charges registry (not to be confused with the Land Registry) at Plymouth. By so-doing, they protected their interest which would then be automatically binding on a purchaser of the land, whether or not they had notice of it. The legislation also established a search facility so that purchasers could check whether any interests had been registered in advance of their purchase. Equally, a failure to register would result in a purchaser taking the land free from the interest. Under this system the enforceability of equitable interests therefore depended entirely on whether or not they had been registered as a land charge.

4.10.2   Registered land

The system of registration of title to land was described in paragraph 4.4.4. Where land is registered in this way the rules regarding the enforceability of third party rights against a purchaser are governed by the Land Registration Act 2002. The significance of the distinction between legal and equitable interests has effectively disappeared. Instead, a purchaser will be bound by interests (whether legal or equitable) which are either protected by an entry on the register or which are capable of overriding the register.

(A) Interests on the register

Almost all the legal and equitable interests we have considered in this chapter are capable of being protected by an entry on the charges register of the title they relate to (see paragraph 4.4.4.B.c). Once protected in this way they will bind a purchaser of the land contained in the title. As the register is a public document it is, however, possible for purchasers to inspect it in advance of their purchase, and therefore to be fully aware of these interests. If an interest has not been registered then it will not be binding on a purchaser unless it is one of a limited number of rights which are capable of overriding the register.

(B) Overriding interests

One of the principles of land registration is that the contents of the register should mirror the actual state of a title, including any third party rights to which it is subject. The existence of overriding interests, which cannot be discovered from an inspection of the register and are nevertheless binding on a purchaser, is therefore often described as a crack in this mirror. The rationale for their existence is that the nature of some interests is such that it would not be reasonable or practical for them to be entered on the register. The most important overriding interests are described below.

(a) Leases of seven years or less

We saw in paragraph 4.4.4.A that leases for terms in excess of seven years are capable of registration as a title in their own right. As part of that process they will also be entered in the charges register of the superior title and are therefore fully protected. Leases of seven years or less are protected by being categorised as overriding interests and will therefore also be binding on a purchaser of the superior title.

(b) Interests of persons in actual occupation

Where someone has a legal or equitable interest in land, and they are in actual occupation of that land, they have an overriding interest in it which will be binding on a purchaser. This typically occurs where a cohabitee contributes money towards the purchase of a house which they subsequently reside in with their partner in circumstances where only their partner's name appears on the title. In these situations the law considers that an implied trust arises (see paragraph 4.6.2.B.b). The cohabitee has an equitable interest in the property which is converted into an overriding interest by virtue of their occupation. Equally, as we have seen (paragraph 4.6.2.C) a purchaser of land acquires an estate contract in the land from the moment that they enter into a purchase contract. If they go into occupation before completion of the purchase their equitable interest would also be converted into an overriding interest.

(c) Easements created by implication or by prescription

As discussed in paragraph 4.7.3 legal easements can be created expressly, by implication or by prescription. Where created by express grant or reservation they must be protected by an entry on the charges register in order to be enforceable against a purchaser. However, it will often not be practical to protect an informally created easement in this way, whether this has occurred by implied grant or reservation or by prescription. These types of easement will therefore bind a purchaser as an overriding interest in any one of the following circumstances:

- Where the purchaser actually knows about its existence.
- Where he does not actually know about it but its existence would have been obvious from a reasonably careful inspection of the property.
- Where the easement has actually been exercised during the year immediately prior to the date of the purchase (for example, the use of drainage easements or other 'invisible' easements that could not have been discovered by an inspection of the land).

(C) Other interests

A small number of interests in land are not capable of protection on the charges register of the title to which they relate. Some of these are instead capable of existing as overriding interests so are protected in this way. Leases of three years or less are an example of this.

However, one of these interests deserves special mention. This is the interest of a beneficiary under a trust. This is neither capable of being protected by an entry on the register, nor (unless the beneficiary is in occupation as discussed above) of existing as an overriding interest.

Instead, the beneficiary's interest is protected by being overreached in the same way as already described in the context of unregistered land. The beneficiary's interest is therefore transferred from the land to the proceeds of sale. As with unregistered land this will only occur if the purchaser pays the purchase monies to at least two trustees. Although this is not essential it is usual to insert a restriction in the proprietorship register preventing any transfer of the land from being registered unless this requirement has been complied with (see paragraph 4.4.4.B.b).

4.11   Commonhold

We have seen how positive covenants, entered into by the owners of neighbouring land, cannot be enforced against the original covenanting party's successors in title (paragraph 4.9.3). This creates a problem for the owners of units (for example flats or business units) forming part of a larger building. The value and amenity of their individual units is very much dependent on the owners of all other parts of the building properly maintaining those parts. Because of the difficulty of enforcing positive covenants this effectively means that there is no means of enforcing the repairing obligations of other owners, once the original covenanting parties have sold their interest in these properties.

The solution to this problem has traditionally been for developers to grant long leaseholds of flats and other such units to purchasers due to the different rules governing the enforceability of covenants between landlords and tenants in leases (see Chapter 5, paragraph 5.13). The tenants of each unit will then covenant with the landlord to repair their original unit. The landlord covenants with the tenants of each flat to repair the common parts of the building (including the structural parts, entrances, stairways and other shared areas) and to enforce the repairing covenants of other tenants if they fail to undertake their repairing obligations. In theory this ensures that the tenant of each individual unit always has a mechanism by which they can enforce the repairing obligations of others in respect of the other units and the common parts.

In practice, there are two major problems with using long leaseholds in this way. The first is that a lease is, by definition, a diminishing asset. As the end of the term approaches lenders become increasingly unwilling to make mortgage loans on the security of the property which therefore becomes unmarketable. The second is that landlords frequently act in their own interest rather than in that of the tenants. They may not take their obligations to maintain the building seriously or, conversely, they may be over zealous in doing so, resulting in excessive service charge demands to the tenants.

Commonhold was introduced by the Commonhold and Leasehold Reform Act 2002 in an attempt to overcome these problems. It provides a mechanism whereby the individual units can be sold as freehold properties in circumstances where the owners can always enforce the repairing obligations of others in respect of all other parts of the building. It achieves this by establishing the 'commonhold' as an entirely new form of landholding, capable of registration at the Land Registry. Freehold titles are registered for each of the 'units' and also for the 'common parts' within the commonhold. The owner of each individual unit owns the freehold in their unit but is also a member of a 'commonhold association'. This is a company which is owned collectively by all the unit owners, and which itself owns the freehold in the common parts, as well as having the responsibility for their maintenance. The division of the building into units and common parts, and the detailed arrangements and responsibilities for maintaining every aspect of it are described in a document called the 'commonhold community statement' (CCS) which also forms part of the commonhold title registered at the Land Registry. This document contains all the legal rules relating to the operation of the building and, crucially, is binding on all existing and future unit owners for as long as they retain their interest in their unit.

5 The Law of Landlord and Tenant

5.1 The leasehold estate

The leasehold is one of two legal estates that can exist in land (the other being the freehold). The nature of the leasehold legal estate was introduced in Chapter 4, paragraph 4.3.3 and readers should refer to that paragraph by way of introduction to the present chapter. Leases (or 'tenancies' as they are also called) are encountered in many forms. They can involve, for example, a private individual paying a weekly rent for living accommodation, a farmer working a farm which is let to him by the freeholder, or a company leasing an office block for the purposes of its business. Long leases (for example, for 999 years) are also sometimes used as an alternative to the freehold estate for certain types of owner-occupied residential property. Leases are characterized by an ongoing relationship between the owner of the estate (the 'tenant' or 'lessee') and the owner of the superior estate out of which it has been created (the 'landlord' or 'lessor'). The law of landlord and tenant is a specialist branch of land law which is concerned with the legal rights and obligations that exist between these parties.

5.2 Types of leases

5.2.1 Fixed-term tenancy

As its name suggests a fixed-term tenancy is one which lasts for a fixed period of time which is stated at the outset. It can be for any length of time specified by the parties, whether for a few days or for hundreds of years.

5.2.2 Periodic tenancy

The length of a periodic tenancy is not fixed at the outset. These tenancies are defined by reference to a particular time period and simply continue on a rolling basis from period to period until terminated by a valid notice to quit by one of the parties at the end of a period. The period can be for any length of time, for example a weekly, monthly, quarterly or yearly tenancy.

Law and the Built Environment   by Douglas Wood, Paul Chynoweth, Julie Adshead and Jim Mason
© 2011 Douglas Wood, Paul Chynoweth, Julie Adshead and Jim Mason

5.2.3 Tenancy at will

A tenancy at will is said to exist where a tenant has exclusive possession of the property, but on terms where either party is entitled to terminate the tenancy at any time. It is typically an interim arrangement where a tenant is in possession pending the negotiation of the terms of a more formal lease. Despite its name it is not strictly a tenancy at all as it lacks certainty of term. We will see below that this is one of the essential elements of a valid lease. A tenancy at will is therefore similar to a licence, but with the added ingredient of exclusive possession.

5.2.4 Other tenancies

Although of little practical significance readers should also be aware of the existence of the following types of tenancy:

- Tenancy at sufferance: although, once again, not strictly a tenancy, a tenancy at sufferance is said to arise where a tenant remains in occupation ('holds over') at the end of a lease without the landlord's consent. In practice this is likely to be very short lived and will usually be terminated by the landlord bringing possession proceedings, or by converting the arrangement into a tenancy at will and eventually into either a periodic or fixed-term tenancy.
- Tenancy by estoppel: this is said to arise where a lease is purportedly granted by someone who has no power to do so. In certain circumstances the lease will nevertheless become enforceable under the doctrine of estoppel.

5.3 Essential elements of a valid lease

5.3.1 Exclusive possession

We saw in Chapter 4, paragraph 4.3.1 that the right to exclusive possession is one of the defining characteristics of a legal estate in land. The right entitles the estate owner to control and manage the property and this includes the right to exclude every other person from it (including, in the case of a leasehold estate, the landlord). A lease cannot therefore exist unless this feature is present. If someone has been granted the right to occupy and use land but does not have the right to exclusive possession then they only have a licence (permission) to do so and not an estate in land.

The distinction between a lease and a licence is of importance as a number of statutory benefits are only available to tenants rather than licensees. Historically landlords have therefore attempted to deny the status of tenant to occupants by granting licences instead of tenancies. The leading case on the lease/licence distinction is *Street v Mountford*[1] where the parties entered into a written 'licence agreement'. Under the agreement Street allowed Mountford to occupy a furnished room at the top of his house in return for the payment of a weekly 'licence fee'. The

---

[1] [1985] AC 809

House of Lords held that, despite its label as a licence, the arrangement nevertheless created a weekly tenancy and that Mountford was therefore entitled to security of tenure under the Rent Act 1977.

The case established that an occupier's status as a tenant or licensee is normally to be decided by the factual question of whether exclusive possession is present rather than by following the expressed intention of the parties. In this case the occupier was held to have exclusive possession notwithstanding a provision in the agreement entitling the house owner to have access to the room for inspection purposes. The case can be contrasted with *AG Securities v Vaughan*[2] which concerned a 'licence agreement' to occupy a room in a house shared by three other people. Three other occupants signed identical agreements under which they each agreed that the owner of the house could introduce new licensees for each of the rooms, as they became vacant. The House of Lords held that the house owner's entitlement to introduce new occupants indicated that he retained exclusive possession of the property. The occupants in this case were therefore licensees rather than tenants.

The courts are, however, wary of landlords' attempts to deny tenancy status to their tenants by the use of sham devices to exclude an entitlement to exclusive possession. In *Aslan v Murphy*[3] a 'licence' to occupy a tiny basement room, allowed the property owner to introduce other occupiers to share the room with the 'licensee'. As the room was barely big enough even for a single bed the Court of Appeal was unconvinced that this provision was genuine. It therefore held that the occupier had exclusive possession and that he was therefore a tenant. The House of Lords came to the same conclusion in *Antoniades v Villiers*[4] which concerned a 'licence agreement' for a cohabiting couple to occupy a one-bedroom flat. A provision purporting to entitle the property owner to move other people into the flat was regarded as a sham and the couple were therefore held to be tenants with exclusive possession.

Although exclusive possession is a prerequisite for the existence of a tenancy its presence does not automatically mean that a tenancy exists. Where it is present it is then also necessary to consider whether there are circumstances which negate the creation of a tenancy. This might be the case if there is no intention between the parties to create legal relations, for example in a family arrangement. Equally, the existence of exclusive possession might be explained on other grounds, for example where premises are occupied pursuant to a contract of employment, or under a contract for the purchase of land where a purchaser has gone into possession prior to completion.

5.3.2 Certainty of term

The law also requires all leases to have a certain start date and for the end date to be ascertainable. Unless stated to the contrary the start date will be the date on which the tenant goes into possession. It is, however, common for the start date to predate

---

[2] [1990] 1 AC 417
[3] [1990] 1 WLR 766
[4] [1990] 1 AC 417

the date of possession, typically by commencing the term on one of the traditional English quarter days:

- 25 March (Lady Day).
- 24 June (Midsummer Day).
- 29 September (Michaelmas).
- 25 December (Christmas Day).

It is also common for the parties to enter into a contract for a lease to start at some time in the future, or indeed for them to enter into an immediately binding lease which starts at some future date (a 'reversionary lease'). However, where they do so, it is important to ensure that the start date is clearly stated.

In *Harvey v Pratt*[5] the parties entered into an agreement for a twenty-one year fixed tenancy of a garage. The agreement contained detailed provisions about the terms of the lease but omitted to state the date of commencement of the term. The Court of Appeal held that this was not a valid contract to create a lease due to the absence of a start date. Any attempt to create a lease with a start date more than twenty-one years in the future will also be void under section 149 Law of Property Act 1925.

As well as having a certain start date, leases must also have an end date which can be identified at the start of the term. In a fixed-term tenancy the length of the term must therefore be clearly stated. In *Brilliant v Michaels*[6] the claimant entered into an agreement to take the tenancy of a flat when it fell vacant. The agreement was held to be void for uncertainty. This was also the case in *Lace v Chantler*[7] where a purported letting was entered into in 1940 'for the duration of the war'.

A similar result was reached in *Prudential Assurance Co Ltd v London Residuary Board*[8] where a letting was to continue 'until the land was required by the London County Council for road widening'. The House of Lords held that the end date of the proposed term was insufficiently certain for it to come into existence. However, in this case, it was nevertheless held that a yearly tenancy had been created as the tenant had actually entered into possession and paid a yearly rent.

This raises the question of how a periodic tenancy can be said to satisfy the requirement for certainty of term as its end date is not strictly ascertainable at the commencement. The answer is that the law treats periodic tenancies as a series of fixed term tenancies rather than as a single open-ended arrangement. Each period of the tenancy equates to a fixed term and on this basis the law is satisfied that the requirement for certainty is satisfied.

One final point concerns so-called 'perpetually renewable leases'. These arise where the lease inadvertently contains an option for the tenant to renew the term at the end of the lease 'on the same terms as those contained in the original lease'. By definition this form of wording would also require the option to renew to be included in the new lease and this would have the effect of making the lease perpetually renewable. In the interests of creating certainty section 145 Law of

---

[5] [1965] 1 WLR 1025
[6] [1945] 1 All ER 121
[7] [1944] KB 568
[8] [1992] AC 386

Property Act 1922 converts such leases into 2000 year terms which are also capable of early termination by the tenant.

5.4   Formalities for the creation of leases

5.4.1   The creation of legal leases

We have seen (Chapter 4, paragraph 4.4.2) that, under section 52(1) of the Law of Property Act 1925, legal estates and interests can generally only be created by deed. The general rule for the creation of leases is therefore that this must be by deed. However, under section 54(2) of the same Act, a lease for three years or less can be created orally or in writing as long as it is at a full market rent and the tenant is immediately entitled to go into possession. Periodic tenancies also fall into this exception to the general rule, even though they may ultimately continue for longer than three years. Note, however, that this exception only applies to the grant of a lease. The transfer ('assignment') of an existing lease must always be by deed, even if it is for less than three years and was created without a deed.

In addition to the requirement for creation by deed, leases of over seven years must also be registered at the Land Registry with their own separate title. Recall that leases of between three and seven years can be protected by an entry on the charges register of the superior title and that all leases of seven years or less exist as overriding interests.

5.4.2   Failure to comply with formalities

(A) At common law

If the parties fail to comply with any requirements for a deed or registration the intended fixed-term lease will be void at law. However, if they were unaware of these requirements it is highly likely that the tenant will still go into possession and start paying rent, and that the landlord will accept the rent and otherwise behave as if there is a valid lease. Where this occurs the law may assume that the parties have instead entered informally into a periodic tenancy under the exception contained in section 54(2).

(B) In equity

In certain circumstances equity might also intervene to assist the parties. It can do nothing for them if their attempt to create the fixed-term lease was simply an oral agreement. However, if there is something in writing (perhaps a deed that was improperly executed, or a valid deed followed by a failure to register it at the Land Registry) it might treat this as a written contract to create the lease satisfying section 2 of the Law of Property (Miscellaneous Provisions) Act 1989 (see Chapter 4, paragraph 4.6.2.C). Either of the parties could, therefore, bring court proceedings to enforce this contract by seeking the equitable remedy of specific performance. If granted, this would compel the parties to complete the required formalities and this would have the effect of converting the agreement into a valid legal lease.

However, if neither party brings court proceedings to enforce the contract, equity may assist the parties in another way. As we saw in Chapter 4, paragraph 4.6.2.C, under the principle that 'equity regards as done that which ought to be done' the contract to create the fixed-term lease will be regarded as a lease with immediate effect. Thus, although void as a legal lease, it will take effect as an equitable lease.

The combined effect of the common law and equitable rules is that a tenant might theoretically end up with both a legal periodic tenancy and an equitable fixed-term tenancy. The potential conflict between the two was considered in *Walsh v Lonsdale*[9]. The case concerned a contract for the grant of a seven-year lease of a mill where rent was to be paid one year in advance. Pending the formal grant of the lease the tenant went into possession and started paying the agreed yearly rent quarterly in arrears. In the event no deed was ever drawn up but three years later a dispute arose between the parties as to the basis on which rent was payable. The tenant claimed to be in possession as a legal yearly periodic tenant subject to payment of the quarterly rent in arrears. The landlord, however, pointed to the existence of the equitable lease requiring rent to be paid yearly in advance. The Court of Appeal held that the rent was payable in advance. The terms of the equitable lease took precedence because, since the Judicature Act 1873[10], equity prevails where there is a conflict between the rules of equity and the common law.

Since the decision in *Walsh v Lonsdale* it is sometimes said, as between the parties, that an equitable lease is as good as a legal lease. However, it should be remembered that an equitable lease will only exist in circumstances where specific performance is available. The courts will not grant this discretionary remedy to someone who has himself behaved badly and who does not therefore 'come to equity with clean hands'. If the remedy would not be available it follows that the principle that 'equity regards as done that which ought to be done' will not assist either as the equitable interest will not be created. Finally, it should be noted that, for the reasons discussed in Chapter 4, paragraph 4.10, an equitable lease is less likely to be enforceable against a purchaser than a legal one.

5.5   Termination of leases at common law

Leases can be terminated in a number of ways at common law and the most important ones are described here. As will be discussed below, some of these are subject to statutory provisions providing security of tenure for particular types of tenant.

---

[9] (1882) 21 ChD 9

[10] The relevant provision is now contained in section 49(1) of the Supreme Court Act 1981

5.5.1 Notice to quit

This is the conventional method by which a periodic tenancy is determined. Unless the parties have agreed to the contrary, a period of notice equal in length to the period of the tenancy must be served. The notice may be served by either party and must expire at the end of a period of the tenancy.

5.5.2 Effluxion of time

A fixed-term tenancy will automatically determine at the end of the term by a process of effluxion of time. No notice is required at common law.

5.5.3 Break clause

Fixed-term tenancies sometimes contain a break clause (or 'option to determine'). These clauses might allow either or both parties to bring the tenancy to an end before the expiry of the term at a particular time or on the happening of a particular event. The exercise of a break clause will only be effective if it is exercised strictly in accordance with the relevant clause in the lease. The notice to exercise the option must therefore be in the correct form, served at the correct time, and in the correct manner.

5.5.4 Surrender

This arises where the tenant gives up his interest in the property to his immediate landlord. The surrender may be express, in which case a formal deed must be used, or it can arise by operation of law where the tenant does some act which is inconsistent with the continued existence of the tenancy and the landlord concurs. The giving up of possession by the tenant and the return of the keys to the landlord is a classic example.

5.5.5 Forfeiture

As will be discussed below (paragraphs 5.14.1.C and 5.14.2.A) forfeiture is a remedy which is available to a landlord in the event of a tenant's breach of covenant. Where it is available it will bring a lease to an end prematurely.

5.5.6 Merger

If the tenant acquires the estate out of which his lease has been granted (the reversion) the two estates will merge and the tenancy will come to an end.

5.5.7 Removal of tenants' fixtures

We saw in Chapter 4, paragraph 4.2.2 how chattels can sometimes become classed as a 'fixtures' by being attached to land. At the end of a tenancy the general rule is that the tenant may remove chattels but that he must leave any fixtures as these will have become part of the land, and therefore the landlord's property. This rule is relaxed in landlord and tenant situations in the case of what are referred to as 'tenant's fixtures'. These consist either of those items that can be described as 'ornamental and domestic fixtures' or as 'trade fixtures'. The tenant is free to remove these types of fixtures at the end of the term provided he makes good any damage caused thereby.

5.6   Covenants in leases

5.6.1   Express covenants

We saw in Chapter 4, paragraph 4.9.1 that covenants are strictly the promises which are contained in a deed. The term is used more loosely in the law of landlord and tenant to refer to any promise made between the parties concerning the terms of the lease, whether in a deed, in a written tenancy agreement, or made orally. Where the promises are expressed by the parties in any of these ways they are referred to as express covenants. Some of the express covenants that are typically found in leases are described in paragraphs 5.7 to 5.12.

In a limited number of areas the law will imply covenants in circumstances where the parties have neglected to address these by express covenants. However, if an express covenant deals with one of these areas it will almost always take precedence over the implied covenant, even if it is more limited in scope that the implied covenant. The relevant areas are considered in paragraphs 5.6.2 and 5.6.3.

5.6.2   Landlord's implied covenants

(A) Quiet enjoyment

Despite its name, the covenant for quiet enjoyment is not a promise that the tenant will be allowed to enjoy the property free from noise. In *Southwark LBC v Mills*[11] a claim by tenants in a local authority block about inadequate soundproofing between the flats therefore failed. The covenant is, in fact, a promise by the landlord that the tenant will be allowed to enjoy the possession of the property without physical interference by the landlord, or by those deriving title from him, such as the tenants of adjoining properties.

Harassment by the landlord would therefore certainly amount to a breach of the covenant. This was held to be the case in *Kenny v Preen*[12] where the landlord sent threatening letters to a residential tenant, banged on her door and shouted threats at her to the effect that he would physically throw her and her possessions into the street. The harassment of a tenant will have other legal consequences as well as being a breach of this covenant. The Protection from Eviction Act 1977 (as amended by the Housing Act 1988) renders the harassment of a residential tenant

---

[11] [2001] AC 1
[12] [1963] 1 QB 400

a criminal offence. Section 27 of the Housing Act 1988 also creates a new tort of unlawful eviction if a residential occupier is driven out of his home as a result of harassment by his landlord. The Act provides for the payment of substantial damages, representing the difference between the value of the property with the tenant in occupation and their value with vacant possession.

Physical interference with the tenant's enjoyment of the property which does not constitute harassment will, however, also be a breach of the covenant. In *Owen v Gadd*[13] the covenant was held to have been breached where the landlord erected scaffolding outside the tenant's shop, obstructing his shop window, interfering with access and thereby causing a loss of trade. However, where the tenant merely suffers inconvenience which falls short of a physical interference with his property this will not amount to a breach of the covenant. This question arose in *Browne v Flower*[14] where the tenant complained to the court about a new external staircase which ran past her bedroom window. The court held that a mere loss of privacy was not sufficient to constitute a breach of the covenant and rejected her claim.

(B) Not to derogate from grant

This covenant consists of an implied promise by the landlord that he will not do anything which detracts from the value of the lease he has granted. It is not appropriate for a landlord to take away with one hand what he has granted with the other. The practical application of the covenant concerns the use of adjacent land by the landlord, or perhaps by persons deriving title from him. He must not use the adjacent land, or permit it to be used, in a way that is inconsistent with the purpose for which the property has been let.

The leading case is *Aldin v Latimer, Clark, Muirhead*[15] where the landlord was held liable when, having let premises for the purposes of timber drying, he built on adjoining land and interrupted the flow of air to the tenant's premises. A similar conclusion was reached in *Grosvenor Hotel Co v Hamilton*[16] where the landlord leased an old house to a tenant and then used machinery on adjoining land which caused the house to be unstable.

A landlord is not liable under this covenant if nearby property is let for a similar purpose and, as a consequence, a tenant suffers financial loss. Nevertheless, there is some obligation on the landlord to ensure that tenancies of adjacent properties are let for purposes which are compatible with the use of the subject property. For example, in *Chartered Trust plc v Davies*[17] the Court of Appeal held that the landlord was in breach of the covenant to the tenant of a gift shop in a narrow shopping arcade. In that case the landlord had breached the covenant by letting the tiny adjoining shop to a pawnbroker, resulting in queues of people in the arcade spilling over into the tenant's gift shop.

---

[13] [1956] 2 QB 99
[14] [1911] 1 Ch 219
[15] [1894] 2 Ch 437
[16] [1894] 2 QB 836
[17] [1997] 2 EGLR 83

(C) Landlord's limited covenants to repair

(a) Fitness for human habitation at common law

Where residential premises are let on a furnished basis there is an implied warranty by the landlord that they are fit for human habitation at the commencement of the tenancy. This is a very limited warranty as it involves no continuing obligation to maintain the premises, and no obligation at all in the case of unfurnished premises.

The extent of the warranty is also extremely limited. The rule was established in *Smith v Marrable*[18] where a landlord was held to be in breach in circumstances where a house was infested with bugs. There is no requirement that the premises should be comfortable and the basic test of habitability simply requires that the occupants should be free from risk of physical injury or damage to health. Other cases where landlords have been held to be in breach therefore relate to such matters as defective drains[19], poor quality water supply[20] and contamination by tuberculosis[21].

(b) Fitness for human habitation under section 8 Landlord and Tenant Act 1985

This section imposes obligations on the landlords of residential premises let at very low rents. The obligations are that the premises will be fit for human habitation at the commencement of the letting and that they will continue to be so for the length of the term. Unfortunately, the provision is of little use because it only covers lettings where the rent does not exceed £80 per year in London and £52 elsewhere. As there has been no revision of these rental levels since 1957, there must be very few people covered by the provision. Moreover, the landlord must be notified of the defects, and it will not apply if the defects cannot be rendered fit at reasonable expense.

(c) Section 11 Landlord and Tenant Act 1985

This provision applies to 'short leases' of dwelling houses (including flats) of less than seven years. It requires the landlord to keep the structure and exterior of the property in repair and also to keep the services in the property in working order. The landlord is only liable if he has notice of the defect but the parties cannot 'contract out' of the provision, except with the consent of the court.

(d) Common parts

In cases of flats in multistorey blocks the landlord is subject to an obligation to take reasonable care to keep the means of access to each flat in reasonable repair. This common law duty was established in *Liverpool City Council v Irwin*[22] which concerned the claimant's tenancy of a council flat on the ninth floor of a fifteen

---

[18] (1843) 11 M & W 152
[19] *Wilson v Finch Hatton* (1877) 2 Ex D 336
[20] *Chester v Powell* (1885) 53 LT 722
[21] *Collins v Hopkins* [1923] 2 KB 617
[22] [1977] AC 239

storey block. As a result of vandalism the lifts were constantly out of order, the staircases and passages were unlit and dangerous, access to the rubbish chutes was dangerous, and the chutes themselves were constantly blocked. The House of Lords held that, as all these facilities were essential to the use of the flats, the landlord owed a duty to take reasonable care to keep them in repair. Nevertheless, it emphasized that this was not an absolute obligation to repair and, in this particular case, the Council had exercised reasonable care. The extent of the problem was due to the scale of the vandalism rather than a failure by the Council to fulfil its obligations.

5.6.3 Tenant's implied covenants

(A) To pay rent

In those cases where the rent is not agreed between the parties expressly and it is obvious that the parties envisage a tenancy coming into being, it is implied that the landlord is entitled to a reasonable sum for the use and enjoyment of the land.

(B) To pay rates and taxes

Unless the lease provides to the contrary, such payments fall on the tenant.

(C) Tenant's limited covenants to repair

(a) To use the premises in a tenant-like manner

This obligation simply requires the tenant (a) to take reasonable care of the premises and (b) to undertake minor odd jobs or day-to-day maintenance that is consistent with this duty of care. Note, however, that it does not include any liability for fair wear and tear. The classic statement of the tenant's duties is found in Lord Denning's judgment in *Warren v Keen*[23]:

> 'The tenant must take proper care of the premises. He must, if he is going away for the winter, turn off the water and empty the boiler; he must clean the chimneys when necessary and also the windows; he must mend the electric light when it fuses; he must unstop the sink when it is blocked by his waste. In short, he must do the little jobs around the place which a reasonable tenant would do. In addition he must not, of course, damage the house wilfully or negligently......but, apart from such things, if the house falls into disrepair through fair wear and tear or lapse of time or for any reason not caused by him, the tenant is not liable to repair it.'

(b) Duty not to commit waste

This is not strictly a covenant as it is an obligation that arises in tort. As such, it applies whatever the parties expressly agree. Waste is the causing of damage to

---

[23] [1954] 1 QB 15, at 20

property which reduces the value of the reversion (defined in Chapter 4, paragraph 4.3.3). The duty not to commit waste overlaps with the obligation to use the premises in a tenant-like manner. The most important types of waste in the current context are:

- Voluntary waste – positive acts which destroy or damage or alter the premises.
- Permissive waste – acts of negligence or omission which allow the building to fall into disrepair due to neglect.

A tenant for a fixed term is liable for voluntary and permissive waste. A periodic tenant is probably only liable for voluntary waste although he must, of course, also use the property in a 'tenant like manner'.

(c) Duty to allow the landlord to discharge his repairing obligations

Where the landlord is subject to an obligation to maintain the property he has an implied licence:

- To view the state of repair.
- To execute the necessary repairs.

5.6.4   *The usual covenants*

If the parties enter into an agreement for a lease in advance of the creation of the lease itself it will contain an implied term that the lease will contain 'the usual covenants'. What is 'usual' will depend on the type of premises, the purpose for which they are let and the geographical location. However, subject to contrary agreement this will always include the landlord's covenants for quiet enjoyment and non-derogation from grant, as well as the tenant's covenants to pay rent, rates and taxes and to allow the landlord to enter and view the state of repair of the premises. In addition, also subject to contrary agreement, the following provisions will also be included:

- A covenant by the tenant to keep the premises in repair.
- A forfeiture clause, entitling the landlord to re-enter and terminate the lease in the event of the tenant failing to pay the rent (but not for breach of other covenants).

This can be of particular significance if the parties subsequently fail to enter into a formal lease. Under the equitable principles discussed in paragraph 5.4.2.B the parties could nevertheless be held to be bound by the 'usual covenants' implied in the earlier contract.

5.7   Rent

Rent is the payment by the tenant for the right to exclusive possession of the property. All leases will invariably contain an express covenant for the tenant to pay rent but as we have seen, in the rare situations where this is overlooked, this will be implied. Where an express covenant is included in the lease the amount of the rent must be clearly stated (or capable of being ascertained if a fixed sum is not stated) or the whole lease will be void for uncertainty under normal contract law principles (see Chapter 2, paragraph 2.4.1).

Where the rent payable under the lease represents the full market rent for the property it is described as a 'rack rent'. However, in some cases the rent might be capitalized and a lump sum consideration (known as a 'fine' or a 'premium') will be paid at the beginning of the term instead. Where this occurs it is also usual that a small amount of rent will also be paid during the term and this is known as a 'ground rent'. This is a common situation where a developer sells off leasehold flats or houses on an estate to owner occupiers. In circumstances where no rent is really expected over and above the payment of a premium the lease would nevertheless still contain a requirement for payment of a nominal financial sum, or possibly for payment, literally, of a peppercorn.

If there is no contrary provision in the lease the rent will be payable in arrears at the end of each period of a periodic tenancy or at the end of each year of a fixed-term tenancy. In order to improve the landlord's cash-flow situation leases therefore usually contain express provisions that rent will be payable in advance, and that it should typically be payable quarterly on the usual quarter days (see paragraph 5.3.2). Because rent is paid in return for the exclusive possession of the land it continues to be payable even if the buildings are damaged or destroyed and therefore become unusable by the tenant. It is therefore usual for leases to contain an express proviso to the effect that payment of rent becomes suspended on the occurrence of certain events, including damage or destruction by fire.

5.8   Rent review

5.8.1   Nature and purpose of rent review

It is common practice, in leases of commercial premises, for the level of rent payable by the tenant to be reviewed periodically rather than remaining static throughout the term. The purpose of rent review is to enable the landlord to obtain the market rent for the property from time to time throughout the term rather than being locked into a rent based on market conditions at the time the lease was granted. Upwards only rent reviews are the norm so that, on review, if the market rent is higher than the amount currently payable, then the existing provision will be replaced by the higher sum. If not, the former sum will continue to be payable.

The machinery for rent review will be contained in a rent review clause within the lease. Recall that the rent must be capable of being ascertained with certainty or the lease itself will be void for uncertainty. The clause must therefore provide a clear mechanism for ascertaining the new rent and it will typically deal with the following five issues:

- Frequency of rent reviews.
- Method of valuation of the market rent.

- Method of initiating rent reviews.
- Provision for agreement of market rent between the parties.
- Procedure in default of agreement.

Each of these issues will now be examined in more detail.

5.8.2 Frequency of rent reviews

The review periods vary from lease to lease. Five years is common but it is not unusual to find shorter periods.

5.8.3 Valuation of market rent

(A) The hypothetical letting

The purpose of the rent review is to provide the landlord with a rent that he could obtain if he offered the property for rent on the open market with vacant possession. This is obviously an artificial situation as he is not actually free to do so until the current lease expires. In order to satisfy the purpose of rent review the valuation must nevertheless be based on this artificial situation. This is an important principle of rent review. Property valuers do not value the property itself. They value an interest in property. In a rent review it would make no sense to value the current tenant's interest in the property. The valuation must therefore be of a hypothetical letting to a new tenant in a situation where the existing tenancy is not currently in existence. This hypothetical letting will typically be described in the rent review clause in similar terms to the following:

> 'Market rent means the rent at which the demised property might reasonably be expected to be let as a whole in the open market with vacant possession by a willing landlord to a willing tenant without a premium upon the terms of this lease (other than the amount of rent).'

(B) The presumption in favour of reality

Precisely because the actual letting to be valued is so hypothetical it can sometimes be extremely difficult to know how to define every single aspect of the imaginary situation that the valuer is being asked to consider. The courts therefore take the view that anything specifically referred to in the rent review clause must be taken into account but that, apart from this, the valuation should be on the basis of the reality of the situation as it actually affects the property being valued. In *Co-operative Wholesale Society Limited v National Westminster Bank plc*[24] this was described by Lord Justice Hoffman in the following terms:

> 'This approach has produced what is sometimes called the 'presumption in favour of reality' in the construction of rent review clauses. In the absence of clear contrary

---

[24] [1995] 1 EGLR 97, at 99J

words or necessary implication, it is assumed that the hypothetical letting required by the clause is of the premises as they actually were, on the terms of the actual lease and in the circumstances as they actually existed.'

By way of example a question will often arise regarding the length of the term to be valued. Traditionally, the longer the term, the greater the security for the tenant and therefore the higher the rent would be. However, in a recession the opposite might be the case as tenants might be reluctant to take on long-term commitments in those circumstances. In the absence of a clear statement in the lease regarding the length of the term to be valued the valuer might legitimately decide to undertake his valuation on the basis of either:

- The original term of the lease, or;
- The period until the next rent review, or;
- The unexpired term of the lease at the review date.

Although the correct approach will inevitably depend in the precise wording of the rent review clause the decision in *Norwich Union Life Assurance Society v TSB*[25] is indicative of the approach often taken by the courts. In that case the review took place in the twelfth year of a twenty-two-year term with valuation being required 'on the terms of this lease'. The court applied the presumption in favour of reality and held that the unexpired term of ten years should be valued rather than the original twenty-two-year term.

(C) Assumptions and disregards

If the valuation was simply to be made on the basis so far described the presumption in favour of reality would lead to injustice in a number of situations. For this reason, in addition to describing the hypothetical letting, it is also common for rent review clauses to require the valuer to take account of certain 'assumptions' and 'disregards'. Some of the common assumptions and disregards are discussed below.

5.8.4 Common assumptions

(A) 'That the tenant has complied with his covenants'

Because of the presumption in favour of reality if the property is in a state of disrepair at rent review the market rent will be lower than if it is in a good condition. A tenant who had not complied with his covenants to repair the property would gain a benefit from this. To prevent this injustice occurring it is therefore common for the rent review clause to require market rent to be valued on the assumption that the tenant has complied with his covenants.

---

[25] [1986] 1 EGLR 136

(B) 'That the premises are fully fitted out and ready for immediate occupation and use'

We have seen that the hypothetical letting requires the property to be valued with vacant possession. However, in *99 Bishopsgate v Prudential Assurance Ltd*[26] the court applied the presumption in favour of reality with unexpected results. It held that vacant possession meant, not only that the tenant had vacated the property, but that he had also taken all his fittings with him, leaving nothing but an empty shell. In these circumstances it is common for new tenants to be given a rent-free period at the start of the lease to fit out the premises. Because of this convention the court held the rent at rent review should be discounted to reflect this rent-free period. As a response to this decision it is therefore now common for rent-review clauses to include an assumption that the property is fully fitted out and ready for immediate occupation.

5.8.5 Common disregards

(A) Tenant's occupation

The requirement for valuation to be on the basis of vacant possession relates to the physical nature of the property. However, in order to ensure that a true market rent is arrived at that does not prejudice the existing tenant a similar hypothetical approach has to be made with regard to the bidders in the market. This is because the existing tenant is likely to be willing to pay a higher rent than most others in the market in order to avoid the expense of having to move to other premises. Thus, a requirement in the rent review clause that the tenant's occupations should be disregarded ensures that the existing tenant is simply treated as one notional bidder in the hypothetical market, rather than one whose personal circumstances would otherwise cause the market rent to be increased.

(B) Goodwill

If the tenant's business has been successful this may have generated goodwill which might increase the rent that bidders would be prepared to pay in the market. It would be unfair to penalise the tenant for his success at rent review so rent review clauses will usually require goodwill to be disregarded when valuing the new rent.

(C) Improvements

The market rent will also be increased in situations where the tenant has carried out improvements to the property during the lease. In *Ponsford v HMS Aerosols Ltd*[27] the House of Lords, again applying the presumption in favour of reality, held that

---

[26] [1985] 1 EGLR 72
[27] [1979] AC 63

the new rent at rent review should therefore take the tenant's improvement into account. In fairness to tenants it is therefore usual for the rent review clause to require these to be disregarded.

5.8.6 Method of initiating rent review

The traditional method of initiating rent reviews is by service of a review notice (often described as a 'trigger notice') by the landlord setting out his proposals for the new rent. The time for service of the trigger notice has traditionally been laid down in the rent review clause. If the tenant wishes to challenge the landlord's proposals he has traditionally been given the right to serve a counter-notice to this effect within a certain time scale. One issue which has been of importance in rent review cases for many years is whether a failure to serve a notice within the specified time limit thereby precludes a party from serving the notice at all. In the language of the law the question was therefore whether 'time is of the essence' in rent review clauses.

The matter was finally resolved by the House of Lords in *United Scientific Holdings v Burnley Borough Council*[28]. The rent review clause in that case provided that the landlord's trigger notice was to be served during the year immediately preceding the review date. Burnley Borough Council (the landlord) in fact served the notice six weeks after the review date and the tenant argued that it was therefore invalid. It was held that the notice was, in fact, valid as there is a presumption in rent review procedures that time is not of the essence. This presumption can, however, be rebutted by evidence that the parties had a contrary intention (i.e. that they intended time to be of the essence). Evidence may be in the form of an express provision in the lease to this effect or implied from what have been called 'contra-indications' in the lease or in the surrounding circumstances.

An example of a contra-indication is what is referred to as a 'deeming provision'. This is a provision that the new rent will be deemed to be that stated in a landlord's trigger notice or tenant's counter-notice unless the other party responds within the stated timescale. Such an arrangement existed in *Starmark Enterprises Ltd v CPL Distribution Ltd*[29]. The landlord served a trigger notice within the required timescale proposing a rent of £84 800 per year. The tenant then served a counter-notice proposing that the rent should be £52 725. However, as the tenant had served the notice six weeks after that required by the lease the Court of Appeal held that it was invalid. The deeming provision provided the necessary contra-indication that the parties intended time to be of the essence and the rent was therefore deemed to be that stated in the landlord's trigger notice.

5.8.7 Provision for agreement of market rent

The rent review clause will provide some form of mechanism for the parties to reach agreement amicably before resorting to some more formal mechanism for determining the new rent. Traditionally, a set period was allowed following service

---

[28] [1978] AC 904
[29] [2001] EWCA Civ 1252

of a tenant's counter-notice for this to take place. Today, as a result of the decision in *United Scientific Holdings*, there has been a move away from rigid timescales and even from the requirement to serve notices at all, in favour of an informal approach to reaching agreement by consensus.

5.8.8 Procedure in default of agreement

If, however, the parties are unable to reach agreement within a certain period, the lease will provide that the dispute should be referred to an independent third party for determination. This will invariably be a surveyor who has significant local valuation experience of the relevant type of property. The lease will either require the surveyor to be appointed as an arbitrator, or as an expert. The nature of arbitration has already been considered (see Chapter 1, paragraph 1.13) and, significantly, an arbitrator is generally immune from claims for negligence, but the parties have a right of appeal against an arbitrator's award to the High Court. An appointment as arbitrator will be appropriate for the more complex or high value cases. For conventional properties at modest rents it will often be more appropriate to appoint the surveyor to determine the new rent in a less judicial manner and he will therefore often be appointed simply as 'expert'. The role of an expert in an expert determination is not to hear evidence and to make a quasi-judicial award but simply to make a decision on the basis of their own professional expertise. The parties are then bound by the expert's decisions. Although there is no right of appeal against his determination he is not immune from suit and can therefore be sued for negligence if he makes a mistake.

5.9   Repairing covenants

5.9.1 Nature of repairing covenants

If there is no express repairing covenant in a lease then, subject to the law of waste and the limited circumstances in which a landlord impliedly agrees to repair (paragraphs 5.6.2 and 5.6.3), neither party is liable for repairs. However, most leases contain express covenants imposing repairing obligations on the landlord, the tenant, or dividing the responsibility between them.

The task for the built environment professional, when confronted by a leasehold property that is in disrepair, is to determine each party's liability for repair under the covenants in the lease. Over the years the courts have unfortunately explained the correct approach to this task in a number of different ways. The reported cases also address an infinite variety of factual situations, none of which is identical to any other. The result is that it is often extremely difficult to assess the liability for repair in a particular instance by reference to the decided cases. The task can be made easier by following a logical approach to the task, such as that proposed by Dowding, Reynolds and Oakes in their book, *Dilapidations: The Modern Law and Practice*[30] and discussed in more detail below.

---

[30] Nicholas Dowding, Kirk Reynolds and Alison Oakes, *Dilapidations: The Modern Law and Practice*, Fourth Edition, Sweet & Maxwell, 2008

5.9.2 Meaning of disrepair

For a repairing obligation to arise it is first necessary to understand that it will only extend to those parts of the property which are within the ambit of a particular repairing covenant. The Dowding book refers to this as 'the physical subject matter of the repairing covenant'. The terms of the lease should therefore be checked to establish the physical extent of the building which is included within the lease and whether, for example, the covenant extends to the whole of these parts or is confined, for example, to its internal or external, or structural or non-structural parts.

Having established the extent of the physical subject matter of the covenant it should then be established whether some part of it is actually in a state of *disrepair*. This implies some damage or deterioration from a previous physical state and is implicit in Lord Atkin's observation in *Calthorpe v McOscar*[31] that repair 'connotes the idea of making good *damage* so as to leave the subject so far as possible as though it had not been *damaged*' (emphasis added). There can therefore be no obligation to repair where there has been no physical deterioration but simply a lack of amenity or inefficiency. In *Quick v Taff-Ely Borough Council*[32] a severe condensation problem caused by metal window frames and a lack of insulation was therefore held to fall outside the repairing covenant. Similarly, in *Post Office v Acquarius Properties Ltd*[33], the repairing covenant was held not to include an obligation to remedy a flooding problem in a basement which was caused by defective workmanship to the floor slab at the time of the building's construction.

5.9.3 Standard of repair

Once it is established that the physical subject matter of the covenant is in a state of disrepair the next question is whether it is in a sufficiently bad state to take it below the *standard of repair* contemplated by the actual words of the covenant. The covenant may, for example, only require the premises to be kept 'wind and watertight' or it may exclude 'fair wear and tear'. In some cases the covenant may define the required standard of repair by reference to a schedule of condition which records the condition of the property at the start of the lease.

In most cases, however, there will simply be a general repairing covenant ('to keep in good and substantial repair' etc.) without any detailed reference to the required standard. In these situations, whilst the condition of the property at the commencement of the lease may be of some relevance in ascertaining the parties' intentions, it does not conclusively define the standard of repair contemplated by them[34] as the property might already have fallen below the required standard. Instead there is an objective benchmark standard which is illustrated by the following two cases.

In *Proudfoot v Hart*[35] the court had to consider whether the tenant of a house was liable for the cost of repairs at the end of a three-year lease in circumstances where

---

[31] [1924] 1 KB 716, at 734
[32] [1986] QB 809
[33] [1987] 1 EGLR 40
[34] *Stanley v Towgood* (1836) 3 Bing. NC 4
[35] (1890) 25 QBD 42

the house had already been in a poor state of repair at the beginning of the term. The words of the tenant's repairing covenant required him 'to keep and leave the premises in good tenantable repair'. The Court of Appeal held that the tenant was indeed liable. The express obligation to *keep* in repair included an obligation to first *put* the premises into the standard of repair contemplated by the covenant, and thereafter to keep them in this condition. The standard of repair in a general repairing covenant was 'that which, having regard to the age, character, and locality of the house, would make it reasonably fit for the occupation of an incoming tenant of the class who would be likely to take it'. On the facts, the condition of the house was below that contemplated and the tenant was therefore liable under the repairing covenant - it was irrelevant that it had already been below this standard at the time that the tenancy commenced.

In *Calthorpe v McOscar*[36] the issue was whether the standard of repair described in *Proudfoot* should be measured according to the prevailing conditions at the commencement, or at the end of the lease. The case concerned a ninety-five-year lease of some high-class country houses. During the ninety-five-years of the lease the quality of the neighbourhood declined considerably. The result was that, upon termination, only tenants requiring short-term social housing would be likely to take the houses and they would only require a standard of repair that would ensure that the premises were kept wind and watertight. The Court of Appeal held that the tenant was responsible for maintaining the property to the standard contemplated when the covenant was entered into. Subsequent changes in the character of the neighbourhood (either for the better or the worse) could have no bearing on what was actually contemplated.

5.9.4 Necessary repairs

If the subject matter of the repairing covenant has indeed deteriorated below the standard of repair contemplated by the covenant, the covenanting party (whether the landlord or the tenant) becomes obliged (and entitled) to carry out some form of repair. The type of repair which is appropriate is obviously a technical question but it is nevertheless subject to a number of legal principles, including the following:

- Where it is possible to repair the subject matter of the covenant the covenanting party cannot choose to discharge his obligations in some other way. Therefore, in *Creska Ltd v Hammersmith & Fulham Borough Council*[37] the Court of Appeal held that the landlord was obliged to undertake expensive repairs to an electrical under floor central heating system even though it would have been cheaper to install an entirely new heating system.
- Where there are several equally valid ways of remedying the defect, the covenanting party can choose which to adopt[38]. A covenanting landlord who can recover the cost under the service charge provisions is therefore justified

---

[36] [1924] 1 KB 716
[37] [1998] EGCS 96
[38] *Plough Investments Ltd v Manchester City Council* [1989] 1 EGLR 244

in choosing the most expensive option. Likewise, a covenanting tenant at the end of his lease is justified in choosing the cheapest method.

- Where repairs are necessary these can quite legitimately include the *renewal* of subordinate parts of the premises, even where these are quite extensive. For example, in *Lurcott v Wakely & Wheeler*[39] the necessary repairs involved the complete demolition and rebuilding of one of the walls of a house. The Court of Appeal held that there was no clear distinction between a repair and a renewal and the works therefore fell within the scope of the repairing covenant. 'Repair' and 'renewal' were not words expressive of a clear contrast as the process of repair always involves the renewal of subordinate parts of a building. The question of what legitimately constitutes a 'repair' is therefore always one of degree according to whether the work genuinely involves the renewal or replacement of defective parts or it instead amounts to the renewal or replacement of substantially the whole building (see paragraph 5.9.5).

- In contrast to the situations encountered in *Quick v Taff-Ely Borough Council* and *Post Office v Aquarius Properties Ltd* (see paragraph 5.9.2), once there has been some damage to the subject matter of the covenant, the repairs can quite properly include works of *improvement* to the original design. So, in *Minja Properties Ltd v Cussins Property Group plc*[40] the landlord was entitled to replace the single glazed windows in a block of flats which had become rotten with double glazing, and to collect the cost of this from the tenants under the service charge provisions.

- Legitimate *improvements* might also include upgrades to take account of technological and legislative changes since the original construction - see *Minja Properties* (above), *Postel Properties* (below) and *Elite Investments v T I Bainbridge Silencers Ltd* (below).

- Again, in contrast to *Quick* and *Post Office v Aquarius*, once there has been some damage to the subject matter of the covenant, the repairs can include repairs to as yet undamaged parts of the premises in addition to those that have already suffered damage. In *Postel Properties Ltd v Boots*[41], as part of a major roof replacement project, the landlord was therefore held to be entitled to renew some parts that still had a maximum life expectancy of twenty years as part of the totality of the works, and to recover the whole cost as part of the service charge.

5.9.5 *Scope of repairing covenants*

Even where the subject matter of the repairing covenant is in disrepair and the necessary remedial work has been identified the covenanting party may still escape liability if that work is so extensive that it goes beyond what is contemplated by the covenant as constituting a 'repair'. We have already seen that there is no clear distinction between a 'repair and either a 'renewal' or an 'improvement'. Instead, the courts apply what is known as the 'test of fact and

---

[39] [1911] 1 KB 905
[40] [1998] EGCS 23
[41] [1996] 2 EGLR 60

degree'. This means that they consider all the relevant facts in any particular case. They then decide whether the proposed works can properly be described as a 'repair' or whether they would actually involve the tenant in giving back to the landlord a wholly different property from that which was originally leased to him[42]. The following cases provide an indication of the approach taken by the courts in this context.

(A) Works falling outside the repairing covenant

In *Lister v Lane*[43] a very old house built on timber foundations had become unstable as the foundations had rotted. The necessary repairs effectively required the whole house to be demolished and rebuilt with new foundations. The Court of Appeal held that this fell outside of the repairing covenant. To have held otherwise would have required the tenant to hand back an entirely different thing to that which he took at the start of the lease. A similar situation arose in *Brew Brothers Ltd v Snax (Ross) Ltd*[44] where a longstanding problem with leaking drains caused a building to subside. The extensive underpinning and partial demolition required to remedy the problem would have cost almost as much as a new building. The Court of Appeal held that the work went far beyond what any reasonable person would have contemplated under the word 'repair'. In *Halliard Property Co Ltd v Nicholas Clarke Investments Ltd*[45] the wall of a 'jerry built' utility room at the rear of a shop collapsed. The landlord required the tenant to rebuild it in accordance with current building regulations and this would have cost about one third of the cost of rebuilding the whole shop premises. The court considered this to be a borderline situation but nevertheless held that the works fell outside the scope of the covenant.

(B) Works falling within the repairing covenant

We have already seen some examples of cases where the works were held to fall within the scope of the covenant in paragraph 5.9.4. Two other cases should also briefly be considered. In *Elite Investments Ltd v T I Bainbridge Silencers Ltd*[46] the roof of a large industrial unit required replacement at a cost of £85 000. The roof had been in a poor state of repair at the commencement of the lease and, when re-roofed, the unit would only have a value of some £140 000. The court rejected the tenant's argument that the cost of repair was disproportionate. The works did not involve handing back to the landlord an entirely different thing but merely the same industrial building with a new roof. They involved the replacement of a subsidiary part of the building rather than substantially the whole of it. The decision in *Ravenseft Properties Ltd v Davstone (Holdings) Ltd*[47]

---

[42] Forbes J in *Ravenseft Properties Ltd v Davstone (Holdings) Ltd* [1980] QB 12, at 21
[43] [1893] 2 QB 212
[44] [1970] 1 QB 612
[45] (1983) 269 EG 1257
[46] [1986] 2 EGLR 43
[47] [1980] 1 QB 12

is also of interest for its treatment of what used to be known as the 'doctrine of inherent defect'. Advocates of the doctrine maintained that works that were required to remedy a defect in the original design of the building (an 'inherent defect') will necessarily fall outside the scope of a repairing covenant. The case concerned a large block of flats whose stone cladding panels were in danger of falling off due to a failure to install expansion joints at the time of the original construction. The tenants objected to meeting the cost of the repairs from the service charge as they argued that they had no liability for the remedying of an inherent defect. The court held that the doctrine of inherent defect had no place in the law of landlord and tenant and found the tenant liable for the cost of the repairs.

5.10   User covenants

5.10.1   Nature of user covenants

If there are no restrictions as to use in the lease, the tenant may use the premises as desired, subject to compliance with planning legislation, with any covenants affecting a superior title, and with any common law restrictions (for example, the law of nuisance). However, in practice, the landlord will generally also wish to control the way that the tenant uses the premises by imposing what are known as 'user covenants'. These will either require the property to be used for a particular purpose, or will impose restrictions on certain types of use. As with other types of covenant that we will encounter in subsequent paragraphs the covenant may be either 'absolute' or 'qualified'. Absolute covenants impose an absolute requirement on the tenant to behave (or not to behave) in a certain way. Qualified covenants impose a similar obligation on him but provide that he might be permitted to depart from the obligation with the landlord's prior (usually written) consent.

5.10.2   Restriction on charging for consent

Section 19(3) of the Landlord and Tenant Act 1927 provides that the landlord is not entitled to demand payment for the giving of consent to a change of use where this is required as part of a qualified covenant. The section applies notwithstanding any contrary provision in the lease so the parties cannot 'contract out' of this requirement. Note, however, that the section does not prevent the landlord from charging for such consent:

- In the case of absolute covenants, or;
- Where the change of use also involves the making of structural alterations.

It also does not prevent the landlord from requiring the tenant to pay:

- A reasonable sum by way of compensation for any diminution in the value of his reversion that will be caused by the change of use, and;
- Legal expenses.

5.11   Covenants against alterations

5.11.1   *Nature of covenants against alterations*

An alteration is a change in the actual fabric or form of a building, such as converting a house into flats or subdividing existing rooms. A change in appearance, on its own, will not suffice if it does not affect the fabric. So in *Bickmore v Dimmer*[48] the erection of a large external clock supported by iron stays and bolted to the side of a building was held not to amount to an alteration.

Unless the lease contains some provision to the contrary the tenant is free to carry out alterations to the property. However, in practice, the landlord will want more control over the tenant's actions than this and covenants against alterations are commonly included. As with user covenants these can be either absolute (imposing a prohibition on alterations) or qualified (requiring the landlord's consent to alterations).

5.11.2   *Unreasonable withholding of consent for improvements*

Where a covenant requires the landlord's consent for the making of alterations, and an alteration amounts to an improvement to the property, section 19(2) of the Landlord and Tenant Act 1927 provides that the landlord's consent shall not be unreasonably withheld. Once again, the parties cannot 'contract out' of this requirement by including a contrary provision in the lease. The question of whether an alteration is indeed an improvement, thus triggering the section, has to be considered from the tenant's point of view rather than from that of the landlord. In *Woolworth & Co v Lambert* [1937] Ch 37, a tenant wished to remove the back wall of the shop in order to connect it to another shop leased from a different landlord. The landlord claimed to be entitled to refuse consent to the alteration as its effect would be to reduce the value of his reversion and it could not therefore be an improvement. The Court of Appeal rejected this argument, holding that any alteration which increases the value or usefulness of the premises from the tenant's point of view is an improvement, whatever its effect on the landlord's reversion. Section 19(2) therefore applied and, in the circumstances, the landlord had unreasonably withheld his consent.

The section does, however, include some protection for the landlord by providing that he is entitled to make his consent conditional upon the tenant:

- Paying a reasonable sum by way of compensation for any diminution in the value of his reversion caused by the improvement, and;
- Undertaking to reinstate the premises at the end of the term.

The section does not apply to absolute covenants and once again, the landlord is also entitled to require the tenant to pay his legal expenses incurred in connection with the giving of consent.

---

[48] [1903] 1 Ch 158

5.12 Assignment and sub-letting

5.12.1 Nature of assignment and sub-letting

An 'assignment' of a lease occurs when a tenant transfers his rights in the premises to another tenant for the remainder of the term of the lease. This must be distinguished from a 'sub-letting' (or 'under-letting') which arises where a tenant retains his leasehold estate but lets the whole or part of the premises to another tenant. In such circumstances the sub-letting must be for a period less that the initial grant (see Chapter 4, paragraph 4.3.3). Assignment and sub-letting are collectively referred to as 'alienation'. An assignment must always be made by deed but the formalities for the creation of a sub-lease are exactly the same as for the creation of any other form of lease (see paragraph 5.4.1).

Unless the lease contains a provision to the contrary the tenant is free to dispose of his interest in the property in any way he chooses. However, it is common for express covenants to be imposed on the tenant which prevent alienation altogether (an absolute covenant), or which require the tenant to obtain the landlord's consent before being allowed to assign or sublet (a qualified covenant).

5.12.2 Unlawful discrimination

In most circumstances it is unlawful to refuse to allow someone to occupy a property on the grounds of their sex, race, religion or disability (Sex Discrimination Act 1975, s.31; Race Relations Act 1976, s.24; Disability Discrimination Act 1995, s.22). Therefore it will be unlawful to refuse to grant consent to assign or sublet to someone on this basis.

5.12.3 Restriction on charging for consent

As we saw with user covenants, Parliament has also intervened to prevent landlords charging for the granting of consent to alienation in certain circumstances. The relevant provision is contained in section 144 of the Law of Property Act 1925 and once again the restriction only applies to qualified covenants. In contrast to the situation with user covenants the parties are, however, free to 'contract out' of the provision by inserting a contrary provision in the lease. Where the provision applies no form of charging is permitted although the landlord is still permitted to require the tenant to pay his associated legal expenses.

5.12.4 Unreasonable withholding of consent for assignment and subletting

(A) Section 19(1)(a) of the Landlord and Tenant Act 1927

There are also similarities to the statutory requirements affecting qualified covenants against alterations. Where a covenant requires the landlord's consent for alienation, section 19(1) of the Landlord and Tenant Act 1927 provides that the landlord's consent shall not be unreasonably withheld. Once again, the parties cannot 'contract out' of this requirement by including a contrary provision in the lease.

(B) Landlord and Tenant Act 1988

Where a covenant prohibits alienation without a landlord's consent it is important to the tenant that the landlord deals with his request for consent fairly and expeditiously. If the landlord fails to do so the prospective assignee or subtenant is unlikely to wait around for things to be sorted out. Thus, in practical terms, the landlord's failure to act can effectively deprive a tenant of his right to alienate, even where this right is contained in the lease. Tenants had very little power in these situations at common law so Parliament enacted the Landlord and Tenant Act 1988 to provide them with some protection. Where the tenant has served a written application for consent, section 1(3) of this Act now imposes the following duties on the landlord:

- To serve a notice on the tenant within a reasonable time setting out his decision about the granting or withholding of consent.
- To grant consent where it is reasonable to do so (and to only impose such conditions on that consent as are reasonable to impose).
- To set out the reasons for withholding consent in the notice where consent is withheld.

Section 1(6) also places the onus on the landlord to prove that he has complied with these duties rather than on the tenant to prove that he has breached them. There is therefore a powerful incentive for the landlord to comply as a failure to do so would make him liable to the tenant in damages for breach of the statutory duty.

(C) Reasonableness of landlord's withholding of consent

The purpose of alienation covenants is to prevent the property being used in an undesirable way and by an undesirable tenant. The reasonableness of a landlord's decision to withhold consent will therefore be judged according to the extent to which it relates to these purposes. In order to be reasonable a withholding of consent must also be based on some aspect of the landlord and tenant relationship. The landlord has no right to withhold consent in order to achieve some 'collateral' advantage which is unconnected with the parties or the terms of the lease.

By way of example, in *Parker v Boggon*[49] an unreasonable withholding of consent was held to have occurred where this was due to the proposed assignee having diplomatic immunity from legal proceedings. In *Bates v Donaldson*[50] the withholding of consent in order to enable the landlord to obtain possession for his own use was also unreasonable. The landlord was also held to have unreasonably withheld consent in *Re Gibbs and Houlder Brothers and Co Ltd's Lease*[51]. In that case the proposed assignee had a tenancy of an adjoining property from the same landlord and planned to serve notice to quit this tenancy following the assignment.

---

[49] [1947] KB 346
[50] [1896] 2 QB 241
[51] [1925] Ch 198

The landlord refused consent as this would leave him with a vacant property which would be difficult to let. Not surprisingly the court held that the landlord's refusal of consent was unreasonable. His reason for refusal had no reference either to the personality of the proposed assignee or to the subject matter of the lease.

Examples of reasonable withholdings of consent include *Ashworth Frazer Ltd v Gloucester City Council*[52] where the proposed assignee had already applied for planning permission to use the premises for recycling metal, indicating an intention to breach the user covenant in the lease. Equally, in *British Bakeries (Midlands) Ltd v Michael Tester & Co Ltd*[53] the landlord was held to have acted reasonably in withholding consent due to the incomplete and unreliable nature of the financial references provided by the proposed assignee. The withholding was also held to be reasonable in *Pimms v Tallow Chandlers Co*[54] where the proposed assignee wanted to exploit the lease to obtain participation in the landlord's future development of the property.

Traditionally, the question of what amounts to a reasonable withholding of consent by the landlord has been a matter for the courts. It has not therefore been possible for the parties to agree these and to specify them in advance. This situation has now changed, at least for commercial leases granted on or after 1 January 1996. Section 22 of the Landlord and Tenant (Covenants) Act 1995 now provides that a withholding of consent to assign shall not be unreasonable where the reasons had been specified in the lease or some other prior agreement. It has therefore now become standard practice for commercial leases to include a list of circumstances in which consent to an assignment can be refused, and of conditions to which any consent may be subject.

Typical stated reasons for refusing consent might include:

- Where the proposed assignee is not a public company quoted on the London Stock Exchange.
- Where the proposed assignee's pre-tax profits are less than three times the rent payable under the lease.

Typical stated conditions to which consent may be subject might include:

- A requirement that the assignee must provide a rent deposit or guarantor.
- A requirement that the former tenant must enter into an authorised guarantee agreement (see paragraph 5.13.2).

Finally, a device which can assist landlords in alienation cases is the use of a so-called '*Bocardo*' clause (named after the decision in *Bocardo SA v S & M Hotels Ltd*[55]). This is where the lease provides that the tenant must offer to surrender the tenancy as a precondition to any dealing, whether assignment or sub-letting. If the landlord does not approve of the identity of the proposed assignee, he can accept a surrender of the lease. Such a provision is not invalidated by section 19(1) of the 1927 Act.

---

[52] [2002] 1 All ER 377
[53] [1986] 1 EGLR 64
[54] [1964] 2 QB 547
[55] [1980] 1 WLR 17

5.13   Enforceability of covenants in leases

5.13.1   Leases granted before 1 January 1996

The enforceability of leases granted before 1 January 1996 depends on the traditional rules relating to 'privity of contract' and 'privity of estate'. Privity of contract exists between the original parties to the lease and all covenants are therefore mutually enforceable between them, in theory, for the whole of the term of the lease. However, once one or both of the original parties has assigned their interest in the lease the question of enforceability will be of more concern to the new landlord or tenant than to the original parties. Although there will be no privity of contract between them there is nevertheless always said to be privity of estate between the parties for the time being to a lease. In these situations the covenants will be mutually enforceable as long as they touch and concern the land[56]. This means that they must affect the land itself rather than being merely personal covenants between the parties. All the normal covenants in a lease will be included within this requirement but a tenant's covenant to pay money to someone other than landlord[57] and a landlord's covenant to repair property not included within the lease[58] have been held to fall outside it.

5.13.2   Leases granted on or after 1 January 1996

The Landlord and Tenant (Covenants) Act 1995 applies to leases commencing after January 1 1996. Enforceability of covenants in these leases is no longer governed by the rules relating to privity of contract and privity of estate. Instead the general rule is that covenants are mutually enforceable between the landlord and tenant for the time being and the original or former parties to the lease generally cease to have any liability once they part with their interest in the property. In practice the situation is slightly more complicated than this. Former landlords are not automatically released from liability under the covenants but have to follow a notice procedure laid down by the Act. The Act also introduces the concept of the authorized guarantee agreement whereby a tenant can be made to guarantee the performance of his assignee when the landlord requires this as a condition of granting consent to the assignment.

5.14   Remedies for breach of covenant

Remedies are the mechanisms used by an injured party to enforce their legal rights, either through the courts, or in some other way. A variety of remedies are available, according to the nature of the covenant which has been breached.

---

[56] *Spencer's Case* (1583) 5 Co Rep 16a
[57] *Mayho v Buckhurst* (1617) Cro Jac 438
[58] *Dewar v Goodman* [1909] AC 72

5.14.1   Landlord's remedies for non-payment of rent

(A) Action for recovery of rent

The landlord can bring a court action against the tenant for rent arrears. By section 19 of the Limitation Act 1980, the action must be brought within 6 years from the date it fell due or will be statute barred.

(B) Distress

Distress is an ancient common law remedy which allows a landlord to recover rent by seizing goods found on the leased premises. It does not require the landlord to proceed through the judicial process. If within five days of the goods being seized the rent remains unpaid, the goods may be sold to pay off the rent arrears. The landlord may levy distress in person or he may employ a certificated bailiff. If the landlord is a company then it must always use a certified bailiff. Certain items may not be seized, including loose money, perishable goods, clothing, and the tools of the tenant's trade.

At the time of writing there are proposals to abolish the landlord's right to distress entirely for residential premises, and to replace it by a more limited remedy of Commercial Rent Arrears Recovery (CRAR) for business premises. In a departure from the process adopted when recovering rent by distress, CRAR would require the landlord to serve notice on the tenant before being entitled to take control of a tenant's goods. The proposals are contained in Part 3 of the Tribunals, Courts and Enforcement Act 2007 but have not yet been brought into force.

(C) Forfeiture

Forfeiture is the right of the landlord to terminate the lease following a breach of covenant by the tenant. It is sometimes called a proviso for re-entry. The right to forfeiture will generally only exist if the lease expressly provides for it.

It can theoretically be exercised either by peaceable re-entry (where the landlord simply physically re-enters the property) or by bringing possession proceedings against the tenant. In practice, forfeiture is normally exercised by possession proceedings. This has to be the case for residential properties due to the requirements of the Protection from Eviction Act 1972. It is also highly advisable for all other types of property as the use or threats of violence whilst attempting peaceable re-entry amounts to a criminal offence under section 6 of the Criminal Law Act 1977.

If, following a breach of covenant by the tenant, the landlord nevertheless elects to treat the lease as continuing he is said to have waived his right to forfeiture. Waiver typically takes the form of a landlord demanding or accepting rent falling due after the date of the breach. In *Central Estates (Belgravia) v Wolgar*[59] this was

---

[59] [1972] 1 QB 48

even held to have occurred where the rent was demanded due to a clerical error by the landlord's managing agents. Similarly, in *Segal Securities Ltd v Thoseby*[60] where the landlord accepted rent 'without prejudice to the landlord's right to forfeit' he was nevertheless held to have waived his right to forfeiture.

There is no requirement for the landlord to serve a section 146 notice (see paragraph 5.14.2.A) before exercising his right to forfeiture. However, at common law he first had to make a formal demand for the rent although, in practice, forfeiture clauses often expressly dispense with this requirement. In any event if at least six months' rent is in arrears the Common Law Procedure Act 1852 removes this requirement. Once the landlord begins to enforce his right to forfeiture the tenant can apply to the court for 'relief' against forfeiture. This means that, if the tenant pays the arrears and legal costs owing, any proceedings will be stayed and his tenancy will be reinstated.

5.14.2   *Landlord's remedies for breach of other covenants*

(A) Forfeiture

Before a landlord can exercise his right to forfeiture for breach of a covenant other than for payment of rent he must first serve a notice on the tenant under section 146 of the Law of Property Act 1925 (a 'section 146 notice'). The notice must specify the breach complained of, require the breach to be remedied and, if this is desired, require the tenant to pay compensation. The purpose of the procedure is to give the tenant an opportunity to put things right, and hence to avoid the lease being forfeited. Once the notice has been served the landlord must allow the tenant a reasonable time to comply with it before exercising his right to forfeiture.

The tenant also has a right, under section 146, to apply for 'relief' against forfeiture at any time between the service of the notice and the landlord actually re-entering the property. The court has a wide discretion to grant relief and may, for example, order a stay of any forfeiture proceedings upon condition that the tenant remedies the breach within a specified period of time.

Parliament has also provided additional protection for tenants where breaches of repairing covenants are alleged. Section 1 of the Leasehold Property (Repairs) Act 1938 applies to leases of at least seven years with at least three years left to run. In these situations a section 146 notice must also advise the tenant of his right to serve a counter-notice within twenty-eight days. If the tenant does then serve a counter-notice the landlord is prevented from exercising his right to forfeiture without the leave of the court. This will only be granted if the landlord can prove that one of the following statutory grounds applies:

- That the value of the reversion has already been substantially diminished, or;
- That the immediate remedying of the breach is required in order, either:
  - to prevent such substantive diminution;
  - to comply with statutory requirements;

---

[60] [1963] 1 QB 887

o to protect the interest of an occupier other than the tenant;
o to avoid a much heavier repair cost in the future.

The purpose of the 1938 Act is to protect tenants from pressure from landlords to carry out non-essential repairs during the course of their lease. As the lease nears its end (in the final three years) the landlord has a greater interest in the state of the property and the tenant loses this protection. Additional protection is also available under section 147 of the 1925 Act where the section 146 notice relates only to internal decorative repairs. In these circumstances the tenant has an additional right to apply for relief and, if the court considers that the notice is unreasonable, it has the power to relieve the tenant from liability for these repairs entirely.

(B) Damages

A landlord might choose to bring a court action against the tenant in order to obtain an award of damages to compensate him for the financial losses he has suffered. These would be assessed on ordinary contract law principles (see paragraph 2.12). Where the claim relates to the breach of a repairing covenant, section 1 of the Leasehold Property (Repairs) Act 1938 applies in exactly the same way as it does to forfeiture. The landlord must therefore serve a section 146 notice advising the tenant of his right to serve a counter-notice and, if necessary, seek leave of the court before he can commence proceedings for damages.

At common law, if the landlord sues for breach of a repairing covenant during the term, damages are calculated by reference to the diminution in the value of the reversion rather than the cost of the repairs themselves. This reflects the loss actually suffered by the landlord at that time. However, if the landlord sues at the end of the term, as he is then responsible for undertaking the repairs himself, damages are calculated by reference to the actual cost of repairs.

To protect tenants from excessive claims at the end of the lease in circumstances where the landlord might have plans for redevelopment rather than for repair, section 18 of the Landlord and Tenant Act 1927 imposes a statutory ceiling on the amount of damages that can be awarded. It provides that damages shall never exceed the diminution in the value of the reversion caused by the breach and, in particular, that no damages shall be recoverable at the end of a term where the landlord intends to demolish or structurally alter the premises in such a way that the effect of the repairs would be negated.

(C) Repairs notice

In the absence of an express provision in the lease the landlord has no right to enter the property to carry out repairs which the tenant has failed to undertake. However, leases will often include such a right, following service upon the tenant of a notice (described by built environment professionals as a 'repairs notice'). The landlord can then undertake the repairs and recover the costs incurred from the tenant in the courts. The case of *Jervis v Harris*[61] established that such costs are recoverable as a debt, rather than by an action for damages and the Leasehold Property (Repairs) Act 1938 does not therefore apply. The remedy is therefore particularly appealing to landlords as it allows them to dispense with the need to serve a section 146 notice and the possibility of having to obtain the leave of the court before commencing proceedings.

(D) Specific performance

Until relatively recently it was generally accepted that tenants' repairing covenants could not be specifically enforced[62]. The objections to specific performance in these circumstances included the difficulty in defining the work and the need for constant supervision by the court to ensure compliance. However, although specific performance will rarely be a suitable remedy it is available in appropriate circumstances. In *Rainbow Estates Ltd v Tokenhold Ltd*[63] the court ordered the specific performance of the tenant's covenant where a Grade II listed building was in serious disrepair and, unusually, the lease contained no forfeiture clause or clause entitling the landlord to undertake repairs under a repairs notice. An order for specific performance was therefore the only remedy available to bring about the necessary repairs.

5.14.3   Tenant's remedies

(A) Damages

Where the tenant suffers financial and other losses as a result of a landlord's breach of covenant, damages, under normal contract law principles, might be an appropriate remedy. Damages will be awarded according to the actual amount of the losses suffered by the tenant as a result of the landlord's breach of covenant. Where a landlord breaches a repairing covenant a residential tenant will be entitled to the cost of carrying out the necessary repairs. In addition, damages will also include the cost of restoring any internal decorations, the cost of alternative accommodation and compensation for living in unpleasant surroundings. However, where the tenant holds the lease as an investment, damages will be calculated on the basis of the diminution in value of his estate which has been caused by the landlord's failure to repair.

(B) Specific performance

Under section 17 of the Landlord and Tenant Act 1985 the court has discretion to order the specific performance of a landlord's repairing covenant in a lease of a

---

[61] [1996] 1 EGLR 78
[62] *Hill v Barclay* (1810) 16 Ves 402
[63] [1998] 2 EGLR 34

dwelling. The remedy is also available for business leases under the court's general equitable jurisdiction[64].

(C) Self-help

Where a landlord is in breach of his repairing covenant the tenant can give him notice that he intends to do the repairs himself. If he does so, and subsequently undertakes repairs that were the landlord's responsibility under the covenant, he is then entitled to deduct the reasonable costs of the repairs from future payments of rent[65]. If the landlord subsequently sues the tenant for failure to pay the rent the tenant can counterclaim for the repair costs which he has incurred[66].

5.15   The statutory codes

We have so-far considered the various common law rules affecting the landlord and tenant relationship, as amended in some areas by statutory provisions. However, in addition to these rules, there are also a number of major statutory codes which affect certain types of tenancies. Where these codes apply the common law rules have to be read in the context of the detailed statutory arrangements imposed by them. There are separate codes affecting residential, business and agricultural tenancies. They operate in different ways but they all provide tenants with security of tenure (the right to a new lease or to stay in possession of the premises at the end of the lease). In addition, some of them have also provided mechanisms for the control of rent, for succession by relatives, for the payment of compensation at the end of the lease, and for leasehold extension and enfranchisement. In the remainder of this chapter we consider the operation of the relevant statutory codes for private sector residential tenancies and for business tenancies.

5.16   Private sector residential tenancies

5.16.1   Introduction

Between 1915 and 1977 successive legislation was enacted which gave qualifying residential tenants in the private sector unprecedented levels of protection in terms of rent control, security of tenure and succession by relatives. From 1980 onwards a distinct change of policy emerged due to a perception that the existing legislation leaned too far in favour of tenants, and that this had limited the availability of residential property being placed on the rental market by landlords. A number of reforms were introduced over time which progressively eroded the tenants' rights

---

[64] *Jeune v Queens Cross Properties Ltd* [1974] Ch 97
[65] *Lee-Parker v Izzet* [1971] 1 WLR 1688
[66] *British Anzani (Felixstowe) Ltd v International Marine Management (UK) Ltd* [1980] QB 137

in this area and the relevant legislation is now contained in the Rent Act 1977, the Housing Act 1988 and the Housing Act 1996. As a result of these Acts the level of protection afforded to a residential tenant depends on the date on which their tenancy was created.

5.16.2 *Tenancies commencing prior to 15 January 1989*

Tenancies created prior to 1989 are still subject to the Rent Act 1977 and provide high levels of protection for tenants. Although of decreasing significance over the years, thousands of properties are still subject to Rent Act tenancies. They have the following characteristics.

(A) Security of tenure

Rent Act tenancies are described as 'protected tenancies' and once terminated according to the common law rules are immediately transformed into 'statutory tenancies'. A landlord can only bring a statutory tenancy to an end by obtaining a possession order from the court. This will be granted if the landlord can demonstrate that suitable alternative accommodation is available for the tenant and the court is satisfied that it is reasonable to make a possession order. Alternatively, the landlord will be able to obtain a possession order if he can establish one or more of certain statutory grounds for possession. Some of these grounds are mandatory and some are discretionary. In the case of the discretionary grounds the court will also have to be satisfied that it is reasonable to make an order for possession.

A mandatory ground will normally only be available where the landlord has served notice on the tenant before the tenancy commenced that possession would be obtained on that ground. Mandatory grounds include:

- Where the landlord is a returning owner-occupier.
- Where possession is required of an off-season holiday let.
- Where the landlord wishes to obtain possession of a home bought as a retirement home.

Discretionary grounds generally relate to some default or misconduct by the tenant and include:

- Breaches of an obligation of the tenancy or rent arrears.

(B) Rent control

Either the landlord or the tenant has the right to apply to the rent officer for registration of a 'fair rent'. Once registered the rent attaches to the property rather than either of the parties and the landlord is prohibited from charging a higher rent. Registration lasts for two years. Fair rents are significantly lower than market rents.

(C) Succession provisions

On the death of a protected or statutory tenant the tenancy will pass either to the tenant's 'spouse' or to some other family member where they have been residing with the tenant for a certain period before the death. Two statutory successions are possible so these far-reaching provisions can prevent a landlord from regaining possession of his property for three generations. Because of the controversial nature of these rules they have now been slightly modified by the Housing Act 1988. In addition, the courts' recognition of the changing nature of society and the combined effects of the Human Rights Act 1998 and the Civil Partnership Act 2004 mean that 'spouse' also now includes unmarried cohabitees (whether or not of the opposite sex to the original tenant) as well as same sex civil partners.

5.16.3   Tenancies commencing between 15 January 1989 and 27 February 1997

Tenancies created during this period are regulated by the Housing Act 1988. Unless certain requirements were complied with (discussed in paragraph D below) these tenancies take effect as 'assured tenancies'.

(A) Security of tenure

Similar security of tenure provisions apply as under the Rent Act 1977. A notice to quit which is served in respect of a periodic tenancy has no effect under the Act. The original tenancy simply continues regardless of any attempt at common law to terminate it. Where a fixed-term tenancy expires a statutory periodic tenancy arises and continues the tenancy.

A landlord can only regain possession by obtaining a court possession order. Before starting possession proceedings he is required to serve a notice on the tenant stating his intention to commence proceedings and informing the tenant that they will not be started before a certain date. Proceedings must then be commenced within twelve months or a further notice must be served.

As with the Rent Act a possession order will only be granted by the court on certain statutory grounds. These are more numerous than the grounds under the Rent Act and include both mandatory and discretionary grounds. Possession will not be granted on the basis of a discretionary ground unless the court is also satisfied that it would be reasonable to do so.

(B) Rent control

Assured tenancies are not subject to a system of fair rent registration. The basic principle under the 1988 legislation is that the rent payable should be the market rent, preferably one agreed between the parties. Hence, unless there is a rent review provision within the tenancy agreement, the rent for a fixed term assured tenancy must remain as originally agreed between the parties. Once the fixed term comes to an end the statutory periodic tenancy commences and different rules apply as described below.

Under periodic tenancies (whether contractual or statutory) there is provision within the legislation for the landlord to increase the rent. The landlord is required to serve a notice on the tenant stating the proposed new rent and the date on which it is proposed to take effect. If the tenant takes no action the new rent will simply take effect on the date included in the notice. If the tenant disagrees with the proposals he has until the date that the rent is due to take effect to apply to a rent assessment committee to determine the rent. The committee will then determine the open market rent for the assured tenancy of the property.

(C) Succession provisions

The Housing Act 1988 provides some limited statutory succession provisions in the case of periodic tenancies. A single statutory succession is permitted in favour of a deceased tenant's spouse, cohabitee or civil partner. (An assured fixed-term tenancy falls outside these provisions and will form part of the deceased's estate and pass according to his will or intestacy.)

(D) Assured shorthold tenancies

During the period under consideration (15 January 1989 to 27 February 1997) it was also possible to create an 'assured shorthold tenancy'. These differ from assured tenancies in two respects:

- The landlord is entitled to possession at the end of the contractual tenancy without having to prove any of the statutory grounds required to obtain possession of an assured tenancy. This, of course, is the major attraction of this type of tenancy from a landlord's point of view.
- The tenant also has a limited right to apply to the rent assessment committee for the rent to be reduced. Where he does so, the committee will reduce the rent only if it is satisfied that the rent is too high by comparison with similar properties let on assured shorthold tenancies in the locality of the subject property. If there are no comparable properties it will take no action.

During the period under consideration a tenancy could only become an assured shorthold tenancy if:

- It was for a fixed term of six months or more, and;
- The landlord had served a notice in prescribed form before the commencement of the tenancy, warning the tenant about the nature of the tenancy and providing advice about the entitlement to apply for a rent reduction.

If a landlord failed to comply with these requirements (and many landlords got them wrong) an assured tenancy would be created inadvertently and the tenant would obtain security of tenure. If a validly created assured shorthold tenancy came to an end and a new tenancy of the same premises was then granted to the same tenant the new tenancy would also be an assured shorthold tenancy regardless of the fact that no notice had been served.

5.16.4 Tenancies commencing after 27 February 1997

These tenancies are regulated by the Housing Act 1988 as amended by the Housing Act 1996. Changes were introduced by the 1996 Act to prevent assured tenancies from being created inadvertently instead of assured shortholds. From 27 February 1997 the two conditions for the creation of assured shorthold tenancies (fixed term of at least six months and prior service of notice) therefore no longer apply.

Residential tenancies will now automatically become assured shorthold tenancies unless the landlord serves notice before the tenancy to the effect that it will be an assured tenancy. All tenancies (including periodic tenancies and very short fixed terms) now come within the definition of assured shortholds. Note, however, that, as an order for possession of an assured shorthold tenancy cannot be made earlier than six months after the beginning of the tenancy, the six month minimum term still exists in practice if not in theory.

5.16.5 Leasehold enfranchisement and extension

The Leasehold Reform Act 1967 allows a residential tenant holding under a long lease and at a low rent either to purchase the freehold (enfranchisement) or to the grant of an extended lease for a period of fifty years (extension). To obtain the benefit of the Act, the tenant must have a lease which was originally granted for a term exceeding twenty-one years and be paying a rent of less than two-thirds of the property's rateable value.

The lease must be of a house (not a flat) which the tenant occupies as his main residence. This means his residence for the last three years or for periods amounting to three years in the last ten years.

The Act was passed to circumvent the problems caused to leaseholders where the original tenant had bought the property as an owner occupier, but with leasehold rather than a freehold title. Towards the end of the lease, a tenant could easily end up with little in the way of a saleable asset because of the diminishing nature of the leasehold estate and the reluctance of mortgage lenders to lend on the security of such assets. A tenant can therefore use the Act to ensure that his home continues to be a saleable asset.

The price for the freehold or extended term will be as agreed between the parties, or as determined by the Leasehold Valuation Tribunal in default of agreement. The basis of the valuation for the purchase of the freehold is that the leaseholder is morally entitled to the ownership of the building while the freeholder has similar rights to the ownership of the land on which it stands. Tenants of flats have now been given similar rights by the Housing and Urban Development Act 1993. This provides individual tenants of flats with an entitlement to a ninety-year extension of their leases. It also grants a right to the enfranchisement of the freehold by the tenants on a collective basis. Finally, readers are referred to the Commonhold and Leasehold Reform Act 2002 which was designed to address some of the same problems as the legislation considered here (see Chapter 4, paragraph 4.11).

5.17   Business tenancies

5.17.1   Security of tenure

The statutory code for business tenancies is contained in Part II of the Landlord and Tenant Act 1954, as amended by the Regulatory Reform (Business Tenancies) (England and Wales) Order 2003. Where the Act applies section 24 provides that a tenant will have security of tenure in two ways:

- The tenancy can only be brought to an end by one of the methods prescribed by the Act. Failing this, on the termination of the contractual tenancy (that actually agreed between the parties), the tenancy will simply continue indefinitely as a 'continuation tenancy'.
- The tenant has the right to apply for a new tenancy in the circumstances set out in sections 25 and 26 of the Act.

5.17.2   Tenancies protected by the Act

Before we examine each of the above mechanisms in more detail it is first necessary to identify the types of tenancy falling within the Act.

(A) Essential requirements

The Act applies to any 'tenancy' which is 'occupied for business purposes' (s.23). The requirement for a tenancy to exist therefore excludes licences from the Act's protection. However, both periodic and fixed-term tenancies are protected. Business purposes are defined within the Act as including 'any trade, profession or vocation'. The courts have, however, interpreted this widely to include any activity which is carried on for payment. By way of example, in *Addiscombe Garden Estates Ltd v Crabbe*[67] a private tennis club, and in *Parkes v Westminster Roman Cutholic Diocese Trustee*[68], a charitable recreational club for children and the elderly, were each held to satisfy the definition of business purposes.

(B) Exclusions from the Act

Apart from those tenancies which fail to satisfy the essential requirements there are others which are excluded from the Act's protection, either by the Act itself, or because of cases decided in the courts. These include:

---

[67] [1958] 1 QB 513
[68] (1978) 36 P&CR 526

- Fixed-term tenancies of six months or less.
- Tenancies at will (see paragraph 5.2.3).
- 'Contracted out' tenancies:
  - As a general rule the parties cannot 'contract out' of the Act and any agreement which attempts to exclude or modify the tenant's security of tenure will be void (s.38). However, section 38A provides a statutory mechanism which allows the parties to agree to contract out as long as they comply with the following requirements:
  - Before the tenancy is entered into the landlord must serve a notice (colloquially called a 'health warning') on the tenant advising him of the consequences of entering into the contracting out agreement.
  - The tenant must then sign a declaration acknowledging service of the notice and confirming his understanding of, and consent to, the agreement. Where the notice was served less than fourteen days before the commencement of the tenancy the declaration must be in the form of a statutory declaration (sworn in front of a solicitor).
  - The lease document must contain a reference to the notice and the declaration.

5.17.3   *Continuation tenancies*

(A) The nature of continuation

If the contractual tenancy comes to an end by a method which is not prescribed by the Act (for example, by effluxion of time for a fixed-term tenancy or by a landlord serving a notice to quit in the case of a periodic tenancy) the tenancy simply continues. Continuation is, in principle, a continuation of the contractual term (rather than a new 'statutory tenancy') and hence the tenancy continues on substantially the same terms as the original tenancy.

(B) Termination of tenancies protected by the Act

The Act provides that the only ways that the contractual tenancy (or the continuation tenancy, if it has already started) can come to an end are as follows:

(a)   Forfeiture (see paragraphs 5.5.5, 5.14.1.C and 5.14.2.A).
(b)   Surrender (see paragraph 5.5.4).
(c)   Tenant's (but not landlord's) notice to quit a periodic tenancy (see paragraph 5.5.1)
(d)   Tenant's notice to terminate under section 27. In the case of fixed-term tenancies a tenant can prevent the continuation tenancy from running by serving not less than three months notice to this effect on the landlord. He can therefore prevent the continuation tenancy from ever starting by serving the notice towards the end of the contractual term. Alternatively, once it has started, he can still serve notice in order to bring the continuation tenancy to an end.

(e) Agreement for the grant of a new tenancy under section 28. If the parties agree to enter into a new tenancy the old tenancy will terminate on the date of commencement of the new tenancy.

(f) Landlord's notice under section 25 (see paragraph 5.17.5).

(g) Tenant's request under section 26 (see paragraph 5.17.6).

5.17.4   The statutory notice procedures

Under section 25 the landlord can serve a notice to terminate the tenancy and under section 26 the tenant can serve a request for a new tenancy. Once service has taken place under either section the other party is no longer entitled to serve under the other. In fact there is no need to do so because, contrary to initial impressions, the effect of service under either section is identical. Once service has taken place under either section a statutory procedure commences which, in all cases, will bring the continuation tenancy to an end but which will have one of two possible outcomes. Either a new tenancy will be granted, in which case the relationship of landlord and tenant will continue between the parties as before, or the tenant will be required to vacate due to the landlord's effective refusal to grant a new tenancy. The nature and workings of the statutory procedure are explored below.

5.17.5   Landlord's Notice to Terminate the Tenancy under Section 25

(A) Reasons for service

The landlord may decide to serve a section 25 notice because he genuinely requires possession of the property. However, it may simply be the case that he wants to increase the rent and that he therefore wishes to grant a new tenancy which will be subject to new terms (including a revised rent).

(B) Form of notice and date of service

The notice has to be served between six and twelve months before the 'date of termination' specified within it. The date of termination cannot be earlier than the contractual date of termination (either by effluxion of time in the case of a fixed-term tenancy or by notice to quit if a periodic tenancy). The notice must be in a form prescribed by regulations[69] and must state:

- The date of termination.
- Whether the landlord opposes the grant of a new tenancy and, if so, on which of the statutory grounds (see paragraph 5.17.8) he relies.
- If the landlord does not oppose the grant of a new tenancy, his proposals for the rent and other terms of that tenancy.

---

[69] Landlord and Tenant Act 1954, Part II (Notices) Regulations 2004

5.17.6   Tenant's request for a new tenancy under section 26

(A) Entitlement

The right to request a new tenancy under section 26 is restricted to tenants whose contractual tenancy was granted for a fixed term exceeding one year (although periodic tenants and fixed-term tenants for terms of less than a year are still entitled to request a new tenancy following service of a landlord's notice under section 25).

(B) Reasons for service

In many cases it will not be in the tenant's interest to make a request under section 26. He will have the benefit of the continuation tenancy in any event and, if a new tenancy is granted, it is likely to be at an increased rent. A tenant might nevertheless wish to apply for a new tenancy in order to create the certainty necessary for him to make long-term decisions about his business. Alternatively, if a tenant has plans to sell his business, potential purchasers will be also be more attracted to a new fixed term rather than having to rely on a continuation tenancy.

(C) Form of notice and date of service

The request has to be served between six and twelve months before the tenant's proposed 'date of commencement' of the new tenancy specified within it. As with the date of termination specified in a landlord's section 25 notice, the date of commencement cannot be earlier than the contractual date of termination of the existing tenancy. The notice must, once again, be in prescribed form, and must state:

- The proposed date of commencement of the new tenancy;
- The proposed rent and other terms of that tenancy.

Following service of a section 26 request the landlord must serve a counter notice within two months, stating the statutory grounds (see paragraph. 5.17.8) that he intends to rely on, if he wishes to oppose the tenant's request.

5.17.7   Applications to the court

Following service of a section 25 notice or a section 26 request the parties will enter into negotiations about the terms of any new tenancy, or indeed, if there is to be one at all. However, at any time after service under either section the parties each have a right to apply to court in order to bring matters to a head. The tenant can apply for a new tenancy or the landlord can apply for the termination of the tenancy without a new one being granted. In either case an application invites the court to consider both possibilities. Unless the parties agree to an extended deadline in writing, the deadline for making an application to the court is the 'date of termination' or the 'date of commencement', depending on whether the statutory procedure was started under section 25 or section 26. A failure to apply to the court by the deadline results in the tenancy coming to an end on that date.

5.17.8 Landlord's grounds of opposition

If the tenant applies to the court for this the court is obliged to order the grant of a new tenancy unless the landlord establishes that at least one of the statutory grounds applies. The most important grounds are discussed below.

(A) Breaches of tenant's covenants

The following three grounds fall into this category:

- Ground (a) - Failure to repair.
- Ground (b) - Persistent delay in paying rent.
- Ground (c) - Substantial breaches of other covenants.

These grounds are referred to as discretionary grounds because, even if the facts are established, the court still has discretion as to whether the tenant ought not to be granted a new tenancy in view of all the circumstances. The following grounds are described as the mandatory grounds because, if the landlord can establish one or more of them, the court is obliged to refuse to grant a new tenancy.

(B) Suitable alternative accommodation

Ground (d) is satisfied if the landlord offers suitable alternative accommodation to the tenant. It must be suitable for all the tenant's requirements, including the requirement to preserve goodwill.

(C) Demolition or reconstruction

Ground (f) is the most litigated of all grounds. It is stated in the following terms:

> 'On the termination of the current tenancy the landlord intends to demolish or reconstruct. . . .the premises or to carry out substantial work of construction. . . .and that he could not reasonably do so without obtaining possession.'

In order to establish this ground the landlord must establish a firm and settled intention. This means that he must not simply be contemplating the works but must have made a decision to carry them out based on the knowledge that it is practicable to do so. In practice, the landlord must show that the scheme is commercially viable and that he has the means to carry it through, together with the necessary statutory consents (planning permission/building regulations approval etc.). The landlord must also show that he could not reasonably carry out his work of demolition or reconstruction without obtaining possession of the premises.

(D) Occupation by the landlord

Ground (g) is also a frequently used ground that leads to much litigation. Its requirements are:

> 'On the termination of the termination of the current tenancy the landlord intends to occupy the [premises] for the purposes....of a business to be carried on by him therein, or as his residence.'

As in the case of ground (f) above, the burden is on the landlord to establish the necessary intention at the time of the hearing.

5.17.9 Grant of a new tenancy by the court

The parties will continue to negotiate even after an application has been made to the court. Even where the court does make an order for a new tenancy the terms of that order will therefore often have been agreed between the parties. In default of agreement the terms of the new lease will be determined by the court.

The length of the tenancy will be 'such as is reasonable in all the circumstances' although this cannot exceed fifteen years (s.33). The rent will be an open market rent, assessed on the basis that certain factors ('the statutory disregards') are disregarded:

- Any effect on the rent of the fact that the tenant or his predecessors in title have been in occupation.
- Any goodwill attaching to the holding on account of the tenant's business.
- Any improvements made under the current tenancy.

Surveyors will give evidence as to rentals based on comparables. Provisions exist for fixing an interim rent.

Apart from length and rent, regard must be had to the terms of the current tenancy and 'all relevant circumstances'. In practice, the court will follow the terms of the current tenancy unless there is a good reason for not doing so. The decision in *O'May v City of London Real Property Co Ltd*[70] enshrines this principle.

5.17.10 Compensation for failure to obtain a new tenancy

The tenant has a limited right to compensation (for 'disturbance') where the court refuses to grant a new tenancy in circumstances where the tenant is blameless and he suffers loss. No compensation is therefore available where refusal is on grounds (a), (b) or (c) as the tenant is at fault, or where it is on ground (d) as the tenant will have suffered no loss. However, compensation is available for refusal under:

---

[70] [1983] 2 AC 726

- Ground (f) demolition or reconstruction, or;
- Ground (g) occupation by the landlord.

The amount payable is the rateable value of the premises. If the business has been carried on at the premises, whether by the tenant or a predecessor for more than fourteen years, the compensation will be twice the rateable value.

5.17.11 *Compensation for improvements*

Under Part 1 of the Landlord and Tenant Act 1927 business tenants also have the right, at the end of their tenancy, to receive compensation for certain improvements that they have made to the property during the term. To qualify for compensation the improvements must add to the letting value of the premises and must have been undertaken following compliance with a statutory procedure. This requires the tenant to serve notice of the proposed improvements on the landlord and either that the landlord has not objected or that the court has issued a certificate to the effect that they are qualifying improvements under the Act. In practice, due to the complexity of the procedure, it is rarely used and the Law Commission has recommended its abolition.

6 Public Law and Regulation

6.1 Introduction

This chapter examines some selected elements of public law. Public law is concerned with the relationship between the state and individuals or organisations. Criminal law falls in the category of public law. In criminal law, the state determines a standard of acceptable behaviour for its citizens and proceeds against those who do not meet that standard. Another important part of public law is the area referred to as *administrative law*. This is the law that governs the bodies that administer government policies. It is concerned with how these bodies are made up, their powers, duties, rights and liabilities. Over recent years, judicial review (see Chapter 1, paragraph 1.8.2.C.a) has become an increasingly important aspect of administrative law. In an action for judicial review, the court reviews the legality of decisions made by government and public bodies.

The chapter begins with an overview of judicial review. The grounds for a judicial review action are considered with reference to some relevant case law and an outline of the judicial review procedure is provided. Certain selected areas of public law are then considered. These include the planning process and areas of state regulation that are of particular relevance to those operating within the built environment such as building regulations and environmental law. Health and Safety law and the regulations that relate to safety in the work place and occupational health are also an important feature of public law and these are also considered in this chapter.

6.2 Judicial review

Judicial review is the jurisdiction over the legality of decisions made by those with public power. A judicial review action can only be taken against a public body. Remedies against private bodies lie in private law. The extent of the power held by a public body can be reviewed as can the procedural correctness of the decision and the fairness of the process. Judicial review does not consider the merits of the decision, which is a political consideration. In reviewing a decision, the court will consider the statute that grants the particular power in question and principles derived from previous cases and determine firstly, what the rule is and secondly,

Law and the Built Environment by Douglas Wood, Paul Chynoweth, Julie Adshead and Jim Mason
© 2011 Douglas Wood, Paul Chynoweth, Julie Adshead and Jim Mason

whether it has been correctly applied. The rules concerned can be contained in a wide array of statutory provisions in a range of areas, for example, housing, planning, environment, education and immigration. There are currently more judicial reviews of immigration decisions than any other area.

6.2.1   *Grounds for review*

Lord Diplock in the case of *CCSU v Minister for Civil Service*[1] identified three *heads* of review: illegality, irrationality and procedural impropriety. It is clear, however, that further grounds can be added and indeed this has happened with the introduction of the Human Rights Act 1998, which allows for judicial review to protect ECHR rights[2]. The review can be of the content of the decision (substantive grounds) or of the procedure adopted (procedural grounds). Under substantive grounds there are two main areas of challenge; that the decision maker has gone outside the powers given in the statute or that the decision maker has abused a discretionary power granted by the statute.

(A) Acting outside powers

The term given to acts made in excess of the powers granted by statute is *ultra vires*, meaning literally outside powers. Any such act will be invalid. The doctrine cannot, however, be applied to the validity of an Act of Parliament. An example of a local planning authority acting outside its powers is to be found in the case of *R v Richmond upon Thames Council ex parte McCarthy and Stone Ltd*[3]. In this case the local authority planning department had started to charge a £25.00 fee for informal consultations between developers and planning officers prior to planning applications being made for new developments. There was no provision in the law for such a consultation and indeed the law stated that all applications had to be determined (see paragraph 6.4 below). The House of Lords held that the fee was not lawful as the charge was not incidental to the council's planning functions. It is evident from this case that no charge can be levied by a public body on the public without clear statutory authority.

(B) Abuse of discretionary powers

Statute often provides for very broad discretion to be exercised by the decision-making body. Not all decisions made within such discretion will be lawful. There are a series of grounds on which exercise of discretion can be reviewed:

- Taking into account irrelevant considerations.
- Not taking into account relevant considerations.
- Using powers for improper purposes.
- Making an error of law.

---

[1] [1985] AC 374, 410
[2] Sections 6 and 7
[3] [1992] 2 AC 48

- Delegating power without authorisation.
- Fettering discretion.
- Breaching financial duties.
- Acting unreasonably.
- Breaching the proportionality principle (in cases where rights under EU law or ECHR exist).
- Acting incompatibly with ECHR rights.
- Making a material error of fact.

The case of *R v Home Secretary ex parte Venables and Thompson*[4] provides an example of a number of these grounds being considered. The Home Secretary had increased the tariff (the period before which release from prison will be considered) for the two boys in question from ten to fifteen years. The House of Lords held that there had been an *error of law*. The Home Secretary had stated that the young offenders would be dealt with in the same way as adult offenders and, in this, he had misdirected himself in law. As Lord Steyn said in the House of Lords:

> 'His legal premise was wrong: the two sentences are different. A sentence of detention during Her Majesty's pleasure requires the Home Secretary to decide from time to time.......whether detention is still justified. The Home Secretary misunderstood his duty. This misdirection by itself renders his decision unlawful'.

It was also found that *irrelevant considerations* had been taken into account in the form of public petitions to increase the tariff and the Home Secretary had failed to take account of *relevant matters* (in this case the progress and development of the young offenders whilst in prison).

The *fettering of discretion* refers to over-rigid adherence to policy. It does not mean that a public body cannot adopt a policy and apply it in most circumstances, but the opportunity for the policy not to be applied must be left open. For example, an authority could not adopt a rule that certain applications will always be refused. Policies cannot be treated as binding rules. The case of *British Oxygen Company v Board of Trade*[5] illustrates this principle. There was a scheme in operation by the Board of Trade, which allowed for discretionary grants to be made to industry. The Board introduced a rule that no grants were payable for items costing less than £25.00. British Oxygen had spent more than £4 million on gas cylinders, but each one only cost £20.00. The House of Lords held that the Board was entitled to make the rule, but had to take account of individual arguments with reference to the operation of its discretion.

The standard of *unreasonableness* required in order for a decision to be set aside is a very high one. The test was originally laid down in the case of *Associated Provincial Picture Houses Ltd v Wednesbury Corporation*[6]. Lord Greene, MR, in setting out the test, said that in order for a decision to be set aside as unreasonable, the decision in question had to be 'so unreasonable that no reasonable authority

---

[4] [1998] AC 407
[5] [1971] AC 610
[6] [1948] 1 KB 223

could ever have come to it'. Unreasonableness has also been referred to as irrationality[7]. These quite extreme formulations have been toned down in more recent years. In *R v Chief Constable of Sussex ex parte International Trader's Ferry Ltd*[8], Lord Cooke expressed it more simply in that the decision taken must be 'one which a reasonable authority could reach'.

(C) Procedural grounds

Procedural requirements are frequently laid down in statute and in addition to these, certain rules of fairness (*natural justice*) must be adhered to in decision-making. Decisions can be challenged if the correct procedure has not been followed or if they have been unfairly reached.

An example of statutory procedure not being followed is found in the case of *Ridge v Baldwin*[9]. The Chief Constable of Brighton Police was dismissed following his acquittal on charges of conspiracy. The Police Act 1919 set out the procedure for dismissal of a Chief Constable and this included a formal inquiry into the charges brought. This had not occurred. The Committee that had dismissed the Chief Constable argued that he had been dismissed under other powers (The Municipal Corporations Act 1882). The House of Lords held that the 1919 Act applied and because the procedure had not been followed, the decision was void.

The rules of natural justice derive from common law and have been built up by the courts over centuries to determine fair procedure in the courts. Alongside these rules, there is now the Art 6 (1) ECHR right to a fair hearing incorporated in the Human Rights Act 1998 (see paragraph Chapter 1, 1.19.2.D). The rules of natural justice are nowadays more commonly referred to as *fairness*. The duty upon a decision-maker to act fairly applies to the procedure and not to the substantive decision. There are two main components to fairness; the rule against bias and the right to a fair hearing. When a decision is found to have been reached unfairly, then it is void.

(a) The rule against bias

The rule derives from common law and is now embodied in Art 6 (1) ECHR and the Human Rights Act 1998 in its requirement for an 'independent and impartial tribunal'. There is no necessity to prove bias. There just needs to be a real possibility of bias. The decision-maker must also be seen to be unbiased. In the famous words of Lord Hewart in *R v Sussex Justices ex parte McCarthy*[10], 'justice should not only be done but should manifestly and undoubtedly be seen to be done'. It is, therefore, not just a question of whether or not the decision-maker has an interest in the matter of the decision, but also of him/her not coming to the decision with an open mind. An example of the rule against bias in operation is to be found in the case of

---

[7] Lord Diplock in *CCSU v Minister for Civil Service* [1985] AC 374, 410
[8] [1999] 2 AC 418
[9] [1964] AC 40 HL
[10] [1924] 1 KB 256

R v Secretary of State for the Environment ex parte Kirkstall Valley Campaign Ltd[11], where the planning authority itself had private interests in the relevant planning permission.

(b) The right to a fair hearing

There is no definitive content to this right. As Lord Mustill acknowledged in the case of *R v Secretary of State for the Home Department ex parte Doody*[12], standards of fairness change over time and what fairness demands will differ from case to case. Fairness will often require that an individual can make representations either before or after the decision is made and that they are aware of the case to answer. Although there is no overarching right to an oral hearing or to know the evidence, where disciplinary procedures result in the loss of employment or benefit, there is a right to a decision before an unbiased tribunal, the right to notice and the right to be heard. There is no universal right to representation, regardless of the proceedings in question.

Fairness often requires that reasons be given for a decision, but this is decided on a case by case basis. If the decision has significant impact upon person or property, it is more likely that reasons will be required. This is a general trend with the application of fairness. If reasons are required they must be proper and adequate. They must be understandable and deal with the relevant points[13]. The leading case on the giving of reasons is *Doody*[14]. Doody and three other prisoners were serving mandatory life sentences for murder. The Home Secretary had consulted with the trial judge and set the penal element (the period before parole can be considered). Judicial review was sought on the ground that the Home Secretary had followed an unfair procedure. One of the main arguments was that fairness required the Home Secretary to give reasons when he decided to impose a different penal element to that recommended by the judiciary. Lord Mustill, in this case, posed a simple question 'Is the refusal to give reasons fair?' He concluded in the circumstances of this particular case that it was.

(D) Legitimate expectations

Grounds for judicial review can also flow from the legitimate expectations of a party. The concept of legitimate expectations is an aspect of legal certainty and it is one of the fundamental principles of EC law. It was first articulated by Lord Denning and was recognised in English law from the 1970s[15]. Legitimate expectations can arise in a number of situations:

- An indication has been given that a certain procedure will apply (for example, an oral hearing).

---

[11] [1996] 3 All ER 304
[12] [1994] 1 AC 531, 557
[13] *Re Poyser and Mills' Arbitration* [1964] QB 467
[14] At no. 12
[15] *R v Liverpool Corporation ex parte Liverpool Taxi Fleet Operators Association* [1972] 2 QB 299

- There is pre-existing policy or guidelines upon which an individual or group relies.
- There is consistency of practice, which is relied upon.

In the case of *Attorney General of Hong Kong v Ng Yuen Shiu*[16], an illegal immigrant had been detained and a deportation order made. The Director of Immigration had said that illegal immigrants would not be deported without interview and 'each case would be treated on its merits'. It was held that there was a legitimate expectation and the order was quashed. In a case concerning Liverpool taxi drivers[17], an undertaking had been given that licences would not be revoked without prior consultation. The court held that Liverpool Corporation was under a duty to comply with the commitment to consultation. There was also found to have been a consistency of practice that led to a legitimate expectation in the CCSU case[18]. Invariably, the practice had been to consult with civil service unions before changing the terms of employment for civil servants. It was held that the Unions had a legitimate expectation of being consulted before the government withdrew the right of union membership from GCHQ staff. However, national security proved decisive in this case.

6.2.2 Procedure

The basis for the procedure in applications for judicial review lies in the Supreme Court Act 1981, s.31, which confirmed a 1977 Rule of the Supreme Court (Order 53). The Procedure is now contained within the Civil Procedure Rules 1998 (CPR). Order 53 has been replaced by Part 54 CPR and at the same time a new Administrative Court was created. The Rules allow single judges of the High Court to decide Judicial Review cases. Changes have recently been introduced by the Tribunals Courts and Enforcement Act 2007 s.15, which allow the new Upper Tribunal jurisdiction to grant relief in certain classes of Judicial Review case. The specified classes will be determined by directions of the Lord Chief Justice (or his nominee) with agreement of the Lord Chancellor. The full procedure for judicial review (including pre-action protocols) can be found in the Administrative Court's Notes of Guidance on Applying for Judicial Review[19].

(A) Time limits

Applications for Judicial Review must be brought promptly and the CPR provide that this must be within three months of the decision unless a shorter time period is specified in statute.

---

[16] [1983] 2 AC 629

[17] At no. 15

[18] At no. 7

[19] http://www.hmcourts-service.gov.uk/cms/1220.htm

(B) Permission

There is no automatic right to judicial review and permission (formerly referred to as *leave*) must first be sought. This is a procedural hurdle that does not exist in any other area of law. To obtain permission, an application has to be served upon the defendant and anyone else who the claimant considers to be an interested party. It is necessary to present an arguable case to gain permission. A decision to refuse permission can be subject to reconsideration on the request of the claimant and there is a right to appeal to the Court of Appeal on refusal. Permission will not be granted unless the applicant has *sufficient interest* in the matter to which the application relates. This is also referred to as *standing* or *locus standi.*

(C) Standing

The requirement for a claimant to demonstrate sufficient interest in the matter is designed to filter out frivolous and unauthentic applications. The personal rights and interests of an individual have to be affected or the individual has to be concerned with official decisions which affect the interests of society as a whole. Alternatively, the applicant can be an interest or pressure group whose members' rights and interests are affected or those of society at large.

The original test for sufficient interest was laid down in the case of *R v Inland Revenue Commissioners ex parte National Federation of Self-Employed and Small Businesses Ltd*[20]. The House of Lords set out two stages:

- Leave to apply, which Lord Scarman said 'prevents abuse by busybodies, cranks and other mischief makers'.
- When the merits of the case are known, then the original decision to grant leave can be reviewed.

(a) Individual standing

Students of scientology, in a challenge to the Home Office over refusal to allow them to remain in the country, were found to have sufficient interest and granted leave[21]. A gipsy seeking direction to the local authority to provide an adequate site was also held to have standing[22]. In the case of *Gillick v West Norfolk and Wisbech Area Health Authority*[23], a mother of several daughters sought to challenge the health authority's policy on contraception and was granted standing. However, in the case of *Holmes v Checkland*[24], an anti-smoker was found not to have standing to challenge the BBC broadcast of a snooker contest sponsored by a tobacco company as he had no more interest in the matter than any other member of the public.

---

[20] [1982] AC 617
[21] *Schmidt v Secretary of State for the Home Department* [1969] 2 Ch 149
[22] *R v Secretary of State for Environment ex parte Ward* [1984] 1 WLR 834
[23] [1986] AC 112
[24] [1987] TLR, 15 April

(b) Pressure and interest groups

A group's *own* interests can be affected as in the case of the Liverpool Taxi owners[25] and the Royal College of Nursing in a challenge to a circular on the role of nurses in abortion[26]. In these cases each individual member would also have had sufficient interest in the matter. The *public* interest can also be at stake. In the above-mentioned *Inland Revenue*[27] case, those engaged in casual labour for the newspapers had provided false names in order to avoid the payment of income tax. The Inland Revenue Commission had declared an amnesty, whereby, if details were supplied for the past two years, they would not pursue tax due for previous years. The National Federation of Self-employed and Small Businesses (a tax-payers association) sought to challenge the agreement. The House of Lords held that the National Federation did not have sufficient interest to pursue the case, although their members would have had standing as individual tax-payers.

The courts have, on some occasions, found that public interest groups do have sufficient interest in the matter at stake and on others that they do not. For example, in the case of *R v Secretary of State for the Environment ex parte Rose Theatre Trust Co Ltd*[28], a company that was specifically incorporated to save the historic Globe Theatre site was found not to have standing. The same judge in the case of *R v Poole BC ex parte BeeBee*[29] found that the WWF and the British Heperetological Society did have sufficient interest to challenge the grant of planning permission by the Borough Council to itself for the development of protected heath land. The difference appears to be that, in the latter case one of the pressure groups in question had a financial interest in the matter. The decision whether or not to grant standing to an interest group will depend on the individual circumstances of the case. However, generally speaking, reputable pressure groups of long-standing and with a wide membership are more likely to be seen as having sufficient interest. In the case of *R v Secretary of State for Environment ex parte Greenpeace Ltd (No. 2)*[30], Greenpeace brought a challenge against the siting of a nuclear reprocessing plant at Sellafield. They were found to have standing although they were unsuccessful in their challenge. A significant factor in the decision was the 400 000 strong Greenpeace support in the UK.

6.2.3 Remedies

In actions for judicial review all remedies are awarded at the discretion of the court. Even if a challenge is successful, a remedy is not automatic. The court can refuse to give a remedy for a variety of reasons. For example, delay in commencing proceedings, the unreasonable behaviour of the applicant or if the grant of a remedy is contrary to the public interest. There is a special class of remedies in public law known as the *prerogative remedies*. The names have recently been

---

[25] At no. 15
[26] *Royal College of Nursing v DHSS* [1981] AC 800
[27] At no. 20
[28] [1990] 2 WLR 186
[29] [1991] 2 PLR 27
[30] [1994] 4 All ER 352

changed as part of Lord Woolf's efforts to simplify the language of the courts. Other remedies are also available as appropriate.

(A) Prerogative remedies

- A quashing order (formerly known as *certiorari*) quashes a decision. If part of the decision is good, then an order can be granted to quash just the offending section.
- A prohibiting order (previously prohibition) is similar to a quashing order but affects future action. It prevents a body making a decision, which otherwise would be capable of being quashed.
- A mandatory order (which used to be referred to as *mandamus*) compels action. It can be used against ministers and departmental officials and prevents unlawful failure to act. This type of order is often used in conjunction with a quashing order. Failure to abide by any of the prerogative orders amounts to contempt of court.

(B) Declaration

This is not a legal remedy, but is merely a statement of the positions of the parties. As with a mandatory order (above) it can be used to encourage government ministers to take a particular action. Although there are no legal consequences, public bodies usually respond to a declaration of the court and modify any deficiencies in their decision.

(C) Injunction

An injunction can be of an interim or a permanent nature and can be positive or negative. Again an injunction can be used against the Crown or a government minister and non-compliance can amount to contempt of court. Injunctions are, in fact, rarely utilised because the end result can normally be achieved by a quashing order or a mandatory order. An injunction is sometimes useful, however, as an interim remedy.

(D) Damages

Damages are rarely granted in judicial review actions. Damages are only recoverable if they would be available through a private law action.

6.3   Building regulations

The general purpose of the Building Regulations is to ensure that buildings are constructed so as to be safe and not a danger to the health and safety of occupants. A uniform national system of building control (except in inner London) has existed since 1965. This was radically revised by the Building Regulations 1985.

Building regulations are made under the Building Act 1984 and the current regulations are the Building Regulations 2000 (as amended). The Regulations now include the inner London area which was previously subject to the London Building Acts 1930–78. A separate system of building control applies in Scotland and Northern Ireland.

6.3.1   Content of regulations

The 2000 Regulations are very short and contain no technical detail. They are drafted in such a way that rigid enforcement is discouraged. The general performance requirements are set out in Parts A to P of Schedule 1 and each Part is supported by an approved document that contains non-binding guidance on how to comply. Although use of the approved documents is not mandatory, the documents can be relied upon in legal proceedings where breach of the Regulations is alleged.

The Schedule 1 headings are as follows:

Part A   Structure
Part B   Fire safety
Part C   Site preparation and resistance to moisture
Part D   Toxic substances
Part E   Resistance to the passage of sound
Part F   Ventilation
Part G   Hygiene
Part H   Drainage and waste disposal
Part J   Heat producing appliances
Part K   Stairways, ramps and guards
Part L   Conservation of fuel and power
Part M   Access and facilities for disabled people
Part N   Glazing materials and protection
Part P   Electrical safety

There is a duty upon persons undertaking works that come within the scope of the Regulations to submit plans together with specifications and particulars. The Regulations apply to the initial erection of a building, an extension and any material alteration or change of use. Temporary buildings, those not open to the public and agricultural buildings are exempt.

6.3.2   Local authority control

(A) Deposit of plans procedure (Reg 13)

This is the traditional system of building control, whereby an applicant deposits full plans with the building control department of the local authority. The plans must be either approved or rejected within five weeks. This can be extended to eight weeks with the agreement of the parties. Plans can be approved with conditions. Works should be commenced within three years of deposit of the plans, otherwise the Local Authority can declare that the plans have no effect. This procedure has the advantage of certainty in that the applicant knows that once approval is given, there will be no risk of the works failing to comply as long as they are carried out in conformity with the plans. Once the notice requirements have been complied with (see below), the applicant can commence work (although it is common to await issue of approval because of the protection that this provides). A completion certificate can be requested at the time of deposit of the plans. This confirms that the completed works comply with the Regulations.

(B) Building notice procedure (Reg 12)

This procedure was introduced in 1985. It avoids the need (and the additional cost and time) of preparing plans. It is ideal for smaller projects where the person carrying out the work is familiar with the requirements of the Regulations. However, as no approval is ever issued, the work is at the risk of the building's owner. Also, there is no facility for the issue of a completion certificate confirming that the works are in compliance with the Regulations.

Building notice must be delivered to the building control department at least two days before commencement of the works. There is no prescribed form, but it must contain a description of the proposed work and certain other required information. The notice alerts the building control department to the fact that the works are to take place. Subject to the standard notice requirements (see below), there are no further formalities to be completed and the applicant can commence work.

(C) Notice requirements (Regs 14, 14A)

Whichever of the two procedures above are followed, applicants are required to give certain notices to the building control department to allow them to inspect the various stages of the work. These should be in writing or in such other form as the building control department requires. Commonly departments issue applicants with pre-printed postcards to return at the appropriate time but they will often accept notice by telephone. The requirements are:

- Two day's notice – before commencement of the works.
- One day's notice – before covering up:
  (1) Foundation trenches.
  (2) Constructed foundations.
  (3) Damp proof course.
  (4) Site concrete or floor slab.
  (5) Drains.
- Five day's notice – after completion of the works.

6.3.3 Private certification

The statutory framework for private certification is contained in Part II of the Building Act 1984. It provides an alternative to the local authority control system.

Local authorities do remain responsible, however, for any necessary enforcement action. The Construction Industry Council is responsible for approving inspectors who are then entered on the Construction Industry Council Approved Inspector's Register. An applicant's suitability for appointment is assessed through an application form and a professional interview. There is a different procedure for approval to the local authority one described above. The detailed procedure and prescribed forms are to be found in the Building (Approved Inspectors, etc.) Regulations 2000.

6.3.4 Self-certification

Public bodies and certain competent persons can be empowered to self-certify, although this currently has limited scope.

(A) Public bodies

Regulation 21 of the Building (Approved Inspectors, etc.) Regulations 2000 empowers the Secretary of State to approve public bodies for the supervision of their own work. Very few public bodies have received approval.

(B) Competent persons

A number of more limited forms of self-certification also exist in specific cases of minor work. These include the installation of hot water, heating and air conditioning systems by a CORGI registered person and the replacement of windows, roof lights, roof windows or doors by a person registered under the Fenestration Self-Assessment Scheme. Such registered persons are described as *competent persons*.

6.3.5 Non-notification

There is extremely limited scope for non-notification. There is a non-notification system of building control if work on 'fixed low or extra-low voltage electrical installations' (those generally associated with dwellings) is carried out by *competent persons* registered for the self-certification procedure (above) with the appropriate electrical body.

6.3.6 Enforcement

Contravention of the Building Regulations is dealt with in the Magistrates' Court. In addition to any fine payable, penalties are imposed for each day the default continues after conviction. Within twelve months of the completion of unauthorised works, the relevant authority may require the owner to alter or pull down the works which infringe the Regulations. In default, the authority may do this themselves and charge the cost to the owner. In appropriate circumstances an injunction may be sought.

6.3.7 Civil liability

As far as civil liability is concerned, the 1970s and early 1980s saw numerous cases before the courts where building contractors and local authorities were sued in negligence for breach of the Regulations based on the case of *Anns v Merton LBC*[31] (see paragraph 3.6.1.A). Liability in this area of the law is now covered by *Murphy v Brentwood BC*[32] (see paragraph 3.6.1.A), which for all practical purposes means that there is no claim in negligence in respect of a defective building caused by breach of a Regulation if there is no injury to property or person. Claims for pure economic loss are generally not recoverable in the law of tort. Section 38 of the Building Act 1984 imposes general civil liability for breach of a duty imposed by the Building Regulations but this section has yet to become law.

6.4 Planning law

Over the past century a system of local and, more recently, central control over urban planning has evolved. Planning law is contained in a series of key statutes supplemented by extensive central guidance (in the form of planning policy statements). There is a very limited role for the courts in planning issues. Most planning decisions are made by the local planning authority (on rare occasions by the Secretary of State). The only criminal offences arise from non-compliance with a notice (see paragraph 6.4.3 below). There is no third party right of appeal, so the only route for someone, other than the applicant, to challenge a determination of planning permission is by judicial review if the decision-making process has not been correctly followed (see paragraph 6.2 above). The entire system is driven by national and local planning policy. From 1991 planning decisions have been led by the local development plan. Nowadays determinations follow local development frameworks for local decisions.

The key statutes are:

- The Town and Country Planning Act (TCPA) 1990, which consolidated the previous statutory measures in a single Act.
- The Planning and Compensation Act 1991. This piece of legislation saw the move to planning being led by the development plan.
- The Planning and Compulsory Purchase Act (PCPA) 2004, which introduced the local development framework.
- The Planning Act 2008. This Act introduced key changes to the procedure for major infrastructure projects.

---

[31] [1978] AC 728
[32] [1991] AC 398

6.4.1 The determination of planning permission

(A) Development

The law places an obligation on a landowner to obtain planning permission before a building may be erected or the use of land is substantially altered. S57 (1) of TCPA 1990 states that 'Planning permission is required for the carrying out of any development of land'. The definition of *development* is extremely broad[33] and can be divided into two aspects: *operational development* and *material change of use*.

(a) Operational development

Operational developments encompass engineering, mining and building operations. The latter are defined in s336 TCPA 1990.

> 'Building operations include rebuilding operations, structural alterations of or additions to buildings, demolition of buildings, and other operations normally undertaken by a person carrying on business as a builder'.

(b) Material change of use

For there to be a material change of use to an existing structure, there must be a physical impact on the land, which must be substantial. This impact must be one that is relevant to town and country planning. Material change of use is assessed by *planning unit*, which is the area of occupation prior to the change. Material change of use is a more difficult concept than operational development. Intensification of use may amount to a material change[34]. Whether the change is material is a question of fact and degree for the local planning authority.

(c) Exempted activities

A list of activities that do not constitute development is provided in TCPA 1990[35]. Amongst these are activities that fall in the category of 'a change of use within the same class of the *Use Classes Order*'[36]. These are uses that have a similar land use impact. For example, a change from one type of office use to another type of office use or from one type of shop use to another shop use will not attract the need for planning permission.

(d) Permitted development

Development can be permitted under statute, in which case no express consent is required from the local planning authority. Planning permission is deemed to be

---

[33] TCPA 1990, s55 (1)
[34] *Brooks and Burton v DOE* [1977] 1 WLR 1094
[35] TCPA 1990, s55 (2) (a) – (g)
[36] Use Classes Order 1987 SI 1987/764

automatically granted. There are thirty-three classes of permitted development listed in the General Permitted Development Order (GPDO)[37]. These cover minor developments, developments carried out by public services and favoured activities (agriculture and forestry). Development consent may still be needed if such projects exceed certain thresholds and the right to development can be withdrawn, for example, if an environmental impact assessment is required. Other developments are permitted in *Special Development Orders, Local Development Orders, Enterprise Zones* and *Simplified Planning Zones*.

(B) Application for planning permission

The application is made to the Local Planning Authority with the appropriate fee. The form should be accompanied by plans and drawings indicating the location and form of development. If the applicant is not the estate owner, a certificate stating the applicant's legal interest in the land and, where appropriate, that notice has been given to the owner must also be submitted. In the case of operations development, an intending developer may wish to test the likelihood of whether or not the authority will allow a consent. In such a case an outline application may be made, indicating the proposed development with an appropriate site plan. Any permission granted will be subject to a subsequent approval (within three years) of *reserved matters*, such as landscaping or access which are not referred to in the application.

The local planning authority consults with a wide range of public bodies and any representations made to the authority will be *material considerations* (see below). All applications must be publicised. Unless the parties agree to an extension, the planning authority has eight weeks in which to come to a decision. The application may be refused, granted or granted subject to conditions. Reasons must be provided. If permission is granted, the development that is authorised must be started within five years of obtaining consent. Applicants for substantial projects must now consider the environmental aspects and whether or not the application is subject to an *Environmental Impact Assessment* (see paragraph 6.5 below). Also, major infrastructure projects are now subject to the provisions of the Planning Act 2008. Nearly all applications are decided by planning officers, but the Secretary of State has unfettered power to call in any planning application[38]. On the infrequent occasions when an application is called in for determination by the Secretary of State, there is almost always a public inquiry.

(C) Development plans

Planning determinations are led by the development plan. The old system involved structure, local and unitary development plans. PCPA 2004 saw a change to the development plan regime, with the introduction of regional spatial strategies. These go beyond the prior requirements for development plans and include such

---

[37] TCPA General Permitted Development Order 1995 SI 1995/418
[38] TCPA 1990, s77

issues as infrastructure and environment. Regional Spatial Strategies are, at the time of writing, not operational and the government plans to abolish them in forthcoming legislation and focus planning policy and decisions at a local level. PCPA 2004 also introduced local development frameworks, which amount to a series of documents designed to deliver the spatial strategy (one of which will probably equate to the old local development plan). PCPA 2004 states that

> 'regard is to be had to the development plan, the determination shall be made in accordance with the development plan unless material considerations indicate otherwise'[39].

(D) Material considerations

There is no statutory definition or guidance as to what constitutes a material consideration. Planning policy statements and representations by consultees and third parties are certainly material considerations as are a range of other matters determined by case law. For example, environmental issues can be material considerations[40] as are obligations under EC Law[41].

(E) Planning conditions

TCPA, s.70 (1) allows the local planning authority to impose such conditions 'as it thinks fit'. Guidance is provided in ss. 72 and 75 and there is a policy on conditions published by the Secretary of State[42]. The courts have taken a restrictive view on planning conditions and it is clear that these cannot be imposed for ulterior motives. In the case of *Newbury DC v Secretary of State for the Environment*[43], it was held that conditions must:

- Be imposed for a planning purpose and not for an ulterior motive.
- Fairly and reasonably relate to the development permitted.
- Not be perverse (so unreasonable that no reasonable authority could have imposed them).

(F) Planning obligations and contributions

Such agreements were previously negotiated on a case by case basis and planning obligations under TCPA 1990 raised issues surrounding the legality of planning gain[44], but following PCPA 2004, planning contributions will impose a

---

[39] PCPA 2004, s38 (6)

[40] See, for example, *West Coast Wind Farms Ltd v Secretary of State for the Environment and North Devon DC* [1996] JPL 767, where environmental considerations were just one of a number of material considerations brought into the balancing act

[41] *R (Murray) v Derbyshire CC* [2002] Env LR 28 (EC waste management objectives)

[42] Circular 11/95

[43] [1981] AC 578

[44] *R v Plymouth CC ex parte Plymouth and South Devon Co-operative Society Ltd* (1993) 67 P&CR 78 and *Tesco Stores Ltd v Secretary of State for the Environment* [1995] 1 WLR 759

predetermined charge for services and facilities according to the development plan. There is still room for negotiated agreements in special circumstances, for example, when there is a particularly environmentally sensitive site. Guidance as to what is permissible in planning gain is set out in Circular 05/2005.

6.4.2 Appeals

There is a right of appeal by the applicant to the Secretary of State on a planning determination and/or its conditions. Notice of appeal must be given within six months. Most appeals are dealt with on the basis of written representations made by the parties, but if either side requests it the issue must be dealt with by public local enquiry before a planning inspector. The application is effectively heard afresh with both legal and policy grounds open for consideration. Reasons must be given for the decision. A new fast track procedure for *householder appeals* was introduced in 2009, which relies upon the original application and written representations only[45]. An application can be made to the High Court to review the decision on appeal within six weeks[46]. If planning permission has been refused or granted subject to conditions and the owner of the land can show that the land is incapable of reasonably beneficial use in its existing state, the owner may serve a purchase notice on the planning authority requiring them to buy the land at market value[47].

6.4.3 Enforcement

In the case of 'a breach of planning control' the local planning authority has a discretion to issue an enforcement notice on the owners and occupiers of the land and any other person who the authority considers is materially affected by the notice. If the breach occurs in a conservation area, or the building is listed, a listed building enforcement notice may be issued. The notice must specify the breach complained of, the steps to be taken to remedy the breach, the date upon which the notice will take effect and the period for compliance with the notice. The notice must normally be served within four years of the breach.

In the event of non-compliance with the notice, the planning authority may enter the land and carry out the steps required by the enforcement notice and recover any expenses due. There is a right of appeal against an enforcement notice to the Secretary of State and a further right of appeal, on a point of law, to the High Court. Breach of planning control on its own is not a criminal offence but failure to comply with a valid enforcement notice is.

To avoid the use of delaying tactics, the planning authority may serve a stop notice requiring the offending development to be curtailed. There is no right of appeal in respect of this notice. Although enforcement notices are still the main

---

[45] Town and Country Planning (Appeals) (Written Representation Procedure) (England) Regulations 2009 SI 2009/452
[46] TCPA 1990, s288
[47] TCPA 1990, ss 137 – 148

weapon available to the planning authority, a number of alternative procedures have been devised to cover specific situations instead of relying on the enforcement notice in every case. In particular, a planning contravention notice can be served where there is a suspected breach of planning control, and similarly a breach of condition notice is applicable in breach of condition cases.

6.4.4 Human rights and planning law

The route of appeal from planning determinations to the Secretary of State gave rise to a challenge under human rights law (Article 6, right to a fair trial, paragraph 1.19.3.D above). In the case of *R v Secretary of State for Environment Transport and the Regions ex parte Holding and Barnes plc and others*[48] (the *Alconbury* case) a submission was made that the decision made by the Secretary of State on appeal made him 'judge in his own cause where his policy is in play' and that 'He cannot be both policy maker and decision-taker'. The House of Lords found that Article 6 was not breached as the legality of the planning judgment is open to challenge by judicial review (see paragraph 6.2 above).

6.5 Environmental impact assessment

As noted above (see paragraphs 6.4.1 B and D), as well as environmental effects being material considerations in the planning process, for certain projects and plans/programmes an environmental assessment may be required. If a project falls within the requirements of the EC Environmental Impact Assessment (EIA) Directive[49] as implemented by the Town and Country Planning (Environmental Impact Assessment) (England and Wales) Regulations 1999[50], then the developer will have to produce an *environmental statement*. Large scale plans and programmes are also now subject to strategic environmental assessment (SEA) under a later EC Directive[51]. Both EIA and SEA are procedural mechanisms. There is no obligation upon the decision-maker to refuse a project or amend a plan because of negative environmental impacts highlighted in the environmental statement, nor is there any mechanism to impose conditions upon projects or plans.

6.5.1 Projects

For EIA to apply, there must be a *project* that is subject to *consent*. Project is defined in the EIA Directive as 'the execution of construction works, or of other installations or schemes'. This will normally be the same as a *development* under planning law (see paragraph 6.4.1.A above). Consent is the decision that entitles the developer to proceed with the project, which, more often than not, will be the

[48] [2001] UKHL 23
[49] Directive 97/11/EC
[50] SI 1999/293
[51] Directive 2001/42/EC

grant of planning permission. Some projects such as those serving national defence purposes are exempt from EIA[52]. Applicants can determine whether EIA is required by seeking a *screening opinion* from the local planning authority[53].

(A) Schedule 1 projects

For projects that fall under Schedule 1 to the 1999 Regulations, EIA is mandatory. These include major projects such as thermal power stations, motorways, chemical installations and oil refineries. For most projects falling within Schedule 1, the definitions are self-explanatory, but for some there are thresholds. For example, for a thermal power station, mandatory EIA is only applicable if the heat output is over 300 megawatts.

(B) Schedule 2 projects

Projects falling within Schedule 2 are less environmentally sensitive ones. Examples include food manufacture, golf courses, retail parks and motorway service areas. Schedule 1 projects that fall below stated thresholds come under Schedule 2. For such a project, EIA is only necessary when it is 'likely to have significant effects on the environment by virtue of factors such as its nature, size or location'[54]. Guidance on when an EIA may be required is contained in Schedule 3 of the 1999 Regulations. The decision-making body has quite a wide discretion in determining whether a project falls within Schedule 2.

(C) The environmental statement

There is nothing in the regulations to indicate the form that an environmental statement should take, but it must contain at least:

- A description including design and size information.
- Relevant data to determine the main likely environmental effects.
- Details of measures to avoid, reduce or remedy significant adverse effects.
- An outline of the main alternatives to the site and reasons for the existing choice.

A non-technical summary understandable by non-experts must be supplied for all information provided. A developer can apply for a scoping opinion from the local planning authority on the information to be provided in the environmental statement. When gathering information for the environmental statement, developers are expected to consult a wide range of statutory and non-statutory consultees.

---

[52] 1999 Regulations, reg 4 (a) (ii)
[53] 1999 Regulations, reg 5 (1)
[54] EIA Directive, Art 2 (1)

(D) Determination of EIA applications

The environmental statement is submitted with the planning application. Statutory consultees must be notified and there are increased publicity requirements. The determination period for planning application is extended to sixteen weeks. Any grant of planning permission that does not take account of the environmental information (from the environmental statement and consultations) is invalid[55]. However, as noted above, projects with significantly detrimental effects to the environment can go ahead as long as the requisite procedure has been followed. Reasons must be given whether or not planning permission is granted.

6.6   Water pollution

Water pollution law in England revolves around a consent system for discharges into *controlled waters*. Controlled waters are defined in s.104 of the Water Resources Act 1991 and cover virtually all inland and coastal waters (surface and ground water). The consent system is to be found in Schedule 10 of the Water Resources Act 1991 and the Control of Pollution (Applications, Appeals and Registers) Regulations 1996. Consents are set on an individualised basis, taking into account local conditions and the status of the receiving waters. They are quite flexible and can be altered to respond to changes in the local environment. An application for a consent should be made to the Environment Agency (EA) for:

- Any discharge of trade or sewage effluent into controlled waters.
- Any discharge of trade or sewage effluent through a pipe from land into the sea outside the limits of controlled waters.
- Any discharge where a prohibition is in force.

There is no legal obligation to hold a consent, but it is an offence to discharge into controlled waters without a consent or in breach of the conditions of a consent (see paragraph 6.6.1 below). The consent, therefore, acts as a defence to a potential prosecution under one of the general water pollution offences.

6.6.1   The general water pollution offences

The general water pollution offences under s.85 (1) of the Water Resources Act (WRA) 1991 are 'causing or knowingly permitting any poisonous, noxious, or polluting matter or any waste to enter controlled waters'. 'Poisonous, noxious or polluting' are not defined in the Act but the courts have interpreted the meaning of 'polluting' very broadly. For example, in the case of *R v Dovermoss Ltd*[56], ammonia found its way into spring water used for water supply. The source was a field on which animal slurry had been spread. Heavy rain had resulted in the slurry seeping into the ground near the spring and entering the water supply. The defence argued that no harm had actually been done to the receiving waters and that ammonia

---

[55] 1999 Regulations, reg 30
[56] [1995] Env LR 258

levels did not exceed maximum concentrations permitted under drinking water regulations. The court held that it was not necessary for the prosecution to prove that the substance had actually caused any harm. It was sufficient that there was a likelihood or capability of causing harm to animal or plant life or those who use water. For a successful prosecution, therefore, actual pollution does not have to be proven, or, indeed, to have occurred.

There are actually two offences contained in WRA 1991, s.85 (1). The *causing* offence is strict liability and is the most commonly prosecuted of the two offences. All that is necessary, for a successful prosecution under this offence, is the entry of potentially polluting substances into controlled waters. The leading case on *causing* under s.85 (1) is *Environment Agency v Empress Car Co (Arbertillery) Ltd*[57]. In the *Empress Cars* case, alleged vandalism of an oil storage tank caused entry of oil into controlled waters. A protective bund had been overridden by the owners and an unknown person had entered the premises and opened the tap. The entire contents of the tank overflowed across a yard, into a storm drain and into a nearby river. On appeal, the defence argued that there had been no positive act on the part of the company which amounted to 'causing' the entry and that it had been the act of a stranger. The House of Lords, rejecting the appeal, ruled that a person may be held to have caused the entry of polluting matter if that person did something with or without the occurrence of other facts, which produced a situation in which the polluting matter could escape.

There are limited defences to be found in WRA 1991, s.88. As mentioned above, holding a consent is a defence. There is also a defence in cases of emergency, but the courts have taken a restrictive approach to this and the defence will only apply when human life is threatened[58].

6.7 Contaminated land

The system for identifying and remediating contaminated land in England is a complex one. The regime is to be found in the Environmental Protection Act 1990, Part 2A, which is supplemented by the Contaminated Land (England) Regulations 2006[59]. Of equal importance to these legislative measures is Circular 1/2006[60]. This document contains detailed guidance on risk assessment, allocation and apportionment of liability and strategic identification of sites. There is a statutory obligation upon the relevant authority to act in accordance with this guidance.

The aim of the contaminated land regime is closely linked to the development of brown field sites and it supplements the planning process. As such, it encourages voluntary action and is very much a mechanism of last resort. Consequently, to date, there has been a relatively small number of determinations and notices served and very few cases before the courts. The legislation is unusual in that it is retrospective (applies to past acts).

---

[57] [1998] All ER 481
[58] *Express Ltd v Environment Agency* [2003] Env LR 29
[59] Part 2A of the Environmental Protection Act (EPA) 1990: Contaminated Land, SI 2006/1380
[60] http://www.defra.gov.uk/environment/quality/land/contaminated/documents/circular01-2006.pdf

6.7.1   The definition of contaminated land

EPA 1990, s.78A (2) defines contaminated land as:

'any land which appears to the local authority in whose area it is situated to be in such a condition, by reason of substances in, on or under the land, that;

(a)   significant harm is being caused or there is a significant possibility of such harm being caused; or
(b)   pollution of controlled waters is being, or is likely to be, caused;'

Harm is defined in s.78 (4):

'harm to the health of living organisms or other interference with the ecological systems of which they form part and, in the case of man, includes harm to his property.'

Ways to ascertain whether there is *significant harm* and *significant possibility* are provided in the guidance. A *significant pollutant linkage* or pathway is required and there must also be a target or receptor, which can be any of the following:

- Human beings.
- Nature conservation sites.
- Buildings.
- Other property (including crops and livestock).

6.7.2   The identification of contaminated land

Local authorities determine which land is contaminated. They have a duty to inspect for the purposes of identifying contaminated land and special sites. Special sites are those where there is threat of serious harm or pollution and they come under the control of the Environment Agency. The local authority must act in accordance with Circular 1/2006 (see above). If there is pollution of controlled water or harm to a conservation site, they must consult with the Environment Agency and Natural England (the English nature conservancy body). The local authority has extensive powers of inspection and entry.

6.7.3   Notification and consultation

Once contaminated land is identified, owners, occupiers and potentially liable parties are notified[61]. There will normally be a minimum three month consultation period, which gives the opportunity for voluntary remediation to be undertaken. During this period remediation methods will be identified and a cost benefit analysis carried out. The standard of remediation is a *suitable for use* standard (including planned use under planning application).

---

[61] EPA 1990 Part 2A, s.78B (3)

6.7.4   Remediation notice

There is quite an extensive list of circumstances in EPA 1990 Part 2A, s.78E in which a notice will not be served, which tends to make the process of serving a notice somewhat discretionary. Notice is served on the *appropriate person* and it contains detail of the action to be taken and the time period allowed. An appropriate person can be a *Class A person*:

> 'person, or any of the persons, who caused or knowingly permitted the substances, or any of the substances, that have been the cause of the contamination to be in or under the land'

or a *Class B person*. Class B persons are owners and occupiers and will only be liable if no Class A person can be found. There will be a separate appropriate person for each *significant pollutant linkage* (see above), so there is likely to be a Class A and/or Class B liability group.

Even after a class of appropriate persons has been identified there are exclusion tests applied in an effort at fairness. There are six tests for Class A liability group members and a single test for Class B exclusion. Liability is then apportioned by relative responsibility with consideration being given to timescale of use or occupation. If there is no information available then apportionment is equal. There is a right to appeal against a notice to the Secretary of State within twenty-one days. The relevant authority can carry out the works required in the notice and recover their costs.

6.8   Waste management law

Recent years have seen a shift in emphasis in waste management law. Initially the focus was upon the protection of public health, but nowadays, the primary goal is the prevention of waste in the first place. The current approach taken is a *cradle to grave* one. Waste law now tackles reduction in packaging, recovery and recycling initiatives and the management of waste as well as its ultimate disposal. EU law is an extremely important feature of UK waste law. Much of our waste law is taken directly from Europe and the definition of waste used in the national courts comes from EU legislation and case law.

6.8.1   Definition of waste

There is a tension between preventing the careless and hazardous disposal of waste, which can put health and the environment at risk and encouraging the recovery and recycling of waste products. This is particularly evident in cases coming before the courts on the question of what is and is not waste for the purposes of EU and national legislation.

The definition of waste is to be found in the Environmental Permitting (England and Wales) Regulations 2007. The Regulations refer to 'Directive waste', thus relying upon the EU definition to be found in Article 1 and Annex 1 of the Waste Framework Directive[62].

---

[62] Directive 2006/12/EC

'any substance or objects in the categories set out in Annex 1 which the holder discards or intends or is required to discard'

Annex 1 of the Directive provides sixteeen categories of waste. Category 16 covers materials, substances or products that do not fall under the other fifteen categories. The list is only helpful, therefore, in providing some examples and the key to the definition lies in determining whether there is an *intention to discard*. The question has generated a good quantity of case law. Two fairly recent cases illustrate some of the problems involved.

In the ECJ case of *Van de Walle and others*[63], petrol had leaked accidentally from underground storage tanks. The ECJ held that the spillages were substances that the holder did not intend to produce and were 'discarded'. The court also held that the soil contaminated by the petrol was waste because it could not be recovered or disposed of without remediation and that Texaco was the producer of the waste (as the supplier of the petrol). This case has been widely criticised, not least because it expands waste law into contaminated land and water pollution regimes.

The case of *OSS Group Ltd v the Environment Agency*[64] concerned waste oil that was reprocessed and sold as fuel. The end product was indistinguishable from ordinary fuel oil. The question was whether waste management law applied to the oil and at what point. The Environment Agency argued that the reprocessed oil only ceased to be waste after it was burnt. This would have put very onerous obligations upon customers purchasing the oil. The Court of Appeal held that the oil was not being 'discarded' in the ordinary sense of the word and, therefore, was not waste once it was reprocessed. This seems to be a sensible conclusion made with explicit reference to the purpose of the EU Framework Directive and one that serves to encourage recovery and recycling.

6.8.2 *Environmental permitting*

Waste licensing has now been drawn into a single streamlined environmental permitting system. Permits are required for 'regulated facilities' and these include all waste operations that involve disposal or recovery of *Directive waste*. The new scheme came into being with the introduction of the Environmental Permitting Regulations 2007. Some low level risk waste activities are exempt. For example, sorting, recycling, construction waste and waste storage[65].

(A) Application

An application for a permit is made by the operator, that is, the person in 'control' of the regulated facility or mobile plant[66]. 'Control' is linked to the authority and ability to comply with the permit and its conditions. Once 'duly made', an application will be determined in a period of between two to four months,

---

[63] C-1/03 [2005] Env LR 24
[64] [2008] Env LR 8
[65] 2007 Regulations, Schedule 3
[66] 2007 Regulations, reg 7

depending upon its nature. Applications can be called in by the Secretary of State. There are requirements for public participation, but publication can be circumvented in cases of commercial or industrial confidentiality and national security. A permit may be granted (usually with conditions) or refused. The key consideration in the determination is meeting the objectives of the relevant piece of EU waste legislation. The judgment is an expert technical one and the courts are reluctant to interfere with the expert determination of the Environment Agency[67]. There is a requirement that the operator is competent and the Agency is under a duty to refuse the grant of a permit if, in their view, the operator could not comply with it.

(B) Enforcement

The Regulations allow for the following enforcement mechanisms:

- Enforcement notices (regulation 36).
- Suspension (regulation 37).
- Revocation (regulations 22 – 23).
- Variation (regulation 20).

There is also an element of self-regulation. Operators are required, in the conditions of the permit, to self-monitor and report breaches and if they fail to do so this will constitute a further breach. It is an offence to operate a regulated facility without a permit or in breach of permit conditions. It is also an offence to fail to comply with a notice[68]. A defence is available in emergency in order to avoid danger to human health[69]. There is a right of appeal against refusal to issue a permit within six months.

6.8.3 General criminal offences

The general waste offences are found in the Environmental Protection Act 1990 s.33 (1). It is an offence to:

(a)   deposit controlled waste in or on land, unless it is in accordance with an environmental permit;
(b)   submit controlled waste to any listed operation (other than a disposal operation mentioned above) unless it is under and in accordance with an environmental permit;
(c)   knowingly cause or knowingly permit either of the above;
(d)   treat, keep or dispose of controlled waste in a manner that is likely to cause pollution of the environment or harm to human health.

An environmental permit will serve as a defence in the case of a, b and c above. There is also a due diligence defence to an unpermitted activity[70]. The question of

---

[67] *Levy v Environment Agency* [2003] Env LR 11
[68] 2007 Regulations, reg 38
[69] 2007 Regulations, reg 40
[70] EPA 1990, s33 (7) (a)

what constitutes a 'deposit' has given rise to some case law. In the case of *Leigh Land Reclamation Ltd v Walsall MBC*[71], it was held that a deposit only occurs when the waste reaches its final resting place. This decision, however, proved problematical as it was easy to argue that a deposit was only temporary and thus avoid liability. The decision was overturned in *R v Metropolitan Stipendiary Magistrate, ex parte London Waste Regulation Authority*[72] when the court held that 'deposit' applied to temporary deposits.

As well as traditional sentences, courts can order compensation for clean up and the confiscation of vehicles and the Environment Agency has powers to order clean up on the occupier and in default, carry out the necessary work and recover expenses.

6.8.4 The duty of care

The Environmental Protection Act 1990, s.34 imposes a duty of care in addition to any controls imposed under the permitting system to controlled waste. It applies to everyone in the waste chain. There is also a restricted duty on domestic waste producers. Any person is subject to the duty to take reasonable steps to:

- Prevent any other person contravening s.33.
- Prevent any other person contravening an environmental permit.
- Prevent the escape of waste.
- Ensure that the waste is transferred only to an authorised person.
- Ensure that an adequate written description of the waste is given to anyone to whom the waste is transferred (The Environmental Protection (Duty of Care) Regulations 1991).

There is a code of practice that gives guidance on reasonable steps[73], which must be taken into account in deciding whether the duty has been complied with. Breach of the duty is a criminal offence, even if no harm has been caused. The duty of care has the effect of making the system self-policing and encourages appropriate waste management systems.

6.8.5 Site waste management

In 2008 new site waste management plans regulations were introduced[74]. These regulations place a duty upon clients and principal contractors to have in place site waste management plans for all developments of a value of £300 000 and above. The plans must give estimates of waste volume and waste types and details of how waste will be managed. There is a more detailed reporting system in place for developments of over £500 000 in value. There are offences in place for failure to produce or to implement site waste management plans.

---

[71] (1991) 155 JP 547
[72] [1993] All ER 113
[73] Code of Practice on the Duty of Care Waste Management: The Duty of Care – A Code of Practice, 1996
[74] The Site Waste Management Plans Regulations 2008, SI 2008/314

6.9   Emissions from buildings

The UK has ratified the United Nations Framework Convention on Climate Change (The Kyoto Protocol) and thus committed itself to a 12.5% reduction in carbon dioxide emissions by 2012 (compared with 1990 levels). EU and domestic targets, however, are even more stringent. The UK was the first world-wide to adopt a legally binding long-term framework to cut carbon emissions. The Climate Change Act 2008 imposes a statutory duty upon the Secretary of State of 2050

'to ensure that the net UK carbon account for the year 2050 is at least 80 percent lower than the 1990 baseline'[75].

A series of five-yearly carbon budgets are to be set by order of the Secretary of State. The first three of these for the period 2008-22 have already been published[76]. The Secretary of State is subject to a duty

'to ensure that the net UK carbon account for a budgetary period does not exceed the carbon budget'[77].

Amongst the principal measures recommended by the Climate Change Committee that advises the Secretary of State is 'energy efficiency improvements in buildings and industry'. Controlling emissions from buildings will be a key factor in meeting this commitment. There are two main routes to implement the necessary changes; through the planning system and by standards set in building regulations.

6.9.1   The role of the planning system

The Planning and Compulsory Purchase Act 2004 (see paragraph 6.4 above) sets an aspiration in s.39 for the achievement of *sustainable development*. This has resulted in land use planners taking account of greenhouse gas and renewable energy issues. Guidance was originally contained in planning document PPS1 and this is now supplemented by guidance in PPS22 that encourages planners to seek renewable energy provision. Merton LBC now requires some developments to provide a proportion of their energy from on-site renewables (*The Merton Rule*) and some other local authorities have followed suit. There are also plans in place to permit householders to install microgeneration equipment under a general development order (see paragraph 6.4.1.A.d above). Some local planning authorities are also making it a condition for the grant of planning permission that there is certification in place for new domestic build under the *Code for Sustainable Homes* (see below).

---

[75] Climate Change Act 2008, s1
[76] Carbon Budgets Order 2009, SI 2009/1259
[77] 2008 Act, s4 (1)

6.9.2 The code for sustainable homes

The *Sustainable Buildings Task Group* first proposed a Code for Sustainable Buildings in 2004. The idea was that a voluntary code would be a catalyst for low carbon, low impact building and set vanguard eco-standards for government to follow. The Code was launched in December 2006 and the technical guide followed in April 2007. The Code sets six standards of increasing rigour against which the whole home can be measured. There is a rating of one to six stars, the one star level currently being set slightly above minimum standards for building regulations. The performance standards are closely linked to those in building regulations. The Code has nine design categories, including carbon dioxide emissions. Six stars, in this category of the Code, equates to *true zero carbon*. Zero carbon means that during the course of a year, the net carbon emissions from all energy use in the home is zero. To begin with the Code was entirely voluntary, but from May 2008, sellers of new properties are required to provide information to the purchaser either in the form of a certificate under the Code or a statement of non-assessment.

6.9.3 The role of building regulations

As noted in paragraph 6.3.1 above, Part L of Schedule 1 of the Building Regulations 2000 relates to *conservation of fuel and power*. There is an approved document that gives guidance in this regard. Compliance with the approved document creates a presumption that the works in question comply with the requirements of the Regulations. The scope of the Building Act 1984, under which building regulations are brought into force, has been significantly widened by the Sustainable and Secure Buildings Act 2004 and the Climate Change and Sustainable Energy Act 2006. The first of these Acts extended the range of matters for 'furthering the conservation of fuel and power' in respect of which regulations can be made. Importantly, this includes the regulation of *existing* buildings in matters which relate to energy conservation and carbon emissions. The 2006 Act further extended the powers in the Building Act. Amongst other things, it enables regulations to be made under the Building Act with regards to the installation of microgeneration technologies in buildings[78].

Two new sets of regulations made under the Building Act implement the provisions of an important EC Directive in England and Wales. The Building and Approved Inspectors (Amendment) Regulations 2006 bring into force Articles 3 – 6 of the Directive and the Energy Performance of Buildings (Certificates and Inspection) Regulations 2007 implement Articles 7, 9 and 10. The UK has chosen not to implement Art 8, which deals with the inspection of boilers. The key features of the Energy Performance of Buildings Directive[79] implemented by these regulations are listed below:

- A methodology is to be established for measuring the energy performance of buildings.

---

[78] Climate Change and Sustainable Energy Act 2006, s11
[79] Directive 2002/91

- Minimum energy performance standards are to be set.
- New buildings are to meet the standards and in those larger than 1000 m^2 efficient forms of heating are to be considered.
- In renovation of buildings over 1000 m^2, costing more than twenty-five per cent of the value of the building or involving more than twenty-five per cent of the shell, performance is to be brought up to the minimum standard where practical and economical.
- On construction, sale or rent, an Energy Performance Certificate is to be available. This must be no more than ten years old. Public buildings over 1000 m^2 are to display their certificate.
- Inspection regimes are to be put in place for boilers and air conditioning systems. Inspections are to be carried out by independent experts.

Future plans for building regulations include a government commitment to a programme for *new dwellings*, by which regulations will demand twenty-five per cent lower carbon emissions by 2010, twenty-five per cent lower by 2013 and by 2016 all new dwellings should be zero carbon.

6.10 Health and safety at work

Since the beginning of the nineteenth century, the law has sought to regulate how employers 'manage' safety. As new hazards emerged through the industrial age (mills, factories, offices, mechanised farming) so too did piecemeal legislation to cover the worst abuses of employee safety.

By the early 1970s, it had become evident that insufficient emphasis was being placed upon accident prevention. A committee was set up under Lord Robens to inquire into the recognised problems in health and safety at work and to make recommendations. The subsequent report recommended a lighter touch, goal-setting approach to legislation, with the law serving as a framework for self regulation. The Robens Report[80], which set out the findings of the Committee, had a significant impact upon the development of health and safety law in the UK. Most of the 1972 report was accepted by Parliament and it formed the basis for the Health and Safety at Work etc. Act (HSWA) 1974.

Parliament has recently tried another approach to improving Health and Safety through the Corporate Manslaughter and Corporate Homicide Act 2007. This is a landmark law where for the first time companies and organisations can be found guilty of corporate manslaughter as a result of serious management failures resulting in a gross breach of a duty of care owed to employees which results in death. Companies and organisations that take their obligations under health and safety law seriously are not likely to be in breach of the new provisions. Nonetheless, companies and organisations need to keep their health and safety management systems under review, in particular, the way in which their activities are managed or organised by senior management.

---

[80] Safety and Health at Work. The Report of the Robens Committee, Cmnd 5034, June 1972

6.10.1   The 1974 Act

The Act replaced existing legislation and introduced, in addition, a system of Regulations and Codes of Practice. The operation of the Act is in the hands of the Health and Safety Executive (HSE), while enforcement is the responsibility of Health and Safety Inspectors.

(A) Duties

Employers must ensure, as far as is reasonably practicable:

- The health, safety and welfare of employees at work.
- Other persons are not exposed to health and safety risks.
- That premises are safe and without risk to health.

(B) Inspectors

Inspectors have extensive rights to enter premises to make investigations and require the production of documents and information. An Improvement Notice may be served where a particular practice is required to be remedied, while in serious cases a Prohibition Notice may be served if there is a risk of serious personal injury. The Act provides for criminal penalties in cases of breach and in some instances allows for a civil action for breach of statutory duty (see Chapter 3, paragraph 3.10 and below).

6.10.2   The 1992 'six-pack' regulations

The 1974 Act is an enabling Act (see Chapter 1, paragraph 1.6.3.C) and regulations can be made under it relating to almost any matter connected to health and safety. Thus the bulk of health and safety law is to be found in the form of regulations. Some regulations that pre-dated the Act were brought under its ambit when it came into force and further regulations were brought in to operationalise the framework provided by the Act.

As with many areas of regulation in this country much of our health and safety law derives from the European Union. Over the years many health and safety directives have flowed from Europe. In 1989 a significant directive was adopted by the EU, the Framework Directive (89/391) on health and safety in the working environment. Immediately following this a number of more specific directives on health and safety issues were adopted. This led to the issue, in 1992, of the Management of Health and Safety at Work Regulations, which implemented the substantive provisions of the Framework Directive into English law. Five other sets of regulations were made at the same time, which addressed the other specific directives and these together became known as the *six-pack*. The six sets of regulations were:

- Management of Health and Safety at Work Regulations 1992
- Workplace (Health, Safety and Welfare) Regulations 1992
- Provision and Use of Work Equipment Regulations 1992

- Personal Protective Equipment at Work Regulations 1992
- Manual Handling Operations Regulations 1992
- Health and Safety Display Screen Equipment Regulations 1992

Most of these regulations have since either been updated by revocation and replacement or amendment. Perhaps two of the most broadly relevant sets of regulations deriving from the original *six-pack* are considered below.

(A) Management of Health and Safety at Work Regulations 1999 (as amended)

The original 1992 regulations were replaced and revoked by these 1999 regulations. The Regulations are supplemented by an Approved Code of Conduct (ACoP) containing guidance on the Regulations[81]. The central feature of the Regulations is the duty on employers to make a suitable and sufficient assessment of the risks to employees in the workplace. The Regulations require measures to be identified to comply with health and safety duties and impose general duties on planning, monitoring, reviewing and providing health surveillance. Competent persons must be appointed to assist in the undertaking of measures and information provided to employees about health and safety risks. There is a new provision in the 1999 Regulations that did not appear in the original 1992 version. Regulation 4 of the new Regulations requires that preventive measures are implemented in accordance with a hierarchy set out in Schedule 1. The top priority is the avoidance of risk. A breach of the Regulations gives rise to potential criminal liability under the HSWA and by a 2006 amendment to the Regulations[82], civil liability for breach (see Chapter 3, paragraph 3.10) is now possible by employees against their employers.

(B) Workplace (Health, Safety and Welfare) Regulations 1992 (as amended)

These regulations apply to workplaces, but specifically exclude construction sites, which have their own set of regulations, dealt with below. The regulations are supported by an ACoP, which is published together with guidance and was updated in 1995[83]. The provisions of the Code are admissible as evidence in criminal proceedings and are often received in evidence in civil actions. The focus of the Regulations is upon elements of the structure and layout of the workplace that affect employees and the facilities that are provided for the workforce. As such, it includes provisions on ventilation, temperature, lighting, cleaning, workstations, floors, traffic routes, doors, walls, windows etc. as well as sanitary

---

[81] Management of Health and Safety at Work (L21, 2000)
[82] SI2006/438.
[83] Workplace Health Safety and Welfare, L24

conveniences, washing facilities, drinking water, changing and rest facilities. These regulations replaced extensive parts of the Factories Act 1961 and the Offices, Shops and Railway Premises Act 1963. A breach of the Regulations may lead to civil liability in addition to criminal liability.

6.10.3   The CDM Regulations

Most day-to-day operations in the construction industry, both in building and civil engineering work, are now governed by a single set of regulations, made under HSWA, the Construction (Design and Management) Regulations 2007 (CDM Regulations). The CDM Regulations replace and revoke an earlier version (1994) as well as what remained of some regulations that predated the 1974 Act (The Construction (General Provisions) Regulations, 1961) and the Construction (Health and Safety and Welfare) Regulations, 1996. There are two other sets of regulations that relate specifically to construction, the Construction (Head Protection) Regulations 1989 (as amended) and the Work in Compressed Air Regulations, 1996 (as amended). In addition there are some general provisions that are of direct relevance and some of these are dealt with in more detail below.

Subsequent to the introduction of the 1994 CDM Regulations, concerns were expressed about the complexity and the bureaucracy of the system. These views were supported by an industry-wide consultation in 2002 that resulted in the decision to revise the Regulations. As noted above, the new Regulations amend and amalgamate the two main sets of regulations that previously existed into a single regulatory package. The Construction (Design and Management) Regulations 2007 (CDM 2007) came into force in Great Britain in April 2007 and they are supported by an Approved Code of Practice (ACoP)[84] that has legal status and gives practical advice for all involved in construction work

The CDM 2007 Regulations are divided into five parts:

- Part 1 deals with the application of the Regulations and definitions.
- Part 2 covers general duties that apply to all construction projects.
- Part 3 contains additional duties that only apply to notifiable construction projects.
- Part 4 contains practical requirements that apply to all construction sites.
- Part 5 deals with transitional arrangements and revocations.

The 2007 Regulations provide for legal duties upon any person having construction or building work carried out, unless they are a domestic client.

(A) General duties

Any person placed under a duty by the regulations must ensure:

- Competence (of all appointees and workers).
- Co-operation (of everyone involved in the project).

---

[84] Managing Health and Safety in Construction, L144

- Co-ordination of all activities.
- Account is taken of the general principle of prevention.

(B) Clients' duties

In addition to these general duties, clients in all construction projects are under a duty to:

- Manage the project to ensure that the work is carried out so far as is reasonably practicable without risk to the health and safety of any person and to comply with Schedule 2 (Welfare Facilities) of the Regulations and other legal requirements for health and safety.
- Provide health and safety relevant pre-construction information to designers and contractors.

(C) Duties of designers

Specific additional duties apply to designers. They must:

- Ensure that the client is aware of his/her duties.
- Avoid foreseeable risks in preparing or modifying a design and eliminate hazards or reduce risks from hazards.
- Provide sufficient information on design and construction to enable other parties to comply with their duties.
- Ensure compliance with health and safety related legislation relating to the design of and materials used in the structure.

(D) Duties of contractors

Similar additional duties lie with contractors, who must:

- Ensure that the client is aware of his/her duties.
- Manage the project to ensure that the work is carried out so far as is reasonably practicable without risk to the health and safety of any person and to comply with other legal requirements for health and safety.
- Inform sub-contractors of the minimum period of time allowed to them for planning and preparation before work commences.
- Provide all workers with training and information for work to be carried out safely and without risk to health.
- Ensure other legal provisions for health and safety training are in place.
- Take reasonable steps to prevent access by unauthorised persons to the site.
- Ensure compliance of those working under their control, with Schedule 2 (Welfare Facilities) of the Regulations.

(E) Additional duties where project is notifiable

(a) Clients

There are additional duties for clients of *notifiable construction projects.* These are projects where either the work lasts longer than thirty days or it involves more than 500 person days of work. For notifiable projects, a client must:

- Appoint a CDM co-ordinator.
- Appoint a principal contractor.
- Provide the CDM co-ordinator with pre-construction information.
- Ensure that the principal contractor has prepared a construction phase plan before construction commences.
- Keep a health and safety file.

(b) Designers

Additional duties also exist for designers, who must:

- Not commence work unless a CDM co-ordinator has been appointed.
- Provide sufficient information about the design to assist the CDM co-ordinator to comply with his/her duties under the Regulations.

(c) Contractors

For notifiable projects, contractors must:

- Not commence work until the names of the CDM co-ordinator and the principal contractor are available, there is access to the construction phase plan and notice of the project has been given to the Health and Safety Executive (HSE).
- Provide the principal contractor with relevant information.
- Identify any sub-contractors to the principal contractor.
- Comply with directions of the principal contractor and site rules.
- Comply with reporting requirements for death, injury etc.
- Take reasonable steps to ensure that work is carried out in accordance with the construction phase plan to ensure health and safety.

(F) Duties of CDM co-ordinators

Under the Regulations, CDM co-ordinators have a duty to:

- Give advice to the client on compliance with the Regulations.
- Ensure arrangements are in place for co-ordination of health and safety measures during planning and preparation for the construction phase.
- Liaise with the principal contractor on health and safety matters.

- Take reasonable steps to identify, collect and disseminate pre-construction information.
- Ensure designers comply with their duties and that there is co-operation between designers and the principal contractor.
- Prepare or review and update the health and safety file and pass this to the client at the end of the construction phase.
- Notify the project to the HSE.

(G) Duties of the principal contractor

The duties of the principal contractor are extensive and include:

- Managing the construction phase to ensure, so far as is reasonably practicable, it is carried out without risk to health and safety.
- Liaising with the CDM co-ordinator.
- Ensuring welfare facilities are in place.
- Drawing up rules and giving directions.
- Ensuring sufficient time is given for preparation and planning.
- Providing induction, information and training for workers.
- Preparing, reviewing and implementing the construction phase plan.
- Ensuring cooperation and consultation with workers.

(H) Duties relating to the health and safety of construction sites

Part 4 of the CDM Regulations deals with those issues previously contained in the 1996 Construction Regulations. The duties contained in this part of the Regulations apply to contractors and any other person who controls construction work. There are detailed requirements in respect of duties falling within the following categories:

- Safe places of work.
- Good order and site security.
- Stability of structures.
- Demolition or dismantling.
- Explosives.
- Excavation.
- Cofferdams and caisons.
- Reports of inspections.
- Energy distribution installations.
- Prevention of drowning.
- Traffic routes.
- Vehicles.
- Prevention of risk from fire.
- Emergency procedures.
- Emergency routes and exits.

- Fire detection and fire-fighting.
- Fresh air.
- Temperature and weather protection.
- Lighting.

(l) Enforcement

The Regulations are enforceable under the 1974 Act by the HSE, providing for criminal penalties in the event of non-compliance. The Regulations specifically exclude civil liability in respect of an action for breach of statutory duty for some elements of their content, but a civil action is possible, for example, for breach of a part 4 duty and duties under Schedule 2 (Welfare Facilities) (see Chapter 3, paragraph 3.10)

6.10.4   The Control of Substances Hazardous to Health (COSHH) Regulations 2002 (as amended)

The COSHH Regulations introduced another approach to safety on site, based on limiting the risks of exposure to hazardous substances. Hazardous substances are defined as 'any natural or artificial substance whether solid, liquid, gas or vapour (including micro-organisms)'[85]. The Regulations are supported by an Approved Code of Practice[86]. A breach of the Regulations is a potential criminal offence under s.33 (1) of the Health and Safety etc. Act 1974 and can also give rise to civil liability in so far as it causes damage[87].

The Regulations prohibit exposure to certain substances and aim to protect the health of persons exposed to other hazardous substances. This is achieved by means of the requirement for risk assessments to be carried out when exposure may occur. Employers are then required to either prevent or control exposure. Control systems are to be maintained, examined and tested and exposure in the workplace is to be monitored. In addition, the Regulations require that health surveillance is in place and that information, instruction and training is provided for persons who may be exposed to substances hazardous to health and that arrangements are in place to deal with accidents incidents and emergencies.

6.10.5   The Control of Asbestos at Work Regulations 2006 (as amended)

Asbestos has been responsible for more work-related deaths than any other cause and the mortality rate is still rising. The control of asbestos is not dealt with under COSSH, but under a separate set of regulations. The 2006 Regulations revoke and replace three prior sets of regulations, providing one single piece of legislative control. The regulations are principally, but not exclusively, aimed at employers.

---

[85] Reg 2 (1)
[86] The Control of Substances Hazardous to Health Regulations 2002 (as amended) Approved Code of Practice and Guidance, L5
[87] HSWA s 47 (2) and see Chapter 3, paragraph 3.10

The general requirement is that an employer must not undertake work with asbestos unless there is a licence in place. There are exceptions to this, where the exposure is sporadic and of low intensity and does not exceed a defined *control limit*[88]. The fundamental duty is for an employer to prevent exposure to asbestos so far as is reasonably practicable. If this is not possible, there is a duty to reduce exposure to the lowest level reasonably practicable by means of the use of respiratory and other protective equipment. An employer must not allow his/her employee to be exposed to concentrations above the control limit.

In addition, the regulations provide that an employer must make an assessment for the presence of asbestos before undertaking demolition, maintenance or other work which is likely to expose employees to asbestos. In cases of doubt it should be assumed that asbestos is present. The employer must not undertake work with asbestos without a written plan and must give information, instruction and training to employees. ACoPs are in place to support the Regulations[89]. Breach of the Regulations can constitute an offence under HSWA. Regulation 37 provides a defence if all reasonable precautions have been taken and all due diligence exercised to avoid the commission of the offence in question.

6.10.6   The Work at Height Regulations 2005 (as amended)

Falls from height remain one of the single biggest causes of workplace deaths and major injuries. The Regulations apply to all work at height where there is a risk of a fall liable to cause personal injury. The Regulations place duties on employers, the self-employed and any person that controls the work of others. They are supplemented by the Work at Height Regulations 2007, which apply to those who work at height providing instruction or leadership in caving, climbing, sporting, recreation or team-building activities

As part of the Regulations, duty holders must ensure:

- All work at height is properly planned and organised.
- Those involved in work at height are competent.
- The risks from work at height are assessed and appropriate work equipment is selected and used.
- The risks from fragile surfaces are properly controlled.
- Equipment for work at height is properly inspected and maintained.

The overriding principle is that a person to whom the Regulations apply must do all that is reasonably practicable to prevent anyone falling. The regulations set out a hierarchy for managing and selecting equipment for work at height. Duty holders must:

- Avoid work at height where they can.
- Use work equipment or other measures to prevent falls where they cannot avoid working at height.

---

[88] Reg 2 (1)

[89] Work with Materials Containing Asbestos (L143, 2006) and The Management of Asbestos in Non-domestic Premises (L127, 2006)

- Where they cannot eliminate the risk of a fall, use work equipment or other measures to minimise the distance and consequences of a fall should one occur.

The Regulations include Schedules giving requirements for existing places of work and means of access for work at height, collective fall prevention (e.g. guardrails and working platforms), collective fall arrest (e.g. nets, airbags etc.), personal fall protection (e.g. work restraints, fall arrest and rope access) and ladders.

6.10.7 The Notification of Conventional Tower Cranes Regulations 2010

These new regulations require conventional tower cranes used on construction sites to be notified to the HSE. These are the type of cranes that are usually installed with the assistance of another crane and are sometimes, therefore, also known as *assisted erected cranes*. The duty does not apply to other types of tower cranes such as self-erecting tower cranes. The duty applies to employers and any person in control of the use of such cranes. In practice, this means that whoever has the responsibility for ensuring that the crane is thoroughly examined by a competent person[90] should also ensure that notification is made to HSE. This will normally be the principal contractor or the contractor appointed by the principal contractor to provide all on-site crane services.

Notification should be writing within fourteen days of LOLER examination. The crane can be utilised during this period. Details of the notification include the name and address of the owner or lessor, address of the construction site, information about the crane and the date of the examination. Notification can be made online or by post, accompanied by the applicable fee.

---

[90] As required by the Lifting Operations and Lifting Equipment Regulations (LOLER) 1998, Reg 9

Index

Law and the Built Environment   by Douglas Wood, Paul Chynoweth, Julie Adshead and Jim Mason
© 2011 Douglas Wood, Paul Chynoweth, Julie Adshead and Jim Mason

**7 DAY
BOOK**

This book is due for return on or before the last date shown below.

0 8 DEC 2011

2 4 JAN 2013

- 7 FEB 2013

1 2 APR 2016

2 3 FEB 2017